FOURTH EDITION

US

NATIONAL

SECURITY

Policymakers, Processes, and Politics

Sam C. Sarkesian
John Allen Williams
Stephen J. Cimbala

LYNNE
RIENNER
PUBLISHERS

BOULDER
LONDON

100598151+

Published in the United States of America in 2008 by
Lynne Rienner Publishers, Inc.
1800 30th Street, Boulder, Colorado 80301
www.rienner.com

and in the United Kingdom by
Lynne Rienner Publishers, Inc.
3 Henrietta Street, Covent Garden, London WC2E 8LU

Library of Congress Cataloging-in-Publication Data
Sarkesian, Sam Charles.
  US national security : policymakers, processes, and politics / Sam C.
  Sarkesian, John Allen Williams, and Stephen J. Cimbala. — 4th ed.
     p. cm.
  Includes bibliographical references and index.
  ISBN 978-1-58826-416-9 (pbk. : alk. paper)
1. National security—United States—Decisionmaking. 2. United
States—Military policy—Decisionmaking. I. Williams, John Allen,
1945– II. Cimbala, Stephen J. III. Title. IV. Title: US national security.
UA23.S275 2007
355'.033073—dc22
                                                                2007022727

British Cataloguing in Publication Data
A Cataloguing in Publication record for this book
is available from the British Library.

Printed and bound in the United States of America

     The paper used in this publication meets the requirements
     of the American National Standard for Permanence of
     Paper for Printed Library Materials Z39.48-1992.

   5   4   3   2

Contents

Part 4 Conclusions

Tables and Figures

Tables

Figures

Preface

ASSESSING THE INTERNATIONAL CONTEXT AND ISSUES OF US national security in the twenty-first century, we conclude that much of what we wrote more than ten years ago remains relevant today. Nonetheless, the new era has created a strategic landscape that requires a rethinking of US national security, particularly with respect to international terrorism and homeland security. Any study of US national interests must encompass questions of values and interests about unconventional conflict. The involvement of the US military in operations short of war (such as low-intensity conflict and peacekeeping missions) has become commonplace. This development has complicated the relationship of policy, strategy, national interests, and the use of force, and it highlights the need for an expanded and effective intelligence apparatus. All of this is even more complicated by the impact of globalization, the information age, and the myriad uses of cyberspace.

The main themes and reference points in the third edition remain relevant and served as the basis for this edition. We have assessed the new era, however, and examine how the challenges in the past years have magnified and complicated those themes and reference points. Our focus remains the same: how the national security system works and its effectiveness in responding to current and future global challenges.

We address these matters by examining the following questions: How relevant are the institutions of the national security establishment in responding to the strategic landscape of the twenty-first century? How well do they function? How do those in the national security system assess the international strategic landscape? What is the US grand strategy and policy in the twenty-first century? What role does public opinion play in US national security policy? And particularly important, what are the US national interests that must form the basis of national security policy?

As with the previous edition, the three of us have combined our research and teaching experience, as well as our working experience in various parts of the national security system, and hope that we have provided a balanced assessment of the strategic landscape of the twenty-first century.

In writing the book, we had the invaluable help of colleagues and students past and present, particularly Robert A. Vitas, Michael P. Noonan, Mary Frances Lebamoff, Stephen J. Guerra, Peter M. Swartz, Steven Michels, Michelle Johns, and John Wood. Their comments on various parts of the manuscript were extremely helpful. We stress, however, that this book represents only our own views and assessments.

PART 1

Introduction

1

National Interests and National Security

THE INTERNATIONAL STRATEGIC LANDSCAPE OF THE TWENTY-first century is shaped by complex and contradictory forces. The world is characterized by turmoil, and changing patterns of state-to-state relationships as well as conflicts within states caused by ethnic, religious, and nationalistic differences have become commonplace. International terrorism, drug cartels, and threats created by information-age technology add to the turmoil. Earlier, there was a widespread sense of optimism about peace, but that was all shattered on September 11, 2001, by the terrorist attacks on the United States and the long war against international terrorism. A United States at war against terrorism and the notion of a new concept of war have become intermixed with globalization, economic expansion, homeland security, and the attempt to pursue US values peacefully.

In this new environment, US national security policy and priorities have become complicated, often ambiguous, and even inconsistent—not because of immediate threat of major conventional war but rather the unpredictable, uncertain, and confusing characteristics of the international arena. Disagreements and disputes within the national security establishment, Congress, and the public were muted temporarily in response to the September 11 attacks and the resulting war in Afghanistan.[1] But now the US involvement in Iraq and the continuing concerns about Iran and North Korea magnify the challenges to US national security policy and have caused a great degree of turmoil in the US political system and in US foreign relations. Although questions have been raised about national interests, national security, and the US role around the world, the terrorist threat and the proliferation of nuclear weapons technology seem to have overshadowed much of the traditional perspectives also, at least for the foreseeable future.

3

National Security

The international security landscape of the initial years of the twenty-first century has clouded the concept and meaning of US national security. The integration of national interests into meaningful national security policy has become more difficult. Recognizing the problems of defining and conceptualizing national security, we offer a preliminary definition that includes both objective capability and perception: *US national security is the ability of national institutions to prevent adversaries from using force to harm Americans or their national interests and the confidence of Americans in this capability.*

There are two dimensions of this definition: physical and psychological. The first is an objective measure based on the strength and military capacity of the nation to challenge adversaries successfully, including going to war if necessary. This also includes a more prominent role for intelligence, economics, and other nonmilitary measures as well as the ability to use them as political-military levers in dealings with other states. The psychological dimension is subjective, reflecting the opinion and attitudes of Americans on the nation's ability to remain secure relative to the external world. It affects the people's willingness to support government efforts to achieve national security goals. Underpinning this is that the majority of people have the knowledge and political will to support clear policies to achieve clear national security goals.

National Security, Foreign Policy, and Domestic Policy

National security must be analyzed in the context of foreign policy, defined as the policies of a nation that encompass all official relations with other countries. The purposes of foreign policy are multidimensional. For the United States, the purpose is to prevent conditions detrimental to the United States and maintain relations with other countries to enhance conditions favorable to US national interests. The instruments of foreign policy are primarily diplomatic and political and include a variety of psychological and economic measures.

In the immediate past, national security differed from foreign policy in at least two respects: national security purposes were more narrow and focused on security and safety, and national security was primarily concerned with actual and potential adversaries and their use of force, whether overt or covert. This means there was a military emphasis, which usually is not the case in foreign policy. National security policy now overlaps with foreign policy, however, sometimes blurring any distinction. But much of foreign policy requires compromise and negotiations—the dynamics of give-and-take—as well as all of the techniques and subtleties associated with traditional diplomacy. This kind of work is primarily a matter for the

US Department of State, with long-range implications for national security policy. These relationships are shown in Figure 1.1.

Until recently, most Americans felt that US values could not be imposed on other states unless survival was at stake. National security is now seen by many to include the projection of US values abroad (see Chapter 2). This adds to the confusion and highlights the interrelationship among foreign, domestic, and national security policies. "America's concept of national security today is infinitely more complex than at any time in its history. The same is true for the relationship between the foreign and domestic components of national security."[2] Although this observation was made a decade ago, it remains relevant today.

The difficulties of determining US national interests and establishing national security priorities are compounded by the increasing linkages between a number of national security and domestic policies. The domestic economic impact of certain national security policies links US domestic interests and policies to the international security arena. This is seen in economic sanctions, embargos on agriculture exports to adversaries or potential adversaries, diminished foreign oil sources, border security, and the export of technologically advanced industrial products. And in a dramatic way, September 11 obscured dramatically the distinction between domestic and national security policy.

Owing to the special characteristics of our democratic system and political culture, it is increasingly difficult to isolate national security issues from domestic policy. Besides the relationship and link between foreign and national security policies, domestic interests are important in establishing national security priorities and interests. Some scholars call these "intermestic" politics and policies.[3]

Nonetheless, national security policy by definition involves military force. Distinctions must be made between foreign and domestic policy and national security. The primary distinction rests in the likelihood of military force as well as in use of the military as the primary instrument for implementing national security policy. Although many other matters are important in the overall notion of national interests, they are best incorporated into foreign policy and the overlap between such policy and national security.[4]

These observations are the basis for defining national security policy, expanding on the concept of national security: *National security policy is primarily concerned with formulating and implementing national strategy involving the threat or use of force to create a favorable environment for US national interests.* An integral part of this is to prevent the effective use of military force and/or covert operations by adversaries or potential adversaries to obstruct or deny the ability of the United States to pursue national interests.

Figure 1.1 National Security and Foreign Policy

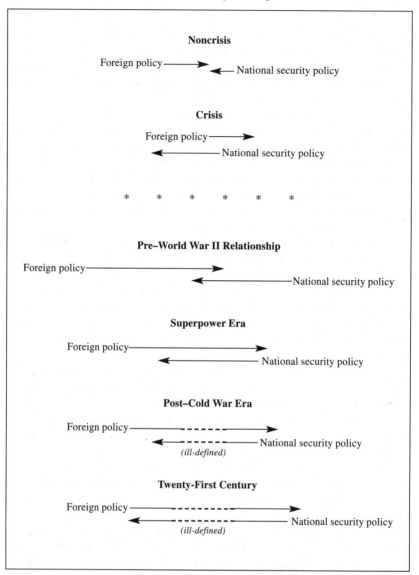

Source: Adapted from Col. William J. Taylor Jr., "Interdependence, Specialization, and National Security: Problems for Diplomats, Soldiers, and Scholars," *Air University Review* 30, no. 5 (July–August 1979): 17–26.

Note: The gap between foreign policy and national policy indicates the relative degree of "closeness" between foreign and national security policy. The arrows indicate the relative degree of overlap. As shown, during times of crisis, the gap between foreign and national security policy is minimal and virtually nonexistent. In the twenty-first century it is often difficult to clearly separate foreign policy and national security because the use of force has become closely connected with a variety of peacekeeping missions, humanitarian crises, operations of war, and operations other than war; many such missions are extensions of foreign policy or a combination of national security and foreign policy, particularly in combating international terrorism.

National security means more than the capacity to conduct international wars. In light of the characteristics of the international arena and contemporary conflicts, challenges to US national security might take any number of nontraditional forms, from economics to unconventional operations. Of course, the capacity to deter nuclear war and wage conventional conflicts remains essential for the conduct of US national security policy, even in the twenty-first century. In this new era, international terrorism, weapons of mass destruction (WMD) (including chemical and biological warfare), and information warfare have become increasingly important dimensions of national security.

National security policy must be carefully developed and implemented according to priorities distinguishing survival (i.e., vital) interests from others. Too often, national security is used synonymously with any interest, suggesting that all interests are survival priorities. Taking a page from Sun-tzu, if almost everything is a matter of national security, then the concept of national security becomes virtually meaningless.[5] If national security policy and strategy followed such a pattern, the United States would have to defend everything everywhere; as a result it would be unable to defend anything. Resources and personnel would be scattered across the globe and rarely be in a position to bring sufficient force to bear, even if survival were at stake.

Short of clear threats to US territory, Americans often disagree over priorities. Even when there is agreement on priorities, there is disagreement on resource commitment and strategy. Yet a system of priorities provides a way to identify levels of threats and helps in the design of strategies. But all this must be guided by the meaning of national security and its conceptual dimensions.

In this new environment, US national security and national interests have become complicated, often ambiguous, and even inconsistent—not because of an immediate threat of major conventional war but rather because of the unpredictable, uncertain, and confusing characteristics of the international arena.

The relationship between national interests and national security is particularly important in this new era. Yet, more than three decades ago, Henry A. Kissinger wrote, "What is it in our interest to prevent? What should we seek to accomplish?"[6] This was written before Kissinger became assistant to President Richard Nixon for national security affairs (a position that is known widely as national security advisor) and then secretary of state. The same questions continue to challenge policymakers, scholars, and elected officials. The answers were elusive at the start of the post–Cold War period and became even more complicated after September 2001.

Although the US war against terrorism became the dominant theme in 2001, spelled out in the Bush Doctrine of President George W. Bush, such matters now are magnified and complicated by the US involvement in Iraq and Afghanistan and the troubling issues with Iran and North Korea, among others, and a variety of issues linked to homeland security.[7] All of these issues go beyond the new kind of war. Why? Do Americans not know what is in their national interest? At first glance the answer seems relatively simple. The US national interest is to promote US values and objectives. To promote these means to protect them by establishing and implementing effective national security policies.

Upon closer examination, however, these answers are inadequate, and they raise additional questions. What are US values? How are they reflected in national interests? What is the relationship between national security and national interests? What is national security? How should US national security policy be implemented? For the past three decades these questions have been addressed by many US politicians and scholars. If they agree on anything, it is that there is no agreement.

Each generation of Americans seeks to interpret national values, national interests, and national security in terms of its own perspective and mindset. Although there is agreement about core elements such as protection of the US homeland, interpretations differ about the meaning of national security, the nature of external threats, and the best course of conduct for security policy. Combined with changes in the world environment, the answers to the dynamics of Kissinger's questions are even more elusive today. To be sure, the war against terrorism became the key focus of national interests beginning in September 2001 and has been magnified with the US involvement in Iraq. But such interests encompass a wide range of elements that underpin an open system and society such as the United States.

It is to be expected that in a country with multiple power centers and shifting focal points there will be different interpretations as well as outright differences. Recognizing that these matters are rarely resolved by onetime solutions and that they are, at best, ambiguous, we explore the concepts of national security, national values, and national interest. In the process, we design a framework for analyzing national security policy.

In any case, the United States is in the world to stay. Whether Americans like it or not, they can neither withdraw from external responsibilities nor retreat to isolation. Regardless of the policies of any administration, the United States has links to most parts of the world: politically, economically, culturally, and psychologically. What the United States does or does not do has a significant impact on international politics.

National Interests

US national interests are expressions of US values projected into the international and domestic arenas. The purpose of interests includes the creation and perpetuation of an international environment that is most favorable to the peaceful pursuit of US values. It follows that interests nurture and expand democracy and open systems. Similarly, the United States wishes to prevent the expansion of closed systems by their use of force or indirect aggression. In the twenty-first century, the domestic arena has become an important consideration in pursuing national interests because of asymmetrical threats, the information age, and international terrorism.[8] Such concerns were heightened by the September 11 terrorist attacks and increased with the US involvement in Iraq.

Three statements serve as reference points. First, US values as they apply to the external world are at the core of national interests. Second, pursuing national interests does not mean that US national security strategy is limited to the homeland. This may require power projection into various parts of the world, especially when combating international terrorism. Third, the president is the focal point in defining and articulating US national interests.

National interests can be categorized in order of priorities as follows:

First Order: vital interests. This requires protection of the homeland and areas and issues directly affecting this interest. This may require total military mobilization and resource commitment. In homeland defense, this also may require a coordinated effort of all agencies of government, especially in defense against terrorist attacks and information warfare. The homeland focus was highlighted by the creation of a new cabinet-level Department of Homeland Security by President George W. Bush following September 11. The purpose is to coordinate the efforts of a number of agencies in countering terrorism in the United States.

Second Order: critical interests. These are areas and issues that do not directly affect the survival of the United States or pose a threat to the homeland but in the long run have a high propensity for becoming First Order priorities. Critical interests are measured primarily by the degree to which they maintain, nurture, and expand open systems. Many also argue that moral imperatives are important in shaping national interests.

Third Order: serious interests. These are issues that do not critically affect First and Second Order interests yet cast some shadow over such interests. US efforts are focused on creating favorable conditions to preclude Third Order interests from developing into higher-order ones.

All other interests are peripheral in that they have no immediate impact on any order of interests but must be watched in case events transform these interests. In the meantime, peripheral interests require few, if any, US resources.

Categories of priorities such as these can be used not only as a framework for systematic assessment of national interests and national security but also as a way to distinguish immediate from long-range security issues. Such a framework can provide a basis for rational and systematic debate within the national security establishment regarding the US national security posture and is useful in studying national security. Today there is rarely a clear line, however, between categories of interests. Many changes have expanded the concept of national interests to include several moral and humanitarian dimensions, among others. As some argue, where can the line be drawn among categories of interests?

A realistic assignment of priorities can be better understood by looking at geopolitical boundaries of core, contiguous, and outer areas (see Figure 1.2). In specific terms, at the core of US national interests is the survival of the homeland and political order. But survival cannot be limited to the "final" defense of the homeland. In light of international terrorism and today's weapons technology, weapons proliferation, and chemical/biological warfare, homeland survival means more than retreating to the borders and threatening anyone who might attack with total destruction. By then it is too late for national security policy to do much good, and in the new war, the attacker can be difficult to identify.

If national interest is invoked only when the homeland is directly threatened and survival is at stake, then the concept may be of little use, too late to overcome the peril. If the concept is to have any meaning for policy and strategy, then it must be something more. The interpretation and application of this broader view spark a great deal of debate and disagreement between the executive and legislative branches of government and within the US political arena. The media also become involved frequently with their own agendas.

Figure 1.2 US National Security Priorities

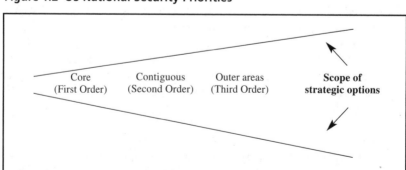

The national security establishment and policymakers rarely have the luxury of endless debate, however; neither do they have unlimited time or all necessary facts in a given situation. Yet policy must be made and strategy options examined, chosen, and implemented regardless of conditions, even while debates and disagreements remain intense.

The fact is that policy must be determined and implemented at some point. Before that, national interests for the particular situation must be identified and articulated. At the same time, national interests over the long range must be considered. Custom, usage, and constitutional powers give the president a basis for articulating their meaning. And though some Americans might challenge this notion today, initiatives in foreign and national security policy usually rest with the president as the commander in chief of US armed forces, the chief diplomat, and the singular expositor and standard-bearer of the US national will.

To be sure, Congress has an important role, but the president must take the lead and is the country's only legal representative with respect to foreign relations. For better or for worse, the president articulates the national interests, and Congress responds. The same holds true with respect to the president and the variety of interest groups in the government bureaucracy and public arena. Members of Congress find it very difficult to force a president to change direction in national security policies if he is sufficiently committed to a course of action—even in the case of the long war that has become unpopular.

US Values and National Interests

US values are based on what is required for the philosophical, legal, and moral basis for the continuation of the US system. These attributes are deeply engrained in our political system and domestic environment; they also apply to the way in which the public perceives justice in the international system and "just cause" in the conduct of war. In other words, values are principles that give the US political system and social order their innate character; they provide substance to US culture and create further principles upon which to base national interests.

The Value System
Modern US values derive from the Judeo-Christian heritage, the Anglo-Saxon legacy (including the Reformation, the Renaissance, the philosophies of John Locke and Jean-Jacques Rousseau, among others, and the principles rooted in the American Revolution), the Declaration of Independence, and the Constitution. From among these many historical reference points, we identify at least six fundamental values that define the United States and its role in the international world.[9]

First, there is the right of self-determination, a dual concept in this context: it applies not only to the nation-state but also to people within that state. It is presumed that each nation-state has the right to determine its own policy and to govern in any way it chooses as long as it does not threaten neighbors or oppress its own people. At the same time, people within that nation-state also have the right of self-determination. From the US perspective, this means that through free and fair elections people in a nation-state have the right to determine how and by whom they will be ruled, with the option to replace rulers as they see fit.

There is another dimension, however: an emerging right claimed by minority groups to demand autonomy as a matter of self-determination. This duality of self-determination and state sovereignty creates serious problems in determining appropriate and legitimate action on the part of the United Nations (UN), regional organizations, and the United States. This duality also has important implications for US military strategy. Moreover, this duality can lead to a dangerous confrontation between minority groups within a state demanding self-determination and the state itself, as occurred in the former Yugoslavia (i.e., between Albanians and Serbians in Kosovo, a province in Serbia) and is occurring in Iraq, among other states. The United States and the North Atlantic Treaty Organization (NATO) intervened on behalf of the Albanian majority in Kosovo at the expense of the sovereignty of Serbia.[10] Ideally, self-determination is accomplished within a system of laws and peaceful change. The peaceful partition of the former Czechoslovakia into the Czech Republic and Slovakia offers a reasonable notion of self-determination, but it is the rare exception.

Second, it follows that there is an inherent worth to any single individual in his/her relationship to others, to the political system, and to the social order. What does this mean? Put simply, every person is intrinsically a moral, legal, and political entity to which the system must respond. Each individual has the right to achieve all that he or she can, without encumbrances other than protection of fellow citizens as well as homeland protection and survival. Individual worth must therefore be reflected in economic, political, and legal systems.

Third, rulers owe their power and accountability to the people, which is the essence of democratic political legitimacy. The people are the final authority: there is a continuing responsibility by elected and appointed officials to rule and function according to the moral and legal principles, and the right of the people to change leaders is absolute. In this respect, no consuming power can dominate government or establish its own rationale for rule. Furthermore, individual worth necessitates limited government with no absolute and permanent focal point of power. To ensure this, rule and governance must be open: decisions and policies must be undertaken in full public view, with input from a variety of formal and informal groups. The system of rule must be accessible to the people and their representatives. This is the essence of what are called "open systems."

Fourth, policies and changes in the international environment must be based on the first three values outlined above. Thus peaceful change brought about by rational discourse among nation-states is a fundamental value. Resort to war can be acceptable only if it is clearly based on home-land protection and survival or other core values, and only if all other means have failed. In this respect, diplomacy and state-to-state relationships must be based on mutually acceptable rules of the game.

Fifth, any system professing such values and trying to function according to their principles must be protected and nurtured. Nation-states whose values are compatible with US values are thought to be best served by an international order based on those same values.

Sixth, US values are grounded in the Judeo-Christian heritage that predated the founding of the republic in the late eighteenth century. For many Americans, this instills a sense of humanity, a sensitivity to the plight and status of individuals, and a search for divine guidance. These precepts add a dimension to what is seen to be proper and just in the minds of many Americans and are considered by many to be beyond the legal definition of government.

We do not suggest that these values are perfectly embodied in the US system. There are many historical examples of value distortions and their misuse to disguise other purposes. But these values are esteemed in their own right by most Americans and are embodied in the political-social system. Furthermore, the system of rule and the character of the political system have institutionalized these values, albeit imperfectly. The expectations of most Americans and their assessment of other states are, in no small measure, based on these values.

American Values: Into the Twenty-First Century and Beyond

The collapse of the old order in Europe following World War I set the stage for the continental evolution of both democratic and tyrannical Marxist-Leninist and Fascist systems. Until that time, Pax Britannica had provided a sense of stability and order to European affairs as well as a security umbrella for the United States in its relationships with Europe. But for many Americans, involvement in a world conflict to save Europe seemed like a mistake. The United States withdrew into isolationism with a failure to join the League of Nations and the Back to Normalcy policy of President Warren Harding in 1920, which ended only with the start of World War II.

Even in the aftermath of World War I, Americans were accustomed to a world dominated by a European order compatible with the general nature of US values and national interests. Although an imperfect order, it did not offend the US value system. At the beginning of the twentieth century, US values were expressed by progressivism, by Theodore Roosevelt's presidency, and later by Franklin Roosevelt's New Deal and the Four Freedoms, focusing on individuals and the government's responsibility to them.

There was little need to translate values into the external world, as the interest of the United States rarely extended beyond its own shores. Yet it was during this time that the United States became a great power, partly as the result of acquiring territory in the Spanish American War. Within two decades, US involvement in World War I was seen as a way to make the world safe for democracy and subdue a tyrannical Old World power.

In the aftermath of World War I, most Americans were glad to distance themselves from the Old World and focus on domestic matters. "It's their problem, not ours," was a common US attitude with respect to Europe and the outside world. US isolationism and demilitarization during the 1920s and 1930s are recognized historical facts, typified by the US failure to join the League of Nations following World War I and thereby renouncing, in effect, President Woodrow Wilson's Fourteen Points for a new world order.[11] World War II changed all that, even though most Americans wanted no part of the "European War" (which started in 1939) until the surprise Japanese bombing of the US Pacific Fleet in Pearl Harbor in 1941.

Between the two world wars, Americans presumed that US interests were also world interests. US values were viewed as morally unassailable and therefore were to be sought after by the rest of the world. In this context, then, US national security was primarily a narrow focus on the protection of the homeland, which required few armed forces and a simple military strategy. Furthermore, there was little need to struggle with issues over US values and how to protect them in the external world, except occasionally for the sake of international economics. We passed to others, primarily Britain and France, responsibility for keeping the democratic peace.

Regardless of the US desire to return to isolation following World War II, US interests were increasingly threatened. Parts of Europe and Asia were smoldering from the war, and it soon became clear that US responsibilities extended beyond the nation's borders. In addition, it was perceived that democracy and US values could not be nurtured and expanded if we simply stayed at home; if democracy was the demand, then it required our presence in all parts of the world. Beyond protection of the US homeland, then, what did the United States stand for? And how did it intend to achieve its goals—whatever they were?

These questions were easier to answer in the negative: the United States was against Marxist-Leninist and other authoritarian political systems determined to subvert or overthrow the international order based on self-determination. The policy of containment reflected a US policy consensus to prevent the expansion of the Soviet Union and its Communist system. Positive responses to such questions were seen in the US role in rebuilding Europe, especially the economic recovery program known as the Marshall Plan. All of this placed the United States in the leadership role of the West and was consistent with the earlier Puritan view of Americans as a chosen people.[12] For many, the second half of the twentieth century was the "American Century"; such a notion would provide the moral basis for involvement in the Korean and Vietnam Wars.

But the end of the Cold War and the emergence of a new security landscape caused many Americans to focus on domestic issues. There was a turning inward, reinforced by the conviction that the United States had won the Cold War and the danger of a major war had diminished considerably. But this new landscape was muddled and obscured by the fog of peace. Indeed, some experts even argued that the United States would miss the Cold War, with its moral certainties and predictable (if difficult) responsibilities.[13]

Turning inward, Americans faced issues of diversity, gender, race, sexual orientation, and the integration of various groups with non-Western linkages. Critics argued that the United States might never have been a true melting pot of culture, yet it had benefited from the waves of immigrants who brought along their rich heritage. But that heritage, according to others, was promoted (as it is today) at the expense of "Americanism." They would argue that US cultural heritage and Western tradition—the bedrock of democracy—risk erosion by an increasing prominence of other cultures, whose loyalties may be rooted in countries other than the United States.[14] An ongoing democratic culture may not be compatible with some versions of multiculturalism, in their view.

The New Era

In the new era—beyond the war against terrorism—it is difficult to agree on the principles of US values as they apply to the international order. Issues of multiculturalism and diversity have called into question the very meaning of Americanism and the US value system. For example, in viewing the US domestic system, former chairman of the US Joint Chiefs of Staff and later secretary of state Colin Powell wrote:

> And Lord help anyone who strays from accepted ideas of political correctness. The slightest suggestion of offense toward any group . . . will be met with cries that the offender be fired or forced to undergo sensitivity training, or threats of legal action. Ironically for all the present sensitivity over correctness, we seem to have lost our shame as a society. Nothing seems to embarrass us; nothing shocks us anymore.[15]

In citing the "balkanization" of the United States, Georgie Anne Geyer argued that we must return to the idea of US "citizenship." She criticized the notion of globalization and the presumed decline of the nation-state as the focus of loyalty.[16] She concluded, "I remain convinced that the nation will rally at this important moment in a Renaissance to preserve the best of the past and to mate it with the best of the present and the future—so that we can and will be *Americans once again*."[17] Others argue, however, that most Americans are in the middle of the political spectrum and embrace God, family, and country. As Alan Wolfe contended, we are "one nation, after all."[18] These disagreements remain unresolved and affect US responses to national security challenges.

As some critics point out, spokespersons for various groups in the United States often use terms such as "our people" or "my people" in referring to their particular racial, ethnic, or religious group to the exclusion of others. This tends to distinguish and separate one group from Americans in general. But as President Franklin D. Roosevelt is credited with saying in 1943, "Americanism is a matter of heart and mind; Americanism is not a matter of race or ethnicity."

Nonetheless, US involvement in foreign lands and non-Western cultures can cause domestic problems because one group within the United States can support a like-minded group in a foreign land regardless of US policy interests. The greatest charge is that such a development can increase balkanization here. But as noted earlier, a number of Americans and policy elites gravitate toward the middle of the spectrum, preferring an inclusive instead of an exclusive definition of Americanism. Clearly, demographics and cultural issues have an impact on US national security policy and strategy. When the national interest is clear and the political objectives are closely aligned with that interest, there is likely to be strong support by Americans for US actions. But US involvement in cultures and religions abroad can have domestic repercussions, such as the conflict in the Middle East between Israel and the Palestinians and US involvement in Iraq and Afghanistan. This makes it more difficult to project US values into the international arena. In sum, the commitment of the US military in foreign areas will not draw support from the public unless it is convinced that such matters are part of the vital interests of the United States.

The Study of National Security

The exploration of national security and all its dimensions—including policy and priorities—leads to some basic questions. How can national security be studied? What fundamental principles provide the bases for US national security policy and strategy?

There are three major approaches to the study of national security: the concentric-circle, the elite-versus-participatory policymaking, and the systems analysis; all concentrate on the way in which policy is made. They should be distinguished from studies that examine national security issues, such as US nuclear strategy or US policy in the Middle East. The three approaches should be further distinguished from studies of government institutions.

The concentric-circle approach places the president at the center of the national security policy process (see Figure 1.3). The president's staff and the national security establishment provide advice and implement national security policy. This approach shows the degree of importance of various groups as the "primary objects" of national security policy. For example, a major objective is to influence the behavior and policies of allies as well as adversaries. At the same time, Congress, the public, and the media have important roles in the national security policy process. But they are not the objects of policy, and so the more distant circles represent government structures and agencies, constituencies, and the media. The farther the institutions are from the center, the less their importance as objects of national security policy. The problem with this approach is its oversimplification of the national security policy process and its presumption of rationality in decisionmaking.

The elite-versus-participatory policymaking approach is based on the view that democracy's basic dilemma is that the policy process is dominated by elites (see Figure 1.4). National security policy is undertaken by elites within the national security establishment, but that elite group must in turn develop support in the broader public. On the one hand, the elites have the

Figure 1.3 Concentric Circle Approach

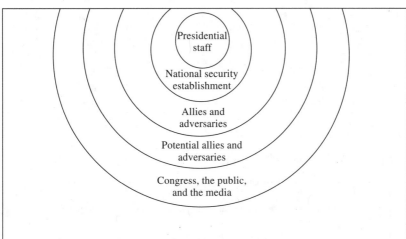

skill and access to information to formulate national security policy, in contrast to an uninformed public. On the other hand, for national security policy to be successful in the long run, there must be some degree of participation by the public and political will within the body politic. The elite model sees national security policy as being made by a small circle that includes the president, his staff, key members of Congress, high-ranking military officers, and influential members of the business community. The assumption is that this is a cohesive elite whose own interests override other concerns. The participatory model assumes the existence of a variety of elites who represent various segments of the public, interest groups, and officials. In this model, the same elites rarely control all aspects of national security policy. Coalitions are formed for particular issues, then reformed for other issues. This approach struggles to reconcile the skill and power of the elite with the demands of participatory democracy.

The systems-analysis approach emphasizes the dynamic interrelationships among variables at all stages of the security decisionmaking process (see Figure 1.5). Many inputs go into the policy process. The policymaking machinery must reconcile competing interests and design a policy acceptable to most. In turn, the impact of policy must be measured by feedback on policy effectiveness and how it is perceived by those affected.

All three approaches, as well as variations, are useful in the study of national security policy; this book incorporates something from each. We

Figure 1.4　Elite and Participatory Models

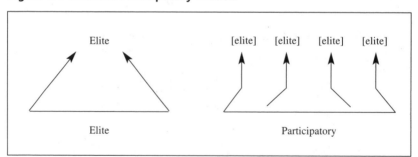

Figure 1.5　Systems-Analysis Approach

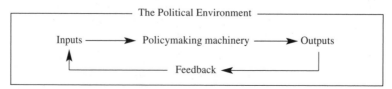

examine the formal national security establishment on the assumption that the president and government entities established by law form that establishment and are at the center of the policy process—the concentric-circle approach. We examine the National Security Council (NSC) and the Department of Defense from the concentric-circle approach and partly from the elite-versus-participatory approach. Finally, as for the formal policy process, most attention is given to the national security network—a systems-analysis approach that considers many power clusters within the governmental structure, the political system, and the international environment that have an impact on the national security establishment and the policymaking process.

National security establishment is a normative-analytical term referring to those responsible for national security decisionmaking as well as a descriptive term that identifies a set of actors and processes that actually produce security policy outcomes. Often, however, the character and personality of the president lead to the creation of informal and parallel structures and processes for developing national security policy. This sets up a series of policy power clusters that form a national security network that drives the national security establishment and the formal policymaking process. The relationships among and within these power clusters and their actual powers are dependent upon the way the president exercises his leadership and views on how the national security establishment should function.

There are four major power clusters within the US command structure, whose powers vary according to presidential leadership and preferences: (1) the policy triad, consisting of the secretary of state, the secretary of defense, and the national security advisor; (2) the director of national intelligence and the chairman of the Joint Chiefs of Staff; and (3) the president's closest White House advisers, such as the White House chief of staff and the counselor to the president; and (4) the secretary of Homeland Security.

These four power clusters are extremely important in shaping national security policy (see Figure 1.6). They represent critical parts of the national security establishment but operate in ways that reflect presidential leadership style and the mind-sets of those within the three power clusters. As such, they may or may not be compatible with the formal national security establishment. Put another way, the national security establishment is fluid and dynamic, and the policymaking process is not as rational and systematic as one is led to believe.

> The defense planning process . . . is beset with multiple dilemmas. Assessing the threat and acquiring the force structure to meet that threat require an efficient crystal ball—not only in the sense of defining the future in the here and now in terms of events and dangers; the process also requires accurately estimating the national mood years before the critical event.[19]

Figure 1.6 Policy Power Clusters and the National Security System

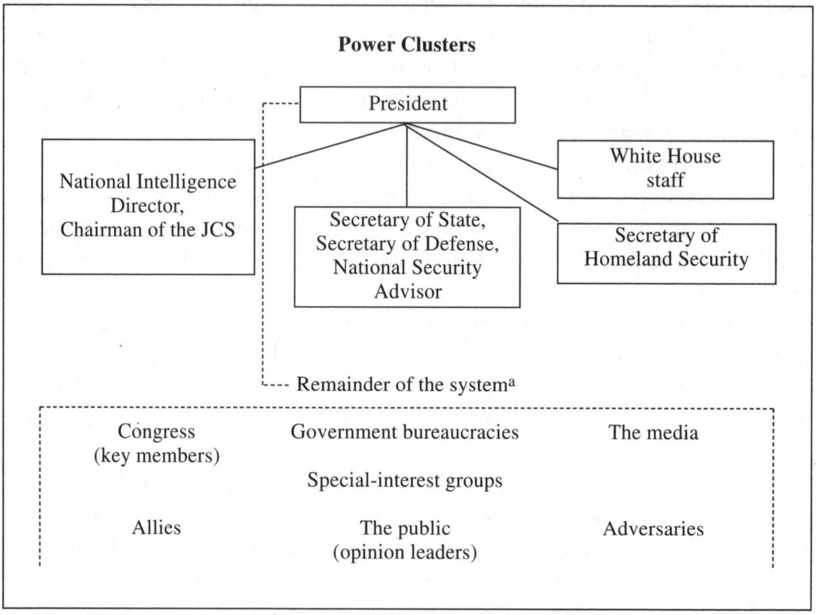

Power Clusters

```
                        ┌──────────────────────┐
                        │      President        │
                        └──────────────────────┘
                                                    ┌──────────────────┐
┌──────────────────────┐                            │   White House    │
│ National Intelligence│                            │      staff       │
│      Director,       │    ┌──────────────────┐    └──────────────────┘
│ Chairman of the JCS  │    │ Secretary of State,  ┌──────────────────┐
└──────────────────────┘    │ Secretary of Defense,│   Secretary of   │
                            │ National Security │   │ Homeland Security│
                            │     Advisor       │   └──────────────────┘
                            └──────────────────┘
```

---- Remainder of the system[a]

```
┌─────────────────────────────────────────────────────────────────────┐
│   Congress           Government bureaucracies        The media       │
│ (key members)                                                        │
│                        Special-interest groups                       │
│                                                                      │
│     Allies                 The public              Adversaries       │
│                        (opinion leaders)                             │
└─────────────────────────────────────────────────────────────────────┘
```

Note: a. Objects of national security policy and inputs into national security policy.

Conclusion

There is a set of boundaries, constraints, and limitations that cannot be separated from the operations of the US national security establishment. The policy process cannot be viewed separately from these considerations. As a result (and aside from real threats to the homeland), there is likely to be internal disagreement and debate within the national security establishment, between the establishment and other branches and agencies of government, and between all of these and the public. The intensity of the disagreement increases in direct proportion to the size of the gap between policies and strategies, on the one hand, and well-established perspectives and the US political-military posture, on the other. When we add the differing views of allies and adversaries and their national security efforts—especially in the new era—it is clear that simply examining the establishment or the policy process does not do justice to the complexities and complications inherent in US national security.

All of this is exacerbated by the diffusion and decentralization of power within the US political system, within and among the branches of government, and also within the general population. Participatory politics and single-issue politics, the erosion of political party cohesion, changing domestic demographics, the policy role of the media, and internal power problems within government have made it almost impossible for the president to undertake any foreign policy or national security initiatives that are perceived as outside the mainstream or as requiring a new kind of military posture or preparedness. The exception may be the war on international terrorism. But even in such cases, disagreements abound regarding the approach and nature of adversaries. To induce changes and to place his stamp on national security policy, the president must build a political base within the government and activate the general public as well as convince the media of the appropriateness of new policies and strategies. This usually means that the matter must be seen as a major national security issue, with the US position clearly proper and morally correct, and must involve acceptable risk and a high expectation of success.

The US fear of concentration of power is engrained in the constitutional principles of separation of powers and checks and balances; these have provided clear limits to the exercise of power of any one branch of government. Yet these restraints can also prevent effective response to challenges that require concentration of power to succeed. Thus the problem is self-contradictory, and the legal niceties of US constitutional practice can have little influence in the international security setting, where power and politics are often inextricable. It is in this context that the US national security establishment and the process by which security policy is formulated and implemented meet their greatest test. Such a test is evident in the struggles between the president and Congress over war power resolutions.

In this book our primary concern is the US national security establishment and the security policy process. In addition, we examine the international security setting, the factors that affect the substance of US national security policy, and the presidential mandate (see Part 2). All of these matters have become exceedingly complicated by the disagreements within the United States over involvement in Iraq and Afghanistan and troublesome issues regarding Iran, North Korea, and nuclear proliferation generally. The chapters on the establishment and the national security process are focused on these issues.

Notes

1. See, for example, "Under Siege," *US News and World Report*, September 24, 2001. The entire issue reports on the September 11 attacks and the US response. Needless to say, there are a variety of reports and assessments of this event in virtually all elements of the media. For example, see Steven Emerson, *Jihad Incorporated: A Guide to Militant Islam in the US* (Amherst, NY: Prometheus

Books, 2006), and Thomas R. Mockaitis and Paul B. Rich, eds., *Grand Strategy in the War Against Terrorism* (Portland, OR: Frank Cass, 2003).

2. David Jablonsky, "The State of the National Security State," in David Jablonsky, Ronald Steel, Lawrence Korb, Morton H. Halperin, and Robert Ellsworth, *US National Security: Beyond the Cold War* (Carlisle Barracks, PA: Strategic Studies Institute, US Army War College, July 26, 1997), pp. 39–40.

3. Charles W. Kegley Jr. and Eugene R. Wittkopf, *World Politics: Trend and Transformation*, 11th ed. (Boston: Bedford/St. Martin's, 2006).

4. Carnes Lord, "Strategy and Organization at the National Level," in James C. Gaston, ed., *Grand Strategy and the Decisionmaking Process* (Washington, DC: National Defense University Press, 1994), pp. 141–159.

5. *Sun Tzu: The Art of War*, translated and with an introduction by Samuel B. Griffith (New York: Oxford University Press, 1971).

6. Henry A. Kissinger, *American Foreign Policy: Three Essays* (New York: W. W. Norton, 1969), p. 92.

7. There are a number of publications and reports regarding the US involvement in Iraq and Afghanistan. See, for example, Lawrence F. Kaplan and William Kristol, *The War over Iraq: Saddam's Tyranny and America's Mission* (San Francisco, CA: Encounter Books, 2003); Lee H. Hamilton, Lawrence S. Eagleburger, and James A. Baker III, *Iraq Study Group Report* (2006); Thomas E. Ricks, *Fiasco: The American Military Adventure in Iraq* (New York: The Penguin Press, 2006); David C. Hendrickson and Robert W. Tucker, *Revisions in Need of Revising: What Went Wrong in the Iraq War* (Carlisle Barracks, PA: Strategic Studies Institute, US Army War College, December 2005).

8. See, e.g., Thomas E. Copeland, ed., *The Information Revolution and National Security* (Carlisle Barracks, PA: Strategic Studies Institute, US Army War College, August 2000).

9. For a useful study, see Eugene R. Wittkopf, ed., *The Domestic Sources of American Foreign Policy: Insights and Evidence*, 2nd ed. (New York: St. Martin's, 1994).

10. David Scheffer concluded, "I propose that we are witnessing the end of sovereignty as it has been traditionally understood in international law and in state practice. In its place we are seeing a new form of national integrity emerging." David Scheffer, "Humanitarian Intervention Versus State Sovereignty," in United States Institute of Peace, *Peacemaking and Peacekeeping Implications for the United States Military* (Washington, DC: United States Institute of Peace, May 1993), p. 9.

11. See James M. McCormick, *American Foreign Policy and Process*, 4th ed. (Itasca, IL: F. E. Peacock, 2004), pp. 28–30.

12. See, for example, Kenneth D. Wald and Allison Calhoun-Brown, *Religion and Politics in the United States*, 5th ed. (Washington, DC: CQ Press, 2006). Also see Douglas Johnston and Cynthia Sampson, eds., *Religion: The Missing Dimension of Statecraft* (Oxford: Oxford University Press, 1994).

13. See, e.g., John Mearsheimer, "Why We Will Soon Miss the Cold War," *Atlantic*, August 1990, pp. 35–50.

14. Samuel P. Huntington, *The Clash of Civilizations and the Remaking of World Order* (New York: Simon and Schuster, 1996). See also Samuel P. Huntington, "The Clash of Civilizations?" *Foreign Affairs* 72, no. 3 (Summer 1993): 22–49. For a critique of the Huntington thesis, see Shireen T. Hunter, *The Future of Islam and the West: Clash of Civilizations or Peaceful Coexistence?* (Westport, CT: Praeger, 1998).

15. Colin Powell, with Joseph E. Persico, *My American Journey* (New York: Random House, 1995), p. 610.

16. Georgie Anne Geyer, *Americans No More: The Death of Citizenship* (New York: Atlantic Monthly, 1996).

17. Ibid., p. 339.

18. Alan Wolfe, *One Nation, After All: What Americans Really Think About God, the Right, the Left and Each Other* (New York: Viking, 1999). See also David Gergen, "One Nation, After All," *US News and World Report*, March 16, 2000, p. 84, and James MacGregor Burns and Georgia J. Sorenson, with Robin Gerber and Scott W. Webster, *Dead Center: Clinton-Gore Leadership and the Perils of Moderation* (New York: Oxford University Press, 2000).

19. Frederick H. Hartmann and Robert L. Wendzel, *Defending America's Security* (Washington, DC: Pergamon-Brassey's, 1988), p. 146.

2

The Conflict Spectrum and the American Way of War

THE AMERICAN WAY OF WAR IS SHAPED BY FOUR CRITICAL dimensions. First, for most Americans there is a clear distinction between the instruments of peace and those of war. The instruments of war remain dormant until war erupts, at which time the instruments of peace fade into the background, allowing whatever must be done to win. This polarization is also reflected in the way Americans tend to view contemporary conflicts. Involvement is seen as an either-or situation: the United States is either at war or at peace, with very little attention given to situations that have aspects of both conditions.

Second, most Americans tend to view conflicts in the world through conventional lenses, with mind-sets shaped by the US experience and by US values and norms. Issues of war and peace are seen in legalistic terms in which wars are declared and conducted according to established rules of law. For many Americans, international behavior must also abide by such rules. Seeing a new basis for US interventionism, one author has written, "The new interventionism has its roots in long-standing tendencies of American foreign policy—missionary zeal, bewilderment when the world refuses to conform to American expectations and a belief that for every problem there is a quick and easy solution."[1] This applies equally well to conflicts in the new era. Yet September 11 made many aware of the new kind of war, one characterized by unconventional strategy and unconventional tactics. It is a war that does not conform to conventional mind-sets.

Third, the Vietnam experience left many Americans skeptical and ambivalent about the overseas commitment of US ground combat forces. This is the case in regard to the continuing US involvement in Iraq and Afghanistan that began in 2003. Even though a new generation is emerging with only vague memories of Vietnam, the Vietnam Memorial in

Washington and several films of varying accuracy promise to keep the Vietnam experience alive. In addition, media coverage of the continuing US difficulties in Iraq and Afghanistan frequently make comparisons to Vietnam. There seems to be an undercurrent of caution—a Vietnam syndrome, if you will—whenever US troops are committed to anything other than conventional war.

Fourth, US involvement must be terminated as quickly as possible, with the victory reflecting clear decisions and final solutions. The fact that the public seeks clear and understandable solutions to complex issues compounds the difficulties inherent in policymaking. This mind-set assumes that every problem has a solution. More than two decades ago, Ernest van den Haag captured this US perspective. He wrote:

> Many Americans still are under the impression that a benevolent deity has made sure that there is a just solution to every problem, a remedy for every wrong, which can be discovered by negotiations, based on good will and on American moral and legal ideals, self-evident enough to persuade all parties, once they are revealed by negotiators, preferably American. Reality is otherwise. Just solutions are elusive. Many problems have no solutions, not even unjust ones; at most they can be managed, prevented from getting worse or from spreading to wider areas. . . . International problems hardly ever are solved by the sedulous pursuit of legal and moral principles.[2]

The consequences drive us to search for the "doable," which in turn leads to oversimplification, whether the issue is strategic weaponry, defense budgets, humanitarian issues, or unconventional conflicts. With respect to unconventional conflicts, most simplistic solutions sidestep fundamental problems and reveal a lack of understanding regarding relationships among culture, modernity, political and economic changes, internal conflicts, and less developed systems. This predilection is reinforced by the fact that many otherwise effective responses to unconventional conflicts might not fall neatly within the framework of values and norms of open systems. The most effective response to terrorist attacks against the US homeland may well require actions that fall outside the norms of democracy. This does not mean that open systems are incapable of effective response. It means that open systems have difficulty in developing policies and strategies for unconventional conflicts owing to the very nature and character of those open systems.

There is increasing disagreement, however, about the appropriateness of the American way of war. Is our traditional way of war relevant in the new era? How should the US military be used in contingencies and missions short of war?

Although military capability remains an essential component of the American way of war and national security, several other components have become important: diplomacy, political power, psychological strategy, intelligence, and economics. In this environment, intelligence capability worldwide takes on an increasingly important role. But the fact is that in some situations none of these components can substitute for the effective use of military power. This is especially important for the United States given its worldwide interests and the security objectives evolving from the new world order. This is not to suggest that military means should be the first or only option, but there may be times when national security and national interests require the use of military force (although this must be tempered by the nature of the conflict and the appropriate use of other instruments). The military is often the instrument of first choice, even in contingencies short of war. This was the case for the Clinton administration (1993–2001) when its security team met to hammer out US policy in Bosnia-Herzegovina. At one point, a discussion took place between UN ambassador Madeleine Albright and the chairman of the US Joint Chiefs of Staff, General Colin Powell. As described by Powell, "The debate exploded at one session when Madeleine Albright . . . asked me in frustration, 'What's the point in having this superb military that you're always talking about if we can't use it?' I thought I would have an aneurysm. American GIs were not toy soldiers to be moved around some sort of global game board."[3] General Powell then explained that US soldiers had been used in a variety of operations other than war as well as outright war during the recent years, but in each there was a clear political goal and the military was structured and tasked to achieve those goals. Powell was clear on the point that the military should not be used until the United States had a clear political objective.[4]

Complicating the issue, the public tends to view war as a clear struggle between good and evil.[5] In this view, the military instrument is an implement of war that should not be harnessed except to destroy evil. This mindset is opposite to the sense of realpolitik and balance of power that characterized the foreign relations of Europe's Great Powers from the seventeenth through the twentieth centuries. In any case, as John Spanier has written,

> Once Americans were provoked, however, and the United States had to resort to force, the employment of this force was justified in terms of universal moral principles with which the United States, as a democratic country, identified itself. Resort to the evil instrument of war could be justified only by presuming noble purposes and completely destroying the immoral enemy who threatened the integrity, if not the existence, of these principles. American power had to be "righteous" power; only its full exercise could ensure salvation or the absolution of sin.[6]

In sum, the ability of the United States to respond to situations across the conflict spectrum (discussed below) is conditioned by historical experience and the American way of war. National interests and national security policy have been shaped by the premises identified here and have influenced the way Americans see the contemporary world security environment. Yet the security issues and conflicts across the spectrum may not be relevant to US perceptions, policy, and strategy. The gap between US perceptions and the realities of the security environment poses a challenging and often dangerous dilemma for US national security policy. This requires a rethinking of the nature of contemporary conflicts and the US national security posture. This rethinking, combined with the turmoil and fog of the international security landscape, is best studied by examining the conflict spectrum.

The Conflict Spectrum

The transformation of the US military to meet the challenges of the twenty-first century has become an indispensable part of its culture. These new directions are intended to ensure that the military remains capable across the conflict spectrum, spelled out by the US Joint Chiefs of Staff in a publication titled *Joint Vision 2020:*

> The ultimate goal of our military force is to accomplish the objectives directed by the National Command Authorities. For the joint force of the future, this goal will be achieved through full spectrum dominance—the ability of US forces, operating unilaterally or in combination with multinational and interagency partners, to defeat any adversary and control any situation across the full range of military operations.[7]

The concept of full spectrum dominance rests on existing as well as evolving military capabilities. Thus, according to *Joint Vision 2020,* the military is expected to be capable in peacekeeping, humanitarian operations, operations other than war (OOTW), unconventional conflicts, and stability operations in addition to all the various dimensions of conventional operations and quick-reaction capabilities. All of this is to be accomplished in a strategic landscape that remains clouded in the fog of peace. In 2001, that fog dissipated somewhat as increasing attention was given to homeland security.[8] As of this writing, however, serious questions remain regarding US capability in Iraq and Afghanistan. Figure 2.1 shows the conflict spectrum into the twenty-first century.

The conflict spectrum is a way of showing the nature and characteristics of international conflicts. It is a useful method for assessing US capabilities and effectiveness. Contemporary conflicts are placed in various categories of intensity. Although the fear of major war between major states has diminished, there is increasing concern about continuous intrastate conflicts as well as unconventional conflicts. Moreover, there is disagreement in the US body politic as well as the national security system about our responses to the turmoil within other states and the international system in general.

Figure 2.1 The Conflict Spectrum

Noncombat: military assistance, peacekeeping, peace enforcement, peacemaking, humanitarian, domestic missions, shows of force[a]	Unconventional: revolution; nationalistic, ethnic, and religious conflicts; terrorism; counterterrorism[a]	Conventional: limited/major war	Nuclear: limited/major war

←——————————————— Asymmetrical[b] ——————————- - - - - - - - - - - - - →

←——————————————— Information-age technology[b] ———————————————→

Challenges and threats to the United States
←—most likely ——————————————————————— least likely —→

Strategic landscape

←——————————strategic reality ——————————————→
←——— likely mission/contingencies ———————→

US effectiveness

←——— good to fair ———►◄—— ? ——►◄——————— excellent ———————→

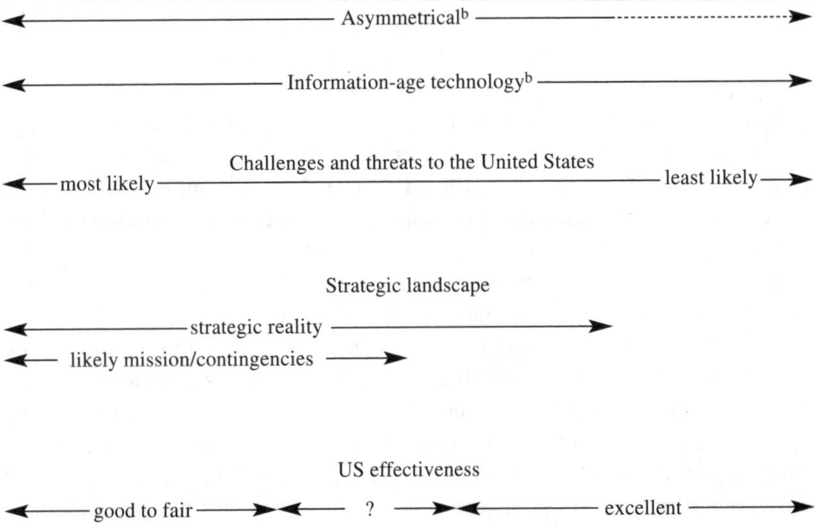

Notes: The complexity of the twenty-first-century strategic landscape and conflict characteristics is reflected in this schematic. This is even more complicated because it is possible that a variety of conflicts can occur simultaneously.

------► indicates an unclear impact and/or end result.

a. There is rarely a clear distinction between noncombat contingencies and unconventional conflicts. The noncombat category includes a variety of humanitarian and peacekeeping operations as well as coalition strategies and military support for UN operations. Virtually all operations other than war have the potential of developing into unconventional conflicts of one type or another. Unconventional conflicts can also take place simultaneously with conventional conflicts.

b. The asymmetrical dimension and threats emanating from information-age technology cut across all the categories of conflict.

Today and for the near term, conflicts are likely to be multidimensional, confusing, and complex. *Three dimensions* have become characteristic of this new international landscape. First, challenges to state sovereignty based on claims of self-determination by groups within a state are becoming international concerns. The United Nations, NATO, and other regional groups such as the European Community are increasingly apprehensive about intrastate conflicts, especially those that are likely to spill over into their areas. This has triggered intervention contrary to the traditional international norm of state sovereignty—the rule of the state over its own habitants. Some argue that state sovereignty has never been an absolute international norm. It certainly is not absolute now, as seen by NATO force involvement in Kosovo and Afghanistan.

Second, there is increasing attention to the impact of information warfare, defined as a range of activities from criminal mischief to technologically sophisticated warfare using computer networks and a variety of communication devices. This was evidently part of the US strategy in challenging Slobodan Milosevic during the Kosovo conflict in 1999 and has been used in the US involvement in Iraq. It was also reported that opponents of the NATO mission in Kosovo temporarily disabled NATO's main website through e-mail bombing (including hacking and flooding of a website). This has also been the case in various parts of the Middle East. In this evolving scenario, it has been argued that proficient computer users, even those living in less developed regions, can prosecute information warfare effectively against the most advanced countries. Indeed, the United States may be the most vulnerable to this kind of attack given its industrial and military dependence on information-age technology.

Third, various types of conflicts can be taking place in one area at any given time. That is, ethnic conflicts might be taking place while terrorism, extrastate intervention, or conventional invasions are occurring. Even more complicating is the fact that information warfare can take place against an adversary in the same conflict arena. This multiconflict scenario makes it difficult not only to pinpoint the specific adversary but also to undertake conflict resolution. The problem of mission creep also enters into the picture, whereby the specific mission assigned to the military becomes enlarged not by choice but by one's efforts to succeed. In the process, the military involvement expands uncontrollably and can lead to unacceptable consequences.

In the conflict spectrum, conflicts are categorized as low intensity or high intensity, primarily for policy and strategy purposes but also in an attempt to distinguish the degree of mobilization and involvement of US forces. The intensity level should in no way be construed as representative of the actual combat area; for US military personnel (as well as for their adversaries), personal combat is high intensity. Too often such categorization is merely a policy posture, with little relevance to the conflict environment.

US competence varies among conflict categories. At the low end of the spectrum, the United States is capable and reasonably effective in OOTW, stability operations, or whatever new missions short of war are labeled. Most of these military contingencies presume that operations are not likely to involve serious combat (or any combat at all). At the opposite end of the spectrum, the United States remains well positioned in nuclear weaponry and strategic forces to deter most adversaries. With the end of the Cold War, the likelihood of a major war or a nuclear exchange between major powers has diminished.[9] In addition, treaties between the United States and Russia to reduce strategic and tactical nuclear weapons have ushered in an era of arms control that is extending worldwide. Many such efforts are a continuation of previous attempts to control nuclear proliferation, yet some states are developing and expanding their nuclear, chemical, and/or biological capability (e.g., China, North Korea, and Iran). In any event, the United States must retain a credible deterrent to counter the use of weapons of mass destruction. Similarly, the US capability in conventional conflict was well demonstrated in the 1991 Gulf War, which was primarily based on operational principles derived from a European-oriented battle scenario. And the air war over Afghanistan in response to September 11 demonstrated a remarkable capability to use high-tech aerial weaponry to incapacitate ground-based forces deployed in difficult terrain. Still, airpower alone was not sufficient; it took Northern Alliance ground forces in Afghanistan to finish the task.

It is in the vast middle area on the spectrum—unconventional conflicts, the most likely conflicts for the foreseeable future—where the United States is at a distinct disadvantage. Most contemporary conflicts are included in this category, ranging from revolution and terrorism to conflicts associated with coalitions of drug cartels and revolutionary groups. The tendency is to see such conflicts in terms of commando-type operations or special operations shaped by counterterrorism contingencies, but there is much more to them than this suggests.

The label *unconventional conflicts* as used here refers to conflicts that do not follow conventional characteristics. In contrast, the 1991 Gulf War was a conventional conflict. Unconventional conflicts include a number of characteristics in which the US adversary employs strategy and tactics that do not correspond to US conventional force dispositions, strategy, and/or tactics. Thus the United States can challenge an adversary on the ground and in the air using conventional means, but that adversary might focus on unconventional strategy and tactics, terrorism, information warfare, and other means. In the case of information warfare, an adversary with information-age technology—a computer hacker, for instance—may be able to do harm to the United States, including its economy, corporations, and the US government itself. At the same time, however, US technology may have little ability to overcome a determined adversary owing to his limited dependence on information-age technology.

It is important to examine unconventional conflicts more closely because they are likely to be based on strategic cultures that do not reflect

Judeo-Christian notions or classic European-type scenarios; neither do they necessarily follow the American way of war. Moreover, competency, indeed, proficiency, in unconventional conflicts and contingencies in the middle areas of the conflict spectrum are necessary if the US military is to be effective in the new era.[10] This will still remain a difficult problem in the foreseeable future.

Unconventional Conflicts

The history of the United States—dating even to the prerevolutionary period—is filled with the exploits of elite units undertaking unconventional operations.

From Rogers' Rangers in the American Revolution, to the First Special Service Unit of World War II and the Tenth Special Forces in Korea, to the Green Berets of the Kennedy era, to the Special Operations Command of the contemporary period, the US military draws from an honored legacy of special operations and low-intensity conflict. Yet too often this experience was placed at the periphery of classic military education, professionalism, and strategy—viewed more as curiosity than curriculum—and was generally considered tangential to real issues of war and peace.

In the 1980s a new counterinsurgency era emerged and, with it, an increased interest in special units and special operations. Resources committed to special operations increased in terms of both logistics and personnel. The creation of the First Special Operations Command in 1982 was a major step in creating a permanent special operations capability within the military. In 1986, Congress provided for an assistant secretary of defense for special operations and low-intensity conflict and established a unified command for all US Special Operations Forces (Army, Navy, and Air Force). By 1990, special forces personnel numbered about 12,000, organized into five active Special Forces Groups. Similar increases occurred in the US Army Ranger battalions; Navy Sea, Air, and Land (SEALS) units; and Air Force Special Operations Forces.[11] This organizational structure remains in place. The organization of the Special Operations Command is shown in Figure 2.2.

Although this recent effort suggests the US position is strong in this area, it was tempered by policy incoherence, flawed strategy, and doctrinal ambiguity. The prevailing view that the US military was capable in unconventional conflicts seemed to apply more to special operations of a more conventional nature. In the Gulf War, for example, special operations forces were involved in long-range reconnaissance and behind-the-line operations—missions within the scope of ranger and commando-type operations. A final judgment on US capability in unconventional conflict will rest on the outcome of such efforts in the war on terrorism that began in late 2001. Preliminary indications are that US forces have improved in this area.

Figure 2.2 Special Operations Command

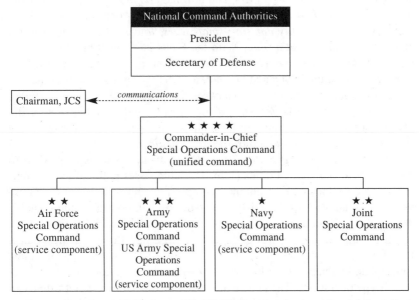

Source: Department of the Army, *FM 100-25: Doctrine for Army Special Operations Forces* (Washington, DC: US Government Printing Office, 1991), pp. 4–19.
Notes: The stars indicate the military rank of the commander.

Since the early 1990s the US Army Special Forces have been in the process of being reshaped into an elite-type conventional force. Furthermore, the Army's efforts at "transformation" and the focus on a variety of missions short of war overlap with the role of special forces. "Threatened with irrelevance by changes that allow conventional forces to conduct missions that were once its exclusive preserve, the Green Berets are refocusing on unconventional warfare."[12] This is the theme of a one-year study by the Army Special Forces as reported in *Army Times* in July 2001. "The changing strategic environment makes unconventional warfare a vital mission for the early 21st century," according to those involved in the study. The report noted, however, that "the shift will require changes in training, and could put Special Forces leaders on a collision course with superiors at U.S. Special Operations Command."[13]

Conceptual Coherence

The most important aspect of developing an effective US political-military posture for unconventional conflicts is conceptual clarity and coherence. During the 1960s counterinsurgency era, a variety of terms came into use to provide some analytical precision to the newfound form of warfare: *insur-*

gency, counterinsurgency, special warfare, guerrilla warfare, wars of national liberation, people's wars, and *internal conflicts.* The 1980s saw the revival of many of these terms and added some new ones, such as *special operations, low-intensity conflict, small wars, low-level wars, operations short of war,* and *secret armies.* With the focus on combating international terrorism, *terror* and *counterterror* have become part of the special operations lexicon. In the 1990s and beyond, a variety of terms have been added, including *stability operations, peacekeeping, peacemaking, peace enforcement, humanitarian missions,* and *OOTW.* Lost are older notions of guerrilla war, insurgency, and revolution; now the tendency is to characterize many such conflicts as *ethnic, religious,* or *nationalistic.*[14]

A case in point is *revolution,* intended to achieve a strategic goal, with both strategic and tactical dimensions. It encompasses political-psychological, as well as social and economic, components and is aimed at the entire political-social order of the existing system. Revolution is a complex, multidimensional phenomenon with origins in the political-social system and a strategy based on a sweeping attack against the existing order. Revolutionary tactics range from terror, assassinations, hit-and-run raids, robbery, and kidnapping to the use of armed force in the conduct of conventional-type operations. The center of gravity of the conflict is not usually in the armed forces but rather the political-social milieu of the existing system. The revolutionary strategy and tactics employed are shaped accordingly.

> A revolutionary war is never confined within the bounds of military action. . . . For this reason it is endowed with a dynamic quality and a dimension in depth that orthodox wars, whatever their scale, lack. This is particularly true of revolutionary guerrilla war, which is not susceptible to the type of superficial military treatment frequently advocated by antediluvian doctrinaires.[15]

Some groups will use revolutionary strategy and tactics to achieve particular political goals that sometimes fall short of taking over the state. This is seen in ethnic, religious, and hypernationalistic conflicts, such as that in the Balkans in 1999–2000 as well as the conflicts in Iraq and Afghanistan in 2006 and beyond.

Terror and Counterterror

In this new era, *cyberterrorism* has become a new phenomenon. Signs already suggest that terrorist groups will try to gain strength and extend their reach by organizing into transnational networks and developing swarming strategies and tactics for destroying targets, entirely apart from whether they can hack into a target's computer system.[16]

In the broader scheme there are at least four categorizations of terror: terror-qua-terror, revolutionary terrorism, state-supported terrorism, and state-sponsored terrorism.[17] All of these can have international dimensions and also be linked to other groups such as drug cartels. *Terror-qua-terror* is violence for the sake of violence, combining tactical means and strategic purposes; that is, the terrorist act is perceived as an end in and of itself. The aim is to strike at the system, to gain recognition for one's terrorist group, to achieve a moral victory, to fulfill a mission in life (e.g., in a religious way), or all of these. There is very little concern about anything beyond the act or state of terrorism itself. In earlier years, factions of the Baader-Meinhof Gang, the Red Brigades, and Direct Action were cases in point. US examples include the Symbionese Liberation Army and the Weather Underground.[18] This is also characteristic of so-called *new terrorism.* According to one account, "the new terrorism . . . appears pointless since it does not lead directly to any strategic goal, and it seems exotic since it is frequently couched in the visionary rhetoric of religion. It is the anti-order of the new world order of the twenty-first century."[19]

Terrorist acts have also been used by individuals or groups as statements against the government. This appears to be the case involving Timothy McVeigh and the bombing of the Murrah Federal Building in Oklahoma City in April 1995. "The bombing introduced many Americans to the disturbing underworld of domestic terrorism while shattering whatever illusions existed about terrorism as only an international or overseas threat."[20]

The September 11, 2001, attacks in New York and Washington introduced Americans to the impact and efficiency of some international terrorist groups. It also shattered some illusions regarding international terrorism. These attacks appeared to be well organized, well financed, and well executed. They created more casualties in the US homeland than any other war, with the exception of the Civil War.

Revolutionary terrorism is a strategic as well as tactical instrument of the revolutionary system; that is, terrorist tactics and strategies are designed to further the revolutionary cause. The terrorist instrument is usually under the control of revolutionary leadership, and terrorist operations are conducted so as to avoid, as much as possible, alienating the very people at which the revolution is directed. Nonetheless, in light of the international scope of revolutionary strategy, terrorists can cross over into the terror-qua-terror category in the name of revolution. The Palestine Liberation Organization in former years, various groups operating in the Middle East such as Hezbollah, the Vietcong during the Vietnam War, and revolutionaries in El Salvador (i.e., the Farabundo Martí Front of National Liberation and the Popular Revolutionary Army) can generally be categorized as revolutionary terrorism. Perhaps one of the clearest examples is Sendero Luminoso (Shining Path) in Peru. In early 2000 many felt that Sendero Luminoso had been all but eliminated by the efforts of Peruvian president Alberto

Fujimoro, yet it re-emerged in 2002. In Greece, the actions of the November 17 group in 2000 may well be a version of revolutionary terror, although the group has been active on and off for decades.

Another dimension in this category is the coalition between drug cartels and revolutionary groups, as in Colombia, where the United States has been involved militarily as well as financially.[21] This coalition in crime is mutually advantageous to the drug lords and the revolutionaries, at least in the short to middle term. The drug cartels pay protection money to the revolutionaries in order to protect drug operations in outlying areas. The revolutionaries provide protection in order to maintain a dependable financial source. This linkage has created internal turmoil and havoc, with the United States becoming increasingly involved. In the broader sense, revolutionaries can take a certain pleasure as well as strategic advantage in seeing Western systems, such as the United States, undermined by drug trafficking and drug use. Yet the underlying philosophical basis of revolution is contrary to the notion of long-term dependence on drug operations. From another perspective, individual revolutionaries are not immune from drug addiction.

State-supported terrorism is difficult to identify because it is often difficult to directly link terrorist activity to states. This is a result of states' ability to hide their support and involvement using a variety of techniques.[22]

State-sponsored terrorism is one in which a particular state actually organizes, trains, and finances terrorist groups. This includes identifying terror targets and providing recruits. Furthermore, sponsor states are able to engage in a form of psychological warfare by controlling information about their own system while gaining access to the media of open systems to broadcast their own messages. Some states engage in terrorism against their own citizens in order to maintain control or neutralize dissidents and resistance groups; totalitarian and authoritarian systems are especially noted for such activity (e.g., Nicaragua under Sandinista rule, Zimbabwe, and the former Soviet Union).[23] In the Middle East, Iraq under Saddam Hussein, Iran, Libya, and Syria have been accused of such operations.

Some observers have also identified a new dimension, *religious terrorism,* that is linked to the new terrorism. As one observer noted:

> In 1998, when Secretary of State Madeleine Albright announced a list of 30 of the world's most dangerous groups, over half were religious and included Judaism, Islam, and Buddhism. If other violent religious groups around the world were added—including the many Christian militia and other paramilitary organizations found in the United States—the number of religious terrorist groups would be considerable.[24]

The terrorist attacks on the United States in 2001 clearly illuminated the threat of religious terrorism. This has become even more pronounced and more complex in the aftermath of the US involvement in Iraq.

These labels are complicated by the fact that terrorism can be multidimensional, that is, a terrorist act can be a combination of all three categories discussed above. Add to this the possibility of cyberterrorism, and it becomes a difficult challenge for states to design effective counterterrorism strategies.

On the international level, many countries do not hesitate to define terrorist acts such as kidnapping, hostage-taking, assassination, bombings, armed robbery, and so on as criminal in nature. Other states, especially in the developing world, resist any definition, however, that may have legal implications restricting the activities of groups fighting against neocolonial regimes. Moreover, some states see the use of terrorism as a low-risk, high-return policy affording an opportunity to strike the West, especially the United States. This lack of definition also reflects the view that one person's terrorist is another person's freedom fighter. Unfortunately such a perspective ignores the characteristics of terrorist acts and the impact on their victims. Furthermore, this view is based on convoluted moral principles that elevate assassination and murder to humanistic ventures.

Unconventional Conflicts

There is a great deal of published literature on the nature and character of unconventional conflicts, ranging from Sun-tzu and Mao Tse-tung to Che Guevara and Vo Nguyen Giap.[25] The concept now includes a variety of efforts short of taking control of the state and establishing a revolutionary government. An in-depth study of revolution and counterrevolution would require serious reading of the major works. For our purposes, it is important to identify five major characteristics that have an especially significant bearing on the ability of open systems to come to grips with unconventional conflicts.

First, unconventional conflicts are *asymmetrical* and, for those involved, they are "total" wars. Revolutionaries feel that they are waging a life-and-death struggle with the existing system. Terrorists often see themselves as engaged in the ultimate struggle, bringing death to themselves, if need be, to achieve their goals. For open systems, however, involvement in unconventional conflicts is more limited, yet the constraints and restraints of limited wars generally apply. More important, the nature of open systems limits strategy, tactical operations, and overall effort.

Second, unconventional conflicts tend to be *protracted*, as the strategies are long-range. Those who demonstrate infinite patience and persistence are more likely to be successful; the classic example is North Vietnam, which had the staying power to outlast a technologically advanced superpower. Revolutionaries thus often adopt long-term strategies to erode the ability of the existing system to govern. Tactics and doctrines are designed according-ly. But revolutionaries do not necessarily choose a protracted conflict; they are forced into adopting such a strategy because of the initial power of the government they oppose. Yet some revolutionary ideologues idealize the nature of the conflict, even more than outright success. In such cases the protracted war is used to mobilize the masses, establish a revolutionary system, and create a revolutionary myth.

Third, unconventional conflicts are also *tactically unconventional*. This type of conflict is not necessarily ruled by Clausewitzian principles that place the center of gravity within the armed forces of the state; Sun-tzu's formulations are more relevant.[26] The Chinese writer emphasized deception, psychological warfare, and moral influence. Combined with hit-and-run raids, assassinations, ambushes, and surprise attacks, the tactics of unconventional conflicts are difficult for conventionally trained and postured forces to counter.

Fourth, *ambiguity* is another characteristic of unconventional conflicts. It is difficult in revolutionary-type conflicts to separate friend from foe and to develop clear criteria for determining success. As the United States learned in Vietnam and is relearning in Iraq and Afghanistan, the amount of real estate taken, weapons recovered, body count (enemy casualties), and secure areas might not be good indicators of who is winning and losing. Furthermore, the rhetoric of revolution and counterrevolution is difficult to untangle, obscuring a clear understanding of the purposes of the antagonists.

Fifth, unconventional conflicts are also characterized by their high *political content* and *moral dimension*. Although it is true that all wars are political, in unconventional conflicts operations and purposes are shaped and conducted according to political-psychological goals. For example, the deliberate sacrifice of armed revolutionary elements for the sake of a political-psychological victory is not an uncommon occurrence. The Tet Offensive by the Vietcong and North Vietnamese in 1968 is a case in point. Even though the enemy forces were decimated by US and South Vietnamese military forces, the media distortions reported to the public back home gave the impression of a great Vietcong victory. The US and South Vietnamese forces won a major military battle but totally lost the political-psychological battle. In the long run, the latter proved to be the more important of the two, as it marked the turning point in public support for the war.

In sum, the shape and dimensions of unconventional conflicts do not easily fit into long-prevailing US notions of conflict. Moreover, the principles of warfare and battlefield conduct that are part of US military professionalism do not really focus on unconventional conflicts. Although US military professionals seek to increase knowledge and develop skills for success in battle by defeating the armed forces of the enemy, the center of gravity of unconventional conflicts is in the political-social milieu of the contending systems. As General Bruce Palmer noted about Vietnam: "One of our handicaps was that few Americans understood the true nature of the war—a devilishly clever mixture of conventional warfare fought somewhat unconventionally and guerrilla warfare fought in the classical manner. Moreover, from Hanoi's point of view it was an all out, total war, while from the outlook of the United States it was quite limited."[27] This view also described the initial US thinking about the latest conflict arena, but some change resulted in the aftermath of September 11. The US military perspective has become more focused on some combination of conventional and unconventional conflicts.

In the twenty-first century the attention to humanitarian missions as well as to a variety of peacekeeping contingencies, combined with the notion of operations other than war, broadened the concept of low-intensity conflicts and special operations, at least within many policymaking and military circles. This merely adds to the confusion already characterizing unconventional conflict concepts.

From lessons learned in a historical view of the United States and guerrilla warfare and its relevance in the current period, Anthony James Joes concluded, "Dangers lie in the path ahead. To avert or at least prepare for them, Americans need to deepen and sharpen their understanding of what guerrilla war has meant and will mean."[28] In considering involvement of the United States in future guerrilla insurgency, "the presumption should be against committing US ground forces. . . . Military victory is ephemeral."[29]

Unconventional Conflicts: US Policy and Strategic Guidelines

Open Systems and Unconventional Conflicts

Open systems direct policy in their attempt to be decent societies based on values, norms, and an ideology that stresses respect for individual rights, justice, freedom, and equality. Underpinning this is the fact that elected officials are responsible to the people and can be removed if they fail in their duties and responsibilities. And although their goals are imperfectly achieved, the fact is that open systems pursue goals and in the process develop many safeguards that protect against government interference and support individual freedom. The environment of open systems is reinforced and perpetuated by counterbalancing forces, independent sources of information, and constitutionally protected independent political actions. The collectivity is subordinate to the individual. This is in sharp contrast to closed systems and, indeed, to the nature of most revolutionary systems, of which Roberta Goren wrote: "More often than not one sort of repressive regime has taken the place of another repressive regime. Often what has been represented as a left-wing 'liberating' regime overthrowing a right-wing repressive regime is no less reactionary than its predecessor."[30]

Many Americans view revolutions either as "glorious" affairs in which a freedom-loving people rise up against tyrants (e.g., the American Revolution) or as anticolonial affairs in one form or another. Although such views carry an implicit democratic rationalization and justification for revolution, they also reveal a misunderstanding of the prevailing security environment. More commonly, elites who initiate or co-opt revolutions are intent upon establishing rule by strong central government and may fall well short of the democratic ideal. Often, well-meaning groups here in the United States and abroad mistakenly view such revolutions through the lens of nineteenth-century liberalism. Their misperceptions and distortions can become the basis for mobilizing segments of the public against the official US political-military posture.

The very character of open systems and their value base are disadvantages in unconventional conflicts. They give adversaries advantages that they would not enjoy by engaging closed systems. Personal liberty, freedom of movement, unfettered communications—all work to the advantage of the subversive enemy intent upon using those characteristics to his advantage. Complicating this is the fact that minority groups struggling for self-determination may be trying to separate from the authoritarian rule of the state. This makes the state vulnerable to intrusion by international organizations in which the UN and the United States often play a major role. The problem facing the United States is made more difficult by the US way of war. In responding to unconventional conflicts, there is a marked US tendency to overwhelm the conflict area and indigenous allies, imposing a US-favored environment. Policymakers are apt to design political-military responses based on bringing overwhelming US forces to bear for short-term operations designed to solve the problem in one way or another. The result becomes ad hoc, short-term initiatives using conventional US strategies, tactics, and doctrines. Although such approaches can be appropriate in some situations, the key for most unconventional conflicts is to penetrate the political-social milieu so as to influence it more effectively (the famous adage is "winning hearts and minds"). This means that success usually goes to the side with the best people on the ground, not necessarily to the one with the largest battalions or the most sophisticated and massive firepower (such as overwhelming airpower). In the long run, solutions—if indeed there are solutions—probably require staying power over an extended period. In the aftermath of the initial US involvement in Iraq, it is clear that the conflict area is much more complicated than first anticipated by the US military and political leaders.

More than forty years ago, Hannah Arendt had this to say about revolution:

> Revolution, in distinction to war, will stay with us into the foreseeable future . . . those will probably win who understand revolution, while those who still put their faith in power politics in the traditional sense of the term and, therefore, in war as the last resort of all foreign policy, may well discover in a not too distant future that they have become masters in a rather useless and obsolete trade.[31]

The American Way of War and Unconventional Conflicts

Throughout history the American way of war has been based on a moral dimension; going to war had the purpose of achieving some higher good. This usually demanded a clear identification of the enemy and his alleged evil purposes. The American way of war also makes a clear distinction between war and peace. In peacetime, nonmilitary systems prevail; in war, the military prevails. Thus the presumption was a clear separation between institutions for peace and those for war. But in the contemporary international environment the lines between war and peace are not as distinct. This throws into disarray prevailing US notions, and it creates a basic dilemma for the US military. A condition of no war–no peace denies the US military the clear political-psychological sustenance from the body politic to engage in unconventional conflicts. At the same time, the US military must continue to maintain a credible posture for nuclear deterrence and major conventional conflicts, including all that implies for relationships with other states. Open systems also require that their officials and military personnel conduct themselves within the general bounds of democratic propriety. This includes just conduct on the battlefield. Lapses from that standard in Iraq have weakened political support for the war.

Overall strategy and tactical operations must also fit within democratic values and norms, if policy and strategy are to maintain their legitimacy. Operations based on hostage-taking, terrorism, and assassinations to erode support for a revolutionary system or penetrate and neutralize terrorist groups will generally be condemned by open systems. The scope and intensity of intelligence activities, both domestic and foreign, are affected by these considerations. This is extremely important given the role of intelligence in unconventional conflicts.

In responding to unconventional conflicts, US forces will usually operate on foreign soil and in conjunction with foreign governments, especially in the less developed world such as prevails in Iraq and Afghanistan in 2007. Supporting an existing system that counters revolutionary challenges is a difficult proposition at best, and a fundamental problem arises from the fact that US personnel socialized into the norms and values of open systems invariably have difficulty relating to and understanding those of foreign cultures. It is difficult to empathize with cultures whose view of individual worth and human rights is at variance with ours. Indeed, it is conceivable that revolutionary rhetoric such as freedom and equality can strike a more responsive chord than does the ideology of the existing system. The lack of understanding of cultures makes it difficult to understand friends as well as enemies. The same problems arise when the United States supports groups within a foreign state who seek self-determination, such as the Albanians in Kosovo in 1999–2000 and groups in various parts of the Middle East.

Finally, the end of the Cold War and the dissolution of the Soviet Union and the Warsaw Pact changed the equation as to unconventional conflicts. No longer driven by East-West ideological confrontations, such conflicts are likely to reflect indigenous issues, such as ethnic confrontation, religious freedom, and minority-group autonomy, or as Huntington asserted, "the clash of civilizations."[32] Conflicts can occur because elites or controlling groups try to gain power and impose a set of political rules and procedures emanating from their version of society. Yet unconventional conflicts arising from the Cold War period may continue in one form or another, as in the Middle East, Southeast Asia, parts of Africa, and Latin America, where some conflicts are the result of drug cartel–revolutionary conspiracy. Although unconventional conflicts generally evolve from the political, social, and economic turmoil in less developed states, wherever a power vacuum exists—or where the United States is at a distinct disadvantage—regional powers, ethnic and religious groups, nationalistic revivals within states, and indigenous revolutionary groups will attempt to fill that vacuum.[33]

Thus the very nature of open systems makes it difficult to respond to unconventional conflicts, including OOTW, conflicts short of war, stability operations, and the like.

Policy, Strategy, and Military Operations

Virtually any commitment of US military forces abroad now has the potential to turn into an unconventional conflict. It is important, therefore, that US policymakers and the military be prepared for such conflicts, even if the mission is peacekeeping. The conflict spectrum (see Figure 2.1) provides a view of the conflict realities; they have clear political-military implications, especially for unconventional conflicts.[34] Responses can demand a political-military posture that is contrary to the American way of war as well as conventional principles and doctrine. This requires training that goes beyond purely military skills. As President John Kennedy stated in response to wars of national liberation, "pure military skill is not enough. A full spectrum of military, para-military, and civil action must be blended to produce success. . . . To win this struggle, our officers and men must understand and combine the political, economic and civil actions with skilled military efforts in the execution of this mission."[35] Although Kennedy was addressing the armed forces in 1962, his words are appropriate today. The same theme was proclaimed by President George W. Bush in the aftermath of September 11. He created a cabinet-level position to head a new Office of Homeland Security. In a television address to the nation on June 5, 2002, President Bush called on Congress to establish a Department of Homeland Security to replace the Office of Homeland Security. The law that was passed created the third-largest department in the national government and brought about the most extensive reorganization of the government since the Truman presidency.

An effective force structure for responding to unconventional conflicts cannot be wedded to conventional hierarchy or command systems. It requires planning, organization, and operations aimed at the political-social milieu of revolutionary-counterrevolutionary systems. It demands individuals with the requisite military skills who also understand and are sensitive to the cultural forces and nationalistic desires of foreign systems—especially those in the less developed world. They must be self-reliant individuals capable of operating for long periods in small groups isolated from the US environment. It will require patience, persistence, political-psychological sophistication, and the ability to blend in with the indigenous political-military system to prevail.

In this respect, success in revolutionary and counterrevolutionary conflicts is not necessarily contingent upon sophisticated weaponry, large numbers of troops, and massive airpower. Rather, success depends on the quality and dedication of efficient soldiers on the ground who can blend in and function as skilled political mobilizers and teachers, following the perspective of Sun-tzu.

Conclusion

In the final analysis, what does all of this mean for US national security policy and strategy?

First, in order to respond effectively to unconventional conflicts, policy must be based on US national interests. Although this seems obvious, it is not so clear with respect to unconventional conflicts and the less developed world. In this context, national interests and policy should include support of like-minded systems. This does not mean that support should only be extended to democratic or quasi-democratic systems. There are not many of those systems in the third world, although some are moving in that direction. The fact is that true democratic systems need little help from the United States, and limiting US interests to that type of system is tantamount to withdrawing from the less developed world. This does not mean that the United States should become involved in every corner of the third world, however. In fact, US involvement and visible support could tarnish and undermine foreign nationalistic leaders, and in some areas US involvement would achieve little or would make matters worse. US attempts to create a democratic Iraq are instructive in this regard.

When compelling US national security interests are at stake, and where long-term interests can be seriously affected, US involvement should include support of states and groups who are like-minded or are the lesser of evils; this can include support of revolutionary systems. However, the United States should never substitute one tyranny for another. It is conceivable that nominally democratic systems, even certain authoritarian systems, are more susceptible to openness than revolutionary systems. The term used to describe this strategy, in which the United States is compelled to choose among undesirable options, is *suboptimizing*. Suboptimizing accepts the notion that the logic of policy and strategy is often subsumed by actual conditions that defy rational, logical, or just solutions.

Second, it follows that strategies must include a variety of options and phases (see Figure 2.1 on the conflict spectrum) that incorporate political, economic, and psychological components as well as military ones. The use of US ground combat forces must be reserved for special situations in which the existing system is about to collapse and the area is vital to US security interests. If other options are effectively implemented, however, the use of US combat forces could be the exception rather than the rule. Strategic options should be based on support and assistance to expand the governing capacity of the existing system, to broaden its political-psychological base, and to develop a civic culture attuned to openness. Such strategies must not Americanize the conflict or the theater itself, except in unusual circumstances requiring direct involvement of conventional US combat forces.

Third, strategies should be based on civilian-military cooperation and interservice coordination. Command structures, planning, organization, and implementation must reflect these and joint efforts. This is especially true with respect to the intelligence function. Effective intelligence requires not only military but also strategic intelligence and analysis associated with intelligence capabilities. Finally, strategies must include counterterrorism and counterrevolutionary operations in support of existing systems and revolutions against repressive systems that promise to become harsher still. Whether such a strategy could be implemented would depend on the assessment of US national interests.

Fourth, within the US body politic, a new realism must emerge regarding war and peace and the challenge posed by unconventional conflicts.

Within military and civilian policy circles and the body politic (especially the media), there must be greater appreciation for the complexity of the conflict spectrum and a recognition of the long-term threat of unconventional conflicts. Without this new realism, it is unlikely that the necessary national will, political resolve, and staying power can be developed to respond effectively.

Fifth, to dismiss unconventional conflicts as a nonthreatening phenomenon and a natural evolution of political-social turmoil is to ignore the lessons of recent history. To dismiss the susceptibility of open systems to deception, political-psychological warfare, terrorism, and totalitarian revolutionaries as unrealistic is to create a condition described by Jean-François Revel: "Democratic civilization is the first in history to blame itself because another power is working to destroy it."[36] This may well have changed after September 11, when Americans united to combat international terrorism. This relates to the critical issue of staying power and national will over the long haul.

The basic dilemma for the US military grows out of these conditions, especially the fact that US norms and values do not easily match the policy and strategy required for unconventional conflicts. The American way of war virtually precludes a military postured for the kinds of tactical and doctrinal techniques inherent in unconventional conflicts. Fighting without appearing to fight, waging war through peaceful enterprise, using morally acceptable tactics and doctrine against adversaries who abandon any pretense of moral behavior—these are the tasks facing the US military. They become more pressing and dangerous in the long run compared to conventional, even nuclear, war.

The capability and effectiveness of the United States to respond to unconventional conflicts are an important part of national strategy and national security policy. Conflicts in the less developed world have geostrategic as well as political-military and psychological importance. Dangers include conflict escalation, regional destabilization, and the possibility of expansion of autocratic regimes. Yet groups seeking self-determination tend to look to the United States for support in the form of resources, including political-psychological assets. In the broader national security dimension, US capability and effectiveness in unconventional conflicts are part of deterrence.

Perceptions of US strength and political will can have a deterrent effect on those who seek to influence unconventional conflicts from external sources. Furthermore, the US deterrence capacity is strengthened by a balanced capability across the conflict spectrum. Much attention has been focused on unconventional conflicts here because of the conviction that the United States has historically shown weakness in this area. Yet these types of conflict are the most likely ones to occur in this decade and beyond, as triggered by US involvement in Iraq and Afghanistan. By continuing to prove its weakness in this area, the United States contributes, no matter how indirectly, to the perpetuation of ongoing unconventional conflicts and reduces the costs to those who engage in them.

Finally, the decision whether the United States should become involved in unconventional conflicts must be based on national strategy and national security priorities, many of which have already been identified. In several instances, US national interests are best served by avoiding military involvement and security guarantees. In other instances, US national interests are best served by political-psychological support and the more traditional means of assistance (weaponry and humanitarian aid) and intelligence operations. In any case, the United States must be prepared to respond effectively—and not necessarily only with military force (for instance, there can be private contractors working with and for the military)—if it is to strengthen its credibility to pursue national security policy across the conflict spectrum.

Notes

1. Stephen John Stedman, "The New Interventionists," *Foreign Affairs* 72, no. 1 (Summer 1993): 4.

2. Ernest van den Haag, "The Busyness of American Policy," *Foreign Affairs* 64, no. 1 (Fall 1985): 114.

3. Colin Powell, with Joseph E. Persico, *My American Journey* (New York: Random House, 1995), p. 576.

4. Ibid., pp. 576–577.

5. See, e.g., Frederick H. Hartmann and Robert L. Wendzel, *Defending America's Security* (Washington, DC: Pergamon-Brassey's, 1988), pp. 26–38.

6. John Spanier, *American Foreign Policy Since World War II,* 11th ed. (Washington, DC: CQ Press, 1988), p. 11.

7. Chairman, Joint Chiefs of Staff, *Joint Vision 2020* (Washington, DC: US Government Printing Office, June 2000), p. 8, emphasis added.

8. See, e.g., Ian Roxborough, *The Hart-Rudman Commission and the Homeland Defense* (Carlisle Barracks, PA: Strategic Studies Institute, US Army War College, September 2001), and Dr. Earl H. Tilford Jr., Conference Brief, *Redefining Homeland Security* (Carlisle Barracks, PA: Strategic Studies Institute, US Army War College, n.d.). This was a summary of a conference sponsored by the Army War College and the Reserve Officers Association held on March 16, 2001.

9. At the same time, nuclear proliferation has raised the danger of nuclear war between secondary powers such as India and Pakistan.

10. Xavier Raufer, "Gray Areas: A New Security Threat," *Political Warfare: Intelligence, Active Measures, and Terrorism Report,* no. 20 (Spring 1992): 1, 4.

11. For an excellent classic analysis of special operations, see John M. Collins, *America's Small Wars: Lessons for the Future* (Washington, DC: Brassey's US, 1991).

12. Sean Naylor, "A Force to Be Reckoned With—Still," *Army Times,* July 30, 2001, p. 16.

13. Ibid.

14. Bernard Fall, *Street Without Joy: Insurgency in Indochina, 1946–1963,* 3rd rev. ed. (Harrisburg, PA: Stackpole, 1963), pp. 356–357. Fall pointed out years ago, "Just about anybody can start a 'little war' . . . even a New York street gang. Almost anybody can raid somebody else's territory, even American territory. . . . But all this has rarely produced the kind of revolutionary ground swell which simply swept away the existing system. . . . It is important to understand that guerrilla warfare is nothing but a tactical appendage of a far vaster political contest that, no matter how expertly fought by competent and dedicated professionals, cannot make up for the absence of a political rationale."

15. Samuel B. Griffith, ed., *Mao Tse-tung on Guerrilla Warfare* (New York: Praeger, 1961), p. 7.

16. See John Arquilla, David Ronfeldt, and Michele Zanini, "Information-Age Terrorism," *Current History,* April 2000, p. 179.

17. Terrorism can be placed into various categories. See, e.g., Cindy Combs, *Terrorism in the Twenty-First Century,* 2nd ed. (Upper Saddle River, NJ: Prentice-Hall, 2000).

18. Most of these groups emerged from the political and social turmoil of the 1960s and 1970s in Europe and the United States. The Baader Meinhof Gang came out of the radicalization of the German Socialist Student Alliance. This group focused on targets in Germany, whereas the Red Brigade operated throughout Europe. The Italian Red Brigade was responsible for the kidnapping and murder of former Italian premier Aldo Moro in 1978. It was also responsible for the 1981 kidnapping of US Army brigadier general James Dozier, who was subsequently rescued by Italian antiterrorist units. Direct Action had its roots in France. The Symbionese Liberation Army emerged in the San Francisco area and was responsible for the kidnapping of heiress Patty Hearst, who subsequently disowned her family and supported the group until she was captured by authorities. The Weather Underground split off from Students for a Democratic Society and was responsible for terrorist operations against the US government and businesses.

19. Mark Jurgensmeyer, "Understanding the New Terrorism," *Current History,* April 2000, p. 158.

20. Dennis B. Downey, "Domestic Terrorism: The Enemy Within," *Current History,* April 2000, p. 158.

21. See, e.g., Joseph R. Nunez, "Fighting the Hobbesian Trinity in Colombia: A New Strategy for Peace," in *Implementing Plan Colombia: Special Series* (Carlisle, PA: Strategic Studies Institute, US Army War College, April 2001).

22. There are excellent works that provide information linking the Soviet Union to terrorism. See, e.g., Roberta Goren, *The Soviet Union and Terrorism* (Boston: George Allen and Unwin, 1982). See also Claire Sterling, *The Terror Network: The Secret War of International Terrorism* (New York: William Abrahams/Owl Books, 1985), and Ray Cline and Yonah Alexander, *Terrorism as State-Supported Covert Warfare* (Fairfax, VA: Hero Books, 1986).

23. See, e.g., Arkady N. Shevchenko, *Breaking with Moscow* (New York: Alfred A. Knopf, 1985). Also see Andre Sakharov, "My KGB Ordeal," *US News and World Report,* February 24, 1986, pp. 29–35; Humberto Belli, *Breaking Faith: The Sandinista Revolution and Its Impact on Freedom and Christian Faith in Nicaragua* (Garden City, MI: Puebla Institute and Crossway Books, 1985); and Shirley Christian, *Nicaragua: Revolution in the Family* (New York: Random House, 1985).

24. Jurgensmeyer, "Understanding the New Terrorism," p. 158.

25. See, e.g., *Selected Works of Mao Tse-tung,* abridged by Bruno Shaw (New York: Harper Colophon Books, 1970); *Che Guevara: Guerrilla Warfare,* translated

by J. P. Morrya (New York: Vintage Books, 1969); General Vo Nguyen Giap, *People's War, People's Army* (Washington, DC: US Government Printing Office, 1962); and *Sun Tzu: The Art of War,* translated by Samuel B. Griffith (New York: Oxford University Press, 1971). See also Hannah Arendt, *On Revolution* (New York: Viking, 1965), and Jack A. Goldstone, ed., *Revolutions: Theoretical, Comparative, and Historical Studies* (New York: Harcourt Brace Jovanovich, 1986).

26. *Sun Tzu: The Art of War.* According to translator Samuel B. Griffith, "Sun Tzu's essays on the 'Art of War' form the earliest of known treatises on the subject, but never have been surpassed in comprehensiveness and depth of understanding" (from the foreword).

27. General Bruce Palmer, *The 25-Year War: America's Military Role in Vietnam* (Lexington: University Press of Kentucky, 1984), p. 176.

28. Anthony James Joes, *America and Guerrilla Warfare* (Lexington: University Press of Kentucky, 2000), p. 3.

29. Ibid., p. 328.

30. Goren, *Soviet Union,* p. 5.

31. Arendt, *On Revolution,* p. 8.

32. Samuel P. Huntington, "The Clash of Civilizations," *Foreign Affairs* 72, no. 3 (Summer 1993): 22–49.

33. For an analysis of conflicts in the third world, see Donald M. Snow, *Distant Thunder: Third World Conflict and the New International Order* (New York: St. Martin's, 1993). For an analysis of such conflicts in the twenty-first century, see J. Bowyer Bell, *Dragon Wars: Armed Struggle and the Conventions of Modern War* (New Brunswick, NJ: Transaction, 1999). See also Donald M. Snow, *Distant Thunder: Patterns of Conflict in the Developing World* (New Brunswick, NJ: Transaction, 1997).

34. See, e.g., Sam C. Sarkesian, *Unconventional Conflicts in a New Security Era: Lessons from Malaya and Vietnam* (Westport, CT: Greenwood, 1993).

35. *Public Papers of the Presidents of the United States: Containing the Public Messages, Speeches, and Statements of the President, John F. Kennedy, 1962* (Washington, DC: US Government Printing Office, 1963), p. 454.

36. Jean-François Revel, *How Democracies Perish* (New York: Harper and Row, 1984), p. 7.

3

The US Political System

DURING THE 1830S, FRENCHMAN ALEXIS DE TOCQUEVILLE traveled throughout the United States observing its people and their government. He had much good to say about the new democracy. But he also noted some problems with the way the government conducted foreign affairs: "Foreign policy," he wrote, "does not require the use of any of the good qualities peculiar to democracy, but does demand the cultivation of almost all of those which it lacks."[1]

De Tocqueville's observations remain applicable; indeed, in the area of security policy today they are even more relevant. Democracies lack many of the qualities required to cultivate and maintain an effective national security posture; the very nature of democracies works against defense issues and the strategies required for long-range success, especially in view of the challenges of the new security issues. The long-term US response to the September 11 terrorist attacks, the worst ever on homeland soil, will be a test of national will, staying power, and political resolve. As de Tocqueville noted in the case of foreign policy: "Democracy finds it difficult to coordinate the details of a great undertaking and to fix on some plan and carry it through with determination in spite of obstacles."[2] This is especially true when such plans require some degree of secrecy.

In the twenty-first century, the United States and other democracies face threats of international terrorism, unconventional conflicts, and a variety of contingencies short of war. At the same time, surfacing ethnic rivalries, religious conflict, and hypernationalism elsewhere further complicate the new security landscape. Much has changed in the international conflict arena, although the threat of a world war between major powers has diminished, and the likelihood of global conflict in the conventional mode seems remote. But regional and unconventional conflicts in the Middle East and the less developed world have become worldwide in scope (including international terrorism).[3]

In addition, so-called asymmetrical wars now characterize the conflict environment. Given its past experience and the nature of its political system and values, the United States finds the new strategic environment to be difficult, except in terms of conventional response, strategic deterrence, and high-tech warfare. September 11 changed many perspectives on national security magnified by the US involvement in Iraq and Afghanistan. In 2006, this became even more challenging with the Iranian and North Korean efforts to develop nuclear capacity. Events now require the strategy and doctrinal wherewithal to mount an effective campaign against international terrorism and other dangers posed by threats to the US homeland. Except in clear cases of national interests, however, the nature of open systems makes it difficult to develop effective intelligence and military systems to respond to unconventional conflicts.

Why is this so? Why is it that the democratic United States finds it difficult to respond to the variety of threats to its national interests except in clear cases of overt aggression? The international setting and the very nature of national security are part of the explanation, but much of the problem rests with the nature and character of democracy and open systems.

US Democratic Principles

Much has been written about the meaning of democracy and its variations as practiced in the United States and elsewhere. Serious philosophical studies have also examined the evolution of democracy as an ideology and as political doctrine. A thorough analysis of democracy and the concept of open systems would require a lengthy study of those works, but the purpose here is more modest: to touch on critical features of democracy as they pertain to national security. Initially, we need to develop some sense of the meaning of democracy, for it is in that context that US national security policy is made.

The fundamental proposition here is that democracy does not adhere to a dogmatic ideological philosophy. Indeed, one of the most pervasive features of democracy is its pluralistic and pragmatic basis. Democracy is rooted in the idea of political tolerance for many views—even extreme views—as long as they include the notion of political equality, self-determination, and individual worth and do not foreclose the possibility of future peaceful political change. Although many disagree on the specific application of these concepts, there are legitimate and historical bases for assessing the nature and credibility of a political system. Finally, the legitimacy of a system and its leaders rests on the will of the people, a basic tenet of the US

Constitution and the functioning of the US political system. Put simply, the way the system functions, expectations regarding elected officials, and the purposes of the system must reflect the notion of government responsibility and accountability to the people.

To be sure, the US political system is not perfect. And although most of the public recognizes the imperfections, it also sees the merits, as did de Tocqueville: "The vices and weaknesses of democratic governments are easy to see . . . but its good qualities are revealed only in the long run. . . . The real advantage of democracy is not . . . to favor prosperity for all, but only to serve the well-being of the greatest number."[4] Democracy may not be the most efficient system or type of government (indeed, the Founding Fathers went to great effort to prevent government from being *too* efficient), but it is, in the long run, the best when compared to all others.

If we accept the view of some observers, faith in democracy has become even more confusing and fragmented by what one can call "cultural amnesia. . . . What happened before doesn't matter; the past is no longer prologue—it is irrelevant."[5] Moreover, in the new era multiculturalism and diversity politics and their politicization complicate the shaping and nurturing of democratic institutions.

We believe that regardless of what contemporary surveys and polls show, there are fundamental principles at the root of the democratic faith that have lasted for centuries. They are engrained in the US psyche and, indeed, in part of the international order. September 11 may well have reinforced such beliefs. The many disagreements within the US political system regarding the role of the United States in the Middle East, particularly in Iraq in 2007 and beyond, however, have created troublesome issues regarding US national security and foreign policy.

This brief description of the nature of US democracy does not do justice to the rich literature and wide-ranging philosophical studies on the subject. But our observations provide a starting point for an analysis of democracy's relationship to national security in the current era.

There are four fundamental characteristics of democracies that are relevant to the study of national security: *the distribution of power, the democratic faith, multiculturalism and cultural diversity,* and *the messianic spirit.*

The Distribution of Power

The pluralistic nature of the US system institutionalizes the diffusion of political power. This builds into the political system a need for compromise while creating an environment for power struggles among the various branches of government, within the bureaucracy, and among groups in society. Power struggles can be especially severe in cases of foreign and national security policies because the issues involve vital interests and US values that are at the core of differences of political opinion in the United States. Institutionalized confrontation—the product of separation of powers—is epitomized by the struggles between the president and Congress and can become especially contentious when each branch is controlled by a different political party. Such has been the case beginning in 2007, with the Democratic Party in control of both houses of Congress with a Republican president.

This was also the case in the past until the election of Bill Clinton as president in 1992. With that election, the Democratic Party gained control of the Oval Office for the first time in twelve years. The Democratic Party controlled not only the presidency and Congress but also the majority of state houses and governorships. This did not necessarily mean that President Clinton had an easy time of it in Congress, however, as shown in the difficulty he had in passing a budget package in 1993 as well as problems in his own party over health care reform, the North American Free Trade Agreement (NAFTA), changes in the military budget and force restructuring, and the nomination of a secretary of defense.

President Clinton's problems increased in 1994, when the Republican Party gained control of Congress as well as the majority of governorships. This balance of political power continued until the election of President George W. Bush in 2000, although this changed in 2001 when a Republican senator became an Independent and handed control of the Senate to the Democrats (the House of Representatives remained with the GOP). The attempted impeachment of President Clinton in the House and subsequent battles over foreign and domestic policy were clear examples of presidential-congressional power struggles (see Chapter 4).

But even when one party controls the Oval Office and Congress, there are likely to be disagreements. The unity within Congress and its support of President Bush in the aftermath of September 11 were a response to the new threat to the US homeland. But the normal state of affairs in Congress and between Congress and the president is characterized more by debate and disagreement. This became even more apparent in 2007 when the new Democratic Congress subjected the Bush administration to serious scrutiny and undertook efforts to force an end to US military involvement in Iraq.

Over history, efforts by Congress to reassert itself in the making and implementation of foreign and national security policy have led to many confrontations with the executive. There are many examples such as Iraq and Afghanistan: the War Powers Resolution of 1973, which among other things attempted to limit and constrain the intelligence community and the deployment of military force; new initiatives with respect to Cuba; the US-China relationship; the US-Russian relationship; and ongoing battles over the defense budget, military force restructuring, and the commitment of the US military to OOTW. These issues remain unresolved, and so the likelihood of continuing presidential-congressional confrontations remains high.

These congressional efforts to control foreign and national security policy led some to label the body the "Imperial Congress."

> As America begins its third century under the Constitution, presidents might wish the framers had been less concerned with checks and balances in the area of national security. In recent years Congress has challenged presidents on all fronts, including foreign aid; arms sales; the development, procurement, and deployment of weapons systems; the negotiation and interpretation of treaties; the selection of diplomats; and the continuation of nuclear testing.[6]

The "imperial" label has become questionable, however, as members on both sides of the aisle struggle *within* Congress over the parties' agendas, and presidents can use the veto as a major bargaining tool with Congress. The major exception is the response in the aftermath of September 11, a unity shattered by US involvement in Iraq and Afghanistan and the Democratic Party election victory in 2006.

During the Clinton administration, battles with the Republican-controlled Congress were numerous and often rancorous. These included US military operations in Somalia in 1993 and 1994, Bosnia-Herzegovina in 1995, and Kosovo in 1999. In 2000, the last full year of the Clinton administration, executive-legislative struggles sharpened over National Missile Defense (NMD—the latest version of President Ronald Reagan's "Star Wars" initiative in the early 1980s) as well as US relationships with the Russian Federation, China, and Cuba. They remained unresolved during the last years of the George W. Bush administration and will likely continue into the administration of his successor.

The stage thus remains set for continuing power struggles between the president and Congress. In the early part of his administration, George W. Bush faced struggles over his tax-cut plan (although it passed and was considered a victory for the president) and NMD. The fact that President Bush placed experienced individuals at the helm of foreign and defense policy may have made a difference; Secretary of State Colin Powell, Secretary of Defense Donald Rumsfeld, and National Security Advisor Condoleezza Rice had extensive experience in previous administrations. All of this was altered later in the Bush administration, with changes at some of the highest levels.

Regardless of the inherent struggles, the fact is that the president has the lead role in foreign policy and national security, and the greatest source of presidential power is found in politics and public opinion, not the Constitution.

> Increasingly since the 1930s, Congress has passed laws that confer on the executive branch grants of authority to achieve some general goals, leav-

ing up to the president and his deputies to define the regulations and programs that will actually be put into effect. Moreover, the American people
look to the president—always in time of crisis, but increasingly as an
everyday matter—for leadership and hold him responsible for a large and
growing portion of our national affairs.[7]

Nonetheless, in the long term (the united front against international terrorism notwithstanding) the president faces many difficult problems in both
foreign and national security policies, a consequence of the new security
landscape. Although these problems are shaped by threats short of a major
war, they remain relevant to US national interests. Moreover, successful
national security policy could necessitate a judicious use of nonmilitary
instruments and covert operations. This requires especially effective presidential leadership in developing consensus at home for the necessity of a
particular policy—a difficult prospect without bipartisan support in
Congress.

This institutionalized confrontation stems partly from the sharing of
power. The popular notion that the US government has three separate
branches with distinct powers has a corollary: the branches also share
power, which allows each to influence and intervene in the affairs of one or
the other, giving rise to important constitutional questions and different
interpretations regarding the proper exercise of power. The US Supreme
Court's tipping of the scales in the 2000 presidential election (a sharply
divided Court ruled in favor of Republican George W. Bush and against
Democrat Al Gore in a case originating in Florida) is a prime example.
Indeed, some argue that there is a fourth branch of government—the media.

Problems of control and responsibility evolving from power-sharing are
increased by the decentralization of power among the various branches of
government as well as within each branch. Within the executive branch,
there is usually a continuing struggle between the Departments of State and
Defense as well as between the Central Intelligence Agency (CIA) and other
agencies. For example, during the Clinton presidency, problems between
the Justice Department and the Federal Bureau of Investigation became well
publicized. The Iran-contra hearings during the Reagan administration illuminated the conflicts between the president's national security staff and various departments. Similarly, struggles occur within Congress among various
power bases: committee chairs, caucus leaders, and individual members.
Combined with the two-party system, such struggles create and nurture
institutional power plays, and the US federal system of government adds to
the fragmentation. Partisan control and party machines at the state level add
yet another dimension to the power equation at the national level.

Historically only the president has been considered the legal
spokesman of the United States in the international arena. The President
does not have a monopoly of power to carry out policy, however, especially

in today's environment. The very nature of the US system creates checks and balances that can frustrate any policy and strategy. The nature of power in the US system generally favors those who support mainstream policies and oppose major changes to the status quo. It goes without saying that a majority of the public is probably most comfortable with mainstream politicians who focus on bread-and-butter domestic issues.

The Democratic Faith

A historical thread running through US democracy is the commitment to the free market of ideas within the body politic and the various branches of government. This supports the notion of a free press and reinforces decentralization, diffusion, and power-sharing. Linked closely to pluralism and nondogmatic philosophies, the free play of ideas is supposed to lead to the truth.

An informed and educated citizenry is essential to democracy. The citizenry must have access to information in order to exercise the will of the people and to assess the performance of government. It is a basic belief that an educated citizenry can overcome any obstacles to the functioning of democracy. This Jeffersonian notion—that information and education lead to an enlightened public—also reflects a belief in the innate goodness of people and their sense of justice; enlightened people are more likely to act wisely and justly.

Pragmatism is another ingredient of the democratic faith. This is the belief that the search for practical consequences based on common sense is a result of having an enlightened citizenry. Once problems are encountered, Americans, applying their God-given common sense, can find reasonable solutions. This can-do attitude pervades most segments of US society.

Finally, an important part of the democratic faith is the belief that the US system is the best of all choices despite its imperfections. The US public prides itself on the fact that Americans are a decent people living in a decent society. The concern with the quality of life at the community level has a parallel with the concern with individual well-being. This is not to suggest that the culture is without prejudice and narrow-mindedness, but a constant in US society is our concern for the individual and continuing efforts to rectify past and prevailing injustices. This is embodied in the US Constitution and reflected in the way that the government functions. Accordingly, the concern with individualism and quality of life shaped by the political system and reflected in the goals of our democratic ideology brings out the best in individuals and serves them most effectively.

Multiculturalism and Cultural Diversity

The modern United States has its roots in the immigrant society. Since the 1960s, changing immigration patterns have affected US society. Today, many immigrants are from the Southern Hemisphere and the Far East rather than from Europe, as was the case for decades. They bring a culture that differs from Anglo-Saxon and Western traditions, yet the United States has not become the great melting pot of historical rhetoric. Rather, it is a system in which each culture and language exists within the broader scheme of Americanism. The motto on U.S. currency—*E pluribus unum,* or "One out of many"—expresses this sentiment.

Efforts have been made to promote cultural diversity and gender equality, especially in institutions of higher education. To be sure, cultural diversity lends a uniqueness, richness, and strength to the notion of Americanism. But for any number of Americans the fear is that multiculturalism can be taken to such extremes that the concept of Americanism is eroded and lost in the maze of cultural diversity, politicization, and polarization. There is also a fear that cultural diversity will bring cultural confrontation and the continuation of age-old animosities that spill over from foreign homelands. This is complicated by the fact that some cultural precepts are difficult to change, limiting assimilation into the US mainstream.

Yet assimilation into that mainstream has been the backbone of the immigrant society. This was based not on destroying old cultures but on learning the English language and understanding the meaning of US citizenship, heritage, and culture. Such an approach placed values and the system above any particular culture. It was best expressed by President Franklin Roosevelt, who in the midst of World War II was said to have stated that "Americanism is a matter of heart and mind. Americanism is not a matter of race or ethnicity." But now concern is often expressed over the label "our people," used in reference to a specific ethnic or racial group, not to Americans as a people. The issue of illegal immigration and the perpetuation of specific cultures and languages separate from traditional US concepts became critical concerns in the first decade of the twenty-first century.

How all of this will play out in the next decades is unclear, as are the ways in which it will shape US values and national security.

The Messianic Spirit

Throughout US history, religion has been an important component in shaping national values and in reinforcing the messianic spirit. This is seen in the view, held by many, that the United States as the leader of the West must be a moral as well as political-military leader and that moral principles must guide the behavior of governmental officials and the military. Although some feel that religion has no place in a secular democratic system, history suggests otherwise. The messianic spirit is reinforced by the historic role religion has played in the evolution of the US system.

Viewed against the backdrop of history, the recent rise in political activism among some religious groups is not a departure from national tradition but only the renewal of a long-standing pattern in American political life. . . . Religion was present at the creation of the American political system, and was one of several elements contributing to the design of the governmental institutions and to the core beliefs that grew into national political culture.[8]

For many Americans, the logical extension of this belief from the individual to the political results in a messianic spirit—the notion that Americans and the political system are ordained to be "the light" for other nations, lending moral weight to the notion of democratic faith. This messianic spirit may partly explain US attempts to spread democracy in the Middle East.

The Impact on National Security

These considerations—power distribution, democratic faith, multiculturalism and cultural diversity, and the messianic spirit—create contradictory forces. On the one hand, they strengthen US ability to respond to national security challenges. On the other hand, they reveal weaknesses and disadvantages, especially if multiculturalism detracts from national unity.

The power distribution that is characteristic of the US political system provides a basis for its legitimacy and precludes a centralized power base from forming in any one branch or individual. Furthermore, it allows inputs from many interest groups, people, and elected officials—the foundation of representative government. The strength created by this base of power makes the US political system and government resilient, capable of responding to mistakes, problems, and failures in a fashion not easily matched by other systems.

In developing national security policy, the president faces many constituencies and must try to build a consensus throughout the political system. This makes it difficult to design new policies and strategies or ones that appear to challenge the prevailing democratic faith. Furthermore, maintaining a degree of secrecy and yet operating within traditional democratic parameters requires delicate maneuvering; covert operations, for example, tend to be perceived as undemocratic, often for good reason. But the need to respond to unconventional conflicts and terrorism may require these very activities. This view is not universally shared, however. The late US senator Daniel Patrick Moynihan argued that there is little need for secrecy in a democracy.[9] The four fundamental characteristics of democracies relevant to the study of national security are repeated for this discussion: the distribution of power, the democratic faith, multiculturalism and cultural diversity, and the messianic spirit.

The Distribution of Power

The way power is distributed creates a condition in which those responsible for foreign affairs and national security do not control all the structures and resources needed to carry out policies and strategies. The exception, of course, is when the United States faces serious threats to its existence, as on September 11. Matters of foreign affairs and national security are susceptible to political opposition within the government and public, bureaucratic foot-dragging, policy distortions, and opposition. Foreign powers may see such internal US political struggles as vacillation, weakness, and divisiveness. This has become even more complicated as information-age technology opens up the system, and foreign governments, nongovernmental organizations, business corporations, international terrorists, and individuals gain access to policy issues that formerly existed within the closed realm of the bureaucratic establishment.

In the process of trying to fulfill their responsibilities, members of Congress and officials in the executive branch can inadvertently serve the purposes of adversaries. The same is true with respect to interest groups, the media, and other segments of the public. For example, during the Nicaraguan conflict in 1984, key members of the Democratic-controlled House, including the Speaker of the House, sent a special message to "Commandante Daniel Ortega, Managua, Nicaragua," supporting his efforts against the US-supported freedom fighters.[10] Later, the election of Violeta Barrios de Chamorro and the defeat of the Sandinistas in that election seemed to underscore congressional misjudgments. In addition, during the Iran-contra hearings in 1987, indications were that certain members of Congress had used their official stationery to support groups sympathetic to the Sandinista regime, in direct opposition to publicly stated US policy. Some aspects of all of these actions continue today.

In another example, a noted expert documented the fact that a 1978 report issued by the House Intelligence Committee regarding Soviet active measures deleted references to important aspects of a World Peace Council meeting attended by some members of Congress. The same report deleted important facts revealed by the hearings. The World Peace Council had been identified as a "major Soviet-controlled international front organization with headquarters in Helsinki."[11] Interestingly, Representative Edward P. Boland presided over the committee hearings and made a public statement denying Soviet involvement in the nuclear freeze movement. "His statement received the widest national publicity," which was not in accord with the official record; however, "even those who do read the entire record of the hearing still will be denied certain facts because the House Committee under Chairman Boland withheld them."[12] Boland also initiated the Boland Amendment prohibiting US aid to the groups fighting the

Sandinista government in Nicaragua, which was a bone of contention in the 1987 Iran-contra hearings. And in the George W. Bush administration, debate and controversy continued over China and Taiwan, NATO enlargement, NMD, the US role in the Middle East, and relations with Russia over its use of force in Chechnya. These issues provided ample opportunity for criticizing US proposals and policy.

But such activities do not rest solely with Congress; presidents also attempt to maintain a degree of secrecy in matters of national security. The Iran-contra affair, whereby the administration was trying to trade arms for hostages and use the profits to support paramilitary groups opposing the Sandinista government of Nicaragua, was but one example. In the Nixon administration, for example, much of the conduct of foreign and national security policy was cloaked in secrecy. In fact, "the administration was predisposed toward a secretive policy by its distrust of the State Department and intelligence community, by the convoluted personalities of its leaders, and by its belief that certain of its goals required extreme confidentiality and centralized direction of policy in the White House."[13]

In the latter part of the Reagan administration, William Casey, director of central intelligence, was renowned for his efforts to limit any information to Congress, even if it was unclassified. Casey

> had developed nonresponsiveness to oversight into an art form. The Senate Select Committee on Intelligence had even built a special amplifying system into its bug-proof hearing room in an effort to make Casey's muttering intelligible. What the senators did not realize was that, when he wanted to be understood, Casey spoke as clearly as John F. Kennedy. That kind of arrogance had gotten the agency involved in the Iran-contra mess in the first place.[14]

During the first George Bush administration, some members of Congress decried the secrecy surrounding weapons deliveries, among other efforts, to Iraq shortly before that country invaded Kuwait. And a continuing chorus of criticism surfaced in 1994 as to the Clinton administration's conduct of foreign and national security policy. Although such criticism had been voiced earlier during the Clinton administration, the catalyst for this round was the spy scandal involving a career CIA officer, Aldrich Ames, who passed along classified information to the Soviet Union and later to Russia.[15]

Serious questions were also raised about President Clinton's friendship with Russian president Boris Yeltsin and US foreign aid to Russia. Earlier, criticism was directed at Clinton for his vacillation on Haiti, Bosnia-Herzegovina, and North Korea. Near the end of his second term in 2000, Clinton was also criticized by some in Congress for his lukewarm support of the NMD system. Clinton ultimately chose to defer the decision as to whether to deploy NMD to the next administration. The criticism of the Bush administration's Middle East policy and involvement in Iraq has raised even greater concerns, but the brief history cited above shows that such criticisms are not a new phenomenon.

These are some examples of the continuing struggle between Congress and the president over national security policy. In this context, it is not unusual for the president to go to extraordinary lengths to develop support for administration policy and strategy. Proposed changes to the existing order, especially changes that promise to be innovative, involve some degree of political risk, however, both domestically and internationally. Furthermore, attempts at change invite the exercise of power by others to frustrate or blunt the initiatives. This leads to the conclusion that the safest political course is to maintain existing policy and strategy and seek only incremental changes to dilute the exercise of power by those outside the Oval Office. Otherwise, a president who seeks new directions must be prepared to deal with a variety of power centers that can seriously challenge his authority. Again, international terrorism might require covert operations and a higher degree of secrecy.

There are exceptions to this generalization, of course. Nixon's détente with China was a distinct change in policy that carried national security overtones, yet it received universal acclaim. In addition, after President Jimmy Carter's ill-fated attempt to impose human rights criteria upon national security and foreign policy, President Reagan won praise for changing the course of the Cold War by first denouncing the Soviet Union as an "evil empire," then fostering a cordial relationship with Mikhail Gorbachev, the leader of the Soviet Union. In the new era, George W. Bush's speech to a joint session of Congress in the aftermath of September 11 won high praise. He spelled out a strategic course of action that was supported by a great majority of the US public. Problems of implementation caused this support to diminish, leading to the 2006 takeover of Congress by the Democratic Party.

Secret diplomacy, the purpose of which is a major change in policy and strategic direction, carries great political risks. And unless the effort has an immediate, positive impact on US ability to protect vital interests—and is perceived as such by the public—then the various power clusters are likely to diminish any chance for success. Even the militarily successful operations in Grenada (1983), Panama (1989–1990), and the Gulf (1990–1991) had their share of critics; less successful missions such as Somalia (1993), Haiti (1998), Afghanistan (2001), and especially Iraq (2003) came under harsher criticism, not only from Republicans in Congress but also from Democratic rank and file and the general public.

These are but a few examples of how congressional agendas, oversight, and power plays can highlight or restrict information according to the interests of politicians—sometimes to the detriment of publicly proclaimed US policy. Congressional maneuvering, however, does not start and end with any single presidential administration.

The Democratic Faith

The democratic faith creates similar dilemmas. On the one hand, the country's commitment to individual worth, justice, and fairness strengthens the credibility of its policy and strategy; it also taps a wellspring of support from the public. On the other hand, the same commitment makes it difficult to address national security issues that require the use of force or alliances with nondemocratic systems (e.g., Saudi Arabia), although these may be necessary in responding to terrorism and unconventional conflicts. Those types of conflicts invariably encompass the political-social structure and make the population at large combatants whether they like it or not. Moreover, involvement in unconventional conflicts requires interjecting US political-military forces into the political-social milieu of other countries, few of which may be democratic in the Western sense. The United States often has few options other than to support the lesser of evils, but relations with regimes that violate human rights run counter to US morals and foster divisiveness within our political system.

The premise that we know best—part of the democratic faith—makes it difficult for many to establish realistic perspectives on the motivation and nationalistic aspirations of other peoples. Madeleine Albright, secretary of state during the Clinton administration, was quoted as saying "if we have to use force, it is because we are America. We are the indispensable nation. We stand tall. We see further into the future."[16]

Many Americans, perhaps adopting the American Revolution as the frame of reference for all revolutions, thus fail to realize that contemporary revolutions may evolve out of considerably different circumstances. The presumption that revolutions ultimately lead to democratic systems reflects the view that the American Revolution represents the path that others should follow and marks the primacy of hope over experience.

The openness of US affairs, even on the most sensitive issues, provides an opportunity for adversaries to use the media as a strategic asset to further their own cause. In the twenty-first century, the access to technology offers even greater opportunity for this information-age strategy. This includes attempting to sway public opinion and elected officials and to support sympathetic interest groups. In addition, the level of debate within the system itself can send the wrong signals to adversaries regarding our political will. If adversaries incorrectly read the US policy posture, it could lead to dangerous strategic choices that could force a US military response. It is likely that many adversaries do not understand the United States any better than the United States understands them.

Still, the US public's commitment to the democratic faith remains a pillar of the system, an inherent strength that provides the endurance to prevail over the long pull. Although the democratic faith may not result in success in every venture, especially in the short term, it minimizes the impact of failure as well as the formulation of unjust policies and strategies.

The Messianic Spirit

The messianic spirit pervading US political culture also has strengths and weaknesses. The concern with moral and ethical issues evolving from our Judeo-Christian heritage provides strength in dealing with national security issues because its humanistic orientation strikes a sensitive chord that is beneficial to US policy and strategy. The downside is that the belief in our messianic mission causes many foreign states and peoples to perceive us as self-righteous and arrogant; we ignore other cultures in trying to rule the world. Some countries, especially those in the less developed world and, increasingly, some in Europe and in the Middle East, see this as imperialistic, further fueling anti-US sentiment. At the very least, US moral and ethical views can be disturbing to hundreds of millions of people, including many populations in geostrategically important areas whose heritage is not Judeo-Christian.[17] This provides ample opportunity for US adversaries to take advantage of differences between Americans and other people.

National Security in a Democracy

De Tocqueville's assessment of democracy's ability to conduct foreign policy is especially relevant to US national security policy today. The US political system is not well suited to timely and thorough development of policy and strategy to create the most effective national security policy; in many ways the US system responds only at the last minute. This is not to say that policy and strategy have not been developed and implemented in a deliberate and timely way, but that is most likely to occur when the security issues are clear, the adversary is identifiable, and general support exists within government and the general public. Unfortunately, many serious threats to US national security do not adhere to this optimistic view; the short-term threat to vital US interests is not always easy to comprehend, even though we may be threatened in the long run.

The real issue, then, is how to reconcile the demands of national security with those of democracy. There are trade-offs, to be sure, but how should one balance the protection of democracy and US values, on the one hand, with the threats to national security that are not amenable to democratic processes and principles? US national security policy and process are bound by all the forces and power clusters characteristic of the US political system, and most Americans expect the government to conform to democratic proprieties. Yet if success is to be achieved, something must give if the goal is to further democracy. This is not to suggest that the United States should design conspiratorial policies that seriously undercut moral principles and tenets. But to assume that the United States must not engage in secret or covert operations in support of its national interests is a journey through the Looking Glass. Furthermore, to presume that such initiatives cannot be undertaken in our governmental system is a simplistic misreading of the nature and character of that system. Moreover, the simplistic argument that political ends can never justify covert means precludes a nuanced and calibrated approach to subtle and complex security dilemmas. Laws and procedures are ambiguous, and policies and strategies are shaped by power struggles within the US government. That is the pragmatic truth of the system. Put differently,

> if the current trends continue, the [United States] will not be the pre-eminent economic or military actor in the twenty-first-century international affairs. It will not exercise global leadership or hegemony in the West, and possibly not even unchallenged hegemony in the Americas. The programme to establish a "New World Order" will have failed, if it has not already. . . . Social polarisation may lead to increased class tensions and conflict between cultural groups and to more civil disorder. Geographical zoning may reflect social and cultural distinctions and economic differences.[18]

Although this book focuses on policy and process, our study is pursued in the context of the US political culture. Those involved in designing policy and exercising power to influence the approval process operate within that context. To examine policy and process separate from US political culture is not only sterile; it is likely to distort the nature of policymaking and the character of the approval process.

With all the disadvantages open systems face in their dealings with authoritarian systems, rogue regimes, and international terrorists, in the long run democracy has the advantage. The involvement of people in the governing process, their ability to voice their views freely, and the ultimate responsibility of those in office to the people establish stability, legitimacy, and capability like no other system. Therein lies the true strength of open systems: little can prevail against the strength of people who, having examined and debated the issues, are convinced of the right policy and strategy.[19]

In Part 2 of this book, we examine the institutions, offices, and individuals involved in policymaking. Similarly, we look at nongovernmental groups, the media, and the US public regarding their respective roles in national security policy and the policy approval process.

Notes

1. Alexis de Tocqueville, *Democracy in America,* ed. J. P. Mayer, trans. George Lawrence (Garden City, NY: Anchor Books, 1969), pp. 228–229.

2. Ibid.

3. See Donald M. Snow, *Distant Thunder: Third World Conflict and the New International Order* (New York: St. Martin's, 1993). Also see J. Bowyer Bell, *Dragonwars: Armed Struggle and the Conventions of Modern War* (New Brunswick, NJ: Transaction, 1999). See also Bruce Berkowitz, *The New Face of War: How War Will Be Fought in the 21st Century* (New York: The Free Press, 2003), and Colonel (Retired) John R. Martin, *A Nation at War,* Seventeenth Annual Strategy Conference (Carlisle Barracks, PA: Strategic Studies Institute, US Army War College, 2007).

4. De Tocqueville, *Democracy in America,* p. 233.

5. Bob Greene, "You Must Remember This (Unless You Don't)," *Chicago Tribune,* Sunday, April 9, 2000, sec. 1, p. 2.

6. Robert L. Lineberry, George C. Edwards III, and Martin P. Wattenberg, *Government in America: People, Politics, and Policy,* 6th ed. (New York: HarperCollins, 1994), p. 467. Also see George C. Edwards III, Martin P. Wattenberg, and Robert L. Lineberry, *Government in America: People, Politics, and Policy,* brief ed. (New York: HarperCollins, 2007).

7. James Q. Wilson, *American Government: Institutions and Policies,* 5th ed. (Lexington, MA: D. C. Heath, 1992), pp. 328–329.

8. Kenneth D. Wald, *Religion and Politics in the United States,* 2nd ed. (Washington, DC: CQ Press, 1992), p. 338.

9. Daniel Patrick Moynihan, *Secrecy: The American Experience* (New Haven: Yale University Press, 1998).

10. "Ten Congressmen Send a Message to Managua," *Wall Street Journal,* April 17, 1984, p. 1.

11. John Barron, *KGB Today: The Hidden Hand* (New York: Berkley Books, 1985), p. 244.

12. Ibid.

13. Terry L. Deibel, "National Strategy and the Continuity of National Interests," in James C. Gaston, *Grand Strategy and the Decisionmaking Process* (Washington, DC: National Defense University Press, 1992), p. 48.

14. Ronald Kessler, *Inside the CIA: Revealing the Secrets of the World's Most Powerful Spy Agency* (New York: Pocket Books, 1992), p. xxv.

15. See, e.g., Sam Vincent Meddis, "CIA Officer Charged as Spy," *USA Today,* February 23, 1994, pp. 1A, 3A, and a variety of TV news reports during the same week.

16. Ray Mosley, "What Went Wrong with Pax Americana," *Chicago Tribune,* February 22, 1998, Perspectives, p. 1.

17. See, e.g., Samuel P. Huntington, *The Clash of Civilizations and the Remaking of World Order* (New York: Simon and Schuster, 1999).

18. K. R. Dark, with A. L. Harris, *The New World and the New World Order: US Relative Decline, Domestic Instability in the Americas, and the End of the Cold War* (New York: St. Martin's, 1996), p. 144.

19. See de Tocqueville, *Democracy in America,* p. 244. For a well-reasoned view of the challenges facing democracy, see Jean-François Revel, *How Democracies Perish* (New York: Harper and Row, 1984).

PART 2

The National Security Establishment

4

The President and the Presidency

SEVERAL YEARS AFTER HE LEFT OFFICE, PRESIDENT LYNDON Johnson wrote, "No one can experience with the President of the United States the glory and agony of his office. No one can share the majestic view from his pinnacle of power. No one can share the burden of his decisions or the scope of his duties."[1] Not only did Johnson capture the essence of the presidency with these few words; he put his finger on the reason why it is difficult for others to comprehend the power and responsibilities of the position. Thus in studying the president and the presidency, we must exercise caution regarding the many relevant perspectives and recognize the considerable disagreement over the power, limits, and responsibilities of the office as well as the characteristics of the most effective type of executive.

All these factors make it especially difficult to develop a sense of the presidential role in national security, except in cases of serious threats to our national interests, as on September 11. As we saw in earlier chapters, security policy is complex, and when studying the president and national security policy it must be understood that concerns and problems are usually linked to domestic issues. This makes it difficult to isolate national security policy from other policy issues under the president's authority and control. During the Cold War, with its enormous problems related to nuclear weapons and superpower conflicts, national security issues took on a dimension rarely known in the past. In the twenty-first century the possibility of world wars between major powers has diminished considerably. The end of the superpower era brought with it a tendency for the US public to focus on domestic issues, at least until September 11, but that does not make it any easier for the president. The world remains a dangerous place: the many conflicts in progress, including international terrorism, within the changing strategic landscape have created a host of new challenges for national security policy.

Another important factor is Congress, which is increasingly assertive in the foreign and national security policy process. With the inauguration of Bill Clinton as president in 1993, the view of many members of Congress was that given the end of the Cold War, domestic issues should have priority over national security. Although the Clinton administration came into power in 1993 with Congress in the hands of the Democratic Party, the 1994 congressional elections swept the Republican Party into power with control of both houses of Congress. This situation continued throughout the Clinton administration and created a different atmosphere in congressional-executive relationships. It also ushered in growing partisanship over domestic policy as well as foreign and national security policy. A similar political condition developed when the Democratic Party came into power as a result of the 2006 congressional elections. After twelve years of control of Congress, the Republican Party lost and the Democratic Party took over control of both houses of Congress. Many regarded this change of power as a result of diminishing support for President Bush's policy in the Middle East, particularly US involvement in Iraq and Afghanistan.

Yet it is ironic that the responsibilities of the president in national security have become more complex even while the power of the office to make and implement decisions has become increasingly difficult, mainly owing to the countervailing power of Congress and the unsettled international landscape. Although the impact of September 11 changed all of this, at least in terms of a unified counterterrorism effort, the US involvement in Iraq beginning in 2003 undermined US public support of President Bush's policy.

In the 1980s, one author had this to say about presidential power, a comment that remains relevant today: "Presidential power may be greater today than ever before . . . it is misleading, however, to infer from a president's capacity to begin a nuclear war that the chief executive has similar power in most policy-making areas. . . . Presidents who want to be effective in implementing policy changes know they face a number of constraints."[2]

Although the primary purpose in this chapter is to study the president and the presidency in terms of national security policy, this cannot be done without an understanding of the nature of the office. Below we identify some benchmarks that help define the Oval Office and its occupant, with particular reference to national security in the contemporary period.

Evolution of the Office: An Overview

Political struggles over the nature of the presidential office are part of US history; indeed, the disagreements began with the Constitutional Convention and the founding of the nation. Many delegates were wary of investing too much power in the executive, but they also realized that a strong executive was necessary for the government to take action. What resulted was a series of compromises leading to the establishment of the basic structure as we know it today. The acceptance of a single executive and its powers were, in no small way, influenced by the fact that most delegates used George Washington as the model for the office they created.

George Washington won admiration for his fairness, honesty, and integrity as well as his leadership in the battlefield in the drive for US independence. He seemed to stand above politics. For most delegates, Washington epitomized what a president should be and the role he should fulfill. Yet upon assuming the presidency, Washington commented that he felt not unlike a "culprit who is going to the place of his execution." Other presidents have had similar feelings upon assuming office. William Howard Taft thought it was the "loneliest place in the world"; Warren Harding referred to the White House as a "prison"; Harry Truman declared that being president was "like riding a tiger. A man has to keep riding or be swallowed."

Whereas most who have held the office have commented on its demands and problems, some have aggressively tried to expand its power. George Washington, Andrew Jackson, Abraham Lincoln, Theodore Roosevelt, Woodrow Wilson, and Franklin Roosevelt used their presidential powers extensively and actively, and their incumbencies are usually identified as "strong" or "expansionist" periods of the presidency. In the modern period, Harry Truman and Ronald Reagan have been identified as men who actively used their office to expand the scope of presidential power—even though each represented a different political party and philosophy. This was also true with respect to the Clinton presidency. Ironically, "Bill Clinton surprisingly retained and even gained popularity the longer he was in office. Indeed, the more personal trouble Clinton got into, the more his public approval ratings went up—even after he was impeached by the US House of Representatives."[3]

It is paradoxical that the presidency, even though it was fashioned by men who had a deep mistrust of executive power, has become the focal point of national politics and the center of the national policy process. The president is the only nationally elected public official, and he is usually the most recognized public leader in the country, often referred to as the "leader of the free world." Yet the president depends on many other political actors to accomplish his political goals and implement policy. Although he has the power, for example, to order a worldwide alert of US armed forces and the deployment of the military, he can meet overwhelming resistance in simply trying to remove a controversial bureaucrat from office or gain the approval of a Supreme Court nominee. He can submit programs to Congress, but he cannot allocate money to them without congressional approval. Truman identified this anomaly when discussing the problems his successor in office, Dwight Eisenhower, would face upon moving into the Oval Office: "He'll sit here [tapping his desk], and he'll say, 'Do this! Do that!' And nothing will happen. Poor Ike; it won't be a bit like the army. He'll find it very frustrating."[4]

The frustration is compounded by struggles between the executive and legislative branches of government over presidential authority and initiative—a conflict especially visible in national security policy. For example, the 1987 Iran-contra hearings, although focusing on covert operations and illegal transfers of funds, were at their core a struggle over presidential power and congressional attempts to control that power. This was also seen in the confrontation between President Clinton and Congress over committing the US military to Haiti, Somalia, Bosnia-Herzegovina, and Kosovo. The same problem developed regarding the use of the US military to support the Colombian government against the drug cartel–revolutionary coalition. And it is clear that these issues have been magnified and compounded during President Bush's terms in office, particularly with respect to US policy in the Middle East. Clearly, in responding to serious threats, the president is accorded almost absolute power, but the point is that today the line is fuzzy as to what the president can and cannot do in foreign and national security policy, absent a clear and immediate threat to US interests.

The extent of presidential power is not determined solely by legal grants of power, by the Constitution, or necessarily by political skill. Traditions, custom, and usage play important roles in determining the power of the Oval Office. The way in which political parties operate, the relationship of political actors to the executive office, the political climate, the functioning of the federal bureaucracy, and the nature of security threats—all impact presidential powers (see Chapter 3). A realistic study of the presidency and national security thus requires an appreciation of the complex nature of the office and the presidential power base. But any study must also be based on the realization that the success and impact of the office depend on the personality, character, and leadership style of the president.

Theodore Sorenson, special counsel to President John F. Kennedy, put it this way:

> Self-confidence and self-assertion are more important than modesty. The nation selects its President, at least in part, for his philosophy and his judgement and his conscientious conviction of what is right—and he need not hesitate to apply them. He must believe in his own objectives. He must assert his own priorities. And he must always strive to preserve the power and prestige of his office, the availability of his options, and the long-range interests of the nation.[5]

Beginning with Andrew Jackson, who sowed the seeds of the so-called modern presidency, many presidents have used a variety of methods to expand the power of the Oval Office, including appealing directly to the people and broadly interpreting the Constitution to favor presidential power. For example, Jackson rationalized his view of the presidency this way: "Each public officer who takes an oath to support the Constitution swears that he will support it as he understands it, and not as it is understood by others." The growth of the power of the presidency accelerated in the twentieth century to the point where Arthur Schlesinger labeled it the "Imperial Presidency."[6] But as President George H. W. Bush (Bush I) learned in dealing with Congress over the US response to China, "Congress . . . restricted the president's conduct of the executive branch by involving itself extensively in the details of domestic and foreign policy."[7] Moreover, "it should be understood that the pendulum of power swings, only to swing back somewhat later. . . . Eventually Congress has always moved to reassert its position."[8] Presidents Bill Clinton and George W. Bush faced the same problems regarding their policies on China, Cuba, and National Missile Defense, among others. Nonetheless, they expanded presidential powers by utilizing the executive order, a presidential prerogative that usually does not require congressional approval. Yet, the US involvement in Iraq in 2003 and beyond is increasingly challenged by Congress and many in the US public.

How does the president exercise power in pursuit of US national security and national interests? What power does he have, and how does he deal with constraints and limitations on that power? What leadership style is effective in developing a coherent policy posture and strategy in national security? Any serious examination of the Oval Office and national security policy must begin with some attention to models and approaches. By first studying the broad dimension of the presidency, we design some method of linking to it the specifics of national security policy.

The Study of the Presidency

Virtually all studies of the presidency incorporate the various formal roles of the president (usually referred to as "institutionalized roles").[9] The most important institutionalized roles are chief of state, chief executive, commander in chief, chief diplomat, chief legislator, and party chief. The president's national security powers derive mainly from the duties of chief executive, commander in chief, and chief diplomat.

Scholars have designed several theoretical models to study the presidency.[10] Many focus on one or two important roles, showing how they affect the political system and political actors. For example, the view of the president as manager focuses on a bureaucratic model of the office. Another approach is based on personality and character and identifies the passive or active presidents and their consequences for leadership and policies.[11] The president-as-great-man view assesses the officeholder according to his greatness in responding to the political challenges of the time. The president's personal perception of office, which can vary from constitutional to expansionist, offers another approach. Still another approach—one that evaluates leadership style—evolves out of leadership studies that use personality and character to examine the president's ability to develop consensus, loyalty, and commitment in his staff and the executive branch and motivate them to pursue his policies. In addition, the two-presidencies model was advanced to suggest that there is a domestic president and a foreign policy president.

Each model and approach can be relevant and useful depending on the circumstances.[12] Our study is based on two elements common to all: leadership style and personal perception of the office. We take our cue from Sorenson's view that the president's self-confidence, self-assertion, and philosophy are critical in the functioning of the office: "Each President has his own style and his own standard for making decisions—and these may differ from day to day or from topic to topic, using one blend for foreign affairs, for example, and another for domestic. The man affects the office as the office affects the man."[13] As Sorenson pointed out, "White House decision-making is not a science but an art. It requires, not calculation, but judgment."[14]

Our study is based on the view that the character and personality are critical in shaping the moral authority and power of the office. Thus there are *four important components* to a systematic study of the president's role in national security: (1) the president's leadership style, personality, and character as critical determinants of how the Oval Office functions with respect to national security policy and process; (2) how the president views the power and limitations of the office and how he sees his role in furthering its prestige and power; (3) the president's mind-set (or worldview) regarding US national interests and the international security environment and how they affect the posture the administration attempts to put into place; and (4) the president's ability to bring the first three components to bear upon the national security establishment so as to integrate its efforts to develop and implement coherent policy.

These four factors must be used to develop support among Americans, the Congress, and the federal bureaucracy. This is necessary to develop the national will, political resolve, and staying power for the implementation of national security policy and strategy. The president's effectiveness in achieving these ends rests in his ability to deal with all the complex issues we have identified and yet remain within the bounds of democratic proprieties.

Leadership Style

Although in legal and organizational terms the national security policy process appears to be rational and clear, in reality it is a political and, at times, a chaotic process, reflecting the power and interests of many domestic and foreign actors. At the vital center of this process stands the president. Depending upon his leadership style and philosophy and his effectiveness in exercising the power of the office, the president can minimize the influence of other political actors and guide the process to ensure that his own views and policies prevail.

The term *leadership style* is not easy to define. It refers to the president's way of doing business, which evolves from personality and character: it is the way in which the president exercises authority and power to create trust, loyalty, commitment, and enthusiasm within the administration and is crucial for successful policymaking and implementation. The term *personality* refers to the psychological and social behavior that lays the foundation for one's perceptions and worldview. The term *character* is defined as the way in which the "president orients himself towards life— not for the moment, but enduringly."[15] Put simply, personality and character fix the political behavior and shape the way the president views the world and his own role in it. In addition, they determine the way the president relates to subordinates, to the public, and to the nation's governing institutions.

The point to remember is that the way in which a president governs is every bit as important as the inherent power of the office-as-institution. And when we talk about the powers of the presidency, we must consider three factors: sense of purpose, political skills, and character.[16] James Q. Wilson once concluded that "the public will judge the president not only in terms of what he accomplished but also in terms of its perception of his character."[17]

The leadership style that emerges from personality and character determines whether the president will follow a *magisterial, bureaucratic, managerial,* or *corporate* method of governing—or a combination of these. In the magisterial style, the president places himself as the authoritative head of the government. The bureaucratic style is one in which the official leads as the chief bureaucrat, with all the mind-sets and perceptions that that role entails. In the managerial style, the president strives for efficiency in the administration through the close supervision advocated by managerial principles. In the corporate style, the president governs like the chairman of a large business, combining the managerial approach with commitment and loyalty. Most presidents tend to centralize their role around a particular style, although there are elements of each in the way most modern presidents lead. Regardless of the chosen leadership style, it is implemented to establish a presence, so to speak: the president sets policy directions and saturates the administration with his views on world affairs. Yet the president must do this without frustrating the expression of alternative views and options—not an easy task.

A successful president can stamp national security with his personal style and outlook. If the executive is unsuccessful, then policy is likely to be incoherent and ineffective, and other domestic political actors are likely to increase their power. This can only lead to erosion of national will, political resolve, and staying power. This appears to be the case regarding President Bush and US involvement in Iraq during 2007.

Perceptions of the Office

President Johnson perceived the power of the Oval Office this way: "The source of the President's authority is the people. He is not simply responsible to an immediate electorate, either. The President always has to think of America as a continuing community. He has to prepare for the future."[18] President Richard Nixon, reaffirming the national character of the office, stated,

> The first responsibility of leadership is to gain mastery over events, and to shape the future in the image of our hopes. He must lead. The President has a duty to decide, but the people have a right to know why. The President is the only official who represents every American, rich and poor. The Presidency is a place where priorities are set and goals determined.[19]

The perceptions of office that have historically evolved and are applicable in the contemporary period cluster around *three basic types*:

1. The constitutionalist, or Buchanan-type, presidency
2. The stewardship, or Eisenhower-type, presidency (although recent scholarship indicates that Dwight Eisenhower was more activist than originally thought)
3. The prerogative, or Lincoln-type, presidency

Some would add a fourth type of presidency, one designed (intentionally or not) by Bill Clinton: the *public opinion* presidency, or one that follows the whims and desires of the majority of Americans. This type of president comes into office with no commitment to a particular type of role, other than maintaining power in office. In light of President Clinton's record, it would not be surprising if such a label were used by his critics. It is difficult to label the current President George Bush's perception. At the end of his term in office in 2008, it may be more clear, although a number of Americans have probably placed him in one or the other category already. Given his expansive view of presidential power, it is likely that President George W. Bush will be considered a prerogative president.

In the constitutional presidency, the president views the power of the office as strictly bound by the US Constitution: the document must clearly sanction any presidential action. This narrow view of presidential authority limits the president to reacting to the policies of others, with little presidential initiative. President James Buchanan (1857–1861) provides the example: he felt he was simply the custodian of the Constitution and tried to remain aloof from political battles. In 1860, he even denied that he had the power to use force to prevent the secession of southern states.

The stewardship view presumes that the Oval Office is nonpolitical or, at least, nonpartisan. The president acts as an agent of the nation, supervising operations of the state machinery. Dwight Eisenhower (1953–1961) was associated with such a presidency. Standing aloof from party politics and political battles, Eisenhower felt that his veto power over legislative bills was the key to the presidential office. From this he took the position that the president should advise the nation, negate ill-advised legislation and ill-advised policies, and be the chief broker of the political system. This approach borrows some elements from the constitutional as well as prerogative approaches. After the Eisenhower presidency, however, there was growing evidence that he was much more active and politically involved than previously believed.[20]

The prerogative view is that the powers of the presidency are exclusive rights resting in a special trust to the benefit of the nation. This approach is best explained by Abraham Lincoln (1861–1865), who made it clear during the Civil War that the legal limits imposed by the Constitution may have to be transcended during a crisis. He felt that the president was the sole representative of all the people and the office was the only institution capable of dealing quickly and decisively with major national problems. President Theodore Roosevelt (1901–1909), another prerogative president, later put it this way:

> I did not usurp power, but I did greatly broaden the use of executive power. In other words, I acted for the public welfare, I acted for the common well-being of all our people, whenever and in whatever manner was necessary, unless prevented by direct constitutional prohibition. . . . My belief was that it was not only his right but his duty to do anything that the needs of the nation demanded unless such action was forbidden by the Constitution or by the laws.[21]

Many scholars argue that no president today can be successful if he ignores the prerogatives of office; the changed security landscape and uncertainties of the nature of international challenges mandate such an approach.

Mind-Set and External Threats

Another key element is how the president perceives external threats, that is, the president's mind-set regarding the international security environment.

Presidents come to the Oval Office with an established viewpoint. Although some have more experience in foreign and national security policy, each has a set of beliefs that stems from public service, political involvement, and other socialization, shaped by experience with allies and adversaries alike. Some have experience only in the domestic arena, however, which may not be the best background to deal with foreign adversaries and allies. Yet this can be overcome through the appointment of experienced and knowledgeable people to the inner circle. President George W. Bush appointed such people following his election in 2000 to compensate for his limited foreign policy experience. But as the United States became involved in the new war on terrorism and in Iraq, the issue became one of strategic choices and implementation rather than experience.

From the end of World War II (1945) to the end of the Cold War (roughly 1989), the central US preoccupation was the relationship with the Soviet Union as well as the threats that Marxist-Leninist ideology posed to democracy and the West. The primary focus of the conflict spectrum was on nuclear and conventional conflicts, Vietnam notwithstanding. Each type of conflict posed a different security challenge to the United States. How the president viewed the seriousness of these conflicts, what he believed was the proper world order, and the place of the United States in that order were all critical elements in presidential performance. They remain so today.

Many observers, including those in the media, tend to oversimplify a president's mind-set by categorizing it as either "hard-line" ("hawks") or "soft-line" ("doves"). Rarely does an individual's perspective fit neatly into one category or the other. True, each president does have a unique perspective about adversaries and is likely to appoint officials with compatible views to high places in the national security establishment. But the responsibilities of office, the political forces within the domestic system, and the continuities of national security policy prevent the president from establishing and implementing a policy that rests solely on his own preferences and initiatives. In many cases the demands of office require compromises with a variety of political forces, both domestic and foreign.

Finally, the term *mind-set* does not mean strict adherence to past perspectives or a dogmatic ideology. The responsibilities for US national security and protection of the homeland weigh heavily upon any president, a burden magnified by the problems of the proliferation of WMD and an uncertain world. Thus the need to reexamine US security interests and the state of US military posture is critical to the national security equation. In the contemporary period, such is the case because of the uncertain world order and the changing and dangerous security landscape, as well as changing leadership in many states and changing international patterns.

The degree to which the president is able to establish US security policy and strategy according to his own mind-set is contingent upon how he functions in the first two elements of our framework: leadership style and perception of the office. For example, it is unlikely that a president who sees the office from a narrow constitutional perspective will be able to develop innovative policies and tackle the range of conflicts across the spectrum. Additionally, a president who cannot inspire Americans, articulate a vision for US national interests, or develop a consensus within the federal bureaucracy to support presidential policies will be unable to convince adversaries, potential adversaries, and even allies of the seriousness of US interests or of US staying power and political resolve.

The President and the National Security Establishment

The final component of the framework for studying the presidency is the president's need to synthesize the first three components in order to ensure that the national security establishment functions effectively. Thus the president's appointments to key positions are critical in determining the degree to which he will be able to shape the establishment to his own worldview and policy directions. Appointees must have the ability to provide the necessary linkage between the establishment and the president. The assistant to the president for national security affairs (the national security advisor) and the secretaries of defense and state are principal actors in this respect. The individual selected for these positions must have the president's complete trust and must be seen by those on the NSC and by the national security staff, among others, as enjoying a special relationship with the president in national security matters. Equally important, the national security advisor is a key cog in the president's inner circle. Through the national security advisor, the national security staff becomes an extension of presidential power and an instrument to set the tone and style of the administration.

The major problem is to ensure that this special relationship among the president, the national security advisor, and the national security staff is not seen by the secretaries of defense and state and their departments as infringing on their own prerogatives or as a threat to their roles and functions. The president and his inner circle must likewise be cautious in dealing with other political actors; the 1987 Iran-contra affair revealed the problems that can arise from internal political struggles. In 1994, the US response to ethnic conflict in Bosnia-Herzegovina and continuing involvement in the Balkans triggered disagreements within the Clinton administration that continued into the George W. Bush administration's policy in Iraq and Afghanistan.

In sum, the president's ability to control and supervise the national security establishment and to develop national will, political resolve, and staying power are based on his leadership style, his perceptions of the office, and his mind-set. Even if a president sees the world in realistic terms, uses the power of the presidency aggressively, and applies effective leadership, however, he will not always be able to develop the wherewithal within the body politic to carry out national security policy and strategy. Without a reasonably effective synthesis of these components, the president will surely fail.

In another development, the Clinton administration gave special prominence to the role of the first lady, Hillary Rodham Clinton. Some textbooks on the US government have even included the president's spouse within the formal organization of the White House.[22] Hillary Clinton's efforts to design the administration's health care plan and to shape other national policies raised serious questions regarding the appropriateness of her role, which was not based upon elective office or federal civil-service guidelines. Whether this had any impact on national security policy or on appointments to the national security establishment remains unclear. Nonetheless, to understand the totality of the presidential role and power base, one must consider the role of the president's spouse.

Discussions of the George W. Bush presidency must include the expansive role of Vice President Richard Cheney. Contrary to historical expectations of a weak and powerless vice president, Vice President Cheney by all accounts has exerted influence behind the scenes, particularly in the national security arena where Cheney, a former secretary of defense, had significantly more experience than President Bush.

The National Security Establishment

The current structure and most agencies that develop national security policy were established in the aftermath of World War II. The war experience, as well as the belated recognition that a better system of unified command and control was necessary, led to passage of the National Security Act of 1947, amended by Congress in 1949, 1958, the 1980s, and later.

The 1947 act established the NSC, the Office of Secretary of Defense, the US Air Force, the Joint Chiefs of Staff (JCS), and the CIA. For the first time, the president was provided with a principal staff member whose purpose was to give the president advice and assistance in matters pertaining to national security. Although the secretary of defense was to oversee the national military establishment, it was presided over by three cabinet-level officers heading three separate executive departments: the Army, the Navy, and the Air Force.

The 1949 amendments created the Department of Defense, making it an executive department and reducing the services to military departments with no cabinet-level officers except the secretary of defense. The position of chairman of the Joint Chiefs of Staff was created to preside over the JCS, which was to remain a corporate body and principal adviser to the president and secretary of defense.

The 1958 amendments reinforced the secretary of defense by granting legal authority over all elements within the Department of Defense, thereby imposing a degree of unification on the military services (additional staff assistance was also provided). The JCS chairman was given added responsibilities over the joint staff and became a voting member of the JCS for the first time. The 1958 amendments also provided that operational commanders would report to the secretary of defense, not through the military departments and service chiefs (who would be responsible for administration and logistical support). The 1986 Goldwater-Nichols Bill provided additional changes within the Department of Defense by strengthening the position of the JCS chairman to make him the principal military aide to the secretary, creating a deputy chairman of the JCS, establishing the position of assistant secretary of defense for special operations and low-intensity conflict, and requiring joint service duty for future general officers, among other things.

The National Security Act of 1947 established the basis for integrating political, military, and intelligence functions into the national security policy process through the NSC, thereby giving the president a structure for a systematized assessment of policy and strategic options. Although the move toward centralization and unification has achieved a great deal, many internal problems of power decentralization and diffusion remain.

The national security establishment as it exists today is shown in Figure 4.1. An important structural evolution since 1947 has led to the emerging prominence of the national security advisor. The national security advisor is appointed by the president without approval by the Congress, and the position has been held by Henry Kissinger, Brent Scowcroft, Colin Powell, and Zbigniew Brzezinski, among others. The Iran-contra hearings revealed more details about the functioning of the post, thanks to the testimony of National Security Advisor Robert McFarlane and Admiral John Poindexter.[23] In any case, the role of national security advisor goes beyond policy coordination; indeed, some observers feel the power exercised by individuals such as Kissinger and Brzezinski undermined the role of the secretary of state. The fact that the national security advisor can provide the president with a unique view not bound by executive department perspectives makes his or her advice especially important. Thus the national security advisor's own personality and character, perceptions of the role, and personal access to the president provide that person with a power base that translates into prominence in all areas of national security. The extent of that superiority depends on the president's leadership style and his own perceptions of the position. Thus the national security advisor's relationship with the president is much different from that of cabinet-level officers, who must be approved by Congress and may be appointed for any number of political reasons. As Theodore Sorenson has pointed out with respect to the president's personal staff, "we were appointed for our ability to fulfill the President's needs and talk the President's language. We represented no one but John Kennedy."[24]

Figure 4.1 The National Security Establishment

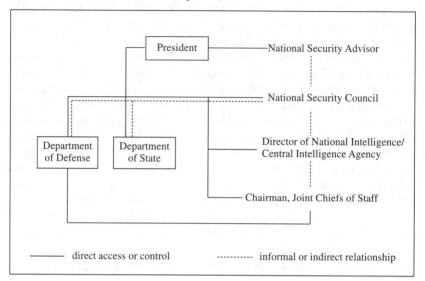

Notes: The four statutory members of the National Security Council are the president, vice president, and secretaries of state and defense. The two statutory advisers are the director of national intelligence and the chairman of the Joint Chiefs of Staff. The national security advisor is an important actor in the national security policy process and usually plans and coordinates the meetings of the National Security Council.

Yet there can be disagreements within the national security establishment as well as the president's own staff. In the Clinton administration, the issue of homosexuals in the military caused serious disagreement within the national security establishment. The disagreements about US counterterror policy and involvement in Iraq will characterize the term of President George Bush through 2008. The president, however, can foster a phenomenon labeled by one scholar as "group-think," in which the group itself takes on a certain mind-set, blocking out or ignoring alternative inputs, even from its own membership.[25] The results can lead to policy disasters and strategic failures.

The NSC, the NSC staff, and other important political actors in the national security establishment are discussed in more detail in Chapter 5.

Constraints and Limitations

The assertion that the president has the preeminent role in national security must be qualified. The *first* qualification is the very nature of the US political system, with its emphasis on democratic proprieties and values. Any president sensitive to domestic politics and public expectations appreciates and understands that the presidency is supposed to symbolize the best of the US system. Behavior and words must be in keeping with the goals and expectations of the people. The constraints this imposes on the president create an inherent dilemma in dealing with national security.

Especially in response to unconventional conflicts, some of the most effective policies and strategies stretch democratic expectations and norms. Even though secrecy and covert operations are part and parcel of the response to unconventional conflicts, current efforts to identify terrorists' plans reveal it is difficult for many citizens, as well as members of ·Congress, to accept the necessity for such operations. The view is that these operations tend to be undemocratic, an un-American way of war. Thus the president must find ways to reconcile democratic norms with acceptable and effective strategic options.

Second, the current distinctions between the national security policy process and the domestic policy process are not as clear as they once were. The turmoil of the 1960s, followed by the US withdrawal from Vietnam, the Watergate affair, and current difficulties in Iraq, eroded public confidence in the presumed preeminence of the president in national security affairs. Neither was their faith restored by later events: US inability to respond to Soviet power projections in Africa and the establishment of Marxist-Leninist regimes in parts of the less developed world, hostilities in the Middle East, US hostages, failures with Iran, the problems with covert operations, questions over US policy in Central America, and so on. More questions were raised about the role of the president in national security concerning US-China relations over Taiwan and US-Russia relations under Russian president Boris Yeltsin, followed in 2000 by Vladimir Putin, a former Komitet Gosudarstvennoy Bezopasnosti (KGB; Committee for State Security) officer. The US role in NATO and in a variety of operations other than war raises further questions about current presidential power and national security. There were limits to presidential power, and some called for more limits to be imposed by the US Congress. This erosion of confidence was reinforced by US involvement in Somalia, the inability to respond effectively to the crisis in Haiti, the commitment of US troops to the Bosnia-Herzegovina conflict in 1995, and the continuing role of the United States in Kosovo and neighboring regions. The war against terrorism and the effort at a global response reinforced and highlighted the presidential role.

The motivations behind a certain national security policy and strategy, as well as the way in which policy is made, have been sensitive issues for Congress and many other political actors. The presumed secrecy surrounding such decisions, and the way the policy process functions, have to a great extent lost their rationale—if for no other reason than fear of the resurgence of an imperial presidency. Writing in 1998, then-senator Daniel Patrick Moynihan argued for more openness in government and for dismantling much of the secret system and apparatus. "*Analysis*, far more than secrecy, is the key to security."[26] The events of late 2001 and beyond, as well as the scope and direction of the US response, muted some of this criticism at first, but with the passage of time it has returned in full force.

In addition, the basis of national security has qualitatively shifted. The clear purposes that characterized the Cold War era have been replaced by the challenge of a more ambiguous security environment. This began with the ascension of Mikhail Gorbachev as head of the Soviet Union. His glasnost and perestroika initiatives paved the way for the dissolution of the Soviet empire, not to mention the Soviet Union itself. In the twenty-first century, the United States and Russia agree on many international issues, as during the 1991 Gulf War, despite some last-minute maneuvering to save Saddam Hussein's hide. This was also the case in the immediate aftermath of September 11 and the call by President Bush for an international response to terrorism. Some former enemies are becoming friends, and friends are becoming economic competitors. At the same time, developing nations, some of which are rich with oil, are not the political-military pawns they once were. Unconventional conflicts, which now characterize much of the security environment, remain difficult security problems. Such conflicts are not easily understood given the American way of war, and the United States is not properly postured to respond quickly and effectively.

Third, any new president inherits his predecessor's budget, structures, commitments, and bureaucratic personnel and so does not have the freedom of action most people would assume, at least initially. Part of this constraint results from the logical reluctance to change national security dramatically early on in an administration. In addition, the continuity of national security policy goes beyond any one president; such continuity is necessitated by the impact of US national security policy on allies and potential adversaries.

Fourth, every new president usually finds it difficult to deal with the national security establishment, especially the military. The character of the military profession and the general orientation of the institution, with its linkage to civilian political actors, preclude the president from becoming a completely free agent. Many items are the province of military experts and civilian specialists who develop a legitimacy from their expertise, and the president depends on them. But members of the military are far from apolitical; they are often drawn into the fray over national security policy, organizational issues, and social issues. Even Eisenhower, whose years of military service should have provided a firm basis for national security policy (he presided over the Allied victory in Europe during World War II), encountered intense political battles. In 1993 and 1994, President Clinton faced serious problems stemming from his avoidance of military service, his anti–Vietnam War activities, and his campaign policy of lifting the ban on open homosexuals in the military. Such views had a troubling impact within the military that dogged him until the end of his administration. An editorial in *Armed Forces Journal International* (speaking specifically to US strategy and policy in committing the military into Bosnia) focused on Clinton's character and judgment:

> Although the majority of the American public has only recently come to realize that their president plays loose with the truth and has a proclivity for inducing others to follow his lead with hair-splitting semantical obfuscation, America's military forces have long seen evidence of those traits in their commander-in-chief. The US military involvement in Bosnia provides abundant illustration of both points.[27]

Again, the response to terrorism in the aftermath of September 11 changed much of this. But many problems of the past have emerged in the current presidency of George Bush.

Fifth, bureaucracies in the national security policy process might resist any change that threatens their authority or budget. At times, bureaucratic loyalty overshadows policy priorities. Of central importance (especially in the military, the Departments of State and Defense, and intelligence) is the maintenance of the stature, role, and budgets of their organizations or subunits. Put simply, their perspectives are affected by bureaucratic affiliation.[28] As Henry Kissinger observed, "The nightmare of the modern state is the hugeness of the bureaucracy, and the problem is how to get coherence and design in it."[29] This has become even more the case in domestic politics with the establishment of the Department of Homeland Security.

Bureaucracies' ability to frustrate a president's national security policy and strategy is reinforced if bureaucrats are able to forge alliances with actors outside the executive office. Equally important are the so-called subgovernments and power clusters that exist within many bureaucracies, which can thwart attempts to design coherent policies and strategies.

The reality of modern US politics is that an opposition government of sorts exists within our federal bureaucracies. Staff members, attorneys, assistant division chiefs, and deputy administrators—a civil service old-boys' network—stand ready to leak embarrassing information to undercut an administration. The motives may vary for this, but every administration understands that it can be sandbagged by one of its own.[30]

Sixth, Congress is more assertive in national security policy through the budget process as well as its role in the policy process. For example, the House and Senate Budget Committees established by the Congressional Budget and Impoundment Act of 1974 provide Congress a structure to examine the administration's budget and prepare an alternative. In addition, Congress has expanded its staff and developed the ability to examine national security policy and strategy. Yet the global counterterrorism strategy that began developing in late 2001 established new procedures and processes that actually expanded presidential power.

The executive-legislative dynamic since the end of the Vietnam War has been affected by a variety of national security problems: questionable CIA involvement in Watergate, presumptions about the CIA as a rogue agency, reactions against military interventions (a hangover from the Vietnam experience), the toppling of the shah of Iran and US hostage-taking, the establishment of authoritarian regimes in parts of the less developed world, and, of course, the continuing difficulties in Iraq and Afghanistan. These events, among others, led many to believe that the country had lost its capacity to affect the international security environment and protect interests abroad. Many feared that a vacuum had been created in national security policy.

Congress attempted to step in, passing legislation to restrict intelligence activities, strengthen congressional oversight, and restrict the president's use of military force (the 1973 War Powers Resolution) and his authority to commit military assistance to other countries (the Clark Amendment and, later, the Boland Amendments). In 2007, Congress began a serious effort to withdraw the US from Iraq. Congress and the country were in the mood to exert control over foreign and national security policies, regardless of the impact they had on adversaries and allies. Although the Reagan administration marked a change—restoring the executive-legislative balance during the early 1980s—the stage was set for continuing congressional involvement in national security affairs. The changes brought on by the post–Cold War period and the concentration on domestic issues and priorities reinforced the congressional role in national security affairs. In the aftermath of September 11, this and the major role of the United States in the Middle East have changed yet again, as President George W. Bush has used some broader powers to counter terrorism, both domestically and in foreign areas. In the long run, national will, staying power, and political resolve will shape the scope and direction of those powers.

In any case, the need remains for flexibility and innovation—to say nothing of usable power—and thus most presidents opt for a trusted staff of advisers to conduct national security policy. For a variety of reasons, ranging from fear of media leaks to distrust of outside political actors, presidents feel more comfortable working with a select group of advisers within a structure that is under their immediate control and supervision. It is this national security establishment that is the primary structure for the president to advance and implement his national security policies.

Conclusion

Lyndon Johnson wrote that the president receives advice from many quarters, "but there is only one [person] that has been chosen by the American people to decide."[31] Decisions on national security were relatively easy to make for the president in the past. Isolationism, distance from the Old World, and military might allowed the United States relative freedom from major external threats. National security issues were relatively clear and far less difficult than domestic problems. Even though World War II and the nuclear era changed all that, there was a sense of clarity that evolved in the era of competing superpowers—a clarity that was missing until September 11. Yet current US policy appears to have developed a new view of the "fog of peace and war."

The changes in the immediate post–World War II environment were retransformed in the 1950s in the aftermath of the Korean War. That conflict showed that beneath the nuclear umbrella the United States still requires usable conventional forces to fight limited wars and deter future ones. The evolution of regional powers, the frequency of nonnuclear conflicts, proxy wars, and the fear of direct US-Soviet confrontation reshaped the international security environment, making it less vulnerable to superpower influence and more vulnerable to the actions of smaller powers and terrorist groups.

Moreover, the impact of events such as Vietnam and Watergate created skepticism and concern about the nature of executive power and triggered the move in Congress to reassert itself in foreign and national security policies. Furthermore, the country's reluctance to undertake foreign ventures, if they meant the use of US military forces, reflected the Vietnam syndrome. It was recognized that there were limits to our ability to affect events in many parts of the world.

Although much of this remains true today, the performance of US forces in the 1991 Gulf War seemed to overcome much of the fear associated with the Vietnam syndrome. Earlier, President Reagan's labeling of Vietnam as a "noble cause" began the healing process. But even in the 1990s, the Vietnam syndrome lurked beneath the surface. Indeed, in the Gulf War the commander of the coalition forces, General H. Norman Schwarzkopf, made a point of noting that US operations and command and control in the Gulf War were not like those in Vietnam. But US involvement in Somalia in 1993 rekindled visions of Southeast Asia, as did our involvement in Bosnia-Herzegovina and Kosovo later that decade. The country's response to September 11 illustrated a focus and unity not seen since World War II, but this has dissipated as more questions have been raised about the US role in the Middle East, especially in Iraq. Future presidents will likely have to deal with an Iraq syndrome historically every bit as constraining as was the Vietnam syndrome.

The Reagan presidency, with its strengthening of the US defense posture and its perceived confidence in dealing with international security issues, changed the pessimism of the late 1970s.

Ronald Reagan established a pattern of leadership which his successors would be prudent to consider. He demonstrated the strength of a simple, straightforward agenda, readily explicable to the public. By concentrating his political resources on that agenda, by defining a mandate and inducing legislators of both parties to accept it, he restored the presidency as the engine that moves government.[32]

But not even Ronald Reagan could revive the earlier US supremacy: "The Reagan revolution was hampered by limitations of power inherent in the presidency and the political system, by private economic decisions, and by events abroad that lay beyond its control."[33]

Following President George Bush's unifying leadership in the 1991 Gulf War, national security seemed to have taken a secondary role to other issues. Indeed, the 1992 presidential election seemed to turn on Bill Clinton's campaign mantra: "It's the economy, stupid!" In the last years of the twentieth century, a healthy US economy, the demise of the Soviet Union, diminished fears of major wars, and the absence of any serious challenge to the US role in the international world, among other factors, refocused the public on domestic issues. Yet the strategic landscape of the twenty-first century poses difficult and challenging problems; the September 11 terrorist attacks were the first shot in a new war: it has grown in intensity since that time, causing serious problems for President George W. Bush.

National security issues in the twenty-first century, although reflecting continuities from the past, have unique characteristics, especially in the nature of conflicts and the relationship between economic strength and national security. This is complicated by the changing relationship between the domestic and national security agendas. The complexity of the issues and their undefined, fluid nature exacerbate the problem of presidential control and direction. In this context, internal struggles among government agencies leave the president vulnerable to agency biases and, in some instances, make him a captive of the bureaucracy. The pressures on the president are magnified by congressional involvement and its advocacy of policies and strategies that may be contrary to those of the administration. Add to this the interests and objectives of allies and adversaries and one must conclude that national security policy is fraught with peril and pitfalls. Yet national security is only one component of the president's total responsibility.

Another major component is that sovereign states can have their own ideologies and conceptions of national security that are in direct contradiction to US goals. Differing strategies can challenge the Western cultural orientation of the United States.[34] Conflict in one form or another is inevitable. Thus declaratory US policy, even when supported by necessary resources, does not guarantee success. There are too many imponderables and uncertainties in the external environment.

According to one assessment, the weakness of the existing state system has a negative impact on leadership:

> Leaders of states in the last years of the twentieth century are weak because the nation-state, as an institution, is weak. There has been a shift of problems from the national to the global arena. . . . The amorphous challenges that have crept up in the present era are not easily countered, or conquered, by simple direct actions. Yet the only leaders in sight with vision and conviction are possessed by some form of fanatical ideology. For most, in these circumstances, muddling through is the only, even if uninspiring, style of leadership available.[35]

In summary, the posture and power of agencies within the national security establishment, the interplay of personalities between the administration and Congress, congressional power in the policy process, the politicization of national security issues, and the changed domestic and international political and security environments have bred issues far different from those of the Cold War era. And therein lies the irony: for many people, the end of the Cold War diminished the importance of national security issues compared to domestic issues. Yet global interdependence, information-age technology, international environmental issues and ecology, the new strategic landscape, and long-term threats to US quality of life have given a new impetus to the link between domestic and national security issues—a brutal reality that hit home on September 11. But it must be remembered that an increasing number of political actors (both domestic and international) affect national security and are beyond presidential control; they are constraints on the use of presidential power despite the new actions in the war on terrorism.[36]

In this environment, US national objectives and interests, as well as political-military policy and strategy, are difficult to define. This applies to adversaries and allies and political actors within the United States. US national security policy often does not have the luxury of clear-cut choices between good and evil. Rather, choices involve living with the lesser of evils. Serious threats are the exception to this general rule.

As Ernest van den Haag has written: "Just solutions are elusive. Many problems have no solutions at all, not even unjust ones; at most they can be managed, prevented from getting worse or from spreading to wider areas. Other problems are best left to simmer in benign neglect until parties are disposed to settle them."[37]

The conclusion is obvious: the models, perspectives, and analyses that are key to presidential performance usually fall short of the mark because there are no simple answers. The interaction among leadership style, perceptions of the office, mind-set, and the national security establishment—in the context of the domestic and international environments—preclude neat paradigms or precise model-building. The forces that affect the president's ability to exercise power and the public's expectations are difficult to integrate. Even the most respected scholars of the presidency do not agree on the power of the office, the capacity of the president to exercise this power, and the best approach to the study of the office.[38] Thus presidential performance in national security does not neatly follow any rational model or specified approach.

Presidents who are successful in the national security area have a deep understanding of the organizational dynamics and interactions within the national security establishment. Yet this should always be tempered by sensitivity to public expectations and appreciation of the system's openness. Furthermore, the president must have a realistic perception of the international scene, adversaries, and allies. Critical to all this are the character and leadership style of the individual presiding in the Oval Office.

This brings us full circle: support and consensus are contingent upon the president's leadership style and ability to set and maintain the tone of the administration. To develop coherent policy and relevant strategy requires articulation of what the United States stands for and the national will, political resolve, and staying power to use the instruments necessary to achieve national security goals. The president's mission is to reconcile the ideals of democracy with the commitment necessary to achieve these goals in the international arena. Unfortunately, this can require the use of the military and loss of life, but only the president is in a position to lead the country to accept such sacrifices and understand why they are necessary.

In the final analysis, the uniqueness of the office, the problems of US national security, and the character of the public interact to create a distinctively US presidency. This is best summed up by the following observation:

> We give the President more work than a man can do, more responsibility than a man should take, more pressure than a man can bear. We abuse him often and rarely praise him. We wear him out, use him up, eat him up. And with all of this, Americans have love for the president that goes beyond loyalty or party nationality [sic]; he is ours and we exercise the right to destroy him.[39]

Notes

1. Lyndon Baines Johnson, *The Vantage Point: Perspectives of the Presidency, 1963–1969* (New York: Holt, Rinehart, and Winston, 1971), preface.

2. Harold M. Barger, *The Impossible Presidency: Illusions and Realities of Executive Power* (Glenview, IL: Scott, Foresman, 1984), p. 2.

3. James MacGregor Burns, J. W. Peltason, Thomas E. Cronin, and David B. Magleby, *Government by the People,* national version, 18th ed. (Upper Saddle River, NJ: Prentice-Hall, 2000), p. 366. There are many published books on the US government and US political institutions. These usually assess the presidency as well as the various institutions of government. One of the more recent publications providing an excellent assessment of these institutions is Barbara A. Bardes, Mack

C. Shelley, and Steffen W. Schmidt, *American Government and Politics Today: The Essentials* (Belmont, CA: Thomas Wadsworth, 2007).

4. Margaret Truman, *Harry S. Truman* (New York: Pocket Books, 1974), p. 603.

5. Theodore Sorenson, *Decision-Making in the White House: The Olive Branch or the Arrows* (New York: Columbia University Press, 1963), p. 84.

6. Arthur Schlesinger Jr., *The Imperial Presidency* (Boston: Houghton Mifflin, 1973).

7. Sidney M. Milkis and Michael Nelson, *The American Presidency: Origins and Development, 1776–2002* (Washington, DC: CQ Press, 2003).

8. Lee Sigelman, "A Reassessment of the Two Presidencies Thesis," in Steven A. Schull, ed., *The Two Presidencies: A Quarter Century Assessment* (Chicago: Nelson-Hall, 1991), p. 60.

9. Burns et al., *Government by the People*, pp. 360–368.

10. See, e.g., Richard E. Neustadt, *Presidential Power* (New York: Wiley, 1960), p. 9; Michael Nelson, ed., *The Presidency and the Political System* (Washington, DC: CQ Press, 1984), esp. pt. 1; and Clinton Rossiter, *The American Presidency,* 2nd ed. (New York: Mentor Books, 1960). See also Steven Kelman, "The Twentieth-Century Presidents," *American Democracy and the Public Good* (Fort Worth, TX: Harcourt Brace College, 1996), pp. 460–468.

11. James David Barber, *Presidential Character: Predicting Performance in the White House,* 4th ed. (Englewood Cliffs, NJ: Prentice-Hall, 1992).

12. See Aaron Wildavsky, "The Two Presidencies," in Wildavsky, ed., *Perspectives on the Presidency* (Boston: Little, Brown, 1975).

13. Sorenson, *Decision-Making in the White House*, p. 5.

14. Ibid., p. 10.

15. See, e.g., James David Barber, *Presidential Character.*

16. Erwin C. Hargrove and Roy Hoopes, *The Presidency: A Question of Power* (Boston: Little, Brown, 1975), p. 47.

17. James Q. Wilson, *American Government: Institutions and Policies,* 5th ed. (Lexington, MA: D. C. Heath, 1992), p. 338.

18. Johnson, *The Vantage Point,* preface.

19. Richard M. Nixon, *Six Crises* (Garden City, NY: Doubleday, 1962), p. 323.

20. Fred I. Greenstein, *The Hidden Hand Presidency: Eisenhower as Leader* (New York: Basic Books, 1994).

21. Theodore Roosevelt, *An Autobiography* (New York: Charles Scribner's Sons, 1913), p. 197.

22. See Robert L. Lineberry, George C. Edwards III, and Martin P. Wattenberg, *Government in America: People, Politics, and Policy,* 6th ed (New York: HarperCollins, 1994), p. 467. Also see George C. Edwards III, Martin P. Wattenberg, and Robert L. Lineberry, *Government in America: People, Politics, and Policy* (New York: HarperCollins, 2007).

23. For a detailed view of this matter, see Oliver L. North, with William Novak, *Under Fire: An American Story* (New York: HarperCollins, 1991).

24. Sorenson, *Decision-Making in the White House,* p. 291.

25. Irving L. Janis, *Groupthink: Psychological Studies of Policy Decisions and Fiascoes,* 2nd ed. (Boston: Houghton Mifflin, 2006).

26. Daniel Patrick Moynihan, *Secrecy: The American Experience* (New Haven: Yale University Press, 1998), p. 222.

27. John G. Roos, "Commander-in-Chief Clinton: The Military Has Already Been Marched Down the Moniker Road," *Armed Forces Journal International* (November 1998), p. 4.

28. Robert L. Gallucci, *Neither Peace nor Honor: The Politics of American Military Policy in Vietnam* (Baltimore: Johns Hopkins University Press, 1975), p. 138.

29. As quoted in Morton H. Halperin, *Bureaucratic Politics and Foreign Policy* (Washington, DC: Brookings Institution, 1974), p. 15. See also Morton H. Halperin, Priscilla Clapp, and Arnold Kanter, *Bureaucratic Politics and Foreign Policy,* 2nd ed. (Washington, DC: Brookings Institution, 2006).

30. Joseph C. Goulden, *The Superlawyers* (New York: Dell, 1973), p. 228.

31. Johnson, *The Vantage Point,* preface.

32. Louis W. Koenig, *The Chief Executive,* 5th ed. (New York: Harcourt Brace Jovanovich, 1986), p. 415.

33. Ibid., p. 2.

34. See, e.g., Adda B. Bozeman, *Strategic Intelligence and Statecraft: Selected Essays* (Washington, DC: Brassey's US, 1992). See also Samuel P. Huntington, "The Clash of Civilizations?" *Foreign Affairs* 72, no. 3 (Summer 1993): 22–49.

35. International Institute for Strategic Studies, *Strategic Survey, 1994–1995* (London: Oxford University Press, 1995), pp. 15–16.

36. For insights into the irony of diffusion and concentration of power, see Wilson, *American Government.*

37. Ernest van den Haag, "The Busyness of American Foreign Policy," *Foreign Affairs* 64, no. 1 (Fall 1985): 114–115.

38. See, e.g., Thomas E. Cronin and Richard E. Neustadt, *Presidential Power: The Politics of Leadership from FDR to Carter* (New York: Wiley, 1980). Also see Edward S. Greenberg and Benjamin I. Page, *The Struggle for Democracy,* 3rd ed. (New York: Longman, 1997), pp. 402–406.

39. John Steinbeck, *America and Americans* (Boston: Little, Brown, 1980), p. 379.

5

The Policy Triad and the National Security Council

AS DISCUSSED IN CHAPTER 4, THE PRESIDENT DEPENDS UPON many people to formulate and implement national security policy, coordinated at the highest level through the National Security Council. Two key presidential advisers—the secretary of state and secretary of defense—are statutory members of the NSC along with the national security advisor. These three individuals form the so-called policy triad. The director of national intelligence is an adviser to the NSC together with the chairman of the Joint Chiefs of Staff. The Central Intelligence Agency's function gives it a critical role in the national security establishment. But that agency's closed nature—the unavoidable legacy of intelligence-gathering and covert operations—means its relationship with the president, the Congress, and the public is quite different; it is isolated from other parts of the administration. In short, the CIA marches to its own drummer (see Chapter 8).

The NSC and its staff are primarily advisory units; even though recommendations can be made by the NSC and approved by the president, their interpretation and implementation rest mainly with the Departments of State and Defense and the CIA. Thus within the NSC the views of operational departments come into play and often clash. And as the United States Commission on National Security/21st Century concluded, "The power to determine national security policy has migrated toward the [NSC] staff. The staff now assumes policymaking and operational roles, with the result that its ability to act as an honest broker and policy coordinator has suffered."[1]

Aside from their advisory functions as statutory members of the NSC, the secretaries of state and defense also play significant roles in the national security establishment as cabinet members and department heads. Furthermore, the Departments of State and Defense have substantial links to Congress and are involved in a variety of formal relationships with other countries. Their perspectives thus reflect many influences.

Whereas these two department heads bring their own worldviews and operational methods, the national security advisor advances the president's perspective and performs an advisory role. This person also sets the agenda and coordinates the activities of the national security staff in support of the NSC.

It is the power and relationships of these three—the two secretaries and the national security advisor—relative to one another and to the president that define the direction of US national security policy. The policy triad is the fulcrum around which the policy process revolves (see Figure 5.1).

The Department of State

The secretary of state is the president's primary adviser on foreign policy and the operational head of the department responsible for its conduct. The department is organized along two broad lines: functional and geographic. Country desks operate under assistant secretaries responsible for a particular region (e.g., the Nigeria country desk would fall under African affairs). The functional areas, such as intelligence and research and political-military affairs, cut across geographic boundaries. In 1993 and 1994, plans were implemented to change the organization to reflect the Clinton administration's foreign policy and to simplify the department's burdensome structure.

Figure 5.1 The Policy Triad

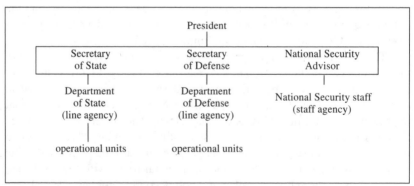

Notes: The secretaries of state and defense each wear two hats: staff adviser to the president and operational department head. Thus their perspectives on national security are usually conditioned by the capability of their departments to implement policy and strategy. The national security advisor, however, has no operational units; the national security staff is just that—a staff agency. The national security advisor and national security staff attempt to provide a presidential perspective and to stand above department issues. Perceptions, mind-sets, and responsibilities differ between the two secretaries and particularly between the two secretaries and the national security advisor.

This included creating the Office of the Secretary to bring together separate groups within the department and to clarify the reporting process. Efforts were also made to give more power to undersecretaries of state.[2] In addition, several embassies and consular offices were closed.

Despite such efforts, some have concluded that during the Clinton administration the department's role in foreign and national security diminished. Indeed, the NSC's role in national security subsumed many aspects of foreign policy. "In sum, the secretary of state in the Clinton administration, like other recent administrations, will continue to be prominent, but will not dominate policy formulation, instead policy making will increasingly be a shared responsibility."[3]

In an especially critical assessment, the United States Commission on National Security/21st Century stated, "The Department of State is a crippled institution that is starved for resources by Congress because of its inadequacies and is thereby weakened further. The department suffers in particular from an ineffective organizational structure in which regional and functional goals compete, and in which sound management, accountability, and leadership are lacking."[4] The organization of the State Department is shown in Figure 5.2.[5]

The end of the Cold War ushered in a changed security environment, one that continues to evolve. Yet the national security establishment created by the National Security Act of 1947 in the aftermath of World War II remained in place for the most part with only slight changes until the 1990s. At that time, the role of the secretary of state became more visible, and during President Clinton's second term some felt that it was the dominant player in the policy process. At the same time, the decline of serious threats and the drawdown of the US military—combined with deep cuts in the defense budget—crimped the scope and power of the secretary of defense. Thus, whereas national security issues were a driving force in US policy during the Cold War, the post–Cold War shift put more attention on foreign policy. In the twenty-first century and after September 11, the focus has once again been on national security policy, with Secretary of Defense Donald Rumsfeld taking center stage behind only the president and vice president. This further marginalized the Department of State. In 2006, Rumsfeld resigned and Robert Gates became secretary of defense. Many noted that Rumsfeld's resignation was due primarily to the US military problems in Iraq. But foreign policy and national security policy are increasingly intertwined. The irony is that both Secretary of State Condoleezza Rice and the secretary of defense have become involved in policy that interlocks foreign policy as well as national security issues.

At the same time, other players took the stage in foreign policy and national security. Arms-control initiatives and agreements with the Soviet Union and, later, Russia, as well as US relations with China, Russia, and the

Figure 5.2 The Department of State

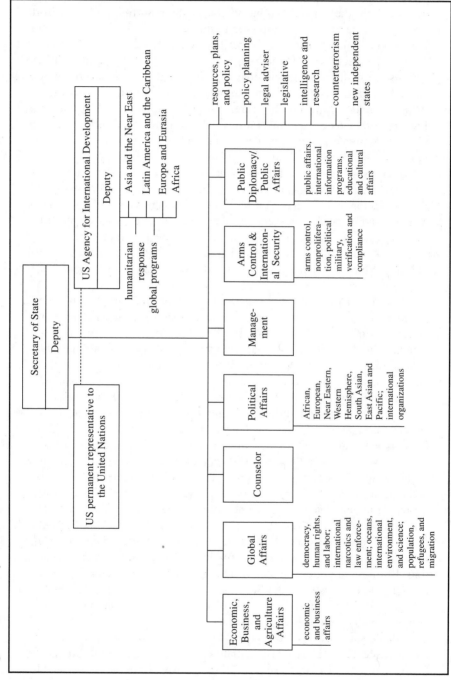

Source: US Commission on National Security/21st Century, *Road Map for National Security: Imperative for Change* (January 31, 2001), p. 57.

Middle East, are many of the primary concerns of the secretary of state. Yet all this has a huge impact on national security issues. As well, peace in the Middle East, primarily a foreign policy matter, has national security implications. And in the 1990s, US involvement in Somalia, Haiti, and Bosnia-Herzegovina intermingled foreign and national security policies. The US involvement with NATO in Kosovo beginning in 1999 also shows the close relationship between foreign and national security policies.

Other State Department activities beyond the realm of national security nevertheless influence the department's perspective on it. The secretary of state is responsible for consular services, aid to US citizens overseas, diplomatic missions, and US embassies—the focal point of the US presence in many countries. Although ambassadors can deal directly with the president, their main contact is the secretary of state. The embassy staffs are typically given the responsibility to coordinate all official US activities in the host country. This country-team concept, first formalized by President Dwight Eisenhower, was an attempt to bring consistency to US activities overseas through centralized control (although US military operations were not included in this concept).

The primary bureaucracy within the Department of State is deeply involved with traditional diplomatic and consular tasks, embedded in traditional notions of courtly, courteous, Old World diplomacy. The focus is on negotiations and compromise. The department's organizational behavior and internal mind-sets stem from these institutional roots, imposing a template of education and socialization that produces foreign service officers and department employees quite different from their counterparts at Defense. The result can be serious disagreements between the two secretaries. The departments at times work at cross-purposes, although accord is usually reached in clear cases of national security and when crises help forge a consensus.

The State Department has been criticized as a bureaucracy committed to stability, the status quo, and self-protection of its organizational integrity and autonomy. According to some, this has produced bureaucratic inertia and burdensome procedures that allow little room for initiative and innovation. The United States Commission on National Security/21st Century had this to say about the reorganization of the Department of State:

> The President should propose to the Congress a plan to reorganize the State Department, creating five Under Secretaries with responsibility for overseeing the regions of Africa, Asia, Europe, Inter-America, and Near East/South Asia, and redefining the responsibilities of the Under Secretary for Global Affairs. . . . The Secretary of State should give greater emphasis to strategic planning in the State Department and link it directly to the allocation of resources through the establishment of a Strategic Planning, Assistance, and Budget Office.[6]

Several studies have also shown that the department has difficulty in formulating long-range policies that link to domestic political concerns as well as foreign policy issues. As Christopher Shoemaker concluded, "this rather important deficiency stems both from the department and from historical proclivities of the Foreign Service."[7] He went on to note that "bureaucratic power within the State Department is normally vested in the regional bureaus, which, despite their staffing by seasoned professionals, are virtually unable to come to grips with the development of long-range policy."[8] Although written in 1991, this assessment remains valid today. Yet with the inauguration of George W. Bush and the appointment of Secretary of State Colin Powell, followed by Condoleezza Rice, important changes were expected.

The Department of Defense

In contrast to the 200-year tradition in the Department of State, the Department of Defense is a relatively new organization, established after World War II by the National Security Act of 1947 and its amendment in 1949. Major problems faced the secretary of defense in trying to centralize defense policy; changes were taking place in the late 1980s and throughout the Clinton administration (1993–2001). These changes reflected the diminished threat of war and administration efforts to reduce the military to reflect that new perception. The Department of Defense is still involved in changes in response to information-age technology and the changing international security landscape. More changes were implemented in the George W. Bush administration with Secretary of Defense Rumsfeld's own defense review and the 2001 Quadrennial Defense Review (QDR). These changes were re-revised in response to September 11; the latest organization of the Department of Defense is shown in Figure 5.3.[9] See also the Pentagon's view of the 2005 QDR.[10]

The president's responsibility as commander in chief is usually exercised through the secretary of defense and the operational elements of the Department of Defense. Like the secretary of state in the foreign policy area, the defense secretary performs dual functions in defense policy: as primary adviser to the president on defense policy and as head of the operational elements of the department. In the advisory capacity, the secretary focuses on the types of forces and manpower levels needed to pursue the goals of US national security policy effectively. Among the secretary's concerns are the composition of forces, weapons acquisition, training, planning, and operational implementation. The operational arms of the Department of Defense are highly visible: coercive military forces. Their symbolic—as well as substantive—role plays a great part in the perceptions of allies and

Figure 5.3 The Department of Defense

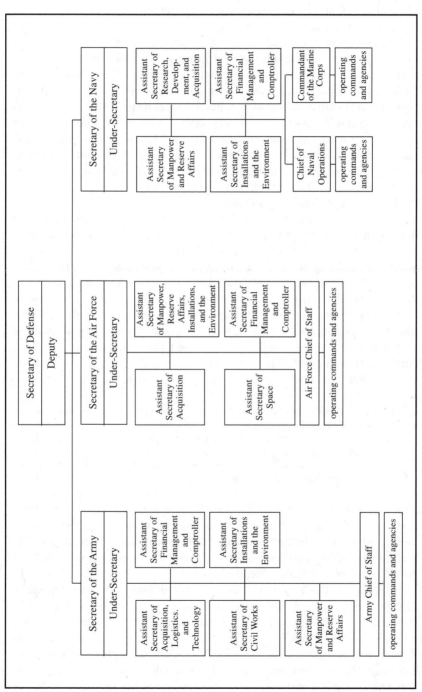

Source: William S. Cohen, Secretary of Defense, *Annual Report to the President and the Congress*, p. A-3. Available online at www.dtic.mil/execsec/adr2001.

adversaries regarding US capability. Thus statements of the secretary of defense are important in shaping policy.

The structure of the Office of the Secretary of Defense (as distinct from the service branches) includes several functional units supervised by assistant secretaries (for example, regional affairs). In 1993, Secretary of Defense Les Aspin changed the department's structure to overlap with certain responsibilities associated with the Department of State, such as democracy and human rights. In early 1994, Secretary of Defense William Perry, who succeeded Aspin, reduced this overlap by shifting the department toward traditional roles and concerns. In addition, the service branches, as well as the Defense Intelligence Agency (DIA) and National Security Agency (NSA), operate or collect information that has a direct bearing on the function of the State Department.

Former US senator William Cohen became Clinton's third secretary of defense in 1996 after Perry had refocused the department on its traditional missions and stabilized what many felt was disarray created by Aspin. Aspin's Bottom-Up Review—a strategy for restructuring US forces and a response to contingencies in the post–Cold War era—drew much criticism. This was compounded by Aspin's effort to develop a military capable of responding to two regional conflicts simultaneously.[11] Nonetheless, the need to prepare for twin conflicts, as well as other contingencies, remained part of military strategy until the end of the Clinton presidency. The Bush administration changed all this yet again.

In a June 1998 review of Secretary Cohen's tenure, one author wrote,

> Nearly 18 months into his initial tour of military service, US Secretary of Defense William S. Cohen has become an enigma. In contrast to his 24 years of service on Capitol Hill, where he was quick to step forward and voice opinions about controversial issues, he now seems to relish the fact that the legions surrounding him provide convenient cover for avoiding the public spotlight. That's too bad.[12]

The author does credit Cohen for appointing a qualified and capable inner circle of civilian advisers yet criticizes Cohen for isolating himself from the uniformed services. In 1999 and into 2001, Cohen did attempt to link with the uniformed services and made a highly publicized trip to meet with North Vietnamese defense officials.

George W. Bush's veteran secretary of defense, Donald Rumsfeld, brought a more cautious and selective view to the use of the military establishment as well as extraordinary bureaucratic skills. He underscored the administration's approach to defense policy and strategy. In his Senate confirmation hearings in January 2001, Rumsfeld stated that "US military forces can best be used when the military mission is clear and achievable and when there is a reasonable exit strategy. . . . When the main burden of the US presence shifts to infrastructure and nation building . . . we are into missions that are not appropriate for the US military."[13] Donald Rumsfeld resigned in 2006 and was replaced by Robert Gates. Rumsfeld was criticized by many Democrats as well as some Republicans in Congress for a so-called failed military policy in Iraq.

Major strategy reviews in the Bush administration redefined the requirements for military forces and their structures. The war on terrorism has placed much attention on the capability of the military to undertake nonconventional missions.

The Quadrennial Defense Review

Questions raised by many outside the Department of Defense regarding US military capability led to legislation that established the Quadrennial Defense Review. This legislation directed the secretary of defense and the JCS to conduct a defense review and provide a report by 1997 and every four years thereafter. QDR 1997 reflected the status quo, retaining the focus on two major regional conflicts and conventional forces.[14] In 2000, Steven Metz wrote, "consensus is emerging that this QDR should be strategy driven rather than budget driven like the QDR 1997."[15] That appeared to be the case with QDR 2001, as Secretary Rumsfeld spelled out a new direction, shifting focus from two major regional conflicts, establishing guidance for transforming the military, budget guidelines for 2003, and so-called terms of reference for the military (these include reassuring friends and allies of US commitments, dissuading adversaries of US resolve, deterring threats and countercoercion, and defeating adversaries if deterrence fails). The 2006 Quadrennial Defense Review made it clear that the war against terrorism was likely to go on for a number of years and required the use not only of the military but also of US intelligence, economic, and diplomatic institutions.[16]

September 11 focused attention on homeland defense, with the establishment of the cabinet-level Office of Homeland Security. Former Pennsylvania governor Tom Ridge was appointed director of homeland security, and he immediately began coordinating agencies' activities for purposes of counterterrorism. The Office of Homeland Security was replaced by the Department of Homeland Security in 2003. In 2007, Michael Chertoff was the secretary of homeland security. The organizational chart of the department is shown in Figure 5.4.

The nature of the military profession, as well as the education and socialization of civilian officials and employees, shapes the institutional posture of the Department of Defense. Logically, the posture leans toward the military solution in responding to national security issues. In turn, there is an orientation within the department to ensure adequate staffing levels, resources to develop sophisticated weaponry, and satisfactory compensation

Figure 5.4 The Department of Homeland Security

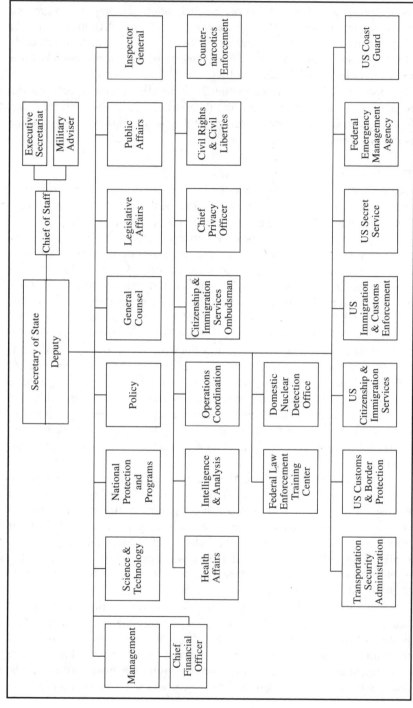

Source: US Department of Homeland Security, available at http://www.dhs.gov/xlibrary/assets/DHS_OrgChart.pdf.

and benefits for service personnel. This fits hand in glove with the effort to develop a skilled military that can effectively perform in war. Increasingly, these efforts have expanded to include operations other than war, unconventional conflicts, and political-military situations that in the past were primarily Department of State concerns.

The New Strategic Landscape

In the strategic landscape of the twenty-first century, the focus has turned to various types of missions—peacekeeping, peacemaking, peace enforcement, and humanitarian. Each has its own character, yet all can overlap to a degree when forces are deployed in the field. "Although the primary purpose of the armed forces is the preparation and conduct of war, the most likely future missions of the armed forces of the industrial democracies are not classic inter-state war fighting but a variety of peace support missions."[17] And as one journalist wrote, "Only a few years ago, our world was a bipolar nightmare in which two superpowers threatened a fight to the finish and the soldier was seen as the bringer of destruction. No longer: The relevance of the soldier today is increasingly as a bringer of peace."[18] Yet September 11 refocused the US military on contingencies and missions overseas. In addition, the tragedy rekindled a fighting spirit to engage terrorism and the states that sponsor or harbor terrorists. As noted in earlier chapters, much has changed since September 11.

Given the nature of its participation in recent conflicts, ranging from ethnic cleansing and religious struggles to nationalistic movements and a variety of unconventional conflicts, the United States is driven by moral imperatives rather than clear national security interests. Yet the primary role of the military remains success in battle to defend vital national interests. The so-called warrior mentality required of combat soldiers is not an artifact of times past; it is a necessary corollary of the professional military ethos and a prerequisite for the use of force to support diplomacy.

In the past, the institutional orientation often placed the Defense Department at odds with the State Department. If negotiation, compromise, and diplomacy characterize the latter, then displays of force, military assistance, coercive diplomacy, and military conflict characterize the former. This is not to suggest there is no mutually acceptable goal to solve problems peacefully if possible. But the "stick" component of the carrot-and-stick approach among states and groups within states is often in the hands of Defense, and its operational arm is the ultimate big stick if military confrontation is inevitable. This overriding mission dominates the rationale for the department's existence, and it strongly influences its organizational behavior (see Chapter 6, "The Military Establishment").

The new strategic landscape requires that the Department of Defense be more adaptable and flexible in the use of military force, that is, less concerned with actual combat and more attuned to the use of the military as a diplomatic instrument prepared to engage in multinational efforts. At the same time, unilateral use of the US military as a humanitarian and peace-keeping instrument has become more frequent. One author has labeled this the "do-something syndrome."[19] All of this suggests that the department is becoming a "shadow" State Department poised to carry out political and diplomatic missions using the military as the operational instrument. This has further marginalized the Department of State.

Colin Powell's views on the use of the military, as expressed to UN ambassador Madeleine Albright when he was JCS chairman, were quoted in Chapter 2. He clearly believed that the use of military force should follow, not precede, the setting of political goals.[20]

Until the 1990s, a large part of the US military was deployed overseas on a semipermanent basis in Europe, South Korea, and Japan. Although military personnel had been reduced overall by more than 25 percent during previous years, commitments to overseas missions increased—and were overstretched, according to some. In March 2001, the number of military personnel in all services committed to overseas missions was more than 257,000. Yet the reduction in the number of military personnel, combined with the increase in deployed forces, changed the strategic configuration of the US military. In addition, military contingencies and strategic perspectives are being reshaped by the strategic landscape of the twenty-first century. Many of these changes have their roots in the late 1990s (see Chapter 6).

Because the likelihood of global conventional war has been considerably reduced, many within the Department of Defense question the commitment of US forces outside existing treaty areas. This has been the general view since the end of the Vietnam War. The Gulf War was an exception, although many within the military initially favored the extensive use of sanctions. But the Gulf War was planned and analyzed as a desert version of a European scenario in which US forces, based on traditional strategic and operational concepts, brought sophisticated weaponry to bear against a clearly identifiable and conventionally postured adversary. The caution and reluctance to engage in military operations are conditioned by the fear of involvement in situations without clear political objectives as well as outcomes that might not be resolved by military force. Equally important is the underlying concern that involvement in ambiguous operations will lead to political opposition at home and the undermining of military capability.[21] But today many are contemplating the use of military force in response to international terrorism. Although much of the action has focused on special operations and relatively casualty-free air operations, follow-on conventional forces have become part of the overall strategy, and major battles involving US ground forces have ensued.

Because there is no sharp delineation of responsibility and power in several policy areas between the Departments of Defense and State, there is often disagreement on policy preferences. This is magnified when the departments are headed by strong personalities with their own views on the international security environment and their own policy agendas. If sufficiently strong, one secretary can dominate and impose one department's approach. In any case, traditional models of national security policy, relationships among cabinet officers, and the power and responsibility of departments rarely go by the book.

The National Security Advisor

President Eisenhower was the first to create the position of special assistant for national security affairs, later to be retitled assistant to the president for national security affairs, and now commonly known as the national security advisor. According to an authoritative study of US foreign policy, by the mid-1970s the national security advisor had become a "second secretary of state."[22] The authors pointed out, however, that this was not the original intent. In the administrations of Harry Truman and Dwight Eisenhower, the role was simply to "arrange meetings of the [NSC] and manage the paperwork."[23] During the early years of the NSC, the secretary of state was the prominent figure in national security policy.

Several factors helped to elevate the national security advisor to prominence by the 1970s. President John F. Kennedy, frustrated by the bureaucratic inertia at the State Department, sought a more streamlined and responsive system for foreign policy advice and implementation. Furthermore, the relatively quiet days of the Eisenhower administration were replaced by the US-Soviet confrontations over Berlin, the Bay of Pigs, the Cuban missile crisis, and the beginning of US involvement in Vietnam. President Kennedy, wanting more direct control over US foreign policy strategy, appointed McGeorge Bundy as assistant to the president for national security affairs. The combination of Bundy's strong personality, expanding US involvement overseas, the increased complexity of national security issues, and the difficulty in developing flexibility and responsiveness within existing departments placed the NSC and the national security advisor in a more prominent policy position.

The post assumed its greatest importance under Presidents Richard Nixon, Gerald Ford, and Jimmy Carter; Henry Kissinger occupied the position, followed by Brent Scowcroft and Zbigniew Brzezinski. Strongminded, covetous of their prerogatives, and enjoying direct access to the president, Kissinger and Brzezinski expanded the power of the position and tried to impose their personal policy preferences on the national security establishment. Under Carter, there was considerable friction between Brzezinski and Secretary of State Cyrus Vance, leading to the latter's resignation in the wake of the failed 1980 attempt to rescue US diplomats held hostage in Iran.

Since then, there has been considerable debate regarding the proper role of the national security advisor. During the first term of Ronald Reagan, there was an attempt to restrict the role to coordinator and expediter rather than initiator and innovator. Some argued that this downgrading allowed lesser personalities to occupy the position and may have led to some of the excesses revealed in the 1987 Iran-contra hearings. The argument is that a strong personality and leader is needed to ensure the proper functioning of the national security staff. This is true whether the adviser has a high-profile style, such as Kissinger and Brzezinski, or a low-profile style, such as Scowcroft.

In 1993, for the first time in twelve years, the Democratic Party controlled the Oval Office and Congress. President Clinton appointed Anthony Lake as national security advisor and Sandy Berger as deputy national security advisor. Later Lake resigned and was replaced by Berger, who remained in that position until the end of the Clinton administration. In 2001, Condoleezza Rice was appointed national security advisor in the George W. Bush administration. She was the first female to hold the post and brought a vision of national security that coincided, as expected, with that of Secretary of State Colin Powell. Condoleezza Rice is the secretary of state as of this writing. This role presumes a more cautious and selective approach to national security commitments, something that also reflected President Bush's perspective. September 11 changed everything, however, leading to long-term military engagements in Afghanistan and Iraq.

The role and power of the national security advisor depend upon the president. Even though the NSC was established by Congress, the way in which it is used is almost entirely in the president's hands. In any case, the national security advisor is in a position to make a major impact on national security policy. This is true for several important reasons. First, that person is the president's personal confidant, as the post is filled without Senate consent, as required for cabinet secretaries. Second, the office is located inside the White House, so the person has direct access to the president and usually sees him every working day; this fact alone creates a perception of power not accorded other officials. And third, the national security advisor is not tied to any agency, which grants a degree of flexibility that secretaries usually cannot match. In addition, the national security advisor is not encumbered by operational responsibilities, and the NSC staff is relatively small—usually about fifty—and thus more controllable than the huge bureaucracies at State and Defense. And finally, the national security advisor represents the president's views, in contrast to the organizational tendencies represented by the secretaries of state and defense.

It is apparent that a strong personality can shape national security policy like no other official. Furthermore, the intermixing of foreign policy, national security, and domestic issues enhances the role. That person is in a position to synthesize these policy issues and bring to bear a perspective that is closely linked to the president's perceptions of office and mind-set. This presidential confidant is appointed by him, works for him, and owes allegiance to him.

The National Security Council

It is useful to examine the organization and function of the NSC in detail, especially with respect to the policy triad and the NSC system. Figure 5.5 illustrates the organization of the NSC, the relationship of the NSC staff, and the procedures for making recommendations and input.

The president determines how the NSC is used—even whether it should be used. Each president from Harry Truman to George W. Bush has shaped the NSC and used it according to his leadership style and perceptions of the office. Truman, the first president to interact with the newly established NSC, made clear that he considered it to be a strictly advisory body and did not regularly attend its meetings until the Korean War. He maintained that a president could not abdicate his responsibilities in foreign and national security policy to a structure such as the NSC.

Figure 5.5 The National Security Council

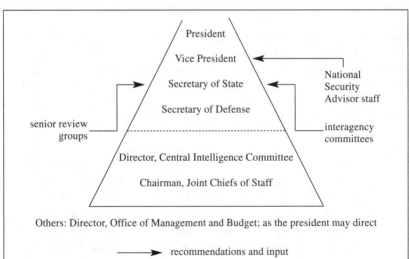

President Eisenhower possessed unmatched military experience and established a formal and systematic method for using the NSC. Besides creating the post that would eventually become known as national security advisor, he set up a system of committees to serve the NSC. As many scholars agree, Eisenhower's preference for complete staff work and well-defined procedures gave the NSC and its staff previously unknown prominence in national security. Following military procedures, Eisenhower wanted options exhaustively discussed within the NSC, with clear recommendations presented to him identifying the best policy.

President Kennedy, however, preferred a smaller and more streamlined staff and eliminated much of Eisenhower's machinery. Kennedy's appointment of McGeorge Bundy reflected the importance he attached to integrating foreign and defense policies. His disdain of formal procedures and rigid bureaucracy made him rely more on the NSC staff and his personal staff, such as Bundy, than on the executive departments. The Bay of Pigs fiasco in April 1961 seemed to confirm Kennedy's distrust of the established bureaucracy.[24] But that event also exposed the weakness in Kennedy's approach to managing the bureaucracy. Eisenhower's more formal approach to reviewing policy proposals would have revealed the inherent absurdity of the CIA plan to invade Cuba with a small exile detachment and overthrow Fidel Castro. The diminished importance of the NSC continued under Lyndon Johnson, who also relied on a network of informal advisers.

Expansion of the NSC

The NSC did not regain its prominence until President Nixon restored much of the machinery established under Eisenhower (Nixon had served two full terms as vice president under Ike). This included a system of interdepartmental groups at the assistant secretary of state level and senior committees at the undersecretary and deputy secretary levels to examine and coordinate policies on defense, intelligence, covert operations, and other national security matters; Vietnam received special attention. This structure continued for the most part under President Ford but changed under Carter, who retained the procedures but reduced the committees to two and gave more authority to the executive departments. Nonetheless, the strong personality and views of Brzezinski under Carter tended to prevail, placing the NSC staff in a powerful position vis-à-vis the executive departments.

The Reagan administration strengthened the NSC committee system and established interagency groups at the assistant secretary level to focus on defense policy, foreign policy, and intelligence. Problems surfaced, however, as Reagan's personal staff became involved and made decisions outside the purview of the established structure. Friction between the national security advisor and the secretaries of state and defense dogged several issues, leading to the resignation of Secretary of State Alexander Haig.

Turnover was high: Richard Allen, William Clark, Robert McFarlane, John Poindexter, Frank Carlucci, and William Powell all served as national security advisor under Reagan.

The George Bush administration brought in new personalities in 1989, including Brent Scowcroft. In the first Bush administration, the roles of the national security advisor and his deputy were strengthened, as each chaired an important interagency committee within the NSC. This internal restructuring was expected to provide better coordination and sharply define policy options. In late 1991 and into 1992, Bush's national security establishment was put to the test as a range of new issues emerged that did not fit easily into the Cold War perspective. Many of these issues continued until the end of the Clinton administration and into the George W. Bush administration.

The Current Period

In 2001, President George W. Bush and his inner circle made an early impact on the NSC and staff:

> The first few weeks of President George W. Bush's tenure as Commander-in-Chief portend significant changes in the national security arena. Old hands in dealing with both the domestic and international ramifications of defense affairs—Cheney, Rumsfeld, Rice, and Powell—are contributing their collective expertise in fashioning the national security construct that will frame the political boundaries of America's military-engagement policies during the next four years. . . . A top-to-bottom scrub of the National Security Council has already occurred, and about one-third of the NSC positions have been eliminated. . . . The size of the professional staff at the NSC doubled under the former president, from about 50 to more than 100 full-timers.[25]

A new superstar emerged: Colin Powell, who as JCS chairman had played a visible role in the 1991 Gulf War and in the transition to the Clinton administration. The more powerful political role that General Powell fulfilled was the result of the 1986 Goldwater-Nichols Act, which made the JCS chairman the principal military adviser to the president and gave him more power in dealing with senior military commanders and the military system in general. Although the exercise of this newfound power is contingent upon the personality and character of the JCS chairman, Powell's superb political savvy established a precedent in the national security process. In 2001, Powell was appointed secretary of state by President Bush, although after September 11 he was eclipsed in influence by Secretary of Defense Donald Rumsfeld.

The creation of the Office of Homeland Security in September 2001 added yet another dimension to the NSC and the formulation of national security strategy. Coordination with the NSC, as well as with a host of agencies, is part of the office's responsibilities. The Department of Homeland

Security was created by Congress to replace the Office of Homeland Security. It has the power, authority, and budget to make it one of the largest departments in the government (see Figure 5.4).

The NSC Staff

The NSC staff is an arm of the NSC. As such it not only performs administrative duties but also is involved in policy-related functions. Muddling the policy process is the fact that the national security advisor lacks a legal basis for operational action. "The National Security Council (NSC) should be responsible for advising the President and for coordinating the multiplicity of national security activities. . . . The NSC Advisor and staff should resist the temptation to assume a central policymaking and operational role."[26] The effectiveness of the staff is limited if it becomes too large and unwieldy, yet it must be large enough to respond to the tasks at hand. As pointed out earlier, the real source of power in the NSC staff rests in its relationship to the president. As such, it has a great degree of bureaucratic freedom and flexibility and reflects the presidential view.

After reviewing the history of the NSC staff to 1987, the Tower Commission concluded:

> What emerges from this history is an NSC staff used by each President in a way that reflected his individual preferences and working style. Over time, it has developed an important role within the Executive Branch of coordinating policy review, preparing issues for Presidential decision, and monitoring implementation. But it has remained the President's creature, molded as he sees fit, to serve as his personal staff for national security affairs. For this reason, it has generally operated out of the public view and has not been subject to direct oversight by the Congress.[27]

The Iran-contra hearings brought the role of the NSC staff into full view as Congress attempted to uncover violations of law by members of the NSC staff, specifically Lieutenant Colonel Oliver North.[28] As intelligence historian John Prados concluded, "ultimately it is the President's responsibility to keep his house in order and banish the conflicts among unruly subordinates. Presidents have compiled a rather poor record in this regard."[29] This was no less true during the Clinton administration.

The NSC and its staff are a well-established structure with statutory authority. It has proven to be a useful and important structure when used as an advisory agency that is allowed to analyze policy and strategy options. The way the NSC and its staff function in any administration is complex and subject to personal preferences, mind-sets, and leadership styles—including those of the policy triad. To be sure, the president is central, and the NSC cannot substitute for his central role. Yet as one authority concluded:

The decision-making process is always problematical and often controversial. The process requires the interaction of people with differing personal, political, and institutional perspectives on policy issues. By design and evolution, the system promotes rivalry among the branches of the government and within those branches as policy questions move toward resolution.[30]

Need for Change
The United States Commission on National Security/21st Century concluded:

> The dramatic changes in the world since the end of the Cold War of the last half-century have not been accompanied by any major institutional changes in the Executive Branch of the US government. Serious deficiencies exist that only a significant organizational redesign can remedy. Most troublesome is the lack of an overarching strategic framework guiding US national security policymaking and resource allocation. Clear goals and priorities are rarely set. Budgets are prepared and appropriated as they were during the Cold War.[31]

Other analysts have also pointed out that changes are taking place in the system of government.

> Not only has the environment changed (and is changing), but so, too, must the mechanisms by which the United States interacts with the world change. The Cold War mechanisms worked admirably to keep that competition from going hot (war). The disappearance of that threat suggests the need to adapt and fine-tune those mechanisms for a "new world order."[32]

All this must be qualified by the realities of the political process and the number of actors involved in the national security system. Examining the role of the power centers in the US political system and their role in foreign and defense policies, Roger Hilsman wrote: "The president and his staff in the White House constitute the most powerful of these power centers, but the presidency is far from being all powerful. . . . [A] political system composed of multiple power centers gives a veto to a relatively small coalition of those power centers who oppose some new initiative."[33] Nonetheless, the policy triad in concert with the president forms a formidable power center that is at the core of national security policy and is the driving force behind the national security establishment. It becomes even more formidable when one party controls both the Oval Office and Congress. As Hilsman concluded, "Policy is made through a political process. Power is an element in politics. But power diffused can lead to evil as surely as power concentrated. Herein lies the irony."[34]

Conclusion

This overview of the primary structure for advising the president on national security provides the basis for several conclusions:

1. The president by law and of necessity has the central role in national security policy.

2. The informal policy triad is critical in shaping national security policy. The interactions among the secretaries of state and defense and the national security advisor strongly influence the way policy is formulated and the kind of advice given to the president.

3. All of the primary players on the NSC have their own constituencies and bases of power. Strong personalities can impose personal policy preferences on the NSC and the system, at times making it more difficult for the president to consider the full range of options.

4. Those in the policy triad and on the NSC can mobilize in a variety of ways to oppose policy options they disagree with. Adding to the problems of coordination and consensus is the fact that the secretaries of state and defense have different organizational goals and may well view problems through different lenses.

5. The NSC does not have an operational arm. If its recommendations are approved by the president, they must be implemented through the two departments—the Departments of State and Defense—and at times through the CIA. Departmental and agency perspectives and preferences come into play in this process. The way that decisions are interpreted and implemented can take on unintended directions.

6. When the interplay of power relationships within the NSC and the policy triad gives rise to multiple advocacy, the president will find it difficult not to become involved in the policy formulation process.

Strong personalities can pose a dilemma for any president, but appointing people who simply parrot the president's version of national security—the "group-think" mentality—can lead to dangerous weaknesses in national security policy. Yet the president cannot constantly interject himself into the policy formulation process to resolve differences among his top personnel. Honest disagreement can be valuable, but he should expect some fundamental meeting of the minds. Reconciling disagreements is the responsibility of the president. For this reason, presidential leadership is critical to effective national security policy formulation and execution.

Notes

1. United States Commission on National Security/21st Century, *Road Map for National Security: Imperative for Change,* final draft report (January 31, 2001), p. 47.

2. See, e.g., John M. Goshko, "State Department Reorganizes Ranks," *Washington Post,* February 6, 1994, sec. A, p. 8.

3. James M. McCormick, *American Foreign Policy and Process,* 3rd ed. (Itasca, IL: F. E. Peacock, 1998), p. 390.

4. United States Commission on National Security/21st Century, *Road Map,* p. 47.

5. Ibid., p. 57.

6. Ibid., p. 54.

7. Christopher C. Shoemaker, *The NSC Staff: Counseling the Council* (Boulder: Westview, 1991), p. 42.

8. Ibid.

9. William S. Cohen, Secretary of Defense, *Report of the Secretary of Defense to the President and Congress* (Washington, DC: Department of Defense, 2001), p. A-1.

10. Jack Spencer and Kathy Gudgel, "The 2005 Quadrennial Defense Review: The View from the Pentagon," WebMemo #682, available at http://www.heritage.org/Research/NationalSecurity/wm682.cfm.

11. John G. Roos, "First Glimpse of Bottom-Up Review Was a Nice Job of Packaging, Anyway," *Armed Forces Journal International* 132, no. 3 (October 1993): 17–18.

12. John G. Roos, "Another Bridge Too Far; It's Time for the SecDef to Fight Some Close-In Battles," *Armed Forces Journal International* 144 (June 1998): 2.

13. Vince Crawley, "Bracing for Change," *Army Times,* January 22, 2001, p. 8.

14. See Steven Metz, ed., *Revising the Two MTW Force Shaping Paradigm* (Carlisle, PA: Strategic Studies Institute, US Army War College, April 2001).

15. Steven Metz, *American Strategy: Issues and Alternatives for the Quadrennial Defense Review* (Carlisle, PA: Strategic Studies Institute, US Army War College, September 2000), p. ix.

16. US Department of Defense, *Quadrennial Defense Review Report* (Washington, DC: Department of Defense, 2006), p. 9.

17. Christopher Dandeker and James Gow, "Military Culture and Strategic Peacekeeping," in Erwin A. Schmidl, ed., "Peace Operations Between War and Peace," *Small Wars and Insurgencies* 10, no. 2 (Special Issue, Autumn 1999): 58.

18. Sina Odugbemi, "Intervention: The Lure—and Limits—of Force," from *Guardian* (Lagos, Nigeria), as published in *World Press Review* 40, no. 3 (March 1993): 9–10.

19. Donald M. Snow, *Peacekeeping, Peacemaking, and Peace-Enforcement: The US Role in the New International Order* (Carlisle Barracks, PA: Strategic Studies Institute, US Army War College, February 1993), p. 6.

20. Colin Powell, with Joseph E. Persico, *My American Journey* (New York: Random House, 1995), p. 576.

21. See Alan Ned Sabrosky and Robert L. Sloane, *The Recourse to War: An Appraisal of the "Weinberger Doctrine"* (Carlisle Barracks, PA: Strategic Studies Institute, US Army War College, 1988).

22. John Spanier and Eric M. Uslaner, *American Foreign Policy Making and the Democratic Dilemmas,* 6th ed. (New York: Holt, Rinehart, and Winston, 1993).

23. Ibid.

24. Although President Kennedy publicly accepted the blame for the Bay of Pigs failure, privately he placed much of the blame on the poor planning and cumbersome procedures in the military and the CIA, as well as the staff procedures of existing agencies.

25. John G. Roos, "A New Beginning," *Armed Forces Journal International* (March 2001): 2.

26. United States Commission on National Security/21st Century, *Road Map,* p. 50.

27. *President's Special Review Board* (Washington, DC: US Government Printing Office, February 26, 1987), generally referred to as the Tower Commission Report.

28. See, e.g., *Report of the Congressional Committees Investigating the Iran-Contra Affair with Supplemental, Minority and Additional Views,* 100th Cong., 1st sess., House Report No. 100-433 and Senate Report No. 100-216 (Washington, DC: US Government Printing Office, 1987), esp. pp. 36–51.

29. John Prados, *Keepers of the Keys: A History of the National Security Council from Truman to Bush* (New York: William Morrow, 1991), p. 561.

30. Donald M. Snow, *National Security: Defense Policy in a Changed International Order,* 4th ed. (New York: St. Martin's, 1998), p. 100.

31. United States Commission on National Security/21st Century, *Road Map,* p. x.

32. Donald M. Snow and Eugene Brown, *Puzzle Palace and Foggy Bottom: US Foreign and Defense Policy-Making in the 1990s* (New York: St. Martin's, 1994), p. 274.

33. Roger Hilsman, with Laura Gaughran and Patricia A. Weitsman, *The Politics of Policy Making in Defense and Foreign Affairs: Conceptual Models and Bureaucratic Politics* (Englewood Cliffs, NJ: Prentice-Hall, 1993), pp. 340 and 343.

34. Ibid., p. 349.

6

The Military Establishment

THE MILITARY ESTABLISHMENT IS A CRITICAL OPERATIONAL ARM of the national security system. How it is organized and its relationship to the president and other political actors are necessary considerations in the study of national security policy. Furthermore, the education, socialization, and mind-sets of military professionals are important in shaping the military establishment and in determining its ability to pursue the goals of US national security policy.

Since the end of World War II, the US military establishment has gone through several important changes in organizational structure and notions of military professionalism. This continued during the post–Cold War era, as it does today in the post–September 11 era. The size of the military has been reduced, and it must reconcile itself to a variety of political and social forces that have affected its structure and missions. At the same time, it must adjust to an ill-defined security landscape and fight wars in Afghanistan and Iraq that are proving difficult to sustain, especially from a personnel perspective. Aimed at making the military more responsive to prevailing threats and preparing it for future conflicts, these changes have made the conflict spectrum, as well as military organizations and professionalism, enormously complicated. Military success requires highly skilled and competent individuals at all levels in the military hierarchy. This in turn has made the president and the national security establishment heavily dependent upon the military for sound advice.

The concept of national security has expanded to include military participation in humanitarian and peacekeeping missions and in combating international terrorism (see Chapter 1). As a result, military force has been used in missions and contingencies that are contrary to the traditional views of the military establishment. All of this tends to dilute any notion that the president and Congress are captives of the military, as the use of force in the new era has become engulfed in civilian cultures and nontraditional missions. At the same time, the US military is in the process of transformation—preparing for wars in the twenty-first century. This envisions changes in strategy, doctrine, and weaponry, among other factors.

The Command-and-Control Structure

The military establishment's focus of power shifted to the secretary of defense when that office was given control of the military departments; changes in 1986 further expanded his power as well as that of the JCS chairman. These changes have had an impact on the development of strategy and the formulation of national security policy as well as on presidential control over the military establishment.

Several reference points need to be reviewed with respect to the structure of the Department of Defense (see Figure 6.1). First, the secretaries of the military departments (Army, Navy, and Air Force) have no operational responsibilities; revisions to the National Security Act of 1947 downgraded their executive department status to that of military departments (1949) and later removed them from the chain of command (1958). The primary responsibilities of the service secretaries are in administrative and logistical areas: manpower, procurement, weapons systems, service effectiveness, military welfare, and training responsibilities, among other duties. A strong personality in the service secretary's office can have a decided influence and political impact, however, in shaping the posture and operational capability of the service.

Second, the role of the JCS chairman has been strengthened. Formerly, the JCS was a corporate body, and the chairman served principally as spokesman. In addition, the chairman had little control over who served on the joint staff from the services, whose commanders also rotated the chairman's functions among themselves in his absence. The chairman held a symbolic rather than a substantive position.

The 1986 Defense Reorganization Act (the Goldwater-Nichols Act) made the JCS chairman the primary military figure in the defense establishment. It gave him direct access to the president and assigned him responsibilities not only for strategic thinking but also for a range of other matters (including budget assessments and readiness evaluations), affording him a more direct relationship with the commanders in unified combatant commands. He now has direct control over assignments to the joint staff. Also created by this legislation are several responsibilities assigned to the JCS vice chairman. The chairman no longer must accept joint staff members selected by the various services. In short, the chairman is now the most important member of the JCS, responsible only to the secretary of defense and the president.

Figure 6.1 The Chain of Command

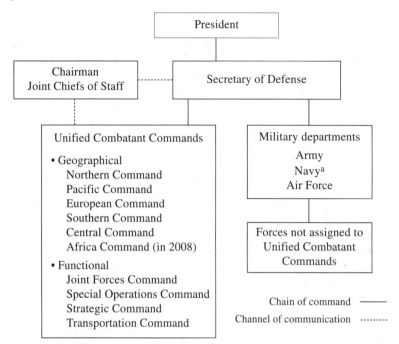

Sources: Joint Chiefs of Staff, US Department of Defense, *Joint Publication 0-2: Unified Action Armed Forces (UNAAF),* July 10, 2001; and US Department of Defense, *Unified Command Plan,* February 7, 2007. Available at http://defenselink.mil/specials/unifiedcommand.

Note: a. Administratively, both the Navy and Marine Corps are in the Department of the Navy.

Third, a new officer specialty was created by Congress.[1] This joint specialty provides for a lifetime career path for officers qualified as staff officers in joint staff positions. The objective is to have a pool of officers from all services qualified to serve on joint staffs, although it was not intended to create a general staff corps on the old German army model. The program has led to important changes within the profession and in the functioning of the joint staff. Education and experience in matters of joint staff responsibilities, as well as socialization processes, are likely to develop a staff mindset on a long-term basis and inculcate some officers with a general staff mentality.

The chain of command and control of the operational arm of the military runs directly from the commander in chief to the secretary of defense through the JCS chairman to the commanders of the Unified Combatant Commands (see Figure 6.1).

Unified Combatant Commands

A unified command, as the name suggests, is a joint service operational responsibility. Commanded by a four-star officer from one service, all services are generally represented in each command. There are currently nine unified commands.[2] Five of these have responsibility for US military operations in specific regions of the world (roughly the United States, the Pacific, Europe, Latin America, and Southwest Asia, including the waters adjacent to these areas):

- United States Northern Command
- United States Pacific Command
- United States European Command
- United States Southern Command
- United States Central Command

A new United States Africa command is scheduled for 2008 and will assume responsibility for all of Africa except Egypt, which was formerly covered by the European, Central, and Pacific Commands.

Four of the nine unified commands are defined by their function:

- United States Joint Forces Command (military transformation)
- United States Special Operations Command (special operations)
- United States Strategic Command (global strike warfare, space, missile defense, combating weapons of mass destruction)
- United States Transportation Command (movement of military forces)

Until the 1986 Defense Reorganization Act, the commanders of unified commands had little control over what units were assigned to their command. This was the responsibility of the various services, whose component commanders had to depend on their own services for resources. The composition of forces was determined by each service. Thus unified commands reflected a mix of doctrines, equipment, and missions as determined by the services.

Now the commanders of unified combatant commands have been given more power in budget matters pertaining to their commands, hiring and firing authority over subordinate commanders, and direct access to the secretary of defense and JCS chairman, bypassing the respective services. The president, in turn, can give the JCS chairman primary responsibility for overseeing the activities of these commands. The 1986 Defense Reorganization Act established the JCS chairman as the spokesman for the commanders of the combatant commands, especially in operational requirements. Commanders now have the authority to act as real commanders, independent from control of their respective services. The changes resulting from the 1986 act have had a positive impact on jointness and in the operational direction of the various commands.

It is also the case that in the new strategic environment, interservice rivalries have resurfaced as each service tries to protect its turf in terms of missions and budgets. This remains a characteristic of the military establishment as each service attempts to prepare for twenty-first-century warfare and the new strategic landscape. Congress tried to override interservice squabbles and problems of command and control by imposing a strengthened secretary of defense and JCS chairman, as well as a strengthened command system, on the military establishment. But the problem of internal rivalries remains. In the past, the number of assistant secretaries of defense reflected the variety of matters under the responsibility of the secretary of defense. Indeed, the scope of activities and the amount of resources required to maintain and expand them created a vast managerial complex—perhaps so complex as to preclude an efficient military system.

The inherent rivalries leave the Defense Department vulnerable to politicization of its operational arms and hamper development of coherent policy and feasible options. With the inauguration of George W. Bush in 2001, a new national security team was put into place and, with it, a new defense system under Secretary of Defense Donald Rumsfeld. This included a system designed to operate in several unconventional environments, particularly to combat international terrorism.

Secretary Rumsfeld's goal was to transform the military into a twenty-first-century force designed to respond to threats and potential threats. This encompassed changes in the military system that focus on doctrine, training, and weaponry and incorporate information-age technology. The initial actions in Afghanistan in 2001 and Iraq in 2003 seemed to offer support for Rumsfeld's vision of lighter and more mobile forces at the expense of numbers, but the need for quantity as well as quality of forces soon became apparent. Rumsfeld's replacement by Robert Gates in 2006 may result in a reappraisal of the specifics of military transformation in view of the US experience in Afghanistan and Iraq.

Congress: Guns and Butter

The role of Congress does not stop at legislation to restructure the military. Executive-legislative skirmishes over constitutional roles have already been discussed, but the division of authority over military appraisal and allocation also impacts the formulation of strategy and its operational implementation. This is reflected in guns-and-butter issues: How much should be spent for defense, and how much for nondefense issues? The president may be the commander in chief, but Congress has the power of the purse. The weapons acquisition process, which obviously affects the military establishment's performance, is but one example. Congress allocates funds for research, development, and production.

All these struggles magnify the political dimension of the military establishment. Congressional hearings on strategy, resource allocation, and military performance strike at the heart of the military establishment, requiring operational commanders at all levels to become sensitive to the political nature of their responsibilities. The desire in Congress for more explicit military recommendations and more control over military commitments in contingencies short of war means it struggles with the president, the secretary of defense, the JCS chairman, individual service chiefs, and a variety of high-level operational commanders. This was true even before US forces became engaged in Iraq. In 1993 and 1994, these struggles were especially visible over the reduction of the military and the shrinking defense budget. In the aftermath of September 11, budget allocations for defense increased, but there is still no consensus on the appropriate size of the force, its structure, or its missions. Figure 6.2 presents a recent allocation for the defense budget, showing the relatively large amounts allocated for operations and maintenance, the global war on terror, and benefits. Procurement—necessary if the force structure is to be preserved—is only 14 percent of the budget.[3]

Directly and indirectly, Congress has increased its oversight of the military establishment. Indeed, it can be said that Congress has become *part of* the military establishment. As such, it brings along a variety of political considerations, from personnel issues to base-closure decisions. Its judgments influence not only budget allocations but also the concept of vital interests, the structure of the military establishment, and the development of strategic options.

Figure 6.2 Department of Defense Budget Allocation, 2006 (percentage)

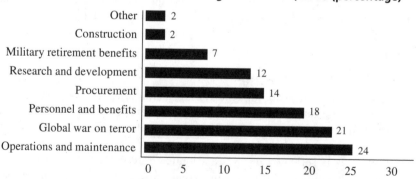

Source: Adapted from Deputy of Defense, *Performance and Accountability Report Highlights, Fiscal Year 2006.* Available at http://www.dod.mil/comptroller/par (accessed April 22, 2007).

Civilians employed by the Department of Defense are an important element in the relationship between the military establishment and other political actors. In 1990, there were more than 1 million civilians working for the department, not counting the more than 1 million employed in defense-related industries. During the Clinton administration, there was a reduction in the number of civilians employed and in the money devoted to defense industries. By 2000, the number of civilians working for the Department of Defense had dropped to about 700,000. Those employed in defense-related industries had also been reduced.[4] To be sure, only a small part of this civilian component has a direct impact on national security policy and the functioning of the national command authority. Nonetheless, close links with the Department of Defense provide a channel for civilian attitudes and mind-sets to penetrate the military profession. Conversely, military attitudes and mind-sets penetrate the civilian component. This interpenetration is greatest at the higher levels, as all appointments at the assistant secretary level and above are political and normally civilian; a more noticeable degree of separation exists at lower levels, where civilians are rarely present in operational units.

Thus the dual influences in the military establishment simply confirm the long-standing norm that civilian control of the US military is a well-established fact in law and reality. Equally important, the military profession has accepted this as a basic premise. Over the years, civilian rule has slowly but surely permeated weapons acquisition, force composition, strategic options, and command-and-control issues. It is in such areas that the president and the military establishment face some of the most serious opposition and disagreements.

Force Restructuring and Composition

The size and composition of US military forces are determined by civilian leaders based on several factors, including the level of resources available, technological developments, and the objective threat. One can never be sure what forces will be required or what the intentions are of potential adversaries, a problem complicated by the very long lead times required to develop new systems. Given the inability to demonstrate conclusively what forces may be needed in the future and given also the vested interests of those who benefit from current procurement, change comes slowly in this area. Much of the US force structure is a "legacy force" designed for the Cold War. It is a force unmatched for high-intensity combat. With the demise of the Soviet threat and the subsequent rise in unconventional and terrorist threats, several attempts have been made to match forces to new missions.

At the end of the Cold War, many hoped for a "peace dividend" by which defense funding could be reprogrammed for other purposes or even left in the pockets of taxpayers. An early attempt to reflect this new reality was made by President Clinton's secretary of defense, Les Aspin. His Bottom-Up Review envisioned the restructuring and reduction of the military by the year 1999, with a reduction in Army active divisions, Navy aircraft carriers, Air Force fighter wings, and Marine Corps personnel.[5] More recently, these plans have been revised by the Bush administration.

For some, the force structure and force composition envisioned by the Bottom-Up Review was driven by budget considerations, rather than serious strategic thought. Then–chief of staff of the Army General Gordon Sullivan and Lieutenant Colonel James Dubik wrote that

> American political leaders expect the military to contract in both size and budget, contribute to domestic recovery, participate in global stability operations, and retain its capability to produce decisive victory in whatever circumstances they are employed—all at the same time. . . . International and domestic realities have resulted in the paradox of declining military resources and increasing military missions, a paradox that is stressing our armed forces. The stress is significant.[6]

All of these changes by the Clinton administration, combined with the president's efforts to lift the ban on homosexuals in the military and expand the role of women in combat, had a decided impact on the military profession. It was feared by some that the military had become more of a social institution than a fighting institution, reinforced by those who challenged the use of the US military in nation-building, peacekeeping, and humanitarian intervention.[7]

Another milestone was, of course, September 11 and the military response to the challenge posed by both irregular military forces and terrorists. The Bush administration entered office in 2001 skeptical of the importance of nation-building, but after the long-term difficulties of the United States in Iraq and Afghanistan, these skills are again seen as important. Defense Secretary Rumsfeld designed his battle plans for both wars to validate his views on the transformation of the US military into a lighter, more agile, and more lethal force—one less dependent on quantity of forces and more dependent on quality.

The Military Profession

If the command-and-control structure is an important ingredient in the formulation of national security policy, the character of the military profession—including its values, norms, and mind-sets—is equally so.[8] How military professionals perceive threats, assess the capability of the military instrument, and develop professional skills and capabilities is a significant determinant of the advice they give. In addition, professional behavior has much to do with the perceptions of Congress, allies, and adversaries regarding US military capability and effectiveness.

Six elements are paramount in shaping the character of military officers: (1) the profession has a defined area of competence based on expert knowledge; (2) there is a system of continuing education designed to maintain professional competence; (3) the profession has an obligation to society and must serve it without concern for remuneration; (4) it has a system of values that perpetuate the professional character and establish and maintain legitimate relationships with society; (5) there is an institutional framework within which the profession can function; and (6) the profession has control over the system of internal rewards and punishments and is in a position to determine the quality and quantity of those entering the profession.

One factor distinguishing the military profession from others rests in its notions of duty, honor, country. Its sole client is the state. The military professional is committed to the ultimate sacrifice—one must be prepared to give one's life for the state. But the characteristic unique to the profession lies in its primary purpose: to win wars. The military is employed as an operational arm to destroy an adversary—in more colloquial terms, "to kill and break things."

Yet the military profession is subject to constraints not found in other callings. For all practical purposes, it cannot publicly or formally engage in political partisanship to secure better wages, conditions of employment, or operational commitments. It must comply with the policy and decisions of civilian officials even if it does not agree with them. Institutional and professional loyalties as well as professional motivations preclude expressing public outrage at orders from above. The military must accept the decision to destroy the enemy with all of the power at hand once the political leadership decides it shall be done.

Professional career patterns and success depend on the ability to work within the system and follow the established path. Professional values and mind-sets, which preclude military professionals from stepping outside the system, also tend to socialize them into an institutional perspective that denotes a particular set of relationships with society. Perhaps most important, there is a system of teaching that establishes the way military professionals view themselves, their institution, society, and the outside world. To be sure, most professions tend to follow somewhat similar patterns. But nonmilitary professions have access to large segments of society and thus can move in a mainstream that has relatively undefined boundaries.

The military profession, in contrast, tends to be a more self-contained community—socially, legally, economically, and intellectually—all of which reinforces the primary professional purpose of success in battle. To be sure, the lifestyles and mind-sets engendered are what civilians find the most difficult to appreciate. This lack of understanding is at the root of the negative (and, at times, antagonistic) views that military professionals hold about self-styled military experts, especially in the media, Congress, and academia. Indeed, many military professionals tend to see such critics as ignorant of the military, which helps perpetuate the self-contained community mind-set of the military and magnifies differences between the operational arm of the military and society in general.

Since the end of the Cold War, however, many voices have demanded that the military reflect society—to become, as one author has put it, a "kinder, gentler military."[9] This is reinforced by the view that the threat of major war has diminished and the military must be more society-sensitive in dealing with noncombat operations such as peacekeeping, humanitarian, and constabulary missions.

Since the 1990s, the military has been struggling with serious internal travails: the role of women and homosexuals, sexual harassment, morale, and recruitment, among others. These internal problems make it difficult to design and commit an effective military force in support of national security policy. All of this is compounded by the argument that the military must more closely reflect society, for example, in its diversity and multiculturalism. These problems remain.[10]

In addition, the profession seemed to be troubled over the direction of political-military policy in the United States. This concern encompassed several issues, ranging from the reduction in the size of the military and the defense budget, to civil-military relations, to the shape of the profession.

The military perspective casts the external environment and the requirements for military effectiveness in a mold that differs, sometimes considerably, from the public's view and that of elected officials. Indeed, it can also differ from views within the executive branch. Evolving in no small part from the Vietnam experience, the mind-set of military professionals has become sensitive to the political dynamics created by military commitment. As a result, they tend toward extreme caution about military involvement in situations likely to generate domestic political opposition, a concern expressed eloquently in 1976 by General Fred Weyand, chief of staff of the Army:

> Vietnam was a reaffirmation of the peculiar relationship between the American Army and the American people. The American Army really is a people's Army in the sense that it belongs to the American people who take a jealous and proprietary interest in its involvement. When the Army is committed the American people are committed, when the American people lose their commitment it is futile to try to keep the Army committed. In the final analysis, the American Army is not so much an arm of the Executive Branch as it is an arm of the American people. The Army, therefore, cannot be committed lightly.[11]

Note, however, that "commitment" has its own spectrum. For example, US Army and Marine Corps combat troops deployed overseas have a distinctly different connotation for the public than do US Navy personnel sailing aboard vessels in international waters.

Yet once committed, most military professionals expect to employ the resources at hand to prevail quickly, believing it unconscionable not to use the most effective weaponry and tactics to subdue the enemy. Furthermore, the principles of war stress that overwhelming firepower and resources should be centered on the enemy's weakest point to achieve victory. One interpretation of this is that military professionals seek overwhelming superiority, not simply adequacy. Military doctrine holds that overwhelming superiority is likely to reduce casualties and be the most economical in achieving success.

The debate regarding the use of force in conflicts short of war focuses not only on the role of airpower but also on combat troops engaged in any variety of humanitarian and peacekeeping missions.[12] Moreover, political fireworks accompany the use of the military in conflicts short of war. This was evident in Kosovo, where objectives became blurred and the use of military force was affected by the political views of allied NATO countries.[13] This also became a major concern in 2001–2002 after US military forces were committed to the war in Afghanistan. More recently, questions of cooperation emerged as NATO assumed security responsibility for part of Afghanistan and as US coalition partners in Iraq became disillusioned with that war.

Homeland security is another mission that complicates the role of the military. Military professionals recognize the need for homeland security but are concerned about command and control and the coordination required among the active military, reserve forces, domestic security forces, and emergency and medical teams.[14] This issue has become more complicated with the creation of the Office of Homeland Security,[15] and will become even more complicated and broader in scope as the most recent department, the Department of Homeland Security, works out its missions and relationships with other national security agencies.

Finally, military professionals expect to be provided clear policy goals, strategic coherency, and operationally precise tasks. Mainstream military posture is shaped best to respond to these dimensions. Contingencies of an unconventional nature are not characterized by these types of considerations. They are likely to be policy incoherent, strategically obscure, and operationally muddled. Security issues in the twenty-first century are largely characterized by unconventional conflicts, and this is likely to continue.

The Weinberger Doctrine

In the 1990s, professional concerns led to the resurfacing of the so-called Weinberger Doctrine, later reinforced by the Powell Doctrine. Events in

Somalia in 1993 seemed to confirm the relevancy of these approaches. During the Somalia mission, the killing and wounding of US soldiers in the failed attempt to capture the warlord Mohammed Farah Aideed led critics to point out that a lack of clearly defined military objectives, inadequate support, and mission creep were fundamental causes of military failure.

The Weinberger Doctrine was established by Secretary of Defense Caspar Weinberger in 1984 during the Reagan administration to spell out the conditions under which US ground combat troops should be committed. The elements of this doctrine include the following:[16]

- There should be no overseas commitment of US combat forces unless a vital national interest of the United States or important US ally is threatened.
- If US forces are committed, there should be total support—resources and manpower to complete the mission.
- If committed, US forces must be given clearly defined political and military objectives, and the forces must be large enough to be able to achieve these objectives.
- There must be a continual assessment between the commitment and capability of US forces and the objectives, which must be adjusted, if necessary.
- Before US forces are committed, there must be reasonable assurance that Americans and their elected representatives support such commitment.
- Commitment of US forces to combat must be the last resort.

Later General Colin Powell spelled out his view on the use of force: "Have a clear military objective and stick to it. Use all the force necessary, and do not apologize for going in big if that is what it takes. Decisive force ends wars quickly and in the long run saves lives. Whatever threats we faced in the future, I intended to make these rules the bedrock of my military counsel."[17]

The 1999 campaign in Kosovo against the Serbs and the regime of President Slobodan Milosevic seemed to contradict the precepts of the Weinberger-Powell perspectives. The seventy-eight-day air campaign led to the end of the Serbian campaign against the Albanians in Kosovo. This was done without the commitment of US ground troops, yet the air campaign was supported by the Kosovo Liberation Army, made up of Albanians armed and supported by outside sources, and the pressure brought to bear by the Russians surely affected decisions. The final status of Kosovo remains unresolved in 2007, but it seems to be moving in the direction of at least de facto independence. The fact is that the massive use of military force at the center of gravity of the adversary remains a clear military prin-

ciple. How this can be applied to operations other than war, stability operations, and unconventional conflicts, including international terrorism,
remains contentious. What, for example, is the center of gravity in such
operations? The US military is unmatched in its ability to destroy regular
military forces, but what if the center of gravity in a conflict is political,
ethnic, or religious?

The Military and the Policy Process

The structure of the Department of Defense and the nature and character of
military professionalism are the primary determinants of the military's role
in the national security policy process. That role has more to do with administrative and operational considerations than with the serious formulation of
national strategy, in which the military is in a distinctly secondary position.

The traditional professional posture rests partly on the premise that military personnel do not become involved in politics. Hence, because the policy process is inherently political, they are expected to keep their distance;
and because formulation of strategy is in turn closely linked to the political
process, they find themselves outside the formulation of strategy.

In addition, the joint perspective necessary for this process is difficult
for military professionals to maintain, as career success typically runs
through the respective services. Even the members of the JCS, with their
dual role, tend first to their service responsibilities. The same is true of joint
staff officers, and although their performance on the joint staff and their relative efficiency are determined by the JCS, service perspectives and career
considerations tend to erode a joint perspective. Service parochialism and
professional socialization instilled over a long career are difficult to overcome by assignment to a joint staff.

Another basic problem is that the role of the military in the policy
process and formulation of strategy is affected by role conflict. The technology drive in the military, reflected in sophisticated battlefield weaponry,
electronic warfare, and the evolution of an intricate organizational defense
structure, has tended to shape the military establishment along the lines of
civilian corporate and managerial systems. Furthermore, great efforts have
been made within senior service schools to develop officers capable of dealing with such complex conditions. As a consequence, military managership
has become an important factor in career success and military efficiency.
But not everyone agrees with this approach. Many military professionals
and critics argue that the real need within the military services is for leaders
and warriors. According to this view, emphasis on managership erodes the
ability of the military services to successfully command and lead operational units in battle. Reliance on technology shifts the focus away from the

psychological-social dimensions of human behavior, thereby reducing competency in the art of leadership.[18]

Notwithstanding its coveted aloofness from politics, the military has been dragged into the fray on many fronts—weapons acquisition, budgets, and relations with Congress, among other things. Furthermore, contemporary conflicts, whether nuclear or unconventional in character, include important political considerations.[19] As some are inclined to argue, the military professional must begin functioning long before the opening salvos of war and operations other than war. Indeed, wars and conflicts in progress in the twenty-first century are characterized by inextricable political and military factors. Cases in point include the monitoring of the Iraqi military and the Kurds in northern Iraq from the end of the first Gulf War and the 2003 invasion of Iraq, continuing involvement in Bosnia-Herzegovina and Kosovo, concern over political developments in Russia, and the China-Taiwan issue, among others. For military professionals to be successful, therefore, they must acquire political as well as military skills. At a minimum, military professionals must be able to deal with the political dimensions of conflict—at least to understand the political dimensions of problems they may be asked to handle militarily. In the twenty-first century, such considerations are no longer distinct from the operational environment.

The fear of many, however, is that attention to politics not only detracts from developing military skills but also exposes the profession to politicization, which destroys professional integrity and autonomy. The only feasible posture, according to this view, is to maintain a clear separation between politics and the military profession. The traditional concept of civil-military relations and an apolitical military associated with democratic systems is based on this separatist view. Yet others argue that there is no such thing as an apolitical military and that the US military is no exception. How these matters can be reconciled with the political character of conflicts and the military's role in a democracy remains a persisting dilemma for the military profession.

According to some, the military must inform the public as well as elected officials about their views regarding the military system and the use of force. As one author suggested, the military profession cannot function as a "silent order of monks."[20] He noted in another context, "The military profession must adopt the doctrine of constructive political engagement, framing and building a judicious and artful involvement in the policy arena. A politics-savvy military profession is the basic ingredient for constructive political engagement."[21]

These characteristics of the military establishment do not allow simplistic views of its role in the national security policy process or in the formulation of strategy. On one hand, the views of the military cannot be ignored; on the other, the character of the military institution, the nature of the military profession, and the way the US political system works preclude a lead role for the military. Research on the matters examined here reveals the following:

> The combination of domestic and international issues promises to weigh heavily on the military profession and its strategic and doctrinal orientation. These issues strike at the core of the professional ethos. Even more challenging is that the military profession must be prepared to respond to a variety of national security challenges with diminished resources and considerably fewer personnel, and it must do so even in the face of skepticism within the body politic regarding issues of national security. Exacerbating all of this is that few politicians and academic commentators in the new era have had any real military experience. Although military experience is not the sine qua non for serious examination and analysis of national security and the military profession, without that experience it is difficult to design realistic national security policies or to understand the nature and character of the military profession.[22]

How the president and the national security establishment incorporate the military establishment into the policy process—while maintaining the character of the profession and not violating the norms and expectations of a democratic system—is a problem facing every president. The challenge surely cannot be met without an understanding of the nature and character of the military establishment and its professionals. The same holds true for anyone studying national security.

Notes

1. A *specialty* is a primary or secondary career pattern for which officers may qualify by virtue of performance and education, among other considerations.

2. Department of Defense, *Unified Command Plan,* February 7, 2007. Available at http://defenselink.mil/specials/unifiedcommand.

3. Gordon England, Deputy Secretary of Defense, *Performance and Accountability Report Highlights, Fiscal Year 2006.* Available at http://www.dod.mil/comptroller/par (accessed April 22, 2007). See also the Department of Defense, *Quadrennial Defense Review Report*, February 6, 2006. Available at http://www.defenselink.mil/qdr/report/Report20060203.pdf, and the Congressional Budget Office, *Long-Term Implications of Current Defense Plans: Detailed Update for Fiscal Year 2007,* April 2007. Available at http://www.cbo.gov/ftpdocs/80xx/doc8018/04-20-Defense.pdf.

4. William S. Cohen, Secretary of Defense, *Report of the Secretary of Defense to the President and Congress, 2001,* Appendix C. Available at http://www.nti.org/e_research/official_docs/dod/2001/101DOD.pdf.

5. Les Aspin, Secretary of Defense, *The Bottom-Up Review: Forces for a New Era* (Washington, DC: Department of Defense, September 1, 1993).

6. General Gordon R. Sullivan and Lieutenant Colonel James M. Dubik, *Land Warfare in the 21st Century* (Carlisle Barracks, PA: Strategic Studies Institute, US Army War College, February 1993).

7. See Gary T. Dempsey, with Roger W. Fontaine, *Fool's Errands: America's Recent Encounters with National Building* (Washington, DC: Cato Institute, 2001).

8. For a detailed study of US military professionalism, see Sam C. Sarkesian and Robert E. Connor Jr., *The US Military Profession into the 21st Century: War, Peace, and Politics* (New York: Routledge, 2006). Also see Don M. Snider and Gayle L. Watkins, "The Future of Army Professionalism: A Need for Renewal and Redefinition," *Parameters: US Army War College Quarterly* 30, no. 3 (Autumn 2000): 5–20. What many consider classics on military professionalism and civil-military relations are Morris Janowitz, *The Professional Soldier: A Social and Political Portrait* (New York: The Free Press, 1971), and Samuel P. Huntington, *The Soldier and the State: The Theory and Politics of Civil-Military Relations* (New York: Vintage Books, 1964).

9. Stephanie Gutmann, *The Kinder, Gentler Military: Can America's Gender-Neutral Fighting Force Still Win Wars?* (New York: Scribner, 2000).

10. Laura L. Miller and John Allen Williams, "Do Military Policies on Gender and Sexuality Undermine Combat Effectiveness?" in Peter D. Feaver and Richard H. Kohn, eds., *Soldiers and Civilians: The Civilian-Military Gap and American National Security* (Cambridge, MA: MIT Press, 2001), pp. 386–429.

11. General Fred C. Weyand, "Vietnam Myths and Realities," *CDRS Call* (July–August 1976). Reprinted in Harry G. Summers, *On Strategy: The Vietnam War in Context* (Carlisle Barracks, PA: Strategic Studies Institute, US Army War College, January 17, 1981), p. 7. General Weyand was the last commander of the Military Assistance Command Vietnam and supervised the withdrawal of US military forces in 1973.

12. See Dempsey and Fontaine, *Fool's Errands.*

13. See, e.g., General Wesley K. Clark, US Army (ret.), *Waging Modern War: Bosnia, Kosovo, and the Future of Combat* (New York: Public Affairs, 2001).

14. See, e.g., Lieutenant Colonel Antulio J. Echevarria II, *The Army and Homeland Security: A Strategic Perspective* (Carlisle, PA: Strategic Studies Institute, US Army War College, March 2001).

15. See ibid. See also Ian Roxborough, *The Hart-Rudman Commission and Homeland Defense* (Carlisle Barracks, PA: Strategic Studies Institute, US Army War College, September 2001).

16. This summary is based on David T. Twining, "The Weinberger Doctrine and the Use of Force in the Contemporary Era," in Alan Ned Sabrosky and Robert L. Sloane, eds., *The Recourse to War: An Appraisal of the "Weinberger Doctrine"* (Carlisle Barracks, PA: Strategic Studies Institute, US Army War College, 1988), pp. 11–12. The Weinberger Doctrine appears in Department of Defense, *Report of the Secretary of Defense to the Congress for Fiscal Year 1987* (Washington, DC: US Government Printing Office, February 5, 1986).

17. Colin Powell, with Joseph E. Persico, *My American Journey* (New York: Random House, 1995), p. 434.

18. Sam C. Sarkesian, "Who Serves?" *Social Science and Modern Society* 18, no. 3 (March/April 1981): 57–60, and Sam C. Sarkesian, John Allen Williams, and Fred B. Bryant, *Soldiers, Society, and National Security* (Boulder: Lynne Rienner Publishers, 1995), pp. 13–17.

19. Sarkesian and Connor, *US Military Profession*. See also Clark, *Waging Modern War.*

20. Sam C. Sarkesian, "The US Military Must Find Its Voice," *Orbis* 42, no. 3 (Summer 1998): 423–437.

21. Sarkesian and Connor, *US Military Profession.*

22. Sarkesian, Williams, and Bryant, *Soldiers,* p. 147.

7

Civil-Military Relations

THROUGHOUT THE HISTORY OF DEMOCRACIES, THE ROLE OF THE
military has rested on absolute civilian control over the military.[1] This is
engrained in the US system, as well as in the US military institution and
mind-set. Although the fear of a politicized military has periodically
emerged in US history, the issue has become more challenging in the
twenty-first century. In turn, it has become a more pressing national security issue. Although the US military must be prepared to respond across
the conflict spectrum, its most likely involvement will be in ethnic, religious, and nationalistic conflicts as in Iraq, Afghanistan, and the former
Yugoslavia. In order to be effective, the military might conduct operations
contrary to the American way of war, undercutting its own credibility and
legitimacy in the US political system.

Even though this dilemma has become a recurring and persistent problem, polls continue to show that the military is among the most admired of
US institutions, respected more than many other (and far more democratic)
institutions such as the Congress. This was true even before the terrorist
attacks on September 11, 2001, and the subsequent response of the US military in Afghanistan and, more controversially, Iraq. Despite the popularity
of the military, however, differences in experiences and culture ensure that
US civil-military relations will remain troubled. This does not mean that the
military is likely to disobey civilian directions or attempt to influence elections, but the degree to which the military can or should try to influence
government decisions (on force structure and force employment) remains
controversial.

Hollywood films are a useful indicator of public opinion, as the media
both shape the public's view of reality and react to it. This is especially true
for cinema portrayals of the military, a subject of strong popular opinion.
The post-Vietnam fall of the prestige of the military, its subsequent rise, and

131

perhaps its coming fall are well chronicled in such films as *Apocalypse Now, Full Metal Jacket, Born on the Fourth of July* (fall); *Officer and a Gentleman, Top Gun* (rise); and *The Siege* (fall). In *The Siege,* the military rounds up Arab residents of Brooklyn in response to a series of terrorist bombings. This suggests that US armed forces would be unresponsive to civilian control in an emergency—although it is more likely that a series of terrorist incidents in the United States would cause public demand for far more restrictive measures than the military would be comfortable in carrying out. One can expect a number of films about the US military experience in Iraq.

In a similar vein, Air Force colonel Charles J. Dunlap Jr. used a hypothetical military coup in 2012 as the backdrop for writing about his concern with the direction of civil-military relations. The coup was sparked by the massive diversion of military forces to civilian uses, the monolithic unification of the armed forces, and the insularity of the military community.[2] Appearing as it did in *Parameters,* the journal of the US Army War College, the article caused quite a stir.

A major question for civil-military relations is this: How can society ensure that military authorities remain in their proper sphere and yet retain the capability to respond effectively across the conflict spectrum? Is the gap between civilian and military society so serious as to pose problems for civil-military relations and civilian control and military effectiveness?[3]

Theories

Two classic discussions of civil-military relations continue to frame the debate on how the military is controlled in a democratic society: Samuel P. Huntington's *The Soldier and the State* and Morris Janowitz's *The Professional Soldier.*[4]

For Huntington, civilian control is achieved through military professionalism. He argued that military officers exhibit three characteristics that define a profession: expertise (the management of violence), responsibility (for the defense of the state), and corporateness (institutional self-awareness and organization).[5] These properties distinguish the military from other professions, and their emphasis serves as the best basis for civilian control. The self-regulating norms of military professionalism ensure that the military will remain obedient to civilian authorities.

In Huntington's view, the nature of the military makes it a poor match with liberal civilian society. Indeed, he suggested that "the tension between the demands of military security and the values of American liberalism can, in the long run, be relieved only by the weakening of the security threat or the weakening of liberalism."[6] As a result, too close an association between the military and society weakens, rather than strengthens, civilian control. The diminished security threat (at least for the moment) brought by the end of the Cold War has eased this dilemma but has not eliminated it.

For Janowitz, the founder of the field of military sociology, civilian control is achieved through the socialization process.[7] Put another way, the military comes from society and reflects its values in important ways. The military's sympathy with the values of society makes it a more willing servant. Although military members cannot enjoy all of society's privileges, they support the democratic system that makes these privileges available to the civilian population. Even so, a distinct military culture is important: "In a private enterprise society, the military establishment could not hold its most creative talents without the binding force of service traditions, professional identifications, and honor."[8]

Thus the degree to which society should impose its values (and culture) on the military is an unresolved question. For example, the degree to which the military should focus on military effectiveness as opposed to civil liberties issues is highly controversial. The military continues to discriminate— that is, make distinctions concerning its members based on gender, sexual orientation, and physical and mental abilities—all in the name of military effectiveness. Many of these distinctions would be illegal in a civilian context but are permitted by the Congress and the courts in a military one. Reasonable people continue to differ on the degree to which these distinctions actually enhance military effectiveness.[9] In any event, the support for the open service of gays and lesbians is gaining ground in US society. Similarly, the sharply increased role of US women service members in Iraq may increase support for an expanded role for women. When these changes inevitably occur, the military can build on its earlier success in ensuring that opportunities are not denied to service members based on their race.

The Gap

Journalist Thomas E. Ricks has noted a widening gap between the military and society. Based on his personal observation of a US Marine platoon during and after basic training, Ricks saw a contradiction between the values inculcated in the military and those increasingly prevalent in civilian society, leading to feelings of estrangement by some in the military. He suggested three reasons for this, including the end of the draft, the "politicization of the officer corps," and a more fragmented, less disciplined US society.[10]

Political scientist Ole R. Holsti confirmed and extended Ricks's analysis. Among other findings, Holsti's extensive survey results documented what he called "a strong trend toward conservative Republicanism among military officers."[11] This is noteworthy in view of the previously nonpolitical nature of the military calling; indeed at one time many officers would even refuse on principle to vote. The military is voting these days, however. Voting officers in all units ensure that all who want absentee ballots receive them and have whatever help they need in meeting state requirements. In the 2000 presidential election, the votes of military personnel outside the country, legal residents of the state of Florida, may well have been the deciding factor in George W. Bush's victory.

The degree and significance of this gap are open to debate. It may be simply a curious result of different socialization processes, but it could also mark a fundamental fault line that has implications for the nature of military service, military effectiveness, and the ability of civilian society to direct the military that defends it. The latter issue is of particular concern here.

There is a danger if society and the military that protects it become too disconnected from one another. Many in the military already feel estranged from civilians, whom they see as undisciplined, irresolute, and morally adrift. They view themselves as the true carriers of US values and tradition, swimming against the tide of a society gone morally soft.

There are also undercurrents of contempt for some civilian leaders. Public demonstrations of disrespect remain rare, but they do occur. An early visit by President Bill Clinton to an aircraft carrier was marred by discourtesy on the part of many crew members. Contemptuous public comments about the commander in chief by an Air Force general resulted in the rapid termination of the latter's service. An op-ed piece in the *Washington Times* written by a major in the Marine Corps Reserve calling for the president's impeachment effectively ended that officer's career. Although many service members felt the piece read well, most felt it went over the line of acceptable commentary by a serving military officer—even a reservist. Wiser commanders pointedly reminded their officers of the provisions of Article 88 of the Uniform Code of Military Justice:

> CONTEMPT TOWARD OFFICIALS: Any commissioned officer who uses contemptuous words against the President, the Vice President, Congress, the Secretary of Defense, the Secretary of a military department, the Secretary of Transportation, or the Governor or legislature of any State, Territory, Commonwealth, or possession in which he is on duty or present shall be punished as a court-martial may direct.

A declining level of support for the Iraq war among service members might have the spillover effect of lower support for the president, but it is unlikely that this would manifest itself in open displays of disrespect or a failure to follow orders.

For their part, most Americans have admiration and respect for the military but are not always eager to put their own civilian pursuits aside to join the military. Recruiting and retaining quality personnel, essential to a modern military, are continuing concerns for military leaders. For many civilians, military life is as unfathomable as life on another planet; military people are outsiders to them. This does not make them expendable—they are, after all, still Americans, and the sight of abused US prisoners of war still strikes a strong nerve—but it does not mean they are part of the mainstream. Military protection is expected, but there is little understanding of the individuals who have chosen the military as a career.

This difficulty in understanding does not equate to dislike, however. There is a sense of respect for the sacrifices military people make that civilians do not, and perhaps could not, make.[12] This is a great improvement from the Vietnam War era, when the military endured great personal sacrifice yet was tainted with the war's unpopularity and returned to a society contemptuous of those who served. After September 11, positive feelings toward the US military as an institution and the people who serve in it became even stronger. Time will tell whether the public's disaffection for the war in Iraq will translate into lower support for the military as an institution or for military personnel.

Civilian and Military Cultures

Many factors drive the civilian and military cultures away from one another. Perhaps the most serious is the diminishing number of civilians—especially elites—with personal exposure to the military, either through their own service or that of a family member. This separation may be modified somewhat as larger numbers of military reservists—with close ties to the civilian communities from which they come—serve on extended combat tours in Iraq.

The draft ended in 1973. The only requirement is to register with the Selective Service System, and even that obligation applies only to males. Compulsory national service plans (usually including a civilian service option) are occasionally discussed, but there is neither widespread political support nor military necessity for any such system. Sociologist Charles Moskos proposed an innovative plan for fifteen-month enlistments to attract college students into the military, but this plan has not received widespread support. Yet as he noted, "if serving one's country became more common among privileged youth, future leaders in civilian society would have had a formative citizenship experience. This can only be to the advantage of the armed forces and the nation."[13]

Bill Clinton's avoidance of service in Vietnam was a lightning rod issue inside the US military, but it goes far beyond that. Today, compared to years past, the president, his major advisers, Defense Department appointees, members of Congress, senators, and their staffs are less likely to have experienced any sort of military service. Media and economic elites, not to mention the general public, are also less likely to have served.

This need not be fatal to military-related policy, for many civilians have a good understanding of military matters. Yet for most people, lack of personal military experience makes it more difficult to evaluate military-related issues, especially those concerning the internal dynamics of the military itself—such as contentious personnel issues.

Such personal disassociation from the military weakens the ability of civilian society to make informed judgments about military issues, let alone influence military decisionmaking. It is not that uninformed civilians will necessarily distrust or dislike the military—indeed, there may be a tendency to like the military too much and to put unwarranted confidence in military solutions to international political problems. All this can have serious implications for establishing effective national security policy and strategy.

In addition, military people perceive a double standard in light of recent scandals. It is disheartening for military personnel, at any level, to see the careers of contemporaries sidetracked or terminated for infractions far less severe than those admitted to by some civilian leaders. The draconian personnel policies of Defense Department appointees and congressional staff members (especially after the 1991 Tailhook scandal, in which naval and other aviators were accused of committing sexual assaults) were widely perceived inside the military as unfair.

Integration in the Military

Because it is subservient to civilian direction, the military often finds itself ahead of society on issues of social change. Some of these policies have worked out better in the military than in civilian society, such as the generally successful attempts to achieve racial fairness.[14]

Perhaps the greatest sociological challenge for the military is the integration of women into the mainstream of military activities, including combat.[15] This is proving to be difficult, especially as pressure grows to permit women into ground combat, with questions about the military effectiveness of mixed units.[16] Civilian and military leaders tend to disagree on this issue: some 57.5 percent of civilian leaders, compared to 37.6 percent of military leaders, supported allowing women to serve in all military roles. Of course, true equality would mean not only that women could *volunteer* for combat but also that they could be *compelled* to serve in combat. Neither civilian nor military leaders are willing to go this far, however: only 13.9 percent of the civilians and 12.7 percent of the military surveyed supported requiring women to serve in all combat jobs.[17]

Still ahead is the inevitable integration of openly gay men and lesbian women into the military, although Charles Moskos's "don't ask, don't tell" policy (adopted by the Clinton administration) has so far withstood judicial scrutiny much better than many had predicted.[18] The issue is not whether there will be gay and lesbian service members—many are on duty now and serving successfully—but how well the military cohesion so crucial in battle can withstand the stress of openly discussed homosexual orientations. This will be especially problematic to the extent that Holsti, Ricks, and others are correct about the increasing conservatism of service members. If the issue were simply civil liberties versus military effectiveness, personnel policy alternatives would be simplified. In the real world, where most of us dwell, the choices are not as stark.[19]

Civilian-Military Connections

Janowitz's advice—that it is best to increase the connections between the military and civil society in order to increase mutual understanding—has serious implications for military recruiting and education. One issue is the source of military officers. An increasing percentage of officers comes from the service academies and, in the case of Reserve Officer Training Corps (ROTC) programs, from less prestigious schools. Meanwhile, Officer Candidate Schools, the least expensive option because the services do not fund candidates' college degrees, have been cut back.

The military services need a variety of sources for their officers, with some of them under their control. Successful efforts at several elite universities to remove ROTC programs from their campuses in the wake of the Vietnam War and disputes about gays in the military are sufficient testimony to this. As a result, it is less likely that the children of civilian elites who go to such universities would enter the military and perhaps continue to influence it through successful careers.

As officers advance in grade, a combination of training and education prepares them to assume higher levels of responsibility. This education needs to reinforce the lessons of proper civil-military relations, which it generally does. Especially at the war colleges, academic standards are comparable to those at civilian universities.[20] Still, there is a strong argument for sending many of the best officers to top civilian universities. The education may well be even better, and military and civilian elites can interact and grow to appreciate and understand the perspective of others.[21]

Another civil-military connection is not as well understood as it should be: the military reserve forces. These part-timers provide an invaluable connection between the active forces and society at large and will be increasingly important as budgets grow tighter and civilian technical and managerial expertise becomes more important for the military.[22]

There is a broad civil-military connection that links the active military to a variety of civil-military groups such as the Military Coalition, which includes organizations such as the Retired Officers Association, Veterans of Foreign Wars, the Air Force Association, the Navy League, the Marine Corps

League, the National Guard Association, the Association of the US Army, the Reserve Officers Association, and the Naval Reserve Association.

The Military and the Media

The gap between the military and society benefits no one, and efforts by both the military and civilians will be required to close it. The military needs to ensure it is training people to understand and respect civilian values, institutions, and prerogatives. This includes inculcating respect for the role of the media and even academic research bearing on military actions and the military as an institution.

In this connection, not all is well. It is too easy for the military to view criticism by outsiders as uninformed and mean-spirited and to see the free press as an enemy. Media coverage of the Iraq war has been detailed, as it should be, and has helped expose a number of improper actions, including the abuse of Iraqi inmates at Abu Ghraib prison and incidents of excessive or unwarranted use of force. Military educators are sometimes so sensitive to media criticism that they inadvertently teach students that such criticism is illegitimate. This is a bad lesson to teach future military leaders who will eventually be charged with defending a society in which a free press is of paramount importance.[23]

Of course, military points of view are not as monolithic as many would expect. Moreover, the degree to which the military should publicly express policy preferences remains controversial. It has been forcefully argued that senior officers should voice their opinions in areas of their expertise. There has been a call for "constructive political engagement," which must steer clear of partisanship on such issues as "military democratization" (the imposition of civilian values and practices on the military institution) and the utility of military force in various contingencies.[24] Conversely, Huntington expressed many doubts about the degree to which the military can "participate in the good-politics of policy without also becoming embroiled in the bad-politics of partisanship."[25] In retrospect, the history of US intervention in Vietnam, in the Balkans, and in Iraq might have been far different had military leaders spoken out publicly.[26]

In the view of many military observers, the handling of the early stages of the 1999 Kosovo crisis helped turn a humanitarian tragedy into a catastrophe, as civilian leaders pushed for a military confrontation with Serbia yet ruled out the use of ground forces. In the minds of many, this showed how badly war can be waged by civilian policymakers who do not fully understand the uses and limits of military power. Perhaps worse, senior military leaders who knew better did not put their careers on the line by putting their doubts on the record in a timely fashion.[27] This is not a call to subvert civilian authority, but more candid advice would have better served the nation. More recently, many military leaders swallowed their professional reservations about plans for the Iraq invasion and subsequent occupation in the face of strong pressure from Secretary of Defense Donald Rumsfeld and other civilian leaders. This is troubling for those who believe deeply in civilian control of the military (including determining strategy). Civilian leaders should listen carefully to military advice, but they retain final authority in the US system.

In assessing the role of the US military in Vietnam, General Fred C. Weyand, US Army chief of staff in 1976, stated, "As military professionals we must speak out, we must counsel our political leaders and alert the American public that there is no such thing as a 'splendid little war.' There is no such thing as a war fought on the cheap." He went on to say that "the American Army is really a people's Army in the sense that it belongs to the American people who take a jealous and proprietary interest in its involvement. . . . The American Army is not so much an arm of the executive branch as it is an arm of the American people. The Army, therefore, cannot be committed lightly."[28]

Conclusion

The real danger in this country is not that military officers will defy civil authority or stage some sort of coup d'état.[29] For reasons laid out some fifty years ago by Huntington and Janowitz, that is quite literally unthinkable. If military authorities ever do think in such terms, the future of US democracy will be in grave doubt. As Justice Robert Jackson noted in his dissent in *Korematsu v. United States,* the Supreme Court case that upheld the internment program for persons of Japanese ethnicity in World War II:

> If the people ever let the war power fall into irresponsible and unscrupulous hands, the courts wield no power equal to its restraint. The chief restraint upon those who command the physical forces of the country, in the future as in the past, must be their responsibility to the political judgments of their contemporaries and to the moral judgments of history.[30]

To the extent that the estrangement of the military and society is real, it is not healthy. Fortunately, the remedies are straightforward. Mutual understanding between the military and society calls for increased linkages at all levels and an understanding that the military is a unique institution with standards that may not always be the same as those of the society it defends.

There is always a balance to be struck between civil rights and liberties within the military, on the one hand, and military effectiveness, on the other. Even within the military, there is a difference in the degree to which forces can or should be expected to mirror society.[31] Ideologues at either end of the spectrum only make it harder to advance sensible policies.

The relationship of the military to society and the civilian-military culture gap is well stated by noted military author John Keegan:

> Soldiers are not as other men—that is the lesson that I have learned from a life cast among warriors. The lesson has taught me to view with extreme suspicion all theories and representations of war that equate it with any other activity in human affairs. War is . . . fought by men whose values and skills are not those of politicians or diplomats. They are those of a world apart, a very ancient world, which exists in parallel with the everyday world but does not belong to it. Both worlds change over time, and the warrior world adapts in steps to the civilian. It follows it, however, at a distance. The distance can never be closed, for the culture of a warrior can never be that of civilisation itself.[32]

Whatever other purposes are served by the military, it must remain a credible fighting force. If it cannot continue to fight and win our nation's wars, including the warlike operations inherent in peacekeeping operations and the new missions dictated by the war on terrorism, its reason to exist is in doubt.

Notes

1. Portions of this chapter first appeared in the September 1999 issue of *The World & I* and are reprinted with permission from *The World & I* magazine, a publication of the Washington Times Corporation.

2. Charles J. Dunlap Jr., "The Origins of the American Military Coup of 2012," *Parameters* 22, no. 4 (Winter 1992–1993): 2–20. This piece is very interesting for a lay audience to read. It was followed by his "Melancholy Reunion: A Report from the Future on the Collapse of Civil-Military Relations in the United States," *Airpower Journal* (Winter 1996): 93–109. A more detailed exposition of his argument, without the literary devices, is in his "Welcome to the Junta: The Erosion of Civilian Control of the US Military," *Wake Forest Law Review* 29, no. 2 (1994): 341–392.

3. For a detailed discussion of military readiness, see Sam C. Sarkesian and Robert E. Connor Jr., *The US Military Profession into the 21st Century: War, Peace, and Politics* (New York: Routledge, 2006).

4. Samuel P. Huntington, *The Soldier and the State: The Theory and Practice of Civil-Military Relations* (New York: Vintage Books, 1957), and Morris Janowitz, *The Professional Soldier: A Social and Political Portrait* (New York: The Free Press, 1971). For a post–Cold War perspective on these arguments, see Peter D. Feaver, "The Civil-Military Problematique: Huntington, Janowitz, and the Question of Civilian Control," *Armed Forces & Society* 23, no. 2 (Winter 1996): 149–178. Although the Huntington/Janowitz distinctions remain the most useful frames of reference for our purposes, those interested in a more detailed discussion of other perspectives should consult Giuseppe Caforio, *Social Sciences and the Military: An Interdisciplinary Overview* (New York: Routledge, 2007). With specific reference to

political science, see John Allen Williams, "Political Science Perspectives on the Military and Civil-Military Relations," in Caforio, pp. 89–104.

5. Huntington, *The Soldier and the State,* pp. 8–18. Although the focus here is on professional military officers, the authors are indebted to Robert B. Killebrew for pointing out that this traditional emphasis is becoming outdated. Senior enlisted personnel look more and more like junior officers in their talents and responsibilities and may be no less "professional" as Huntington uses the term.

6. Huntington, *The Soldier and the State,* p. 456.

7. Janowitz founded the Inter-University Seminar on Armed Forces and Society in 1960. Subsequently led by Sam C. Sarkesian, Charles C. Moskos, David R. Segal, and John Allen Williams, it continues to serve as an interdisciplinary "invisible college" of civilian and military scholars worldwide on issues relating to the interaction of armed forces and the societies they defend. Its journal, *Armed Forces & Society,* was also founded by Morris Janowitz and is a primary scholarly outlet for studies on civil-military relations.

8. Janowitz, *The Professional Soldier,* p. 422.

9. On the issues of gender and sexual orientation and their possible effects on military effectiveness, see Laura L. Miller and John Allen Williams, "Do Military Policies on Gender and Sexuality Undermine Combat Effectiveness?" in Peter D. Feaver and Richard H. Kohn, eds., *Soldiers and Civilians: The Civil-Military Gap and American National Security* (Cambridge, MA: MIT Press, 2001), pp. 361–402.

10. Thomas E. Ricks, "The Widening Gap Between the Military and Society," *Atlantic Monthly,* July 1997, 66–78, and Ricks, *Making the Corps* (New York: Scribner, 1997).

11. Ole R. Holsti, "A Widening Gap Between the US Military and Civilian Society: Some Evidence, 1976–1996," *International Security* 23, no. 3 (Winter 1998–1999): 5–42. Another perspective is that the gap is a good thing but should be managed. See John Hillen, "The Civilian-Military Culture Gap: Keep It, Defend It, Manage It," US Naval Institute *Proceedings* 124, no. 10 (October 1998): 2–4.

12. As a Navy flag officer remarked in a personal communication, "Most civilians equate military service with sacrifice—sacrifice of personal liberties, sacrifice of personal choices, and so on—and they are very much unsure that they could do the same thing, not to mention that the thought of possibly having to would be abhorrent to them."

13. Charles C. Moskos, "Short Term Soldiers," *Washington Post,* March 8, 1999, p. A19.

14. See Charles C. Moskos, with John Sibley Butler, *All That We Can Be: Black Leadership and Racial Integration the Army Way* (New York: Basic Books, 1996), for a positive interpretation of the US Army's attempt to create a "race-savvy" (not race-blind) force that maximizes combat readiness.

15. See Charles C. Moskos, John Allen Williams, and David R. Segal, eds., *The Postmodern Military: Armed Forces After the Cold War* (New York: Oxford University Press, 2000), for a discussion of the many changes in relations between the military and society in twelve democratic states after the end of the Cold War.

16. Graphic reports of women soldiers who are maimed or abused as prisoners of war (POWs) would have an especially shocking effect on the US public, although the loss of two female sailors during a terrorist attack on the USS *Cole* on October 12, 2000, caused no greater outcry than did the loss of fifteen men in the same incident.

17. See Miller and Williams, "Do Military Policies on Gender," for detailed statistics on this issue.

18. Josh White, "'Don't Ask' Costs More Than Expected: Military's Gay Ban

Seen in Budget Terms," *Washington Post,* February 14, 2006, p. AO4. The policy permitting gay and lesbian members to serve so long as they "don't tell" is an institutional version of the personal policy most service members have followed for years. Most can think of military associates whom they knew to be homosexual, or strongly suspected them of being so, but it did not become an issue so long as it did not affect job performance. It did not occur to them to "ask." The continuing high number of discharges for homosexuality is attributed by the services to members "telling" so they can leave the service early.

19. Miller and Williams, "Do Military Policies on Gender."

20. These are the National Defense University (Washington, DC), the Naval War College (Newport, RI), the Army War College (Carlisle Barracks, PA), and Air University (Maxwell Air Force Base, AL). Each of these institutions has an outreach program to civilians involving conferences, publications, and participation in college functions.

21. Such a case is made in Sam C. Sarkesian, John Allen Williams, and Fred B. Bryant, *Soldiers, Society, and National Security* (Boulder: Lynne Rienner Publishers, 1995).

22. As Army chief of staff after Vietnam, General Creighton Abrams integrated Army active and reserve forces so thoroughly that it would be impossible for the Army to fight a major war without calling up the reserves (as President Johnson refused to do in Vietnam, lest it reduce public support for the war). National Guard forces, normally under the control of state governors, are part of this equation as well.

23. See John Allen Williams, "The US Naval Academy: Stewardship and Direction," US Naval Institute, *Proceedings* 123, no. 5 (May 1997): 67–72.

24. Sam C. Sarkesian, "The US Military Must Find Its Voice," *Orbis* 42, no. 3 (Summer 1998): 423–424.

25. Huntington, *The Soldier and the State,* pp. 459–460.

26. For an extended discussion of this issue, see H. R. McMaster, *Dereliction of Duty: Lyndon Johnson, Robert McNamara, the Joint Chiefs of Staff, and the Lies That Led to Vietnam* (New York: HarperCollins, 1997). This book was widely read in Washington in the wake of US military operations in the Balkans.

27. Unidentified leaks from the Joint Chiefs of Staff suggesting they had reservations about the military strategy do not count here. If they had such reservations, they failed to convince the proper civilian leaders in a timely fashion. It is as if senior military officials began to speak on the record only after they feared that the failure of the original strategy would be apparent to all. See Robert Burns, "Reimer Reveals His Views on Kosovo Strategy," *European Stars and Stripes,* May 27, 1999, p. 1. Whatever the details of an eventual cease-fire, the United States is likely to be militarily involved in the region indefinitely. On Iraq, see Thomas E. Ricks, *Fiasco: The American Military Adventure in Iraq* (New York: The Penguin Press, 2006), and Michael R. Gordon and Bernard E. Trainor, *Cobra II: The Inside Story of the Invasion and Occupation of Iraq* (New York: Pantheon Books, 2006).

28. As quoted in Harry G. Summers, *On Strategy: The Vietnam War in Context* (Carlisle Barracks, PA: Strategic Studies Institute, US Army War College, 1981), pp. 7, 25. These originally appeared in *CDRS Call* (July–August 1976). Summers wrote, "General Weyand was the last commander of the Military Assistance Command Vietnam (MACV) and supervised the withdrawal of US Military forces in 1973" (p. 7).

29. There is widespread agreement on this among those who study issues of military and society. See, e.g., Eliot A. Cohen, "Civil-Military Relations," *Orbis* 41, no. 2 (Spring 1997): 177–186.

30. *Korematsu v. United States,* 323 US 214 (1944).

31. See Sarkesian, Williams, and Bryant, *Soldiers, Society, and National Security,* pp. 160–162, for a discussion of the "three-military" idea. In this conception, the support forces can reflect society closely, whereas it is more problematic for regular ground forces and especially the elite and special operations forces to do so.

32. John Keegan, *History of Warfare* (New York: Alfred A. Knopf, 1993), p. xvi.

8

The Intelligence Establishment

AFTER THE ATTACKS ON THE WORLD TRADE CENTER AND THE Pentagon on September 11, 2001, the importance of an effective intelligence establishment is beyond dispute. This lesson was reinforced by intelligence failures prior to the 2003 invasion of Iraq. Accurate and timely intelligence, analyzed realistically and used properly, is an essential ingredient for strong national security. There are various types of intelligence, as indicated in Table 8.1.

The Director of National Intelligence

In the wake of September 11, the Congress established a bipartisan National Commission on Terrorist Attacks on the United States, more popularly known as the 9/11 Commission. It issued a public report on July 22, 2004, followed by two staff monographs on August 21 of that year.[1] Among the recommendations of the commission was the creation of a new post, the director of national intelligence (DNI), to replace the CIA director as the coordinator of the far-flung intelligence community. This recommendation was implemented by the passage of the Intelligence Reform and Terrorism Prevention Act of 2004, and a DNI was appointed.[2]

How the new DNI and his staff will coordinate the intelligence community is still being worked out, and it may take some time before new patterns of operation emerge. The CIA remains the primary intelligence agency and its director retains his important role in that community, but it is the DNI, not the CIA director, who briefs the president. The DNI is the principal national security intelligence adviser to the president.[3] The DNI relates as well to the National Security Council and the congressional intelligence oversight committees: the Senate Select Committee on Intelligence and the

145

Table 8.1 Types of Intelligence

- Human intelligence (HUMINT): Collected overtly or covertly by human agents

- Communications intelligence (COMINT): Collected from intercepting foreign communications, such as radios, the Internet, and telephones

- Electronic intelligence (ELINT): Information from intercepted noncommunications transmissions, such as radars

- Imagery intelligence (IMINT): Collection of photographic or other imagery (such as infrared signatures) from satellite and other sources

- Measurement and signature intelligence (MASINT): Encompasses seismic, radiofrequency, acoustic, optical, and other data

- Signals intelligence (SIGINT): A general term that includes COMINT, ELINT, and MASINT

- Open source: Public domain information, such as in the media or the Internet

Source: Adapted from Central Intelligence Agency, *CIA Today: Different Kinds of Intelligence.* Available at https://www.cia.gov/cia/publications/cia-today/ciatoday-06.shtml (accessed April 22, 2007).

House Permanent Select Committee on Intelligence. The role and importance of the DNI are evolving and are discussed further below.

The Intelligence Community

The term *intelligence community* is a general reference and includes all agencies (or components of such agencies) within the executive branch that deal with intelligence on some level. It refers to the gamut of intelligence agencies and services: the CIA; intelligence agencies organized under the Department of Defense, including the Defense Intelligence Agency (DIA), the National Security Agency (NSA), the National Geospatial-Intelligence Agency, and the National Reconnaissance Office (NRO); and the intelligence agencies within the Army, Navy, Air Force, and Marine Corps. The Federal Bureau of Investigation (FBI) has a particularly important role in counterterrorism and counterintelligence (that is, preventing the penetration of US institutions by hostile intelligence elements). After September 11 the FBI role shifted so that law enforcement considerations would not preclude effective intelligence efforts. The Department of Homeland Security (and the Coast Guard, which is now part of that department) has a growing capability in counterterrorism. The Drug Enforcement Administration and the Departments of State, Energy, and Treasury also have intelligence elements.[4]

There are several important intelligence agencies within the Department of Defense. The NRO is in the category of "offices responsible for the collection of specialized national foreign intelligence." Specifically, it is responsible for satellite reconnaissance used by the intelligence community. The NSA is responsible for electronic intelligence. It intercepts and monitors radio transmissions and other electronic communications (with particular attention to the Soviet Union in the past). The NRO and NSA are especially secretive, given their advanced capabilities. The latter has been under scrutiny by our European allies owing to suspicions that Echelon, the NSA's assumed (but unconfirmed) communications-intercept system, was collecting economic intelligence for the benefit of US corporations. The NSA denied such allegations and would not discuss the possible existence of such a system. More recently, it was revealed that the Bush administration tasked the NSA with intercepting phone conversations between persons in the United States and certain phone numbers abroad linked to terrorist networks. Although this seemed to many to be a good idea, others were concerned by the lack of judicial supervision of the program.

The Defense Intelligence Agency coordinates and controls Defense intelligence sources and agencies and provides the secretary the finished intelligence product required to carry out his responsibilities. The National Geospatial-Intelligence Agency produces strategic and tactical maps, charts, and other data necessary to support military weapons and navigational systems and deals with open-source as well as secret data, some of it collected by the NRO. The NSA and NRO, although within the organizational framework of the Department of Defense, are focused on national-level intelligence.[5]

The military's intelligence agencies—including Army, Navy, Air Force, and Marine Corps intelligence—exist at another level. Each has its own community that includes a variety of subagencies and sources. The service intelligence agencies focus on the battlefield intelligence necessary to support the individual services' tactical plans. This includes enemy order-of-battle information and analysis. Finally, some intelligence services are directly subordinate to unified combatant commands (see Chapter 6). Their purpose is to provide specific information on the command's area of responsibility (e.g., European Command, Southern Command, and so on). In so doing, they serve their own particular departments, services, and commands, but they also provide input into the total intelligence effort through the intelligence community.

Intelligence relationships and responsibilities are difficult to control, a problem magnified by the fact that each intelligence agency and service has its own mind-sets and loyalties. These can affect the intelligence produced, although intelligence is usually passed on to the agency requesting it (the "consumer"). Any distortions in the intelligence process are of concern, given the importance of accurate intelligence for national security and the civil liberties implications of a process that has the potential to become enormously intrusive. Of course, effective intelligence is always likely to be intrusive, which makes problems of control and oversight more critical.

The DNI and other intelligence officials have relationships with the foreign intelligence services of US allies (as well as those of not-so-friendly countries, especially post–September 11). Close coordination is critical to certain clandestine activities, such as counterterrorism operations. They also share intelligence information for less dramatic but mutually beneficial purposes in support of international efforts and treaties.

In recent years, these relationships have been under considerable stress. The intelligence services of US allies were dismayed by the congressional investigations of the CIA in the 1970s, which revealed sensitive information and threatened the exposure of foreign sources. Contemporary revelations by investigative journalists, whether the reports are accurate or not, create embarrassing situations that do little to enhance the CIA's effectiveness. One result is that foreign sources become extremely cautious when dealing with US intelligence groups for fear of exposure. This tends to chill relationships between the US intelligence system and its foreign counterparts.

The key to developing a reasonably effective intelligence system is to create an environment of trust and confidence among national agencies, Defense Department intelligence services, and their subordinate services. The responsibility now rests primarily with the DNI. The structures are in place and the statutes spelling out the power and role of the CIA and other agencies are on the books, but there is a great deal of room for flexibility below the national level. How all of the pieces are brought together is not only a function of managerial efficiency but also of leadership, experience, and professional competence. Equally important, the DNI and other intelligence officials need to develop close relations with foreign intelligence agencies and services. To be sure, Congress, interest groups, and journalists have a great deal of impact on images of the intelligence community that can tarnish and erode US intelligence credibility. But this can be countered to some extent by a competent and skilled US intelligence service led by a DNI whose leadership skills are up to the task. It is too soon to tell how effective the new organizational structure will be.

The Central Intelligence Agency

The key agency for intelligence collection and analysis is the Central Intelligence Agency, established by the National Security Act of 1947. Its charter reads in part:

For the purpose of coordinating the intelligence activities of the several government departments and agencies in the interest of national security, it shall be the duty of the Agency, under the direction of the National Security Council . . . to correlate and evaluate intelligence relating to national security, and to provide for the appropriate dissemination of such intelligence within the Government using where appropriate existing agencies and facilities.[6]

Since its creation, the CIA has been vilified and praised, and some of its more public and legendary activities have raised questions about the proper role of intelligence in a democracy. The CIA has been the subject of many congressional investigations, and there is continuing concern regarding its role and relationship to other instruments of government, especially in light of the war on terrorism. Unfortunately, the contemporary debate is colored by political rhetoric and reveals much misunderstanding. As one scholar has written:

Much of the criticism of the CIA stems from the fact that its activities are secret. The public—and particularly the media—resent its being told that they can not know something. Silence is interpreted as arrogance. Moreover, when people do not know what an agency is doing, they assume it is either doing nothing and not changing with the times, or that it is doing something wrong.[7]

In any case, the requirements of national security have created dilemmas for the CIA, the president, and Congress. Although this has been true for decades, it is especially so in the new strategic environment. On the one hand, national security requires a wide range of intelligence activities, many of them necessarily secret and covert. On the other hand, some of these activities can stretch the notion of democracy and threaten individual rights and freedoms.

At the same time, questions have been raised as to what *strategic intelligence* means today. Should it include industrial espionage? How open should the CIA be now that the Cold War is over? How should the intelligence community respond to international terrorism? How we reconcile these demands yet still maintain an effective intelligence establishment is a persistent problem for the president, Congress, the CIA, and society at large. Issues with respect to covert operations are especially controversial.

Since 1947, many intelligence activities and covert operations—some successful, some not—have been attributed to the CIA. The publicized failures have caused a degree of embarrassment to the entire country, but the public is usually unaware of the successes. Many citizens are uncomfortable with secret intelligence activities, for secrecy, covert operations, clandestine activities, and certain special operations do not easily fit into the moral framework of an open system.

The fact that such problems persist was confirmed by the 1987 Iran-contra hearings (dealing with the Reagan-era scandal of diverting funds from arms sales to Iran to support antigovernment contras—who were rebels or freedom fighters depending on your point of view—in Nicaragua in possible violation of congressional restrictions), which refocused the public spotlight on the activities of some CIA operatives and threatened to expose several covert operations. Critics in Congress, the media, and the public were quick to dramatize and magnify the problems that emerged. Others placed them in a more favorable perspective, noting that virtually all intelligence activities were conducted according to law and in full cooperation with Congress, Iran-contra notwithstanding. Nonetheless, the debate over the intelligence system continues, and it is not likely to be resolved anytime soon—especially in light of the perceived intelligence failure to uncover the September 11 conspiracy beforehand or to note the absence of weapons of mass destruction in Iraq prior to the 2003 invasion. This reflects problems that persist from the Cold War as well as the new problems of the post–Cold War era.

The improprieties identified during the Iran-contra hearings, including the role CIA director William Casey may have played in diverting funds to the contras, were reminiscent of the outcry against the CIA a decade earlier, when Congress passed a series of laws limiting intelligence activities and establishing more rigid congressional oversight. This was a reaction to the CIA role in Watergate and other presumed domestic activities. The Church Committee hearings in the Senate (named for the committee chairman, Democratic senator Frank Church) and its subsequent report in 1976 detailed many congressional concerns.[8]

Control over the intelligence agencies continues to trouble Congress. In an effort to preclude such operations in the future, Congress and the executive branch have attempted to reconcile secrecy and oversight. One example was the Intelligence Authorization Act of 1991.

> [The act] represents the first significant remedial intelligence oversight legislation in more than a decade. The Act provides the first statutory definition of covert action, repeals the 1974 Hughes-Ryan Amendment governing notification to Congress of covert action, requires presidential "findings" for covert action to be in writing, and prohibits the President from issuing retroactive findings.[9]

The act has been considered a "reasonable compromise between divisive political issues and competing interpretations of constitutional responsibilities."[10]

The CIA also made some improvement in its relationship with Congress and its accountability to the public. "The DCI's Office of Legal Counsel now employs 65 attorneys to follow legal matters that relate to intelligence, compared to only 6 in the 1970s."[11] In addition, "the Office of Congressional Affairs relies on a half-dozen personnel (including more attorneys) to focus on legislative relations."[12]

The issue of CIA effectiveness was raised again in February 1994 with the revelation that career CIA officer Aldrich Ames and his wife were arrested for passing classified information to the Soviet Union and later to Russia. He was also charged with aiding the exposure and subsequent execution of several Russians working for the CIA.[13] Although his activities began in 1985, they were not exposed until 1994. This was a serious matter for the CIA, and it had repercussions for US-Russia relations as members of Congress from both parties raised objections to continuing US foreign aid to Russia.

Constraints on intelligence activities expanded during the Jimmy Carter administration, especially with respect to covert operations. The overthrow of the shah of Iran, the abortive hostage rescue in that country, and Soviet activities in Afghanistan drew a great deal of criticism regarding the capability of the intelligence services. Criticism also surfaced as to the quality of CIA intelligence immediately prior to the Gulf War in 1991 as well as the failure to predict the attempt by Soviet hard-liners to overthrow Mikhail Gorbachev that same year (and, for that matter, to predict the collapse of the Soviet Union). Later, a great deal of criticism was directed at the inability of technology to penetrate foreign political-social networks and provide on-the-ground analyses and judgments that can be done only by agents in the field.

Another review of the CIA was by the Commission on the Roles and Capabilities of the US Intelligence Community, led by former defense secretary Harold Brown and former senator Warren Rudman. This commission proposed in 1998 that the amount of funds used for secret intelligence be revealed and that the size of the intelligence agencies be reduced.[14] Given the nature of intelligence operations, however, it is doubtful that there will be a full public accounting of its funding—and in the present circumstances a reduction in funding to the intelligence community seems both unwise and unlikely.

The new administration under President George W. Bush quickly ordered its own review of the intelligence community, led by director of central intelligence (the CIA director) George Tenet. Under National Security Presidential Directive 5, Bush called for the DCI (i.e., Tenet) to form a panel of internal and external members to consider the structure and operations of the members of the intelligence community.[15] This panel was headed by Brent Scowcroft, chairman of the president's Foreign Intelligence Advisory Board and a former national security advisor. Early reports suggested that the panel would recommend major changes to increase the control of the CIA director over all sources of intelligence, including photographic and electronic.[16] Evidence is emerging that indications of impending terrorist attacks were picked up prior to September 11, but their significance was not realized owing to lack of coordination among and within US intelligence agencies.

In a perceptive article written before the September 11 terrorist attacks, one scholar noted the importance of rethinking the intelligence establishment: "Despite the apparent consensus on the need for change, recent intelligence failures suggest that US intelligence has yet to leave its Cold War–era methods and structure behind."[17] Better intelligence and counterintelligence are crucial for effective policy and strategy. But better intelligence and its effective use depend on an understanding of the nature and purpose of intelligence and the knowledge of the intelligence community. Any study of national security policy must include the relationship between the president and the DNI, the structure and purpose of the CIA and the intelligence community, the role of intelligence, the intelligence cycle, and the system that tries to integrate all of these into a coherent whole.

The director of the Central Intelligence Agency is an adviser, a coordinator, and a leader-manager—all in different settings and with different political and professional relationships. His main function is to be directly responsible for the control and operations of the CIA—the center of the intelligence system.

The CIA's organization, resources, and operations cover a range of activities and require a vast managerial effort. Actual figures are difficult to come by, but by one earlier estimate the CIA included "roughly 20,000 employees and a classified budget estimated to fall between $1.5 billion and $2.5 billion. . . . [The director of the CIA] is aided by a 237-member intelligence community staff that coordinates the activities and budgets of all the intelligence organizations."[18] Although "the bulk of the community's financial, human and hardware assets . . . actually reside in the Defense Department,"[19] the importance of the CIA as the lead agency in the intelligence community gives it a stature not enjoyed by other intelligence services.

The CIA is divided into four operational directorates, each headed by a deputy director: the National Clandestine Service, the Directorate of Intelligence, the Directorate of Science and Technology, and the Directorate of Support.

The National Clandestine Service (formerly the Directorate of Operations) "has primary responsibility for the clandestine collection of foreign intelligence." This includes human source intelligence, sometimes referred to as HUMINT. Covert actions are also part of this directorate's responsibility abroad, and domestically it handles "the overt collection of foreign intelligence volunteered by individuals and organizations in the United States."[20]

Within the Directorate of Intelligence, "the DDI [deputy director for intelligence] manages the production and dissemination of all-source intelligence analysis on key foreign problems. The DDI is responsible for the timeliness, accuracy, and relevance of intelligence analysis to the concerns of national security policymakers and other intelligence consumers."[21]

The Directorate of Science and Technology is concerned with "creating and applying innovative technology to meet today's intelligence needs."[22] Finally, the Directorate of Support handles services ranging from security and communications to training and financial management.

These directorates are at the center of the politics and turf battles that occur within the CIA. For example, those in the Directorate of Operations, now the National Clandestine Service, considered themselves to be the cutting edge and looked upon others as paper pushers and administrators. "We got all the action. We make the world go around. Satellites can't tell you what people are doing."[23] The other directorates offer their own assessment of their importance to the overall intelligence effort. Even within the various directorates, separate elements tend to develop their own style.

The Intelligence Cycle

The term *intelligence* refers to the final product that comes from collecting and analyzing all available information on foreign nations and their operations as well as information on group activities (such as terrorism) that are important for national security planning. To be useful, intelligence is dependent upon the intelligence services' fulfilling their responsibilities in what is called "the intelligence cycle" (see Figure 8.1), described as "the process of developing raw information into finished intelligence for policymakers to use in decisionmaking and action."[24]

The intelligence cycle is a useful way to conceptualize the intelligence process. It can be viewed as a process of five steps: (1) planning and direction, (2) collection, (3) processing, (4) analysis and production, and (5) dissemination. The *planning and direction* stage involves "the management of the entire effort, from identifying the need for data to delivering an intelligence product to a consumer."[25] The process usually begins with a request from the National Security Council (or another department or agency) to collect intelligence on particular subjects. Some of these requests may be for onetime intelligence, or they may be a standing request for continuing intelligence on a particular subject, such as the development of Chinese strategic missiles.

The next stage, *collection,* "is the gathering of the raw information needed to produce finished intelligence."[26] Intelligence collection depends on a variety of operations and activities, including private sources and

Figure 8.1 The Intelligence Cycle

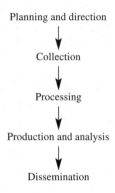

Planning and direction

↓

Collection

↓

Processing

↓

Production and analysis

↓

Dissemination

Source: Adapted from Central Intelligence Agency, *Factbook on Intelligence,* January 2001, p. 14.

media accounts as well as clandestine sources. The methods used for collection are technical, including satellite and electronic means, as well as human.

The large amount of collected raw intelligence must undergo *processing* to make it manageable. This step "involves converting the vast amount of information collected to a form usable by analysts through decryption, language translations, and data reduction."[27]

The *analysis and production* stage "is the conversion of basic information into finished intelligence."[28] It turns the processed intelligence into an understandable and usable form for authorized consumers. All collected intelligence is not of equal quality and so must be evaluated for reliability and credibility (i.e., as to the source of the information) as well as accuracy. The evaluation also includes the examination of other intelligence and sources that corroborate or contradict the original information.

Intelligence must be analyzed with respect to its relationship to US national security, that is, its importance with respect to enemy intentions, strength, and policy. This may be one of the most difficult parts of the process, as the accuracy and reliability of the analysis depend upon the experience, sophistication, and capability of the analysts. It is especially difficult to reconcile contradictory raw intelligence to give it meaning and make it useful for policymakers. A historical note: signals intelligence might have predicted the Japanese attack on Pearl Harbor, but it was not properly analyzed until it was too late. Similarly, hindsight shows several indications of the September 11 attacks that were missed or dismissed at the time as not important. It is sobering to wonder if there are similar indications available now that are also being missed owing to bureaucratic inefficiency, organizational politics, or otherwise beneficial restrictions on the intelligence community.

Production is an inherent part of analysis and refers to the shape and form of the final product. This is followed by the final step: *dissemination* of the final product to the end users and receiving feedback from them as to its utility.

Although this process seems to follow logically from one step to the next, in reality the steps are blurred. Furthermore, it is difficult to manage and coordinate the agencies and services involved in the cycle and therefore to provide accurate and timely information to the consumer. Because the finished product is based on the judgment of analysts, the human equation enters into the picture and, with it, the risk of mistaken judgments and human error.

In the final analysis, regardless of how good the intelligence is, how analytically precise, and how timely, the utility of the finished product depends upon the consumer. Although the use (or nonuse) of intelligence is beyond the control of those in the intelligence system, it is an inherent part of the cycle. This creates dilemmas for the intelligence system. On the one hand, there is professional pride in producing worthy finished products and critical intelligence estimates for national security purposes. On the other hand, if these products are not used or are ignored, then the system is more likely to become self-serving, enmeshed in meaningless operations, and committed more to bureaucratic efficiency than to the purposes of intelligence. It is not difficult to move from this stance to policy advocacy and even operations in the belief that the intelligence generated is correct and that policymakers should act on it in a timely fashion.

Covert Operations

The most controversial aspect of the intelligence system is covert operations. The CIA has not been the only agency involved in such operations, although it is the primary one. Interestingly, covert action as it is now defined was not initially identified as a role for the CIA. That responsibility was assumed under the provision that the CIA was to perform such functions affecting US national security as the National Security Council directed.

The term *covert operations* is a convenient label used to identify a variety of clandestine activities, ranging from propaganda and psychological warfare to paramilitary operations and espionage. Indeed, published reports from post–September 11 actions in Afghanistan revealed that the CIA has a significant paramilitary capability. In the words of one authority: "Covert action is defined in the US as the attempt by a government to influence events in another state or territory without revealing its involvement."[29] The concept also extends to political action and various forms of intelligence-gathering.

At the presidential level, however, the term *special activities* is used to identify a variety of covert operations. In Executive Order 12333, signed by President Ronald Reagan in 1981, special activities were defined as "propaganda, paramilitary and covert political operations. They specifically do not include the sensitive collection of foreign intelligence."[30] Thus the concept of covert operations can be assigned to virtually every part of intelligence activities as well as to some aspects of US military operations. Secret and/or concealed operations and activities are the stuff of covert actions.

The purpose of covert operations is to support the foreign policy of the state engaging in them. There are two major considerations: first, the state may be involved in operations that are best served by secrecy, that is, when the public and policymakers in the target state are not aware of such operations; second, the state may be involved in operations that are public yet wish to conceal or at least deny involvement. Paramilitary operations and political actions, for example, can be quite visible in the target state yet supported and encouraged by another state that does not want to be identified for any number of reasons, such as embarrassment or fear that the success of the operation would be jeopardized. The United States was involved in such operations against Cuba in the early 1960s during the John F. Kennedy administration. There are credible reports of sabotage and multiple attempts to assassinate Cuban leader Fidel Castro. Other examples include US involvement in Chile beginning in 1970 as well as a variety of activities revealed during the Iran-contra hearings in 1987.

As a result of the variety of covert operations in the 1980s, some of which were mismanaged, critics charged that such operations were contrary to democratic norms. In 1992, "a 20th Century Fund 'Task Force Report on Covert Action and American Democracy' blistered covert action as fundamentally at war with democratic norms."[31] Yet covert operations to some extent are an integral part of the intelligence system, often necessary to achieve foreign policy and national security goals. The nature of the United States—an open system committed to law and the norms of democracy and decency—places the US public in an awkward position with respect to certain secret operations. Moreover, official and government representatives who must engage in them are also placed in difficult positions regarding what is proper behavior and moral conduct. A complicating factor is that even effectively managed and "successful" covert operations, such as the 1953 coup in Iran that returned the shah to the throne or the arming of mujahidin forces in Afghanistan in the 1980s with surface-to-air missiles to help defeat the Soviet forces there, may have been unwise from a long-range perspective.

According to a former CIA intelligence officer, one of the major aspects of this "third option"—the alternative to military and diplomatic actions—is "paramilitary operations or the furnishing of *covert* military assistance to unconventional and conventional foreign forces and organizations."[32] The reasoning is that the United States was faced with a variety of "insurgencies" abroad since the 1970s, which may have threatened several US national interests. Thus "the bottom line on the decision to use or ignore the third option will not be based solely on the quality of intelligence, analysis, or organizations. The decision will be made by those who have, or lack, the will to pursue policy goals through techniques that have preserved our interests in diverse areas."[33]

The nature of covert operations and the dilemmas they create highlight the fundamental uneasiness that any open system has with secret intelligence operations and the intelligence system in general. Although recognizing the importance of effective intelligence, critics feel that the requirements of democracy—to abide by the rule of law, adhere to democratic proprieties, and protect individual freedoms and rights—provide ample reason to oppose at least some intelligence activities and to demand oversight and accountability. These criticisms are not confined to the United States, of course; Great Britain's MI-6 intelligence agency and Israel's Mossad have also been subjected to considerable, and often highly critical, outside attention.

Democracy and the Intelligence Process

Many serious problems face any democracy that maintains an intelligence system. Aside from the relationship of intelligence operations to less opaque institutions in the political system, there are moral and ethical issues that compound the legal and philosophical problems inherent in such operations.

Intelligence successes (especially covert operations) are rarely revealed, but failures are often made public to the embarrassment of the United States and to the detriment of foreign and national security policies. The media are quick to point out intelligence failures such as those revealed in the Iran-contra hearings, by September 11, and by the justification for the war in Iraq. It is only a short step from this view to the support of constraints and limitations that preclude a wide range of intelligence activities, thereby reducing national security capability. In addition, revelations can become the focal point of media coverage and book-length exposés that are difficult to counter without revealing sensitive information and sources.[34]

The issue of successes and failures aside, the legality of intelligence operations creates debate. As noted earlier, in the wake of Vietnam and Watergate, Congress and some interest groups attacked the CIA and the US intelligence system, creating an adversarial environment. Indeed, the second half of the 1970s may have represented the nadir of the US intelligence system and marked a significant decline in the US capability to pursue national interests. More than anything else, the Church Committee epitomized the adversarial approach to investigations of the CIA. According to one source, "consideration of the present mechanism of oversight and control of the US intelligence agencies should begin with the final report of the [Church Committee]."[35] The report identified the problems that arise between the executive and legislative branches in their efforts to determine the scope and purpose of intelligence activities.

A series of legislative acts evolved to regulate and control the CIA and other intelligence activities. To the earlier 1974 Hughes-Ryan Amendment were added a variety of procedures—from the expansion of congressional oversight to the Boland Amendments—that were at the root of the Iran-contra hearings.[36] These acts "created permanent oversight committees in both houses of Congress" with "principal budgetary authority over the intelligence agencies." In addition, statutory provisions were enacted to deal specifically "with the provision of information by the intelligence agencies to the two congressional committees"; new groups were added within the executive branch, including "the President's Intelligence Oversight Board, and . . . an Office of Intelligence Policy and Review within the Department of Justice."[37] Other procedures included the issuance of presidential executive orders, a process of judicial review, and the strengthening of the Office of General Counsel of the intelligence agencies with respect to intelligence activities.

The underlying assumption at this time was that Congress did not know about many intelligence activities, some of which did not comply with existing laws. In the majority of cases Congress was informed through its political leadership, yet many members of Congress would prefer to distance themselves from knowledge of such activities for fear that revelations, especially of failures, would harm them politically. Thus denial of knowledge can be a useful political position.[38] This was the case in the controversy that developed over the CIA mining of Nicaraguan harbors to prevent arms shipments to the insurgents in El Salvador.

One authority had harsh words over the attacks on the intelligence community in 1975 in a comment that resonates today:

> No country had ever subjected its secret organs of government to such open and extensive review. . . . The Congressional Committees conducted their business openly and publicly, adopted an adversarial, accusatory, and investigative approach, and, perhaps, inevitably and irresistibly, dramatized its proceedings. . . . It rarely acknowledged any legitimate reasons for clandestine operations and operated under the assumptions that most clandestine or secret activities were indefensible.[39]

This statement is a sharp reminder of the persisting problems inherent in trying to reconcile intelligence needs with the norms and expectations of a democratic political system. Furthermore, it shows the divisiveness generated within the national security establishment over the role of an intelligence community in national security policy. The critical issue, however, is the proper role of an intelligence community that must adhere to the rule of law while remaining an effective instrument of US national security policy. Answers to this dilemma are elusive and will continue to pose problems for the president and the national security establishment.

Another problem is the possibility of intelligence that is fabricated to favor a particular political-military posture or policy. This so-called cooked intelligence is closely related to policy advocacy: intelligence favorable to a particular stance is highlighted while contrary intelligence is ignored, downgraded, or allowed to slip through the cracks. Allegations of cooked intelligence and policy advocacy were leveled against CIA director William Casey with respect to US policy in Nicaragua.[40] More recently, the Bush administration has been criticized for trying to shape the judgments of the intelligence community on Iraq to support the administration's rationale for the 2003 invasion.

In any case, the credibility of the intelligence community rests primarily on its ability to avoid policy advocacy, retain institutional autonomy, and maintain professional competence. Any president who seeks intelligence as a basis for a preconceived policy position not only distorts the intelligence process but also erodes the credibility of the CIA and the US intelligence community. Moreover, for the CIA to take any position—other than the most objective analysis of intelligence and the pursuit of the requirements in the intelligence cycle—will surely raise questions of competence and have a chilling effect on intelligence professionals whose horizons are not limited by agency protectionism or bureaucratic loyalties.

Finally, the relationships among the DNI, the president, and Congress help determine the overall effectiveness of the intelligence community. It is important to note that how the DNI carries out his responsibilities to Congress, his relationships with individual members of Congress, and his relationships with the intelligence oversight committees have much to do with the ability of the president to play an effective role in the national security policy process. The trust and confidence between the DNI and the president remain critical, and an intelligence community without political motivations and purposes is at the base of this relationship. The DNI must therefore be responsive to the president's national security concerns as well as those of the National Security Council while fostering objectivity within the intelligence community and maintaining good relationships with Congress—a task that requires an individual of strong character and personality, as well as competence and integrity.

All these relationships shape the public's image of the CIA and the intelligence community. For example, Senator Church's 1975 comment that the CIA is a "rogue elephant" remains a pejorative used by many critics today. Although such a comment can hardly stand close scrutiny, especially now that the country is conducting a publicly supported war against terrorism, its imagery still has an impact on public perceptions of CIA conduct. Continuing problems with and suspicions of the CIA have been reflected in various publications: "There are limits to human trust and gullibility; intelligence manipulation has more often than not threatened national security and the prospects of world peace. Therefore, the question of the CIA's standing invites close attention—and it cries out for redress."[41] Another study, based on assessment of CIA records and interviews, concluded: "The CIA is one of the most important institutions in American society, one that Americans are fortunate to have. The agency has seen the country through the most difficult times in the nation's history, providing information that has kept the country out of a major war with the Soviet Union and helped the US win smaller ones, including the war in the Persian Gulf."[42]

There is another complicating factor regarding the role of intelligence in a democracy: in the post–Cold War period, some are calling for a redefinition of *intelligence*. According to one account, "the United States Congress and some intelligence experts are now increasingly prepared to use the CIA and the National Security Agency for economic intelligence-gathering."[43] It is argued that one of the most serious threats to US national security is in the economic sphere. Some in the intelligence field are resisting that tack, because moving into the economic intelligence field raises several legal and ethical questions. To whom should the CIA make economic intelligence available? All of the major US corporations? How ethical is it to pry economic secrets from friendly powers, even though they may be attempting to do so from us? Would such an intelligence effort require reshaping of some elements of the CIA? What effect would this have on the willingness of US allies to cooperate? And no matter how *intelligence* is defined, how is the US government to handle the problem of intelligence-sharing with an expanded NATO alliance that includes former enemies?

Others have argued that more effort should be placed on gathering political intelligence in the third world. Only by such efforts will the United States understand internal political realities and be able to choose more intelligently what groups and individuals to support.[44] In any case, the twenty-first century brings with it several questions, not only about the proper role of the CIA in espionage and intelligence-gathering but also about its role in a democracy and the issue of secrecy and covert operations.

Conclusion

In summary, the dilemma of how to maintain an effective intelligence institution in an open system is a continuing one. There are no easy answers in the search for the proper balance between security and civil liberties. Developing an acceptable relationship, delineating proper boundaries and roles, and maintaining a dynamic and continuing assessment begin with the president and his leadership. He must be cognizant of these problems and recognize the need to maintain the moral and ethical credibility of the intelligence function. How this is translated and projected into the intelligence community rests with the leadership of the director of national intelligence and is affected by the president's trust and confidence in that person. Equally important, the most effective intelligence in an open system requires an enlightened Congress and public.

The difficulties involved in maintaining an effective intelligence establishment in an open system are complex:

> To presume, however, that democracies must rigidly adhere to strict application of law, even to the point of self-destruction, is the height of immorality. Equally presumptuous is the view that democracy should take no action unless a clear and present danger exists. . . . To wait until there is a clear and present danger may be too late. Even if it is not too late, waiting for the outbreak of conflict may place the open system in an extremely disadvantageous position, considerably raising the costs of effective response.[45]

Yet at the same time it is imperative that the intelligence establishment function within existing laws and regulations. With proper oversight and skilled personnel, there is no reason to believe that the CIA cannot function in this way and be effective. This might require more effort, a more flexible system of regulations and procedures, and a more understanding Congress and public. It may also mean that the opinion makers, Congress, and the media must understand that the CIA belongs to the US public and serves it and the democratic system. But "the enduring irony of intelligence is its potential to destroy as well as to guard democracy."[46]

Notes

1. National Commission on Terrorist Attacks on the United States, *9-11 Commission Report*, July 22, 2004. Available at http://www.9-11commission.gov.

2. Office of the Director of National Intelligence, *The National Intelligence Strategy of the United States of America*, October 2005. Available at http://www.intelligence.gov/.

3. Information on the role of the DNI and the structure of the intelligence community is from a briefing of the Office of the Director of National Intelligence, *The Intelligence Community: Uncovering the Truth*. Available at http://www.intelligence.gov/.

4. Office of the Director of National Intelligence, *Members of the Intelligence Community (IC)*. Available at http://www.intelligence.gov/.

5. Ibid.

6. National Security Act of 1947, United States Statutes at Large 1947, vol. 61, pt. 1, 1948, pp. 496–505.

7. Ronald Kessler, *Inside the CIA: Revealing the Secrets of the World's Most Powerful Spy Agency* (New York: Pocket Books, 1992), p. 251.

8. For a detailed account of these matters, see Loch K. Johnson, *A Season of Inquiry: Congress and Intelligence* (Chicago: Dorsey, 1988). The volume is essential reading for those interested in the role and power of Congress in dealing with the US intelligence establishment.

9. William E. Conner, *Intelligence Oversight: The Controversy Behind the FY 1991 Intelligence Authorization Act* (McLean, VA: Association of Former Intelligence Officers, 1993), p. 1.

10. Ibid., p. 39.

11. Loch K. Johnson, "Smart Intelligence," *Foreign Policy* (Winter 1992–1993): 68.

12. Ibid.

13. See, e.g., Sam Vincent Meddis, "CIA Officer Charged as Spy," *USA Today,* February 23, 1994, pp. 1, 3A. Virtually all US news networks on radio and television carried the story during the week.

14. Tim Weiner, "Commission Recommends Streamlined Spy Agencies," *New York Times,* March 1, 1996, p. A17. This report is sometimes referred to as the Brown-Aspin Report, as Defense Secretary Les Aspin was originally selected to head the commission.

15. Vernon Loeb, "US Intelligence to Get Major Review," *Washington Post,* May 12, 2001, p. A3.

16. Walter Pincus, "Intelligence Shakeup Would Boost CIA: Panel Urges Transfer of NSA, Satellites, Imagery from Pentagon," *Washington Post,* November 8, 2001, p. A1.

17. Bruce Berkowitz, "Better Ways to Fix US Intelligence," *Orbis* 45, no. 4 (Fall 2001): 609.

18. David C. Morrison, "From Iran to Trade to Soviet Intentions, Can Government Intelligence Officers Keep Their Judgements Free of Politics?" *Government Executive,* June 1, 1987, p. 22. This was prior to the DNI.

19. CIA press release, June 2001.

20. Central Intelligence Agency, *Fact Book on Intelligence* (Washington, DC: Central Intelligence Agency, January 2001), pp. 9–10.

21. Ibid., p. 10. See also Central Intelligence Agency, *CIA Today: Overview of CIA's Organization.* Available at http://www.cia.gov/cia/publications/cia_today/ciatoday_04.shtml (accessed April 22, 2007).

22. CIA, *Fact Book on Intelligence,* p. 10.

23. Kessler, *Inside the CIA,* p. xxviii.

24. CIA, *Fact Book on Intelligence,* p. 13.

25. Ibid.

26. Ibid.

27. Ibid.

28. Ibid., pp. 13–14.

29. Roy Godson, *Intelligence Requirements for the 1980s: Covert Action* (New Brunswick, NJ: Transaction, 1981), p. 1. For post-9/11 information on Afghanistan, see Andrew Feickert, *CRS Report for Congress, U.S. and Coalition Military Operations in Afghanistan: Issues for Congress* (Washington, DC: Congressional Research Service, December 11, 2006).

30. Standing Committee on Law and National Security, American Bar Association, *Oversight and Accountability of the US Intelligence Agencies: An Evaluation* (Washington, DC: American Bar Association, 1985), p. 19.

31. Bruce Fein, "Official Secrecy and Deception Are Not Always Bad Things," *Insight,* June 8, 1992, p. 23.

32. Theodore Shackley, *The Third Option: An American View of Counterinsurgency Operations* (New York: Reader's Digest, 1981), pp. 6–7.

33. Ibid.

34. See Gregory F. Treverton, *Covert Action: The Limits of Intervention in the Postwar World* (New York: Basic Books, 1987), p. 222: "If the United States remains in the business of covert actions, even under restrictive guidelines, it will continue to confront the paradox of secret operations in a democracy. That paradox is, if anything, sharper now because of the changes in the American body politic, particularly relations between Congress and the executive."

35. Scott D. Breckenridge, *The CIA and the US Intelligence System* (Boulder: Westview, 1986), p. 230.

36. American Bar Association, *Oversight and Accountability,* p. 7.

37. Ibid. See also Johnson, "Smart Intelligence," and Breckenridge, *The CIA.*

38. American Bar Association, *Oversight and Accountability,* p. 1.

39. Breckenridge, *The CIA,* p. 249.

40. Stafford T. Thomas, *The US Intelligence Community* (Lanham, MD: University Press of America, 1983), p. 46.

41. Rhodri Jeffreys-Jones, *The CIA and American Democracy* (New Haven: Yale University Press, 1989), p. 251.

42. Kessler, *Inside the CIA,* p. 252.

43. From *Der Spiegel* (Hamburg), as reprinted in the *World Press Review,* March 1992, p. 9. See also Stansfield Turner, "Intelligence for a New World Order," *Foreign Affairs* (Fall 1991): 151–166.

44. See Turner, "Intelligence," pp. 152–153.

45. Sam C. Sarkesian, "Open Society: Defensive Responses," in Uri Ra'anan et al., eds., *Hydra of Carnage: International Linkages of Terrorism* (Lexington, MA: Lexington Books, 1986), p. 219.

46. Johnson, "Smart Intelligence," p. 69.

PART 3

The National Security System and the Policy Process

/

9

The Policy Process

THE POLICY PROCESS THAT EXISTS WITHIN THE US POLITICAL system is extraordinarily complex. Examining it is like trying to find the beginning of a spiderweb. The process might begin as a bureaucrat's idea, be triggered by a special interest group, or set off in a new direction by an adversary's surprise action. Yet the formal process appears to be reasonably straightforward when Congress goes into session and passes legislation. As a policy moves through the process, it sparks different reactions from many political actors—opposition, support, compromise. If a policy emerges at the end of this process, it may bear little resemblance to the original idea.

Scholars have studied the policy process using a variety of perspectives, approaches, and theories. Yet the process remains somewhat of a mystery or a "muddling through." As one authority has observed, "anyone bold enough to undertake a serious analysis of how policy is made in the American political system must begin with the realization that he is examining one of the most complex structures ever conceived by man."[1] In the final analysis, whether a policy is approved and implemented has more to do with political forces and the ability and attitude of leaders than with any formal process. As such, there are many ways to affect policymaking and the process and to shape policy. As noted several years ago by two prominent scholars, "the process is complex because of its many participants and because policy-making procedures cannot be divorced from all of the independent sources that shape decision makers' responses to situations demanding action."[2]

Identifying, tracing, and evaluating US policy are difficult for many reasons that evolve from the characteristics of the system (see Chapter 4). Such characteristics cause pluralistic ambiguity and obscurity out of a seemingly straightforward process. This is not the case for all policymaking, however. Policies that respond to crises or that evolve from a public consensus pass quickly thanks to the massive support. This explains the rapid approval of security and antiterrorist initiatives in the wake of September 11. Nonetheless, some of the most important policies respond to ambiguous situations or those in which there is little agreement on the proper course.

Complexity cannot justify neglecting the study of the US political system, of course. The effectiveness of the national security establishment and the success of the president in furthering his national security objectives depend on his ability to manipulate the policy process.

Several approaches and models may provide some order and manageability to analyzing the policy process. Nonetheless, we need some framework as a starting point to analyze the policy process. We begin by discussing several approaches that serve as an introduction to our approach.

Approaches and Models

There are many major approaches and models to study how policy is made.[3] The differing perspectives discussed here illustrate some of the inherent problems.

Although written in the middle of the twentieth century, two approaches evolved from the distinct philosophical views of C. Wright Mills and Robert Dahl.[4] Mills argued that policy is essentially in the hands of an identifiable elite (high-level bureaucrats, business interests, and the military) that is self-centered and does not necessarily reflect the public interest. Dahl argued that even though policy is made by elites, rarely are the same groups involved with the same degree of intensity; policy therefore emerges as a result of compromise. A third approach is based on the presumption that policy is made by the people through a variety of procedures (public opinion polls, elections, constituent pressure on elected representatives, and interest group advocacy, among other things); "power to the people" takes on a meaningful dimension in this context.

Another approach is *statism,* in which the state is the primary actor with its own characteristics, objectives, and goals. Little attention is given to institutions and agencies within the state or, for that matter, to individual and group behaviors. The *bureaucratic* approach is based on the assumption that policy is driven primarily by the bureaucracies in the government, which create a network of like-minded interests. The *organizational* approach is similar in that it assumes that organizational objectives and purposes drive policy. Thus the Department of State has a particular worldview and focus in determining policy, which can differ from those of the Department of Defense and Central Intelligence Agency. Often it is difficult to make clear distinctions between the bureaucratic and organizational approaches.

Another aspect relates to differing philosophies regarding policy procedures—the mechanics rather than substance. The *rationalist* view presumes that major policy alternatives are developed at the highest levels of government. Then, through a rational process, alternatives are studied, possible courses of action identified, the best course selected, and the policy passed through. In reality, however, policy is usually made incrementally, that is, in a piecemeal fashion. Furthermore, policy initiatives occur at a variety of governmental levels or even outside the government structure. Thus policy is often a piecemeal response to a particular situation, not part of a grand design. Furthermore, important policies can also result from citizen action, bureaucratic activity, corporate lobbying, foreign nations, or presidential initiative. This is not to deny that there are grander schemes, but even they result in piecemeal programs. In times of crisis, policymaking and the policy process follow the rationalist model more closely.

This study does not accept the elitist model; neither does it believe that people can directly control policymaking and the policy process. Although a relatively small group of persons ultimately approves and implements policy, the legitimacy and credibility of policy are usually based on a broad spectrum of the populace. The pattern was well described in the following passage: "Few, if any, of the decisions of government are either decisive or final. Very often policy is the sum of a congeries of separate or only vaguely related actions. On other occasions it is an uneasy, even internally inconsistent, compromise among competing goals or an incompatible mixture of alternative means for achieving a single goal."[5] The author went on to note that policy often emerges by "halting small and usually tentative steps" full of "zigs and zags." Policy can also become the opposite of what was originally intended. And finally, it is possible that "issues continue to be debated with nothing being resolved until both the problem and the debaters disappear under the relentless pyramiding of events."[6]

Is there a more systematic approach? *Policy phases* and *political dynamics,* as well as the dynamics emerging from the *total process,* help us better grasp the big picture. Also, politics nurtures elusiveness, placing an opaque gloss over the entire process. Addressing the role of military officers in the national security policy process, two scholars concluded: "Because of the variety of purposes among subordinate national security professionals and especially among career military officers, the game of politics remains intense, marked always by the presence of vested interests, interorganizational conflict, intraorganizational rivalry, and the elusiveness of a 'best' policy."[7]

Regardless, there are several policy phases, each affected by political actors and leading to an *interconnected process,* so that what occurs in one phase has an impact on the succeeding phases. Policymaking and the policy process are never-ending; established policies are constantly being revised and passed through the process.

Policy Phases

Scholars in this area often focus on the nature and character of the US political system, studying and identifying the various powers, how the public agenda is set, and the results. Some scholars identify how policy is injected into the decisionmaking process as well as the roles of agencies and groups in policy outcomes. Regardless, the approaches and perspectives have much in common regarding how policy flows through the process. Our framework for study is based on four phases: policy issue, approval, implementation, and feedback.

Policy issue refers to the shaping of a policy in response to a problem and its injection into the process. This includes the character of forces mobilized for and against. The important element is how policy is shaped and the source of the initiative—a bureaucracy, the Oval Office, interest groups, the federal court system, or Congress. This affects the environment and establishes the boundaries for struggle and compromise. The role of the media is especially important because of its ability to affect and even set the policy agenda.

Approval is the process by which policy passes through formal executive and legislative procedures. Rarely can a policy be effective without congressional approval, whether direct or indirect. Major policy implementation usually requires the commitment of financial resources, meaning congressional action. Debates in Congress, congressional hearings, interest group mobilization, and corporate lobbying are all part of the picture.

Implementation refers to how policies are carried out. The key is the bureaucracy. It plays the critical role in interpreting congressional and executive intent; it also translates intent into practical rules and regulations and applies them to the real world. Also included in this phase is how supporters and opponents affect how policy is interpreted and applied as well as attempts to revise policy.

Feedback is the response of those affected—that is, the policy impact—and how that response is injected back into the policy process, perhaps triggering new initiatives. The role of the media is also important as a transmitter of information and in focusing public attention on agendas determined by the media elite. The policy phases and their relationships are shown in simple forms in Figure 9.1.

Figure 9.1 Policy Phases

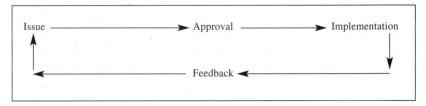

Congress and the Bureaucracy

Congress and the bureaucracy are critical political actors in the policy process. Congress has a constitutional role (see Chapter 10), broadened through oversight as well as constraints and reporting requirements it has imposed on the president and the national security establishment. Although this broader role is a relatively new development with respect to foreign and national security policy, it has always been the case with respect to domestic policy.

The bureaucracy, in contrast, finds its power in the executive branch and the president's constitutional responsibility to ensure the laws are properly administered and carried out. "In the end, the President is heavily dependent upon the ability of bureaucratic organizations for his own success."[8]

The Congressional Factor

The organization of Congress, congressional staffs, and constituent links are important elements of the policy process. Congress operates on the basis of standing committees. Those with the most seniority in the majority party chair the most important committees (Ways and Means, Appropriations, Budget, and Armed Services in the House; Armed Services, Foreign Relations, Budget, and Appropriations in the Senate). Furthermore, the party leaders are critical players (the Senate majority and minority leaders and the Speaker of the House and the House majority and minority leaders). Together with the committee chairpersons, they form an inner sanctum with its own politics and procedures. It is virtually impossible to push a policy through Congress without the direct or indirect support of the leadership.

This does not deny the importance of other members of Congress. The power base of individual members and their staffs makes each one a political entity unto himself or herself. Cooperation among members provides mutually beneficial political rewards, thereby strengthening individual power bases. But the fact is that much of the power of members of Congress resides in their staffs and constituencies. Staffs of twenty to forty spend considerable time strengthening and expanding the power base of each member. The bureaucracy and special interest groups are especially targeted. This all means that congressional staffs have a significant input on policy, and it broadens the political power of members.

The congressional focus is domestic, although that changes in times of international crisis. Most members and their staffs develop their knowledge and political power in the domestic area. Moreover, domestic politics is a direct link between policy and congressional behavior. Bread-and-butter issues determine whether a member of Congress is doing well, as well as his or her chances for reelection. This links the political fortunes of members to constituents, whose concerns are employment, economics, and general well-being. This is not to suggest that foreign policy and national security are unimportant, but in normal times they generally give way to domestic matters in the voting booth.

It follows that most interest groups are concerned with domestic issues, and members must be sensitive to them. The result is a link among a member of Congress, special interest groups, and bureaucrats. Once this link is forged, it provides a basis for advocacy and opposition. Such "iron triangles" create various power bases in the policy process.[9]

Both constituents and national interest groups pressure members. Sometimes a single issue, such as abortion, gun control, or the environment (so-called litmus tests), will impact the record and perceived performance of members. Several critics decry single-issue politics, arguing it distorts the legislative process. Many political action committees (PACs) are single issue–oriented.

Thus several important power clusters within Congress are critical components of the policy process. Although they have an important role in foreign and national security policy, they are especially prominent in making domestic policy.

The Bureaucratic Factor

The bureaucracy affects the way policy is carried out in the end, sometimes differently from the intent of Congress and the president. The bureaucracy also has an important impact on the kinds of policies that are injected into the higher levels of the process, whether civilian or military issues. The power of the bureaucracy rests primarily on its organizational character. The classic description is provided by Max Weber: "The decisive reason for the advance of bureaucratic organization has always been its purely technical superiority over any other form of organization. . . . Under normal conditions the power position of the fully developed bureaucracy is always overtowering."[10] Technical skills, administrative structures, and institutional loyalties are the bases for bureaucratic power.

The tendency for bureaucracies to protect their power base and responsibilities can distort policy goals. Bureaucracies often interpret policy according to organizational predispositions. In so doing they reinforce the existing state of affairs and resist major changes to the internal power structure. The dominance of the organization is reinforced by efforts to make the bureaucratic process a predictable routine. Individuality tends to become subsumed by the collective will of the organization. According to Carnes Lord, "a realistic approach to strategy at the national level must rest on two things, a careful distinction between the types or levels of policy-making and an appreciation of the bureaucratic faultlines that complicate and often defeat the development and implementation of national strategies."[11]

Also reinforcing the power of the bureaucracy is its influence over the emergence of policy. Power clusters within a bureaucracy, most identified with a particular organizational ideology, reflect a bureaucratic mind-set that accepts only those policy goals and procedures reinforcing the organizational posture. Policy that is generated within the organization or its subunits is vulnerable to the action and influence of gatekeepers, or the individuals with decisionmaking power over what is submitted to the higher policymaking levels. They control the flow of information, including recommendations, suggestions, and plans for policy and procedures. Items that do not fit the organizational setting and goals rarely find their way into the policy process.

In the final analysis, it is difficult to change the bureaucracy or persuade it to accept anything other than the existing state of affairs. Even once a policy is implemented, it is difficult to persuade the bureaucracy to change direction. Indeed, the tendency is for the bureaucracy to justify the policy in the most virtuous terms and perpetuate as well as expand the commitment. In other words, established policy becomes legitimized.

National Security Policy and Process

Analysis of the national security policy process can apply the four-phase pattern described earlier, but the nature of national security and related issues shapes the policy process in several important respects. First, secrecy may be needed in order to respond to initiatives planned by an adversary. Second, in crisis or near-crisis situations, there is a need for speed. Third, in most cases national security policy must deal with external groups or foreign states outside the range of US laws. And fourth, the instruments for carrying out national security policy are the foreign service, the military, and intelligence agencies, many of which operate overseas. In summary, national security policy issues evolve out of external sources and necessitate responses by instruments operating outside the United States. This is the context in which one must view the political actors and characteristics of the national security policy process.

The policy phases as they apply to the national security process are intermingled and collapsed into a relatively narrow time span. In addition, power clusters are usually limited to a few high-level political actors at some distance from domestic constituencies. Information is limited and often unavailable to the public, Congress, and bureaucrats outside the national security establishment. In this environment the media play an especially important, and sometimes adversarial, role.

The president usually faces the dilemmas of national security policy. On the one hand, their sensitive nature may dictate quiet diplomacy and secrecy, including undisclosed use of military, diplomatic, and intelligence instruments to affect foreign states. On the other hand, the difficulties in conducting covert operations, maintaining secrecy, and explaining troop commitments after the fact challenge notions of fairness and ethical behavior in an open system. The need to maintain the appearance of normalcy often places the president, other government officials, and bureaucrats in the position of telling half-truths or not informing the public of impending issues. Some domestic opponents of the administration and/or its policies are quick to infer insidious intentions.

The most visible aspect of defense policymaking is the defense budget, which is approved under established legislative procedures in Congress. Although it is a tortuous process, it does provide opportunities for public discussion of national security matters. But the fact remains that the most serious issues are handled through a process that differs from the domestic process (see Figure 9.2).[12]

Conclusion

In normal times, the national security policy process is primarily, but not exclusively, the preserve of the president and the national security establishment. Although this extends to an inner circle of congressional leaders, the president generally has wide discretion in the use of military force. The primary instruments and agencies are under the direct control and supervision of the executive. Congress and the public depend on the president for information and for defining national security interests. But the president does not enjoy complete freedom. Indeed, he is considerably constrained in what he can do. In a time of diminished support for the president's policies, there will be increased challenges from Congress—as was the case during the Vietnam and Iraq wars.

There are several problems associated with developing and implementing national security policy and strategy. First, national security policy affects domestic policy. In many cases, the best national security policy can have a negative impact on domestic policy. For example, punishing an adversary through economic measures can have domestic repercussions, such as the 1980 grain embargo against the Soviet Union, which had a negative impact on US wheat sales. Similarly, national security policy and strategy can trigger domestic reaction, as with US involvement in Vietnam, Nicaragua, and Iraq. In another dimension, a determined president focused on domestic policy can be undermined if he is seen as ineffective on national security and foreign policy. Conversely, presidential effectiveness in national security and foreign policy can be eroded by ineffectiveness on the domestic front.

Second, national security failures are likely to become public and undermine the credibility of an administration. Yet many successes cannot be revealed, limiting the ability of the administration to generate support for some policies and strategies (see Chapter 8).

Figure 9.2 Differences in Policy Phases

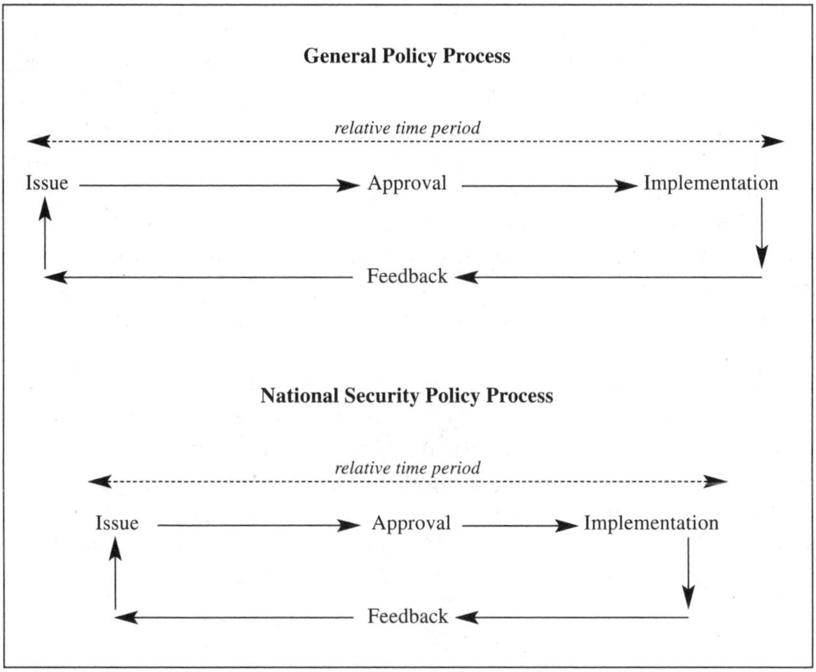

Notes: In addition to the differences in time elapsed for the two policy processes, the figure portrays the relative number of political actors involved. In the national security policy process, the circle of participants is considerably narrower than in the general policy process. It must be understood, however, that in a number of national security policy issues, the process follows a pattern similar to the general policy process. Much depends on whether the issue is a "crisis," whether it requires secrecy, and, in some cases, whether the president feels it is within his existing power to execute a certain policy without reference to Congress.

Third, inherent problems thwart the functioning of the national security establishment as well as policy formulation. The president must deal with the national security establishment, the bureaucratic power structure, and Congress to develop and implement his policies. In this respect, Congress is an important factor in oversight and finances, as well as its ability to affect public opinion. Moreover, PACs and other nongovernmental actors, including the media, play an important role. All of this complicates the development and implementation of an administration's national security policy.

Fourth, the environment and constituencies of national security policy differ from those of domestic policy. Foreign states and groups outside US boundaries are major players. Although there is considerable interdependence between domestic and national security policy, the focus of the latter is on external actors and on deploying US military forces. This is true despite new missions such as humanitarian assistance, peacemaking, peace-keeping, and a variety of other peacetime engagements.[13] In domestic politics, the focus is on a domestic constituency and domestic political leaders and political actors. Thus there may be interdependence between domestic and national security policy, but there are also basic distinctions in the constituencies and in the strategies and instruments to implement policy. The character and power of international actors and the resulting politics differ in most respects from domestic politics and political actors.

Fifth, the strategic landscape is characterized by new challenges and potential threats, many with no direct link to US national security and national interests. In such an environment it is difficult to design national security policy that can be understood by potential adversaries, allies, and the public.

In summary, the president is at the center of the policy process, yet national security is affected by institutional and interagency politics, individual mind-sets, domestic political and social forces, and foreign actors. Coherency in policy, cohesiveness in implementation, and credibility in commitment are presidential responsibilities. All this must evolve from a strategic vision articulated by the president and a leadership style that has a positive impact on the national security establishment.

Notes

1. John C. Donovan, *The Policy Makers* (New York: Pegasus, 1970), p. 16.

2. Charles W. Kegley Jr. and Eugene R. Wittkopf, *American Foreign Policy: Patterns and Process,* 5th ed. (New York: St. Martin's, 1996), p. 16.

3. See, e.g., Larry Berman and Bruce Allen Murphy, *Approaching Democracy,* 3rd ed. (Upper Saddle River, NJ: Prentice-Hall, 2001), pp. 544–548, and James M. McCormick, *American Foreign Policy and Process,* 3rd ed. (Itasca, IL: F. E. Peacock, 1998), pp. 271–274. For more on the incremental nature of the US decisionmaking process, see David Braybrooke and Charles E. Lindblom, A *Strategy of Decision—Policy Evaluation as a Social Process* (New York: The Free Press, 1970). On rationalist (or "rational actor"), bureaucratic, and organizational process models of decisionmaking and their impact on policy, see Graham T. Allison and Philip Zelikow, *Essence of Decision: Explaining the Cuban Missile Crisis*, 2nd ed. (New York: Longman, 1999).

4. C. Wright Mills, *The Power Elite* (New York: Oxford University Press, 1956), and Robert A. Dahl, *Who Governs?* (New Haven: Yale University Press, 1961).

5. Roger Hilsman, with Laura Gaughran and Patricia A. Weitsman, *The Politics of Policy Making in Defense and Foreign Affairs: Conceptual Models and Bureaucratic Politics,* 3rd ed. (Englewood Cliffs, NJ: Prentice-Hall, 1993), p. 347.

6. Ibid., pp. 67, 68, and 69.

7. Richard Thomas Mattingly Jr. and Wallace Earl Walker, "The Military Professionals as Successful Politicians," *Parameters: US Army War College Quarterly* 18, no. 1 (March 1988): 43.

8. Robert T. Nakamura and Frank Smallwood, *The Politics of Policy Implementation* (New York: St. Martin's, 1980), p. 171.

9. For a description of "iron triangles," see Theodore White, *The Making of the President, 1972* (New York: Bantam, 1973). See also B. Guy Peters, *American Public Policy: Promise and Performance,* 2nd ed. (Chatham, NJ: Chatham House, 1986), pp. 21–23.

10. H. H. Gerth and C. Wright Mills, eds., *From Max Weber: Essays in Sociology* (London: Routledge and Kegan Paul, 1984), pp. 214, 232.

11. Carnes Lord, "Strategy and Organization at the National Level," in James C. Gaston, ed., *Grand Strategy and the Decisionmaking Process* (Washington, DC: National Defense University Press, 1991), p. 143.

12. Examples include the policy process in the Bay of Pigs operation, the Cuban missile crisis, and the so-called secret wars in Southeast Asia. See John Prados, *President's Secret Wars: CIA and Pentagon—Covert Operations Since World War II* (New York: William Morrow, 1986).

13. Alexander M. Haig Jr., "The Question of Humanitarian Intervention," *WIRE* (Foreign Policy Research Institute) 9, no. 2 (February 2001).

10

The President and Congress

SINCE THE US CONSTITUTION WAS APPROVED, THE EVOLUTION of power has placed the president in the dominant position in foreign affairs and national security. This remains the case even after passage of legislation, such as the War Powers Resolution, designed to increase congressional power in these areas. Congress has an important role, but the nature of international security issues and the increasing complexity of international politics make it difficult for Congress to lead the nation or, for that matter, to check the president on policy initiatives, especially during a national crisis. In addition, presidential power has grown in response to increasingly complex US economic and social systems, which have indirectly reinforced the president's power in national security policy.

In the post–Cold War era, the traditional notion of national security is being questioned, and as a consequence of this and difficulties in Iraq and Afghanistan, presidential power in national security is undergoing change. Some prefer a stronger congressional role; others see a stronger presidential role. Given the uncertainty, it is small wonder that the powers of the president and Congress are being reexamined. It is too early to predict the long-term effects of the war on terrorism on this balance, but we expect that the president's role will be significantly challenged, at least in the short term.

In any case, "presidents are not kings." To understand the power that they wield we must distinguish between foreign and domestic affairs and specifically what kind of power over what kind of issue and in what circumstances and against the opposition of which other centers of power.[1] Put simply, the exercise of presidential power is a function of the president's ability to understand the nature of the political process, his constitutional power, the international climate, and the power inherent in his own leadership and skills as a politician. At the same time, Congress is increasingly reclaiming its share of responsibility.

179

The Presidential Power Base

Several factors complicate the policymaking process, including the nature of the presidency, public expectations, and the demands of the international security environment. These all have philosophical, ideological, and political overtones. National security goes beyond a strong military and the ability to support it financially. It includes confidence in leadership, staying power, national will, political resolve, and agreement on national security goals. In today's strategic and political climate, it also includes some agreement on the meaning of national security.

The president faces potential opposition from several quarters. Although the president and Congress cooperate in many ways on national security matters, disagreements over policy diverge from the established procedure. Special interest groups, segments of the US public, and allies may also oppose the president. Add to this disagreements within the administration and the national security establishment, and one can appreciate the extent of the problem, especially in the strategic landscape of the twenty-first century.

Aside from the Constitution, the institutional characteristics of Congress and the power of individual members create conflict. Constituencies, terms of office, and mind-sets all play a role. Incumbency strengthens the hand of many members of Congress. Incumbents perpetuate their power to ensure reelection, and few are defeated. Some members of the House of Representatives have been in office for more than thirty years. This has led some to view Congress as an institution of incumbents intent on maintaining office, overriding political party consideration and position on particular issues and categorizations.

The president can use several strategies to overcome opposition in Congress. Many are inherent to the office, whereas others depend on the effectiveness of presidential leadership style and techniques.

Every president, beginning with Dwight Eisenhower, has used a congressional liaison staff to establish and maintain relations. It targets key members in both houses, especially potential allies. The staff keeps the president informed of congressional power clusters and the general mood and recommends tactics to develop support for presidential initiatives. Similarly, the staff keeps members informed about presidential initiatives.[2] Although the liaison staff is usually concerned with domestic issues, national security policy and defense issues are also important.

Other tactics for developing support include bargaining, threats and intimidation, and rewards. For example, the attempt by Congress to invoke the War Powers Resolution over US involvement in the Gulf in 1987 was the focal point of much presidential maneuvering. This ultimately led to a compromise in which the president was simply expected to inform

Congress of developments. The president must be cautious in following certain tactics, however, because Congress can react negatively to extreme pressure from the White House and can undermine the president's domestic and foreign agendas.

The president can decide that the best means to implement national security policy and strategy is to distance himself from Congress and provide minimum information. He can thereby maintain a degree of flexibility. The danger is that members of Congress, as well as the public, may perceive the president as out of touch and isolated from major policy decisions.

In a direct confrontation with Congress, the president can take his case to the people. In 1987, President Ronald Reagan used this tactic to develop support for financial aid to the contras opposing the Sandinista government in Nicaragua. Earlier, he took the case for Vietnam to the people, labeling US involvement as a "noble cause" and honoring those who fought there. Other presidents have adopted this tactic when faced with congressional opposition to important presidential initiatives.

In 2007 President George W. Bush used public speeches, news conferences, and radio addresses to oppose congressional limitations on his freedom of action in Iraq. Indeed, with the 2006 election of a Congress controlled by the Democratic Party, congressional oversight of presidential actions in Iraq and Afghanistan began in earnest, with the Democrats determined to bring US troops back from Iraq on a strict timetable. By mid-January 2007 the Congressional Research Service had prepared an exhaustive study, a compilation of previous congressional attempts to restrict the presidential war-making power by restricting funding and by other means, that could serve as a handbook for future attempts.

The president must also provide a strategic vision for Congress and the American people. Critics of President Bill Clinton felt that there was no clear strategic vision articulated by the Clinton administration.[3] This was seen in the apparently muddled response and misjudgments associated with US involvement in Somalia, where eighteen US soldiers were killed in an engagement in October 1993 (the subject of the popular film *Black Hawk Down*).[4]

The president has an advantage in dealing with Congress in the national security arena, however, because the sources of intelligence, the basis of policy and strategy skills, and the operational instruments are centered in his office. For example, the president's cabinet, presidential advisers, national security staff, and the national security advisor are reinforcing resources of power. Even though expanded congressional staffs are important, the presidential power base—the Departments of Defense and State, the military advisory system, the Central Intelligence Agency, and the National Security Council and its staff—is dominant. Congress must rely on presidential sources for much of its information about national security.

President George W. Bush's efforts to prosecute the war on terror and to depose the Saddam Hussein regime in Iraq provided a dramatic episode in the ongoing struggle for power between the executive and legislative branches of government. The Bush administration put forth an ambitious and controversial agenda for expanded presidential power, including warrantless surveillance of Americans' international telephone calls and e-mails; detention of suspected terrorists as enemy combatants without prompt access to legal counsel or protection of the Geneva Convention; extraordinary renditions of terrorist suspects to foreign countries where barriers against torture were weak or nonexistent; and, against the grain of a US Senate majority led by Republican senator and former POW John McCain, efforts to prevent the application of a congressional ban on torture during interrogations by US intelligence and military personnel. A number of these issues arising between the September 11 attacks and the end of Bush's second term in office would ultimately have to be resolved by the courts.

The attempt of the Democratic Congress elected in 2006 to have a greater say in the conduct of the war in Iraq, at the expense of traditional presidential prerogatives as commander in chief of the military, is an important national security issue with both policy and political dimensions. The Congress and the president struggled not only over specific policies in Iraq but over the constitutional powers of each branch to affect those policies.

The Congress has formidable weapons at its disposal, such as the investigatory power and the power of the purse, included in the Constitution by the Founding Fathers to act as a check on the president. The president has different but similarly effective resources of power, flowing from his many constitutional roles and his ability to take action while Congress deliberates.

The most notable attempt to achieve a compromise short of a constitutional crisis was the 2006 report of the ten-member Iraq Study Group, cochaired by Republican James A. Baker III and Democrat Lee H. Hamilton and including prominent political figures from both parties and a former Supreme Court justice.[5] Both the president and the leaders of Congress gave lip service to this report, but neither's actions or proposals have been completely consistent with it so far.

Congress: The Legislative System

The relationship between the chief executive and Congress has been described as an "invitation to struggle," as Benjamin Franklin said of democracy itself. The US political system has a constitutional basis with separation of powers among the branches of government and resulting checks and balances (see Chapter 3). Although these characteristics are more pronounced in domestic politics and policy, they play an important role in national security policy, as well. To understand the congressional role in national security, we need to review the general features of the institution and the legislative process.

The Founding Fathers expected that Congress would be the most powerful branch of government. Although the president was given important powers in foreign affairs, those at the Constitutional Convention wanted to ensure that he would not dominate the policymaking process. The president would have power to react in emergencies, but Congress would determine war policy. Furthermore, the power of Congress in the legislative process and budget matters was to provide an effective counterbalance to the president.

The scope of congressional responsibilities has increased, yet Congress is finding it more difficult to respond because of the cumbersome legislative process and the characteristics of the institution. As S. J. Deitchman concluded:

> The Congress, representing diverse and often irreconcilable interests, is gaining long-term dominance over the Executive Branch. . . . Decision making in the interest of national security will become more difficult because the conflicts inherent in having a multiplicity of national-security decisionmakers will have the effect of inhibiting, delaying, or distorting decisions that must be made in a world demanding increasing perceptiveness of international trends and more responsiveness and coherence in adapting to or attempting to influence them.[6]

Nevertheless, effective national security policy depends on congressional support and public acceptance. Because of the representative role of Congress and its power over the purse, no successful president can afford to disregard Congress, isolate himself from the legislative process, or distance himself from the leadership in Congress.

The organization and functioning of Congress rest primarily on the committee structure. In the normal course of the legislative process, bills first go to committees, with the chairs of committees and subcommittees exercising considerable power in determining their fate. Chairs are appointed by the majority party in each house, with seniority being critical to appointment. The internal power system of Congress does not rest solely with the committee structure, however. Congressional leadership positions, such as the Speaker of the House and the majority and minority leaders in both houses, carry power that generally exceeds that of committee chairs. Reforms in the 1970s placed final approval of leadership roles in the party caucus and eroded the disciplined party system as well as the authority of the party leadership. Combined with the committee structure and the power of individual members, these reforms have fragmented power within Congress.

Power in Congress thus derives from a mixture of sources: power over the purse, the status of the membership, relationships with colleagues, the party, and the formal leadership offices. As long as constituent support remains high, members are powerful in their own right. Nonetheless, they can accomplish little by themselves; they are dependent upon colleagues to get things done. Every bill needs supporters, and this leads to constant interplay among internal forces seeking accommodation and compromise (or leading to confrontation). Thus even with internal power fragmentation, effective leadership in Congress is essential for the functioning of the legislative process.

Congress and the Executive: The Invitation to Struggle

Congress has a critical role in national security. According to Frederick Kaiser, "national security is not a simple set of well-integrated subject matters neatly arranged along a single, consistent policy continuum. . . . It is a complex set of diverse subject matters that cross into many different policy lines; these in turn raise different issues and concerns, institutional interests, and costs that affect congressional roles."[7] At least two important distinctions need to be made as to the president and Congress. First, the institution of the presidency rests on one individual who heads a hierarchical branch of government. The center of power is clear, and the responsibility for executing the laws of the nation is focused on the president. There is little overt fragmentation of power or responsibility. In Congress a different picture emerges. Not only is there considerable fragmentation of power within the institution, but also it is often difficult to place responsibility in any single member. Responsibility falls on Congress as an institution, making it possible for individual members to shift blame to the institution as a corporate body. This affords members a great deal of flexibility in taking political positions, and they can disclaim responsibility for any institutional outcome that is unacceptable to their constituencies.

Second, the president is the only nationally elected official (aside from the vice president, whose power is dependent on the president[8]). Thus only the president has a national constituency, with all that that suggests with respect to national security policy formulation. Individual members of the House of Representatives represent districts within states, many of which reflect narrow segments of the population. Furthermore, such districts can be dominated by one or two special interest groups. Senators, representing states, also reflect a small part of the total population. Even in states, the political power can rest with a handful of special interest groups.

Congress has attempted to overcome some of the disadvantages by referring to the corporate will of Congress. More often than not, this means little more than the will of a majority coalition, and if Congress is controlled by one party and the presidency by another party, the politics of the corporate will may result in partisan confrontation and gridlock. The differing constituencies between the president and Congress not only reflect different power bases and interests; they create different policy mind-sets and the conditions of struggle over policy, programs, and budgets.

The War Powers Resolution of 1973 is an important reference point. During the Richard Nixon administration, the Democratic Party held majorities in both houses of Congress. Congressional concern over US involvement in Vietnam and the erosion of President Nixon's power as a result of Watergate prompted Congress to pass the War Powers Resolution over presidential veto (many Republicans saw the issue as one of congressional prerogative rather than party loyalty). The resolution required the president to consult Congress prior to committing US troops to hostile action and periodically thereafter. The War Powers Resolution provides that "the President in every possible instance shall consult with Congress before introducing United States Armed Forces into hostilities or into situations where imminent involvement in hostilities is clearly indicated by the circumstances, and after every such introduction shall consult regularly with the Congress until United States Armed Forces are no longer engaged in hostilities or have been removed from such situations."[9]

After sixty days, US forces would have to be withdrawn unless Congress declared war or passed an extension. The president has an additional thirty days to withdraw all US forces if he states in writing that "unavoidable military necessity respecting the safety of United States Armed Forces requires the continued use of such armed forces in the course of bringing about a prompt removal of such forces."[10] The resolution also provided Congress the option of passing a concurrent resolution ending US involvement in hostilities. Such a resolution could not be vetoed by the president. But according to most authorities, "the War Powers Resolution cannot be regarded as a success for Congress. . . . All Presidents serving since 1973 have deemed the law an unconstitutional infringement on their powers."[11] Indeed, even when presidents consult Congress about military actions (as George H.W. Bush did before the Gulf War in 1991 and as George W. Bush did in initiating the war on terrorism after September 2001 and before involving Iraq in 2003), they do not specifically invoke the War Powers Resolution, and Congress is often brought into the process long after it can affect policy.

In his relationships with Congress and in trying to establish the necessary consensus and support for national security policies, the president must deal with a variety of power clusters within the institution. In the past, given party discipline and effective leadership in Congress, the executive could focus his attention on the Speaker of the House and the majority and minority leaders in both houses; today the president must also deal with other important members, especially key committee chairs. The increase in power clusters is especially pronounced in domestic policy, but it also affects national security policy. As some authorities concluded: "With more committees and subcommittees dealing with international issues; more staff and better information facilities at their disposal; more foreign travel by legislators and their aides; more groups, governments, and individuals trying to affect policy judgments, members of Congress, individually and collectively, have become less disposed to acquiesce in the president's initiatives. Some have even taken matters into their own hands."[12]

This was the case during President Reagan's second term in office. Congressman Stephen J. Solarz, for example, was directly involved in the Philippines as Ferdinand Marcos was deposed and replaced by a new government. In another example, Senator Christopher Dodd became the self-appointed spokesman for the Daniel Ortega government in Nicaragua when he visited and dealt directly with Ortega. Before the dissolution of the Soviet Union, members of Congress also visited and met with Soviet president Mikhail Gorbachev. In 1993, Senator Bob Kerrey attempted to take the lead in establishing US policy on prisoners of war/missing in action (POWs/MIAs) in Southeast Asia, visiting North Vietnam in a highly publicized tour to give credence to his effort. In a more recent instance, President George W. Bush was opposed in 2006 by prominent Senate Republicans, including John McCain (Ariz.) and John Warner (Va.), over the issue of interrogation tactics for enemy combatants held at Guantánamo or in other locations. Speaker of the House Nancy Pelosi visited Syria in 2007, against the view of the Bush administration, who wished to help isolate Syria.

If the president loses popular support, or if his initiatives appear vacillating and ambiguous, Congress is more likely to take the lead. For example, following the killing of eighteen US Army soldiers in Somalia in late 1993, Congress set conditions for US involvement there. Some observers noted the marginalization of the presidency in the matter. President George W. Bush maintained high levels of public and congressional support for the war on terror and the war in Iraq during his first term. But second-term setbacks, including rising US casualties in Iraq, drove down his popularity ratings and emboldened congressional critics of his war policies—including some Republicans. Public opinion thus provides the base upon which an assertive president who wishes to expand presidential power can succeed— or from which a president with low ratings can fall and lose control of his agenda.

Nonetheless, the public looks to the president for leadership in national security policy. This is true also for most members of Congress, even though they debate and criticize policy. Part of this acquiescence stems from a recognition that it is difficult for Congress to lead; it is better postured to react and engage in oversight. Another factor is the tendency for Congress to be cautious in initiating national security policy for fear of being associated with failures or controversies that might affect their popularity with constituents. The safest position is to keep some distance from national security policy until it becomes clear whether it is succeeding or failing.

This allows the president some latitude in initiating national security policy, although policy failures are easily attributable to him. Equally important, the complexity of national security issues, the changed external power relationships, and the difficulty the United States faces in trying to control external situations all mean success is never assured. Failure is no longer a remote possibility. One can understand, therefore, the reluctance of members of Congress to become too closely associated, too soon, with presidential positions on national security, save for crises. In the international order of the twenty-first century, this is even more so.

In summary, no president can ignore the congressional role in national security policy. Indeed, most successful policies depend on the bipartisan involvement of congressional leadership. Congress, sensitive to its responsibilities and protective of its prerogatives, demands an equal, if different, role in national security. Because there is ambiguity as to executive power in national security policy, the case is compelling for many members to be deeply involved. Ambiguity, shared power, institutional character, and the nature of national security policy thus create the basis for confrontation between the president and Congress.

The President, Congress, and the Policy Process

The president's ability to deal with Congress and to develop the support necessary for national security policy must be viewed from two dimensions: (1) the element of national security policy being considered, and (2) how the president's sources of strength can overcome the sources of conflict.

National security policy includes a range of subpolicies, from the defense budget and military manpower levels, to executive agreements and treaties, to covert operations. There is a degree of overlap between national security and foreign policy. This overlap has become considerable in the new strategic landscape, in which national security increasingly encompasses nonmilitary matters.

The president has a great deal of latitude in committing and deploying US military forces, especially in the early stages of a crisis. Nevertheless, congressional oversight and budget power restrict the president in the long term. Congress, ever sensitive to negative reaction from constituents about US force commitments, will make its reaction known to the president. To be sure, in short-term commitments where success appears clear, and even in longer-term commitments where there is a clear threat to the nation, as in the current war on terrorism, the president can enjoy popularity and support for his policies. But only he will be blamed for any failure.

Support for the preceding points is evident in the progression of the US decision in 2003 to invade Iraq, depose the regime of Saddam Hussein, and rebuild a stable and democratic Iraq. The US "shock and awe" military machine rapidly blew away the resistance of Iraqi conventional military forces, occupied Baghdad, and overthrew the government. The Bush administration proclaimed "mission accomplished" for Operation Iraqi Freedom on May 1, 2003, in a widely televised "photo op" for President Bush on a US aircraft carrier. To this point, Congress was fully in accord with presidential strategy. On the other hand, the postconflict reconstruction of Iraq was a mixed set of accomplishments and embarrassing setbacks. By the fall of 2005, increased public uncertainty about the stability of Iraq's new government in progress and about the clarity of the "endgame" for US completion of its political mission caused Congress to be much more assertive of its right to question the administration on war policy and military strategy. Congressional assertiveness on this issue increased greatly with the 2007 takeover of both houses of Congress by the Democratic Party. Even the congressional Republican leadership demanded more clarity from Bush about providing an exit strategy that would eventually replace departing US troops with Iraqi military, border guards, and police forces.[13]

An essential part of the national security policy process is reflected in debates over the defense budget and the final shape of the national budget. The annual budget process focuses attention on general issues of national security. This usually does not involve serious discussion and debate over strategy, but there can be exceptions (e.g., the George W. Bush administration, which initially decided not to increase defense spending but was forced by September 11 and other events to seek larger increases).[14] Yet budget debates are usually the most visible part of national security policy formulation, although specific events (e.g., September 11, the anthrax scare, the Iran-contra affair, the Marines barracks bombing in Lebanon, the Gulf War, Somalia, and Bosnia-Herzegovina) focus attention on specific issues that can lead to debate over national security policy. In 1993, the attempt by Clinton's secretary of defense, Les Aspin, to restructure the US military drew criticism in Congress and other quarters and figured in defense budget debates and in national security policy in general.[15] In addition, some issues have gone beyond traditional national security notions (e.g., the Clinton administration's efforts to lift the ban on openly serving homosexuals and to expand the role of women in the military). Such efforts can raise much criticism, with some observers linking issues to problems in national security policy.

Finally, some issues of US national security may be a continual source of debate, but there is continuity in important aspects of US policy, even in the new world order. The fight against terrorism, the close relationship with Western Europe, the concern over weapons proliferation, protection of freedom and nurturing of democratic systems, and control and reduction of nuclear weapons stockpiles will continue to be important priorities.

Well-established and accepted components of national security generally do not create controversial and difficult issues for the president. It is when the president wants to change direction, adds a new dimension to established policy, undertakes new initiatives, or fails to clarify national security policy that he faces opposition in Congress and among the public. In the past, national security included policies long understood by the US public, such as the role in NATO and other security arrangements. But the end of the Cold War has thrown such relationships into disarray, even irrelevance.

NATO, for example, recast its missions and identity from the end of the Cold War through the end of President George W. Bush's first term in office. No longer a political-military bloc aimed primarily at containment of the Soviet Union, NATO expanded its membership among states in East Central and Southern Europe and accepted responsibility for crisis management, contingency operations, and "out of the area" peacekeeping and stability operations, as in Afghanistan following the toppling of the Taliban.

Presidential Leadership and Party Politics

Although developing consensus and support in Congress depends on presidential leadership, the direct involvement of the president in national security policy has an immediate bearing on his leadership style. In this respect, popular support and party politics are important factors in developing effective presidential leadership.

The relative strength of the political parties in Congress impacts the president's ability to shape national security policy through the legislative process. If the same party holds the White House and Congress, the president will likely have the advantage thanks to party loyalty, as in the first six years of the George W. Bush administration. The fact that the president is also the leader of his party reinforces this. A skilled president can use this to strengthen his position on national security policy and strategy, allowing him greater latitude for initiating changes. President George W. Bush used his congressional majority to great advantage in moving forward his agenda in domestic and foreign policy until the Democrats won control of Congress in the 2006 election.

It does not always follow, however, that party support in Congress automatically leads to support for presidential initiatives. Policy and strategy must have a basis in the overall orientation as reflected in general posture, that is, in the mainstream political party orientation. Conversely, lack of party support does not preclude a president from developing consensus and support. As stated before, the ability of the president to use party support in Congress to his advantage is a function of his leadership skills.[16] But in general the advantage is with the president whose party holds both houses of Congress.

There is a close correlation between party support and popular support for the president. A perceived mandate from the electorate can translate into support in Congress. Even if individuals are opposed to presidential policies, they find it difficult to defy a popular president publicly. At the same time, erosion of popular support has a similar impact on congressional support, regardless of party alignments. Lyndon Johnson and Richard Nixon discovered that the hard way. President George W. Bush had extraordinarily high approval ratings in the wake of September 11. But by the fall of 2005 Bush's polling numbers appeared less favorable, in the aftermath of a protracted occupation of Iraq, inept responses to Hurricane Katrina, and criminal investigations of key White House aides.

Sometimes the president can make a personal appeal to members of Congress. By approaching individual members, appealing to their sense of propriety, stressing the need to support the president and the nation in critical national security issues, and even promising support on future issues, the president can overcome resistance to his policies. Lyndon Johnson was the acknowledged master of this tactic. A longtime member of Congress before he became president, Johnson personally knew most members and was keenly aware of congressional dynamics and politics. Making full use of this knowledge, he prevailed upon individual members to garner support for policies ranging from the Great Society to US involvement in Vietnam. But when popular support for the Vietnam War eroded, a similar erosion took place in the president's popular support—causing a reduction in his congressional support.

In 1993 and 1994, President Clinton and his inner circle, though not necessarily attuned to the ways of Congress, employed similar tactics as they cajoled, prodded, and coerced various members to support presidential budget initiatives and (unsuccessfully) health care reform. The administration was more effective in its second term, convincing Congress to support permanent normal trade relations with China and convincing the Senate to ratify an expansion of NATO to include Poland, Hungary, and the Czech Republic. In addition, the Clinton administration was not averse to compromises in developing support among the Democratic Party. Even some Democratic members of Congress opposed to certain presidential initiatives did eventually support him, proclaiming the need to save his presidency or the need to have this president succeed, overlooking policy-specific concerns.

If used cautiously and prudently, personal appeals can be an effective tactic. But if the president resorts to such appeals too often, they lose their effectiveness. Only when individual members of Congress feel that personal appeals are focused on special issues that have a direct bearing on presidential performance and are essential to effective policies will they tend to respond positively. In other words, the president can rapidly deplete the power associated with personal appeals.

In the final analysis, the president may need to stand up for what he believes rather than make concessions. President George W. Bush indicated in 2006 his intent to "stay the course" in Iraq and refused to set a timetable for withdrawal of US forces despite a wavering Congress and plunging public opinion polls. Ultimately it is the president who is held responsible for national security policy, regardless of the actions of Congress. The president "is the only person in the government who represents the whole people."[17] Yet some presidents revel in public opposition to Congress, whether it stems from perceived do-nothingism, incompetence, corruption, or deceptive congressional practices. Some members of Congress will go to extraordinary lengths to frustrate and oppose the president as a matter of political principle.[18]

Covert Operations and Secret Military Deployments

Covert operations are at the root of many controversial national security issues (see Chapters 6 and 8). Many times they reveal serious disagreements between the president and Congress and provide insights into the congressional role in national security issues. This was dramatically exposed during the Iran-contra hearings in 1987.[19] Even though many Republicans felt that the Democratic-controlled Congress tried to exploit the hearings in a partisan way, the matter was a valuable education on certain aspects of national security policy. The hearings revealed the character of covert operations and explained the role of Congress in the process. In addition, the logic of such operations was examined through Oliver North's dramatic testimony in support of the cause of the Nicaraguan contras, whom he portrayed as freedom fighters. The Iran-contra episode highlighted the struggles between the president and Congress over covert actions that had been ongoing since the end of the Vietnam War.[20] A review of this matter will clarify the root of these struggles.

In the late 1970s, on the heels of investigations into alleged CIA abuses and secret operations, a series of legislative bills was passed strengthening the congressional role in intelligence matters. Two of the most important features of this legislation were (1) the creation of permanent oversight committees in the House and Senate and (2) provisions for dealing with the relationship of intelligence agencies and Congress. Although these focused specifically on intelligence agencies, information, and the relationship to Congress, they had a direct bearing on the relationship of the president with Congress on sensitive national security issues. As such, they help identify the direction and substance of the president's ability to deal successfully with Congress on national security policy and strategy.

In 1976, the Senate Select Committee on Intelligence (SSCI) was created, "composed of 15 members drawn from the Appropriations, Armed Services, Foreign Relations and Judiciary Committees, and from the Senate at large. . . . The SSCI [has] full authority to oversee the activities of US intelligence agencies and to authorize their funding."[21] Two years later, the House passed similar legislation creating the House Permanent Select Committee on Intelligence (HPSCI). "The HPSCI consists of 16 members, with membership drawn from Appropriations, Armed Services, Foreign Affairs and Judiciary Committees, as well as from the House at large,"[22] and has essentially the same authority as the SSCI.

The Intelligence Oversight Act of 1980 imposed several reporting requirements on the CIA director (more formally, the director of central intelligence) as well as on "the heads of departments, agencies and other entities of the United States involved in intelligence activities to keep the committees fully and currently informed of all intelligence activities, including any significant anticipated intelligence activity."[23] Presumably this responsibility now transfers to the office of the DNI created by Congress during the administration of George W. Bush. The DNI is now the head of the entire US intelligence community, including the CIA and other organs of intelligence collection and analysis scattered throughout the government. The congressional oversight provision does not require approval of intelligence activities; it is primarily consultative and informative. But a committee member can frustrate any intelligence operation by threatening to leak it to the media; in 1987, a senator acknowledged using this tactic on more than one occasion.

The act requires reporting covert operations in a timely fashion, but it is not clear what that means in this context. President Reagan agreed to make a report within forty-eight hours, and legislation evolving from the Iran-contra hearings placed specific time limits on reporting requirements.[24] Moreover, according to some scholars, Congress does have important powers in reacting to or in limiting presidential initiatives: "It may cut off funding for foreign and defense policies. The Church Amendment to the appropriations bill for 1973 cut off US government support for the Republic of Vietnam . . . and the various Boland Amendments between 1982 and 1986 (named after Representative Edward Boland, D-Mass.) sought to prevent federal funds from being provided to the Contras in Nicaragua."[25]

Congress also passed legislation to restructure Defense Department special operations and low-intensity conflict. In 1986, Senators William

Cohen (R-Maine) and Sam Nunn (D-Ga.) sponsored a bill passed by Congress that mandated an assistant secretary of defense for special operations and low-intensity conflict; a US Special Operations Command, along with a Low Intensity Board as part of the National Security Council; and a deputy assistant to the president for national security on low-intensity conflict. These provisions triggered serious opposition within the military and the executive branch. Some skeptics doubted that the assistant secretary position would develop into an effective instrument for policymaking; others, from a different standpoint, feared that the position would become too influential, improving the bureaucratic clout of "special ops" compared to regular forces.

Covert operations differ from secret military operations in important aspects. In the latter (e.g., the invasions of Grenada and Panama, as well as certain actions in Afghanistan and elsewhere) the initial phase of US involvement was concealed for reasons of security and safety. Secret military operations are difficult to keep under wraps for any length of time and eventually invite public debate and congressional involvement. They are often used to demonstrate US policy. Covert operations, however, are special activities cloaked in secrecy that are intended to conceal US government involvement, among other things.[26] Such activities range from propaganda and paramilitary operations to the use of small special operations forces for extended periods.

The 1990s witnessed, according to some, a downturn in US intelligence performance and competitiveness, compared to the Cold War years. Interest in covert operations seemed less important for a Clinton administration whose guiding policy stance was the promotion of democratic "engagement and enlargement." Nevertheless, the Clinton administration did authorize some collaborative interagency work on counterterrorism, and prior to leaving office it highlighted the danger posed by Al-Qaida and other transnational terrorists. It took the dramatic events of September 11, however, to alter the latter Cold War and post–Cold War relationship between intelligence and policy—changing, as well, the climate for covert action.

In response to September 11, the Bush administration urged and Congress passed the USA Patriot Act in October 2001. The act expedited the sharing of information and analysis across the "red line" that had previously separated domestic intelligence gathered for the purpose of law enforcement and criminal conviction, on one hand, from foreign intelligence collected for the purpose of defeating foreign espionage, on the other. To some extent, this commingling of information from foreign and domestic surveillance had been foreshadowed by the traumatic cases of Soviet spies Aldrich Ames and Robert Hanssen. The CIA's Ames and the FBI's Hanssen passed many vital secrets to Moscow for years until they were unmasked and arrested in the 1990s. Each did considerable damage to

US security and caused the deaths of a number of US agents operating in the Soviet Union. Collaboration and teamwork between the CIA and FBI were required to indict and convict Ames, and Hanssen's case were closed by obtaining his KGB file from a retired Russian intelligence officer resettled in the West.[27]

Leadership and Policy

This study has stressed that the success of national security policy depends on the president's leadership and his relationship with Congress. The president has the key role, the constitutional authority, and much latitude in foreign and national security policy. His ability to build support in Congress, to control and direct the national security establishment, and to gain public acceptance of his policies is a direct function of his leadership style.

No single model of leadership is sufficient (see Chapter 4). Indeed, a variety of leadership approaches can establish a basis for legislative support, just as there are various tangible means by which the president can create and nurture congressional support. Yet certain principles of leadership are essential in dealing effectively with Congress. These principles, and the way they are applied, must lead to the development of trust and confidence. This in turn evolves from the perceptions of members of Congress that the president is in control of the national security establishment, that his presence permeates that establishment, and that he clearly articulates a vision of US strength and commitment. Furthermore, Congress must feel that the president's staff is knowledgeable, skilled, and supportive of his national security policy. Equally important, there must be mutual trust and confidence among the president and the national security staff, the military, and the intelligence establishment. Part of this evolves from the character, background, and experience of the commander in chief. In this respect, there is sometimes a decided gap between the president and the military.[28]

Much presidential strength is a function of personality and character. According to Erwin C. Hargraves and Roy Hoopes, "the point to remember in assessing the presidential power and the ability of a given president to wield it effectively—or perhaps even abuse it—is that the style and character of the president himself is every bit as important as the inherent power of the institution. And when we talk about powers of the presidency, we must consider three factors: a president's sense of purpose; his political skills; and his character."[29]

James Q. Wilson concluded, "The public will judge the president not only in terms of what he accomplishes but also in terms of its perception of his character."[30] To understand the power that presidents wield, we must make some distinction between foreign and domestic affairs, specify the kind of power and the issue, identify the circumstances, and consider the opposition from other centers of power. We must also understand how well the president understands the political process itself, how deeply he feels about achieving the goals being sought, and how much political skill he brings to the job.

Trust and confidence between the executive and the legislature are strengthened by several procedures flowing out of the Oval Office. Members of Congress, especially the leadership, must feel that the president is sincere about consulting Congress and accepts the coequal status of Congress and the president. Furthermore, Congress must feel that the president is providing timely and useful information on matters of national security. This especially applies to covert operations and secret military movements, even though Congress initially is only a recipient of information and not an approving body.

Furthermore, the president must make himself reasonably accessible to members of Congress, especially to the leadership. Members become frustrated if ignored by the president and feel that such a situation damages their ability to deal with their own issues. In such an environment, confrontation and disagreement between Congress and the president are inevitable. The idea of consultation is engrained in the two institutions. Consultation can pave the way for support, provide the perception of congressional power, and become a symbolic tool for fulfilling congressional responsibility.

Even if the president does all these things, he will not be assured of success; but he will have the most favorable environment in which to pursue such goals. Leadership is the key to relationships with Congress, and leadership must begin with an understanding of the important role played by Congress as well as an appreciation for the human motivations of individual members.

The performance of the Bush White House immediately after September 11 showed considerable skill in using the president's central position in the policymaking process for national security to advance his agenda. Bush chose a strategy of invading Afghanistan to dislodge Al-Qaida and the Taliban in 1991 and reprised his policy against Saddam Hussein in Iraq in 2003. Bush also signed a National Security Strategy in 2002 that highlighted preemption as an important option for dealing with terrorists or rogue states bent on attacking the United States. Congress, consistent with Bush proposals, reorganized the intelligence community by creating an interagency intelligence czar: the DNI. Congress also created the Department of Homeland Security as a cabinet-level agency incorporating more than twenty previously separate agencies and departments. George W. Bush did not win everything he sought from Congress in national security, but his scorecard for the first term alone illustrated what an empowered president with a congressional majority can accomplish.

On the other hand, even a Congress with a friendly majority cannot be taken for granted by presidents. An example was provided by an unusual episode in the spring of 2006, when the FBI staged a weekend raid on the offices of a US representative from Louisiana. The Democratic congressman was under investigation, although not then indicted, for corruption. The Republican leadership on Capitol Hill went ballistic—especially Speaker of the House Dennis Hastert, the key figure in pushing George W. Bush's past and future agendas through the House of Representatives. Although narrowly legal, the FBI raid breached a tradition of the separation of powers between the two branches of government and frayed relations between the executive and congressional wings of the Republican Party. President Bush moved quickly to freeze the materials seized in the raid and to set up a review process that would reassure Congress against further usurpation of congressional prerogatives.

Conclusion

The US system of government divides power and authority over national security policy among the various branches of government, especially between the president and Congress for policymaking. The president must exploit the potential power of his office to drive the national security agenda toward his and his party's preferred goals. The Congress must authorize wars and approve treaties, pay the bills for diplomatic and military actions, and hold accountable the performance of the executive by means of hearings, investigations, and reports. The president cannot simply respond to popular passions of the moment; neither can he simply ingratiate himself with Congress. Such behavior can only lead to the erosion of executive credibility and project a picture of a weak leader. Perceptions of presidential weakness at home can have serious negative effects abroad: leaders of states and terrorist groups may be inspired to resist US policy initiatives or, at worst, to attack US vital interests. The president is ultimately responsible for the formulation and implementation of national security policy and strategy. For most elements of his policy, he is in a position to receive the support of Congress and the public. But there are elements of policy in which he may have to stand alone, taking credit for its success but assuming full responsibility for failure. Unpopular wars or military interventions are the most controversial, and lonely, decisions. How these controversies play out within the national security system depends mainly on presidential leadership, congressional reports, and the periodic success of the president's policies.

Notes

1. Roger Hilsman, with Laura Gaughran and Patricia A. Weitsman, *The Politics of Policymaking in Defense and Foreign Affairs: Conceptual Models and Bureaucratic Politics*, 3rd ed. (Englewood Cliffs, NJ: Prentice-Hall, 1993), p. 145.

2. Richard A. Watson and Norman C. Thomas, *The Politics of the Presidency*, 2nd ed. (Washington, DC: CQ Press, 1988), p. 257.

3. This was rectified somewhat later in his administration with the publishing of an annual National Security Strategy report. See, e.g., *A National Security Strategy for a Global Age* (Washington, DC: US GPO, December 2000).

4. Eighteen special operations personnel (sixteen Army Rangers and two members of the elite Delta Force) were killed on October 3 and 4, 1993, in an attempt to capture Somali warlord Mohammed Farah Aideed. He was a general in the Somali army and trained in the former Soviet Union. He was also a student of Mao Zedong and studied the strategic perspectives of Sun-tzu. Many of these matters have to do with guerrilla warfare, but in October 1993 Aideed's background and training were hardly noted by any spokesperson in the Clinton administration or by the media.

5. The report of the Iraq Study Group is available on the website of the United States Institute of Peace, http://www.usip.org/isg/iraq_study_group_report/report/1206/index.html.

6. S. J. Deitchman, *Beyond the Thaw: A New National Strategy* (Boulder: Westview, 1991), p. 34.

7. Frederick M. Kaiser, "Congress and National Security Policy: Evolving and Varied Roles for a Shared Responsibility," in James C. Gaston, ed., *Grand Strategy and the Decisionmaking Process* (Washington, DC: National Defense University Press, 1991), p. 217.

8. The vice president's constitutional power as president of the Senate can be important if the Senate is evenly divided, as it was for a short time after the 2000 election.

9. The War Powers Act of 1973, Public Law 93-148, sec. 3.

10. Ibid., sec. 5(b).

11. Robert L. Lineberry, George C. Edwards III, and Martin P. Wattenberg, *Government in America: People, Politics, and Policy*, 5th ed. (New York: HarperCollins, 1991), p. 486.

12. George C. Edwards and Stephen J. Wayne, *Presidential Leadership: Politics and Policy Making* (New York: St. Martin's, 1985), p. 299.

13. On shortcomings in the US plan for postconflict stabilization following Operation Iraqi Freedom, see David C. Hendrickson and Robert W. Tucker, *Revisions in Need of Revising: What Went Wrong in the Iraq War* (Carlisle Barracks, PA: US Army War College, Strategic Studies Institute, December 2005).

14. See Tom Ricks, "Clinton's Pentagon Budget to Stand," *Washington Post*, February 7, 2001, p. 4. Any military leader who was surprised by this failed to read the tea leaves correctly. Military leaders' visceral dislike of Clinton personally and the Clinton-Gore military policies blinded them to the fact that the militarily hawkish Republicans were primarily *budget* hawks. If the military wanted to continue the status quo, only with more money, they should have hoped for a Gore victory.

15. Les Aspin, Secretary of Defense, "Bottom-Up Review," letter dated June 25, 1993, with enclosure on "Remarks" as prepared by Les Aspin, Secretary of Defense, at the National Defense University Graduation, Fort McNair, Washington, DC, June 16, 1993. Also see Representative Les Aspin, "The New Security: A Bottom-Up

Approach to the Post–Cold War Era," US House of Representatives, Armed Services Committee, October 1993.

16. This is not to suggest, of course, that all such lack of support is political in nature. For many, it is a matter of principle and genuine differences in policy preferences.

17. Merle Miller, *Plain Speaking: An Oral Biography of Harry S. Truman* (New York: Berkley Medallion Books, 1974), p. 445.

18. Ibid.

19. For details on the Iran-contra affair, see *Report of the Congressional Committees Investigating the Iran-Contra Affair* (Washington, DC: US Government Printing Office, 1987), and *Report of the President's Special Review Board* (Washington, DC: US Government Printing Office, February 26, 1987).

20. For a useful study, see Gregory F. Treverton, *Covert Action: The Limits of Intervention in the Postwar World* (New York: Basic Books, 1987).

21. Standing Committee on Law and National Security, American Bar Association, *Oversight and Accountability of the US Intelligence Agencies: An Evaluation* (Washington, DC: American Bar Association, 1985), pp. 7–8.

22. Ibid.

23. Ibid., pp. 11–12.

24. See "Text of the President's Letter on New Guidelines for Covert Operations," *New York Times*, August 8, 1987, p. 5. In this letter to Senator David Boren, chairman of the Senate Select Committee on Intelligence, President Reagan expressed his support for a number of committee recommendations on covert operations, including the following: "Except in cases of extreme emergency, all national security findings should be in writing. If an oral directive is necessary, a record should be made contemporaneously and the finding reduced to writing and signed by the President as soon as possible, but in no event more than two working days thereafter. . . . I believe we cannot conduct an effective program of special activities without the cooperation and support of Congress."

25. Donald M. Snow and Eugene Brown, *Puzzle Palace and Foggy Bottom: US Foreign and Defense Policy-Making in the 1990s* (New York: St. Martin's, 1994), p. 148.

26. Thomas Powers, *Intelligence Wars: American Secret History from Hitler to al-Qaeda* (New York: New York Review Books, 2002), pp. 391–398.

27. American Bar Association, *Oversight and Accountability*, p. 19. See Chapters 2 and 6 in this book for a more detailed discussion of unconventional conflicts and covert operations.

28. David Silverberg, "Clinton and the Military: Can the Gap Be Bridged?" *Armed Forces Journal International* 129, no. 3 (October 1993): 53, 54, 57.

29. Erwin C. Hargraves and Roy Hoopes, *The Presidency: A Question of Power* (Boston: Little, Brown, 1975), p. 47.

30. James Q. Wilson, *American Government: Institutions and Policies*, 5th ed. (Lexington, MA: D. C. Heath, 1992), p. 338.

11

Empowering the People

POPULAR CONTROL OF GOVERNMENT IS A FUNDAMENTAL
principle of democracy. The channels to establish, nurture, and expand
presidential links to the people, and from the people to the president, are
the media, political parties, and interest groups. These are usually considered linkage institutions, linking people to government and the president.
The media transmit images, information, opinions, and the attitudes of the
public to the president and vice versa. Media professionals also advance
their own agendas, even becoming active players in the policy process.
Political parties attempt to mobilize the people to win office and are the
main instruments for organizing Congress and controlling the legislative
agenda and process. Interest groups reflect and shape the attitudes, opinions, and policy positions of important segments of the public. Interest
groups are a means for individuals to have a voice and a channel for
expressing their preferences.

As a general rule, the public holds broad views on policy, rather than
informed opinions oriented toward specific issues. Some scholars are quick
to note that public views are usually inchoate and oversimplified. But public
views can be transformed into specific policy preferences as a result of
interest groups and political parties. Interest groups (i.e., every type of
organization that tries to achieve its goals by affecting policy choices and
policymakers) can be transformed into single-issue groups, mobilizing segments of the populace. In the course of this mobilization and policy advocacy, interest groups provide a means to pressure policymakers and elected
officials.

Public attitudes and the degree of public support are factors in influencing the relative success of a president's policies. This is the case not only in
domestic areas but also with respect to national security policy. Public support over the long run is necessary to the success of national security policy

and strategy. This is emphatically the case when the president seeks to place US armed forces in harm's way or when the public feels directly threatened, as on September 11. Additionally, how these relationships evolve into support for or opposition to the president and national security policy is an important factor in the study of the policy process.

In this chapter we place into context the role of linkage institutions and processes in making national security policy. First, we consider the public and its relationship to national security and defense policy formulation. Second, we discuss the enormous importance of the media and other means of communication on public attitudes and policymakers. Third, we review some important fundamentals about the role of political parties as linkage institutions: some feel that they are in decline relative to other components of the policymaking process. And fourth, we examine the power and influence of interest groups in the US political system generally, national security in particular.

The Public

The ability of the president to deal with Congress and develop support for his policies is contingent in large measure upon perceived and actual popular support. Much of this stems from the mandate the president receives upon election. For example, the 1980 Ronald Reagan landslide became the basis of the so-called Reagan Revolution. Reagan's decisive reelection in 1984 should have provided the basis for continuing and broadening the revolution, but in its second term the administration struggled to maintain momentum. In part, this was owing to a cabinet reshuffling that placed key White House adviser James Baker in the Treasury Department, breaking up the team that had so effectively advanced Reagan's agenda during his first term. The loss of the Senate to the Democratic Party in the 1986 elections also created difficulties for the Reagan program. But the president retained a high approval rating, even though many Americans did not fully support some of his policies.

Bill Clinton, winning the presidency in 1992, did so without a majority of votes, which meant that the president and his administration had to work hard to build credibility in foreign and security policy. This was reflected in several polls in the fall of 1993 in which less than a majority—and at times a bare majority—approved of his presidential performance. Public skepticism about Clinton as commander in chief was a result of ambiguous or vacillating policies in Somalia, Haiti, and Bosnia-Herzegovina, ascribed to the president's lack of military experience and possible distrust of the military profession. The controversy over homosexuals in the military added to the impression that he was tone-deaf on matters affecting the armed services.

George W. Bush was elected to the presidency in 2000 with an uncertain mandate, having lost the popular vote and won a disputed outcome in the electoral college that had to be resolved by the US Supreme Court. Until the terrorist attacks of September 2001, Bush appeared uncertain of his footing in national security and other policy issues. After September 11, however, Bush found his voice as a spokesman for national unity and resolve in the face of the attacks on the World Trade Center and the Pentagon. The Bush reaction to September 11 created a favorable impression of his leadership and ability to protect the nation from further attacks. His image as a guardian of US security held up during his reelection campaign of 2004, when he ran against former Navy Vietnam veteran and current Massachusetts Democratic senator John Kerry. Only in 2005, following a slow and ineffective administration response to Hurricane Katrina and a stalemated war in Iraq, did Bush's polling numbers on national security begin to drop significantly. This continued in 2006 as many in the US public disapproved of the continuing US involvement in Iraq. This was magnified by the Democratic Party control of both houses of Congress following the 2006 congressional elections.

The relationship between the people and the president, which is complicated by the media's role in transmitting information and setting the public agenda, is thus more intricate than many might suppose. As the nation's leading political figure, the president is expected to develop and implement policies that are binding on the entire populace. People respond favorably or unfavorably to his personality and political style and to the events that occur while he is in office. They also assess the president by the way he relates to particular groups, as well as social (religious, ethnic, racial), economic (business, labor), and geographical divisions of the population.[1]

If most authorities agree that public support is an essential part of presidential effectiveness, they disagree as to the specific nature of this support and its relationship to congressional support. How support is translated into presidential effectiveness and performance is subject to dispute. On the one hand, the public gives the president high approval ratings; on the other, it shows less than majority support for specific policies. The inconsistency is more apparent than real, since the public's perception of the president's reputation for success and integrity colors its judgments about individual decisions.

In addition, over time the support for the president and specific policies is affected by shifts in the public mood. Attitudes can change in the face of major policy issues or failures and because of a perception that the president has failed to live up to his promises or seems incapable of leading the nation. At times, the public may seem to act on a whim, shifting attitudes or suddenly dropping support for a president for no clear reason. Because of these intricate relationships, the president needs to be sensitive to the people and beware the fragile nature of public opinion.

This complex arena requires that the president respect the limits of public acceptance for national security policy and strategy. In times of peace and prosperity, it is difficult to energize the public and gain support for any policy and strategy that departs from the mainstream. In times of crisis and perceived national peril, the president can undertake broader initiatives for purposes of national security, defense, and intelligence. Following September 11, President George W. Bush ordered a review of US counterterrorism policies. Some of the proposals, such as arming civilian airline pilots and federalizing airport security, would have been unthinkable prior to the attacks.

Presidents must be especially wary of public sensitivity to secret and covert operations. Many Americans can understand the need for and accept them (albeit reluctantly), but there are limits. Moral and ethical boundaries exist for any operation. And even though the president has flexibility in national security policy and strategy, Americans expect an accounting of his decisions and actions, whether they are successful or not.

The Limits of Public Opinion

National security policy cannot be conducted solely according to public opinion. Public attitudes and opinions, except in crisis, are not geared toward specific national security issues. Moreover, there is some degree of secrecy involved in several contingencies, a double-edged sword: going public might justify the policy and strategy in the eyes of the people, but it would also telegraph US policy and strategy to adversaries, which could lead to failure as well as place our forces in danger.

The president cannot neglect public opinion on national security issues, however. Reaction after the event is an important component of the national security equation, part of the final accounting the public expects. The history of US public opinion in foreign policy demonstrates that presidents have the advantage of initiative and command of detailed and timely information. But the public, the Congress, and the media can define success or failure according to a different standard. The president and the government are sometimes preoccupied with the nuances and subtleties of small policy differences; the Congress, the media, and the public react more sharply to the impact of policy decisions.

From Nicaragua to Bosnia

The president and the national security establishment must be especially sensitive to the fact that interest groups and the media, as well as adversaries and allies, play an important role in influencing the US public. For example, in 1987 the Sandinista regime in Nicaragua made serious efforts to develop political networks in the United States to convince the public of the legitimacy of the Nicaraguan system. Nicaragua hired a US public relations firm to paint the best possible picture and to lobby Congress for favorable legislation. This is not necessarily an unusual or illegal tactic, as several foreign states hire local firms. During the Gulf War of 1991, the government of Kuwait hired a high-profile Washington, D.C.–based public relations firm to coordinate its public opinion campaign against Iraq in the United States. But this strategy is not always available to the United States: a US president or his advisers cannot gain similar access to media in a foreign country with a closed political system in order to publicize US views to the foreign peoples.

In the final analysis, the public usually follows the president's lead in national security policy and overwhelmingly supports any president who takes bold and responsible action, especially during a crisis. President Reagan's orders for the raid on Libya in 1986 and the earlier invasion of Grenada were favorably received by a majority of the public. This was also the case with President George H.W. Bush's initiative in the Gulf War in 1990–1991. With the conclusion of that war, Bush's approval ratings were above 80 percent, and for a time he was considered unbeatable in the 1992 presidential race—which he would lose to Bill Clinton. A decade later, President George W. Bush's approval ratings also reached 80 percent following the September 11 attacks, only to begin an accelerating slide.

But national security policy and strategy can lead to political disaster, such as the debacle at the Bay of Pigs in 1961, the failed attempt to rescue US hostages in Iran in 1979, Iran-contra in the mid-1980s, and possibly the current war in Iraq. Even though John F. Kennedy and Ronald Reagan retained high approval ratings, the credibility of both administrations suffered at home and abroad.

Some mistakes do lead to irretrievable disaster. In the wake of the failed Iran hostage rescue in 1980, the Jimmy Carter administration was voted out of office in November. The credibility of the Clinton presidency suffered as a result of several questionable national security and foreign policy efforts in Somalia, Haiti, and Bosnia-Herzegovina during Clinton's first term, even though a historic Israel-Palestine peace accord was signed at the White House in September 1993 to the applause of many. The George W. Bush presidency may be similarly impaired. When the public begins to lose confidence in the president's ability to respond effectively, or when it perceives that the president cannot respond positively to failure, credibility erodes, as does confidence in the president and US national security policy. This public attitude impacts the national security establishment and congressional attitudes.

In contrast to Clinton's indecisiveness in Bosnia during 1993 and 1994, the administration improved its performance by brokering the Dayton peace accords of December 1995, bringing an end to an exhausting civil war and ethnic cleansing. With NATO partners, the United States established the

Implementation Force (IFOR), a large and highly capable military peace-keeping and peace enforcement operation initially involving some 60,000 NATO troops. IFOR was succeeded a year later by the Stabilization Force (SFOR). Although scaled down from its original size, SFOR remained in place at the dawn of the twenty-first century. The Clinton administration also claimed victory in NATO's US-led bombing campaign against Serbia in 1999, undertaken to end the ethnic cleansing of Kosovar Albanians by Serbs. Even though the air campaign was a one-sided affair, its political effects were uncertain, and the US public was ambivalent.

The Media and National Security

The role of the media in national security policy derives from their important position in an open system. A free press is a fundamental principle of the US system. First Amendment freedoms often have priority, and individual freedom of speech and freedom of the press are two sides of the same coin. Indeed, most would agree that an essential ingredient of any open system is the role and freedom of the media.

This gives the media a degree of power in an open system not enjoyed by other groups and institutions. This is not a new development. In the nineteenth century, the French aristocrat and political essayist Alexis de Tocqueville observed that even with some limitations "the power of the American press is still immense. . . . When many organs of the press do come to take the same line, their influence in the long run is almost irresistible, and public opinion continually struck in the same spot, ends by giving way under the blows."[2] A modern version of this view is described by one scholar as "pack journalism."[3]

There is an inherent dilemma with respect to the role of the media and national security policy. On the one hand, some security policy must be formulated and implemented in secret. On the other hand, the media's mission is a direct challenge to that secrecy. In addition, media technology has changed so drastically that it has become an unwieldy global network of electronic, print, and visual sources of information of varying accuracy and integrity.

The quandaries posed to any administration are numerous. Some administrations have engaged in deception to avoid premature publicity of security strategy. In dealing with the Cuban missile crisis in 1962, for example, the Kennedy administration deceived the media and the public, at least initially (most eventually accepted the need for secrecy in this case). The Iran-contra hearings revealed the half-truths and deceptions of administration officials in dealing with Iran and the Nicaraguan contras.[4] Other administrations have openly tried to prevent publication of sensitive information.

The Pentagon Papers, stolen government documents that revealed aspects of the Vietnam War, were published widely by the media, even though much of the content was classified.[5] When the government brought a lawsuit, the court ruled in favor of the media on the grounds that the First Amendment prohibited prior restraint of publications by government.

The media perform important functions, which affect their role with respect to national security matters and the presidency. The media inform the public about what is going on in government, the country, and the world; they transmit information from political leaders both in and outside government to the public and political actors. The media are also used by political leaders and government officials to signal policy intentions and test reactions. In this sense, the media play a quasi-official role, knowingly or otherwise, and provide a channel to signal foreign adversaries and allies of government policy. For example, once the Cuban missile crisis became public knowledge in October 1962, President Kennedy and Soviet premier Nikita Khrushchev used the media as a means of negotiation: trial balloons were floated in the press, and at least one prominent US media personality was used as a go-between during a sensitive time in diplomatic negotiations.

The media business is highly competitive. Whichever reporter or corporate news structure breaks the news first has an important advantage. Furthermore, television news anchors are rated on physical appearance and their impact on the viewing public, which appears to be more a function of symbols and gimmicks than of substantive news reporting skills. This tends to place television news reporting in the area of entertainment rather than information. Understandably, television ratings are key indicators of commercial success, which influences the way the news is selected and presented. It follows that news events and images of political leaders are shaped by a variety of factors that have more to do with sales than with content.

The role and function of the media in an open system are further complicated by the emergence of investigative reporting and adversarial journalism. Investigative reporting is the aggressive pursuit of news; it is an intense uncovering of facts and is associated with a presumption of wrongdoing. Watergate blasted into the public consciousness thanks to two reporters from the *Washington Post* who uncovered the political connection of breaking into the Democratic Party offices in Washington, D.C.; it was directed by high officials in the White House, ultimately implicating President Richard Nixon in its cover-up.[6] The unnamed source for many facts in the story, "Deep Throat," was revealed only decades later during the administration of President George W. Bush.

Adversarial journalism assumes that the best approach is to view government officials, individuals, and groups under investigation as the enemy. In one sense, the targets are presumed guilty until proven innocent. Presidential press conferences reflect one aspect of adversarial journalism:

it is not uncommon for a reporter to ask the president questions beginning with a statement that presumes a blunder or lack of sincerity. Seeing themselves as adversaries, some reporters focus the spotlight on the president as well as on themselves. A similar dynamic appears in editorials, in the way the news is presented, and in the images of political leaders.

Investigative journalism and adversarial journalism serve a purpose in challenging government officials and policies. Indeed, according to some observers, the media emerge as the only visible counter to the government's national security policy and strategy—the only check on government excesses. Yet journalistic excesses occur as well owing to professional and commercial competition. These excesses can cause a well-conceived policy to fail and even endanger the lives of US officials and agents operating in foreign countries.

In addition, when investigative and adversarial journalism is combined with hidden political agendas, there is the potential for distortion of the political process by interest groups promoting partisan interests. The seemingly unending debate about the personal conduct of President Clinton and his possible impeachment was distorted by many people working in or with partisan media, talk radio, and the Internet. As the president's domestic situation was perceived to have weakened, his ability to conduct foreign and defense policy was impaired. President George W. Bush's administration and supportive television networks complained regularly about a liberal bias among the major news networks and their reporters. A poorly documented investigative report by CBS about President George W. Bush's military service led eventually to the early retirement of its stellar anchor, Dan Rather.

Investigative journalism is a necessary part of media coverage. The government should never be trusted to reveal its own shortcomings, especially corruption and illegality. Yet investigative journalism can become a feeding frenzy, and the willingness to rely on unattributed or dubious sources, combined with a subtle antimilitary agenda, can lead to biased reports. Even history can be reenacted within the framework of a morality play critical of the US armed forces. The combination of the Internet and cable news creates a pressure for immediacy of news and against careful fact checking of the kind that media professionals ought to do.

A complicating factor is the alleged liberal political leaning of media elites. Although it is debatable, there is evidence to suggest the existence of "a media elite with a particular political and social predisposition that places it distinctly left of center of the American political spectrum."[7] One of the most authoritative studies of the media elite concluded, "Today's leading journalists are politically liberal and alienated from traditional norms and institutions. Most place themselves to the left of center and regularly vote the Democratic ticket."[8]

Some journalists undoubtedly tend to see a world that is "peopled by brutal soldiers, corrupt businessmen, and struggling underdogs."[9] From this it is not unreasonable to conclude that such perceptions seep into news reporting, editorials, and the way political leaders are projected to the public. Of particular concern is that these perceptions can set the public agenda. Others have expressed concern that the media's most important potential bias is neither liberal nor conservative: instead, it lies in the media's control over the agenda of public policy debate:

> To control what people will see and hear means to control the public's view of political reality. By covering certain news events, by simply giving them space, the media signals the importance of these events to the citizenry. By not reporting other activities, the media hides portions of reality from everyone but the few people directly affected. . . . Events and problems placed on the national agenda by the media excite public interest and become objects of government action.[10]

Finally, some have questioned whether the allegedly liberal bias of reporters and commentators is offset by the conservative perspective of those who own media as opposed to those who work there. Wealthy entrepreneurs such as Rupert Murdoch and large media conglomerates including ABC/Disney are interested in maximizing ratings and audience sizes. This requires appealing to the centrist or conservative-centrist majority of Americans who channel surf or engage in Internet hopping for video and sound bites.

Reporting and a Political Agenda

The role of the media in a democratic society, the functions they perform, and their agenda-setting establish one set of important considerations. The political predispositions of the media elite establish another set. Combining the two creates a powerful profession, one that is able to set its own agenda and shape the image of reality according to its own views. Fortunately, there are some media professionals who place fairness and objectivity above personal agendas. In addition, the public can access a variety of news sources and has the opportunity to compare news reporting. For the concerned individual, analysis and comparison of news sources and the substance of news reporting can reveal misjudgments, errors, and political bias in reporters and editorial staffs.

A classic example of judgmental reporting was that of the Tet Offensive during the Vietnam War. In 1968, during the Buddhist New Year, Vietcong and North Vietnamese forces launched an offensive across South Vietnam in the hope of triggering a people's uprising. The US and South Vietnamese military reacted, with the enemy suffering a military disaster. Yet the media reported it as a military disaster for the United States. This version was accepted as true by many groups and was publicized by antiwar groups and others to such an extent that it became the common view. This perception played a role in prompting President Lyndon Johnson not to stand for reelection in 1968. As Peter Braestrup concluded: "The general effect of the news media's commentary coverage of Tet in February–March 1968 was a distortion of reality—through sins of omission and commission—on a scale that helped spur major repercussions in US domestic politics, if not in foreign policy."[11] There are other examples of distortions and predispositions coloring the news, but the coverage of Tet stands out for its massive impact on US politics and national security policy.[12]

In the 1991 Gulf War, the media, especially cable television, played an important role in informing an international audience and in shaping the images that impacted the political agenda and public perceptions of the war. "Daily, live coverage briefings from the headquarters in the Gulf and from the Pentagon via television and radio, reports from the 1,500 and then echoes—and there were lots of echoes from columnists, correspondents, consultants and assorted pundits in the United States and abroad—all served to keep the American public informed."[13]

Some critics contended that the US military's controlled press environment in the Kuwaiti theater of operations slanted coverage favorably toward administration policy. Yet there was serious criticism of television reporting from Baghdad, the enemy capital, by a CNN reporter who enjoyed exclusive access.[14] Many argued that his one-sided reporting undermined coalition efforts. Global television news also affected US and international perceptions, much of it based on television-driven strategy and policy. US forces exploited this for the purpose of "perceptions management" by staging amphibious exercises off the Saudi Arabian coast in full view of CNN cameras. Iraq's leadership was thus tricked into believing that an amphibious assault was imminent along the Kuwaiti border, and several Iraqi divisions were tied down awaiting an attack that never materialized.[15]

To say that the president must establish good working relations with the media is an understatement. But the president cannot control all of the news associated with national security policy and strategy. Neither can he control what members of the national security establishment say to the media. Confidential sources and leaks provide the media ample opportunity to gain access to classified material. Furthermore, partisan members of Congress can easily leak information to the media to thwart administration policy. To complicate matters, policy and strategy extend to the international arena, where a variety of sources and events can trigger exposure of US intentions and actions.

At times the president tends to court the media; although unseemly to traditionalists, media savvy is required for holding public office. Even before the advent of television, President Franklin Roosevelt masterfully exploited the media by means of carefully orchestrated fireside chats reaching nationwide radio audiences. Like it or not, the president must assuredly give the media their due, given the important role they play in an open system. It is best for the president to be confident in his national security posture, attuned to the dynamics of the national security establishment, and sensitive to the support of the public and Congress. These factors are not lost on the media. Yet it is also important that the president recognize the media's responsibility as a friendly adversary, remaining skeptical of government claims and actions until shown otherwise.

For their part, the media must be aware of the responsibility to provide objective and fair reporting as well as the risks of reporting classified information and prematurely disclosing policies and strategies that might jeopardize US national security interests. There is no clear line between the people's right to know and US national security interests. Indeed, some argue that there is nothing in the legal domain that makes the media the people's representative or that the public has a right to know anything. The media must therefore police themselves. Legal and political battles over the line between First Amendment freedoms and national security marked the second term of President George W. Bush, especially revelations about domestic spying on Americans without judicial warrants by the NSA.

One media responsibility is not to be a conduit for manipulation of public opinion by foreign adversaries, including state and nonstate actors such as terrorists. For similar reasons, they must not become the mouthpiece for domestic cranks and ideologues. Examples of manipulation of public opinion by foreign powers include atrocity accusations, demonizing the opponent, claiming divine sanction for one's global agenda, and hyperbole that inflates the stakes involved in a conflict ("the war to end all wars").[16] Examples of the unfiltered media transmission include accusations that the US Navy shot down TWA flight 800 in 1996 and the even broader coverage given to reports that the Central Intelligence Agency sold crack cocaine to inner-city neighborhoods in California to raise money for the anti-Sandinista rebels in Nicaragua.[17]

After September 11, experts debated whether US television networks ought to publicize video or audio tapes distributed by terrorists, especially by Osama bin Laden and other leaders of Al-Qaida. Media executives and reporters felt they were informing the public; critics feared that they were providing a global village for the distribution of Islamic extremism.

The Presidential Role

The president's leadership and personality shape the environment in which the media function, at least in terms of the national security establishment. Trust and confidence in the president and the perception of direction and initiative in US national security policy are key ingredients in shaping this environment. Even the best environment does not preclude political disasters and failures, but it does provide the president an opportunity to respond. The best presidents accept responsibility for failure while maintaining public confidence and trust—not an easy challenge but one that has been successfully met. The media's important role in this environment was recognized by Alexis de Tocqueville more than 150 years ago: "I admit that I do not feel toward the freedom of the press that complete and instantaneous love which one accords to things by nature supremely good. I love it more from considering the evils it prevents than on account of the good it does."[18]

All of this became more complex as cable television developed into a major information source, especially internationally, and the Internet and World Wide Web made "connectedness" across the boundaries of time, space, and territory a household word. A major characteristic of the strategic landscape is the role of global television.[19] Many conflicts and international problems become highly publicized, virtually dominating national security and foreign policy agendas. For example, the starvation and conflict in Somalia in 1993 became an international crisis thanks to the tragic images broadcast on cable television. Some in the United States bemoan the fact that national security and foreign policy have become video-driven in this way (the so-called CNN effect).

Another phenomenon is the growing popularity of talk radio. Talk radio has expanded to include discussions on any variety of domestic and international issues. It provides an information source and allows listeners to express personal views over the airwaves. In 1993 and 1994, talk radio became a focus for attacks on the Clinton administration. Liberals complain that talk radio is overwhelmingly conservative in its political slant; conservatives respond that talk radio reflects the grassroots feelings of Americans whose views are not represented by the mainstream press and television media or Hollywood.

A global communications network is in place and continues to expand thanks to the Internet, fax machines, portable phones, computers, copy machines, and satellite television. Indeed, the information age has become a reality, and governments must rapidly respond to events as international audiences are exposed to issues almost instantaneously. With its variety of information channels and news sources, the information age has reaffirmed the case that the media shape the political agenda.[20] If policymakers are not careful, the media will drive, instead of merely influence, the agenda for security decisions. Involvement in major conflicts can be driven by media conglomerates thirsting for news.

It is also the case that "the public's evaluation of the incumbent president rises and falls in accordance with cues provided by the media. The more prominent the coverage accorded critics of the president, the lower the level of presidential popularity will be."[21] To reduce the amount of criticism, the administration can limit information provided to the media and make determined efforts to manage the news or at least shift its focus. Spin-doctoring is a proven White House strategy. In the Clinton administration there were many attempts to mute the criticism over Somalia and Haiti: by focusing on television events such as Hillary Clinton's visit to Chicago for health care reform, conducting a trade fair on the lawn of the White House to drum up support for the North American Free Trade Agreement, and publicizing the need for free mammograms for women.

The George W. Bush administration during its first term succeeded in creating a media narrative that drove its Democratic opponents into defensive and reactive angst. This narrative positioned Bush as the chief warrior against terrorist and other threats to US security. Opponents of the president's way of waging this war on terror were depicted as lacking in patriotism or ignorant of the facts. The Bush White House also succeeded in commingling the war on terror with the invasion of Iraq to depose Saddam Hussein in 2003. Many Americans believed erroneously that Iraq had somehow been involved in the September 11 attacks. Others were convinced that Saddam Hussein would soon acquire a nuclear weapon and pass it to terrorists planning to attack the United States. The Bush military campaign against Iraq (Operation Iraqi Freedom) was thus accompanied by an effective public relations offensive that temporarily isolated Bush's critics and war skeptics as marginal or fringe opinions. Later, however, as public support for continued occupation of Iraq plummeted in 2005–2006, more survey respondents separated their feelings about September 11 from their sentiments toward Iraq—to Bush's detriment.

Public reaction to news good and bad reminds us that "the president is *the* big story in Washington."[22] By his presence and attention to certain events, he can (re)focus the media and the public. The president and the media have a competitive and cooperative relationship in national agenda-setting. The president requires media attention to explain and defend administration policy yet must remain wary of the media's ability to place that same policy under the microscope. The media need the president, a unique focal point for US national politics and a good source for boosting ratings. But the media must always remain alert to the possibility of White House spin-doctoring. This love-hate relationship was especially apparent during Bill Clinton's and George W. Bush's second terms.

Political Parties

The role of political parties needs little review here, but we will summarize the basic essentials. Parties are a vital connection between elected officials and the public; in theory they take positions on important issues of the day. Thus parties, more than politicians, can be held accountable for the passage of or failure to pass programs consistent with their views. Parties also relate to interest groups but perform a different function. Traditionally, US political parties, at least those that aspire to majority party status, have attempted to be large tents that accommodate a diversity of many intraparty factions and viewpoints. When the party's agenda is captured by one faction or wing, as with liberal Democrats in the 1970s and conservative Republicans in the 1990s, presidential hopes dim. Thus parties seeking to win Congress and the White House must promote issues that appeal to the middle of the electorate.

Some points need to be emphasized with respect to national security and parties. Often it is difficult to distinguish the role that political parties play in the national security policy process and in Congress because of the impact of interest groups. But the majority party in Congress has the power to control the legislative agenda and to select the leadership positions. At the same time, the party out of power is supposed to provide the "loyal opposition" essential to the nation's two-party system. It follows that a democratic system presumes that there is a viable two-party system at the national level and the periodic retransfer of power from one party to the other. This is also supposed to be the case for the president.

Thus in terms of national security, political parties are expected to offer viable alternatives when out of power and develop political resolve and strategic visions when in power. During the Cold War, it was generally presumed that partisan politics stopped at the water's edge—that both parties, regardless of their position, would support national security goals and, if necessary, mobilize party and public support for the president. Nonpartisanship did not always hold, of course, as partisan wrangling over national security issues has characterized every administration since Lyndon Johnson's.

In the post–Cold War period, however, with its ill-defined challenges and uncertain "distributed" threats, the Republican and Democratic parties are challenged to fix on a particular national security policy or clearly articulate a strategic vision.[23] The parties do serve as instruments to debate and mobilize party members in focusing on the shape of the military, the defense budget, and responses to immediate national security issues. During President Clinton's two terms in office, immediate issues included humanitarian crises and civil wars in Somalia and Bosnia, the NATO air war against the former Yugoslavia, and relations with Russia as well as the reduction of US military forces. President George W. Bush's agenda of security issues was driven by the attacks of September 11 and the wars in Afghanistan and Iraq. But most of the time, absent clear cases of threats to vital national interests, political parties tend to be driven by domestic issues: for President Clinton they were the economy, health care, education, welfare, and crime. The issues in the 1992 presidential campaign were a case in point.

As the presidential campaign unfolded in the first few months of 1992, debate became increasingly parochial. Voters seemed to care little about foreign policy, except when it impacted domestic issues such as unemployment and trade. The leading presidential candidates—including President George H. W. Bush, an avowed internationalist—pandered to this point of view. Given the self-involved mood of the country, the idea that the US military might function as a global sheriff was simply laughable. The United States was turning inward; the only question was how far the process would go.[24]

In 1992 Ross Perot emerged to energize voters disaffected by the major parties. With many voters alienated by the Republican and Democratic standard-bearers, the multimillionaire won 19 percent of the popular vote, precluding a majority vote for either Bush or Clinton. Bush supporters were quick to point out that Perot took more votes away from their candidate. Perot's use of the media and town meetings bypassed party structures. In the razor-thin presidential election of 2000 between Republican George W. Bush and Democrat Al Gore, Gore supporters resented the Green Party candidacy of Ralph Nader, who siphoned votes from Gore. Nader probably tipped the balance in some swing states such as Florida. Nader, vilified by congressional Democrats, nevertheless committed himself to further pursuit of his environment-friendly and antiestablishment agenda in the twenty-first century.

Public opinion data demonstrate that the two major parties are losing support. The number of voters who decline to express any partisan preference or declare themselves as independents indicates growing alienation toward the party organizations and their principal donors, whether corporate or other special interest groups. The higher visibility of third parties, such as the Reform Party, and its candidates, such as former pro wrestler Jesse Ventura, in the late 1990s reflected dissatisfaction with the partisan status quo at national and state levels. The early appeal of Senator John McCain in the 2000 Republican presidential primary and of former senator Bill Bradley in the Democratic primary suggested flagging enthusiasm for party establishments and their preferred candidates backed by prodigious amounts of so-called soft money. Ralph Nader ran for the White House in 2000 as an antiestablishment candidate, railing against both majority parties. At this time, it is hard to tell how third parties and independent candidacies will affect national security policy. Third parties had negligible impact on the 2004 presidential race in which George W. Bush was reelected running against Democrat John Kerry.

Interest Groups and Coalition Politics

Interest groups provide useful ways to mobilize the public and affect policy. Yet some groups can be more concerned with their own agendas than with serving the public good; some tend to serve their small group of leaders and do not necessarily seek out the public to mobilize votes and influence elected officials. In any case, interest groups serve an important purpose in an open system.

Interest groups have become increasingly important and powerful in the US political system. Part of this is in response to the vacuum left by the decline of political parties. The rise of single-issue politics (i.e., political activism based on one narrow issue, such as abortion) has reinforced the role of some interest groups. The performance of public officials tends to be judged according to that one issue—a litmus test—regardless of their record on other matters. Additionally, single-issue activism can be co-opted by broader-based interest groups to take on a particular policy or official. An example is the 1999–2000 controversy surrounding Elián González. He and his mother fled Cuba by raft in 1999; she drowned, but he was rescued off the coast of Florida. His relatives in Miami then fought a long battle against US immigration authorities and the Justice Department, going to court to prevent Elián's return to Cuba. Court decisions favorable to the Justice Department and a successful night raid to remove Elián from the control of his anti-Castro relatives were required to resolve the episode.

The emergence of PACs and soft money further complicated the relationships among the president, Congress, and interest groups. PACs have become major instruments used by corporations, business, and labor groups to influence elections and remain within the federal election laws. PACs donate to election campaigns and often become the vanguard in establishing political positions for larger groups. As expected, PACs have influence in Congress, partly because direct influence in the White House is difficult; also, the nature of congressional constituencies leaves members of Congress vulnerable to the influence of PACs. Soft money, that is, money not given directly to candidates but to issue development or under other auspices, indirectly, if not directly, supports the conduct of a political campaign. Both Republicans and Democrats have charged the other side with commingling soft and hard money, which is given explicitly and directly to the candidate. Only specialized lawyers fully understand the complexity of campaign finance law and of perennial "reform" efforts in rules affecting campaigns and lobbying. The public's eyes glaze over.

Think tanks of various political persuasions have established themselves not only as idea factories for political parties and candidates but also as political players in their own right. The reports and activities of think tanks can have political consequences and are used by interest groups to advocate their own policies. Yet certain think tanks are identified with partisan worldviews, whether liberal or conservative, such as the Brookings Institution (liberal) and the Heritage Foundation (conservative). The national security establishment as well as important political actors in the policy process can be, and has been, influenced by the research and publications produced by think tanks. In this sense, think tanks can serve, consciously or otherwise, as the basis for positions adopted by interest groups and political actors. Neoconservative pundits based in think tanks contributed much of the philosophical underpinning for the George W. Bush national security strategy, war on terror, and war in Iraq.

The fragmentation of power and the decline of central authority in Congress make it likely that the president will need to become involved in interest group politics. To develop support for legislation and promote consensus for national security policies, the president often must appeal to interest groups and form coalitions with them. Obviously, he seeks the support of groups most likely to favor his policies. For example, the president might turn to defense contractors and politicians in communities where military bases are located in order to build support for favored weapons programs and defense policies. Congress sometimes deliberately spreads defense spending for a new weapons system around as many states and communities as possible to maximize the political reward.

The underlying motivation for presidential involvement in interest group politics is that PACs, lobbyists, and other interest groups have significant influence on Congress, which is vulnerable to persuasion by external actors. In addition, there is a need for the president as well as Congress and the bureaucracy to respond to the growing power of organized interests to develop coalitions for supporting a policy and to thwart those opposed to a policy. The growing power and influence of interest groups was one major factor in establishing the Office of Public Liaison during the Gerald Ford administration. This office was created to help shape friendly relationships between the president and interest groups; its primary purpose is to mobilize support for the president.[25]

Interest groups also attempt to influence public opinion, hoping that public pressure will reach not only Congress but also the White House. For example, during the early 1990s, in the aftermath of the Clarence Thomas nomination fiasco and the Tailhook investigations, feminist groups and their political allies pressured the president and the Pentagon to prevent sexual harassment in the military. And throughout the 1990s, gay-rights groups, with a great deal of support in the Clinton White House as well as Congress, led efforts to sensitize the military chain of command to the problems of discrimination against, and harassment of, gays in uniform. The same groups monitored Defense Department performance and contributed to the revisions of policies affecting women as well as gays in the late 1990s, especially the department's antiharassment directives of 2000. The US political scene is full of such examples, covering issues from the environment and abortion to the Strategic Defense Initiative (Star Wars) and the defense budget.

Domestic and National Security Policies

Some would contend that interest groups have less of an impact in the national security arena than in domestic politics. The intermingling of the two areas, however, blurs the distinction between interest group activity and national security policy. For example, interest groups and PACs involved in the domestic economy invariably become involved in defense spending. In addition, social-issues groups have an impact on the federal budget and defense outlays by demanding spending on welfare and social programs and because of their belief that cuts in defense will help their programs. Unfortunately, few such groups make a serious effort to examine and analyze defense issues and strategy from a balanced perspective.

In some cases, the link between national security and domestic policy is straightforward. For example, it is difficult to boycott a state that imports US goods without causing some economic hardship at home. A case in point: during the Cold War, a decision not to sell agricultural products to the Soviet Union raised protests and triggered opposition by interest groups representing US farmers. Yet this was one method to respond to Soviet policies that threatened US interests. Similarly, restricting imported goods to protect domestic industries can have an impact on US relationships with states that are important to US security policy. In February 1994, for example, President Clinton lifted the trade embargo on Vietnam that had been in place for nineteen years, primarily to stimulate the US economy. POW/MIA groups and several Vietnam veterans strongly opposed such a move. Many interest group activities were seen in the intense campaign by the Clinton administration to pass the North American Free Trade Agreement (NAFTA) in 1993. Labor unions mounted massive opposition campaigns, whereas some business groups as well as congressional Republicans spoke out in support of NAFTA. The agreement was passed by Congress.

During President George W. Bush's administration, the connection between interest group politics and national security was evident in debates about control over illegal immigration. From the standpoint of national security, many advocated tighter border controls and more expedient deportation of illegals to their countries of origin. The governors of two southwestern states, Arizona and New Mexico, declared states of emergency with respect to loss of control over illegal border crossings from Mexico. On the other hand, immigration was also an issue that involved economic and social considerations and resonated with liberal and conservative interest groups. Some liberals supported President Bush's proposal for "guest worker" and amnesty programs that would legalize some previously illegal immigrants provided they met certain criteria. And some conservatives attacked Bush for not providing enough border security against possible infiltrators who could be terrorists or "coyotes" being paid to run terrorists and other illegals across the border. On the other hand, some business groups wanted cheap labor, and some humanitarian groups objected to immigration restrictions as denials of human rights.

Although most interest group activity is focused on domestic issues, some groups can have an important, albeit indirect, role in national security issues. These include church groups, friendship societies, cultural groups, and policy advocacy groups. Interest groups with concerns about national security can make alliances across ideological lines. An example is the coalition of liberal and conservative groups that warned against excessive zeal in prosecuting the war against terrorism. This ad hoc coalition defended US freedoms and included liberal groups such as the American Civil Liberties Union and conservative organizations such as the National Rifle Association. Others reacting to September 11 showed the diversity among US interest groups; some raised humanitarian aid, others rallied patriotic support for the president and nation, and still others clamored for improved security at airports and called for a housecleaning in the US intelligence community.

Other examples of interest group activity are aimed at the US role in the international arena. For example, human rights groups can affect US policy by publicizing human rights violations in other countries, which can lead to moral indignation at home, requiring some response. The events at Tiananmen Square in 1989 led to many demands for US sanctions against China. Amnesty International, which analyzes human rights activities, serves this purpose. Also, veterans' organizations have a similar impact on the use of US military forces overseas. Human rights groups helped publicize widespread ethnic cleansing and humanitarian abuses in Somalia in 1992, in Bosnia from 1992 through 1995, and in the Serbian province of Kosovo in 1999, and presumed excesses by the troops fighting the growing insurgency in Iraq.

Foreign countries also try to influence US public opinion and congressional views. "Large research and lobbying staffs are maintained by governments of the largest US trading partners, such as Japan, Korea, the Philippines, and the European Community. . . . Frequently, these foreign interests hire ex-representatives or ex-senators to promote their position on Capitol Hill."[26]

Bureaucratic Interest Groups

Informal groups and networks within the federal bureaucracy play a less visible but important role in influencing national security policy and strategy. Bureaucratic groups are active in defending parts of the defense budget, especially as part of the iron triangle that includes bureaucracy, defense contractors, and supportive legislators.

Within the administration, power clusters may prefer one policy and strategy over another. During the Reagan administration, there was a considerable amount of infighting regarding the proposed Intermediate Nuclear Forces (INF) agreement with the Soviet Union. On the one hand, some high-level military officers opposed INF, forming an implicit alliance with some members of Congress. On the other hand, at the highest levels of the State Department, there was considerable effort to reach an accord. During the Clinton administration, competing power centers doomed national health care. And pertinent to security issues, Joint Chiefs of Staff (JCS) chairman Colin Powell publicly expressed disagreement with others in the administration on the issue of military intervention in Bosnia. And a 1992 Clinton campaign promise to permit gays to serve openly in the military was strongly opposed by the members of the JCS shortly after Clinton assumed office in 1993. Clinton and the JCS finally settled for the compromise "don't ask, don't tell" policy.

In the early and middle period of the George W. Bush administration, there were clear policy differences between the State Department under Secretary Colin Powell and the Defense Department headed by Donald Rumsfeld. Rumsfeld and Vice President Richard Cheney formed a political alliance that left Powell frustrated on account of the Rumsfeld–Cheney willingness to act unilaterally as opposed to emphasizing consultation with allies. Rumsfeld's dismissive reference to "old Europe" (France and Germany) compared to "new Europe" (former Soviet states now incorporated into NATO and more sympathetic to the US position on Iraq in 2003) spiked diplomatic fevers across the Atlantic. Similar interagency frictions were apparent in the relationship between the vice president's office and the intelligence community between September 11 and the onset of the US military campaign against Iraq in March 2003. Cheney aggressively pressed the view that CIA intelligence needed to be more responsive to policymakers' priorities and preferences, but some highly placed CIA analysts resented this interference with what they regarded as their professional assessments of Iraq's plans and military capabilities.

It is interesting to note that in the early 1990s "the Defense Department [was] assisted by almost 350 lobbyists on Capitol Hill; it maintain[ed] some 2,850 public relations representatives in the United States and foreign countries."[27] During the Clinton administration, groups within the Department of Defense and the military services formed implicit alliances with members of Congress to expedite action on policy issues favored by the military (such as increased readiness spending) and to block unfavored proposals (such as permitting gays to serve openly in the armed forces). The point is that any number of interest groups evolve from the bureaucracy and become involved in advocating and supporting policy or strategy.

Iron Triangles

Domestic politics is characterized by interest groups' attempts to influence the public, Congress, the bureaucracy, and their own constituents. Equally important, interest groups become deeply involved in political campaigns and party politics. Although members of Congress can become captive to interest groups, especially if they dominate the member's district, members use interest groups to support their own legislative agendas. Furthermore, interest groups can become influential within the federal bureaucracy. Individuals with close links to interest groups are often appointed to administrative positions. Moreover, as bureaucrats implement a given policy over the years, they tend to acquire views similar to those of interest groups active in the field.

When the interests of members of Congress, interest groups, and bureaucrats come together, a power cluster results. Such iron triangles are coalitions of interests that are nearly impossible to penetrate and influence from the outside.[28] Throughout the process, several iron triangles may be at work advocating or opposing policy; they can even form a network of triangles that can frustrate almost any policy. Iron triangles confront the theory of democracy with the actuality of elitism and inside-track policymaking.

Put simply, it is a fact of political life that the president faces power clusters and interest group activities while establishing national security policy and directing the policy process. Although far stronger in domestic policy, such influences are affecting national security policy and strategy. Thus the president needs to build a coalition of power clusters for policies that are likely to be debated in Congress or that require resources only Congress can approve. At the same time, if policies are undertaken in secrecy, the president must be sensitive to the fact that publicity, especially occasioned by failure, will require an explanation and taking responsibility. Support from various power clusters and interest groups eases the political damage and makes it less difficult to design and undertake even risky policies.

Conclusion

The impact of public opinion on security policy should not be underestimated. Although only small percentages of voters pay close attention to the details of security and defense policymaking, public awareness of broad trends is stimulated by the media, political parties, and interest groups. The distortion created by media reports, partisan politics, and self-motivated interest groups undermines public understanding of public policy, including security policy. Yet competition among the media, political parties, and interest groups within a pluralistic system ensures that voters are exposed to multiple and competing perspectives. At the ballot box, the voters will have the last word.

The president has more latitude, at least at the outset of a new initiative, in defense and foreign policy, compared to domestic policy. Tradition and the advantages held by executive branch agencies vis-à-vis Congress ensure that a president who gets out in front of events and who seems to lead will have high approval ratings—at least for a while. Whether strong approval ratings can be sustained depends upon a president's skill in getting the message across to the government, Congress, and the media. In security policy, as in other aspects of the US political system, there is no single government policy but an array of competing policy preferences, each supported by powerful internal constituencies. If there is a threat of war or actual hostilities, the enemy and its perceptions and goals need to be taken into account as well.

In the final analysis, the president cannot simply assume that national security policy is self-executing. The president and the national security establishment, as well as other executive agencies, drive the instruments of policy and its supporting strategies. Orders must be passed down to apply the policy; then its implementation must be undertaken. When policies do not require appropriations from Congress or are hidden from view, the president and his staff must recognize that other political actors can shape the final result.

Even with an ethically dubious or controversial policy, the president must be prepared to accept responsibility and the political damage that results. Regardless of the nature and character of national security policy and its strategic implementation, presidents will be judged by their effectiveness in national security and how it furthered democracy and society. In the end, this final assessment is critical in the overall performance and credibility of the president. Even more important, it has a direct bearing on the capability of the United States to effectively pursue its national security interests. Presidential decisionmaking about peace, war, and crisis leaves indelible legacies to successors in the Oval Office.

Notes

1. Richard A. Watson and Norman C. Thomas, *The Politics of the Presidency,* 2nd ed. (Washington, DC: CQ Press, 1988), p. 153.

2. Alexis de Tocqueville, *Democracy in America,* ed. J. P. Mayer, trans. George Lawrence (Garden City, NY: Anchor Books, 1969), p. 186.

3. Doris Graber, "Media Magic: Fashioning Characters for the 1983 Mayoral Race," in Melvin G. Holli and Paul M. Green, eds., *The Making of the Mayor, Chicago, 1983* (Grand Rapids, MI: William B. Eerdmans, 1984), p. 68.

4. Bruce D. Berkowitz and Allan E. Goodman, *Best Truth: Intelligence in the Information Age* (New Haven: Yale University Press, 2000), pp. 133–135.

5. See, e.g., *The Pentagon Papers,* ed. Senator Mike Gravel (Boston: Beacon, 1971).

6. See, e.g., *Watergate Hearings: Break-In and Cover-Up: Proceedings* (New York: Viking Press, 1973).

7. Sam C. Sarkesian, "Soldiers, Scholars, and the Media," *Parameters* 17, no. 3 (September 1987): 77.

8. S. Robert Lichter, Stanley Rothman, and Linda S. Lichter, *The Media Elite* (Bethesda, MD: Adler and Adler, 1986), p. 299.

9. Ibid., p. 95.

10. Thomas E. Patterson and Robert D. McClure, *The Unseeing Eye: The Myth of Television Power in National Elections* (New York: G. P. Putnam's Sons, 1976), p. 75.

11. Peter Braestrup, *Big Story: How the American Press and Television Reported and Interpreted the Crisis of Tet 1968 in Vietnam and Washington* (Boulder: Westview, 1977), p. 184.

12. See, e.g., Editorial, "The End of the 'Jimmy' Story," in *Washington Post,* April 16, 1981, p. A18; Don Kowet, *Matter of Honor: General Westmoreland Versus CBS* (New York: Macmillan, 1984); and Edith Efron, *The News Twisters* (New York: Manor Books, 1972).

13. General Michael J. Dugan, USAF (ret.), "Perspectives from the War in the Gulf," in Peter R. Young, ed., *Defence and the Media in Time of Limited War, Small Wars and Insurgencies* 2, no. 3 (Special Issue, December 1991): 179.

14. A balanced appraisal of this issue appears in McCormick Tribune Conference Series, *The Military-Media Relationship 2005: How the Armed Forces, Journalists and the Public View Coverage of Military Conflict* (Chicago: McCormick Tribune Foundation, 2005). For a particularly scathing criticism of the media, see William V. Kennedy, *The Military and the Media: Why the Press Cannot Be Trusted to Cover a War* (Westport, CT: Praeger, 1993).

15. Dorothy E. Denning, *Information Warfare and Security* (Reading, MA: Addison-Wesley, 1999), p. 6.

16. Alvin Toffler and Heidi Toffler, *War and Anti-War: Survival at the Dawn of the 21st Century* (Boston: Little, Brown, 1993), pp. 167–168.

17. Denning, *Information Warfare,* p. 115.

18. De Tocqueville, *Democracy in America,* p. 180.

19. Donald M. Snow and Eugene Brown, *Puzzle Palace and Foggy Bottom: US Foreign and Defense Policy-Making in the 1990s* (New York: St. Martin's, 1994), pp. 21–22.

20. See Bruce W. Jentleson, *American Foreign Policy: The Dynamics of Choice in the 21st Century* (New York: W. W. Norton, 2000), p. 215, and Stephen Ansolabehere, Roy Behr, and Shanto Iyengar, *The Media Game: American Politics in the Television Age* (New York: Macmillan, 1993), pp. 142–144.

21. Ibid., p. 201.

22. Ibid., p. 199.

23. Daniel Goure and Jeffrey M. Ranney, *Averting the Defense Train Wreck in the New Millennium* (Washington, DC: Center for Strategic and International Studies, 1999), p. 2.

24. International Institute for Strategic Studies, *Strategic Survey, 1991–1992* (London: Brassey's UK, 1992), p. 54.

25. Ansolabehere, Behr, and Iyengar, *The Media Game,* p. 199.

26. Steffen W. Schmidt, Mack C. Shelley II, and Barbara A. Bardes, *American Government and Politics Today, 1993–1994* (Minneapolis–St. Paul: West Publishing, 1993), p. 301.

27. Ibid., p. 253.

28. Theodore White, *The Making of the President, 1972* (New York: Bantam, 1973).

12

Who's Who in the
International System

THE UNITED STATES IS UNDOUBTEDLY A POWERFUL COUNTRY.
As the twentieth century drew to a close, economic strength and military
power both placed the United States in a class by itself. Yet the United
States is powerless to affect many international issues if acting alone.
Potential power does not always translate into influence over policy outcomes.[1] This disparity hit home on September 11, 2001. One reason is that
the United States coexisted with hundreds of other state and nonstate actors
within an international environment or system. The term *system* simply
means that states and other actors interact with one another in more or less
regular and predictable ways.

The international system, with some 190 states and many nonstate
actors, is a complex web and places the United States in relationships that
constrain US goals and the means, including military, to pursue those goals.
Even though the United States is a superpower with vast resources to implement national security policy, its power is limited in the international arena.
First, several major powers (e.g., Russia, China, Great Britain, France,
India, and Japan) have their own agendas and national interests that they
project into the international arena. Second, not all states share the view of
the world held by the United States. US culture, for better or worse, is
unique: a blend of pragmatism, economic and technological assertiveness,
and political inclusiveness, with future-oriented instead of traditional perspectives on social development.

Third, the United States has limited resources and must be judicious
about how and when they are used to achieve national security objectives.
Fourth, regional powers pursue interests that may be contradictory to those
of the United States. Fifth, democratic proprieties require that the United
States use diplomacy, negotiations, and consensus-building as the primary
means to achieve its national security goals—which means compromise and

recognition of the national interests of other states. Sixth, the United States shares power and responsibility with a variety of other states with common purposes and some cultural affinity—the most visible and successful example of which is the alliance.

The United States must operate in a world environment that is disorderly. Many heads of state or government do not share US concepts of world order. Within the context of US national security, sovereign states can be grouped into broad categories: *allies, adversaries, potential adversaries,* and *others.* Allies are best illustrated by fellow members of NATO. With the demise of the Soviet Union, NATO has no clear adversary, which is one of the most important changes from the Cold War era. Potential adversaries include states that have adopted explicit anti-US policies and have the military means to pursue their goals. Some are motivated by strategic cultures exuding suspicion of, and hostility to, Western cultural heritage.[2] Some also have the potential to evolve into a US adversary. "Others" include virtually the entire third world, with the exception of some states in the Middle East as well as other states that have the potential to become adversaries (Iran) or allies (Egypt), depending upon the specific security issue.

In this chapter, we discuss the effect of the international environment on US security policymaking. First, we review major US alliance commitments, especially those related to European security and NATO. Because NATO is exceptional in its durability and success, we also look at other US commitments with the flavor, although not the texture, of an alliance such as NATO. Second, we consider past and possible future US adversaries and some of the problems they might pose for US defense and foreign policymaking. Third, we discuss the other actors who fall outside the category of allies or adversaries as used here but whose relationships with the United States on security matters might be important in the future.

The Current State of Alliances

Historically, the United States has been suspicious of so-called entangling alliances. Even with respect to Europe, whose cultural affinity with the United States has deep historical roots, the United States has tried to keep its distance. Until World War II, Old World Europe retained its tarnished image of monarchy and radical revolutionaries. US isolationism in the 1920s and 1930s was intended to keep the United States at a distance from Europe. Even after World War I the United States did not ratify the Versailles Treaty (which included the League of Nations) but simply maintained its observer status during debates at the League. During this period, US military forces were primarily concerned with defending US boundaries rather than engaging in offensive contingencies and global power projections. There were exceptions, of course, especially at the turn of the twentieth century with respect to the Southern Hemisphere and parts of the Pacific, and Theodore Roosevelt's dispatch of the Great White Fleet to the Far East was a classic demonstration of US military might.

In the aftermath of World War II, an era of permanent US international involvement in peacetime began. The United States became one of the prime movers in the creation and management of the international system. US provincialism gave way in the face of international threats and US involvement in a variety of Cold War confrontations, including several Berlin crises and the Cuban missile crisis. George F. Kennan's grand strategy of containment was the lodestar of US policy planning for the duration of the Cold War: the Soviets were to be fenced within their spheres of interest in Europe and Asia and not permitted to advance their security perimeter against vital US and allied interests. US containment strategy expedited the demise of the Soviet Union and its empire without a World War III.

The end of the Cold War, the dawn of the twenty-first century, and the terrorist attacks on September 11 made it obvious that much of US security strategy, and the assumptions on which it was based, needed rethinking. Various concepts of grand strategy competed for priority among scholars and policymakers. During the 1990s the Clinton administration favored a grand strategy of "engagement and enlargement" that required a robust peacekeeping presence or assertive humanitarian intervention in various countries outside of previously defined US zones of vital interest. The George W. Bush administration favored a higher-profile grand strategy after September 11 characterized by its critics as imperialism and by its advocates as US hegemony or as a United States destined to play the role of "sheriff of world order."[3] On the other hand, some regarded both the Clinton and second Bush presidencies as adopting grand strategies that were inconsistent with the best interests of the United States and with a realistic appraisal of US capabilities. For example, Harvard University professor Stephen M. Walt argued that both the Clinton grand strategy of selective engagement and the George W. Bush grand strategy of global military predominance overextended US commitments and risked alienating allies and potential adversaries. Instead, Walt favored "offshore balancing" as a US grand strategy consistent with US traditions.[4]

A strategy of offshore balancing would limit US military deployments and interventions to those situations in which vital US interests were at risk. Offshore balancing assumes that "only a few areas of the globe are of strategic importance to the United States (i.e., worth fighting and dying for)."[5] These areas include those regions having major concentrations of power and wealth or critical natural resources: Europe, industrialized Asia, and the Gulf. Offshore balancing does not require that the United States control these areas directly: the United States need only ensure that no hostile great power, and especially no adversary "peer competitor," controls these vital regions.[6] Offshore balancing is not isolationism: the United States would still be a major player in world politics and a prime mover in multilateral institutions such as NATO and the United Nations; it would also be able to act unilaterally when necessary in response to threat or attack.

North Atlantic Treaty Organization

The most important alliance for the United States is NATO, formed in the aftermath of World War II. Designed primarily as a defensive military alliance of sixteen countries against the Soviet Union, NATO moved toward a more expansive definition of its purpose in the 1990s following the dissolution of the Soviet Union. In 1994, NATO initiated its Partnership for Peace program, intended to provide a closer relationship with several Eastern European countries and the former republics of the Soviet Union.[7] Somewhat earlier, the North Atlantic Cooperation Council (NACC) had been formed. With regard to NACC, one appraisal suggested: "For the moment, like the [Conference on Security and Cooperation in Europe (CSCE), which evolved into the Organization for Security and Cooperation in Europe (OSCE)], this new organization [i.e., NACC] is more a series of conferences and consultations than formal mechanisms for collective security."[8] Another consultative vehicle was created by NATO in 1997 as a result of the NATO-Russia Founding Act, enabling Russia to be heard on security issues of interest to NATO but without giving Russia a veto over NATO decisions.

Partnership for Peace turned out to be among NATO's most important and successful innovations of the decade. Partner agreements allowed countries not yet eligible for NATO membership to establish routine military cooperation with NATO and, in some cases, helped pave the way for later admission. This was the case, for example, with Poland, the Czech Republic, and Hungary, which joined NATO in 1999. Those on the waiting list, and even those with no aspirations for permanent membership, regarded the joint military exercises and other experiences under Partnership for Peace as favorable to military stability and arms control transparency in Europe. Partner agreements paved the way for NATO to expand its membership to twenty-six countries during the first decade of the present century, with additional candidate members waiting offstage.

NATO Enlargement

NATO's expanded membership in 2007 reflected its success in redefining its Cold War mission for post–Cold War Europe. In addition to its Cold War "Article 5" mission (collective self-defense), NATO announced a willingness to take the lead in conflict prevention, conflict management and resolution, and preventing or assuaging humanitarian disasters. These broader missions were tested in Bosnia, where NATO deployed the 60,000-person IFOR beginning in December 1995 pursuant to the Dayton peace accords. IFOR was changed to SFOR one year later, and SFOR remains in Bosnia at this writing, albeit considerably downsized. Russia and other NATO non-members also participated in the SFOR deployments in Bosnia. Areas of Afghanistan also became NATO's responsibility as noted below.

Throughout the 1990s the subject of Europe's post–Cold War security relationship with North America became an important agenda item. NATO was supportive of the establishment of a "European pillar" within the Atlantic alliance under which Europeans might become more self-reliant in regional security issues that did not call for direct US participation. European members and nonmembers pursued the related but distinct European Security and Defense Identity (ESDI), which has ties to the European Union (EU).[9] NATO's European-pillar concept would permit various coalitions among the European NATO members, probably under the aegis of the Western European Union (WEU), to undertake conflict prevention and conflict resolution missions with purpose-built forces (perhaps combined joint task forces). Arranging for NATO-related or NATO-congruent, but not NATO-controlled, security architectures was complicated by the problem of partially overlapping memberships among NATO, the WEU, and the EU.

An additional problem in integrating European defenses without breaking European ties to NATO is the diversity of competencies among European NATO defense forces. Especially significant is the technology gap relative to high-end conventional warfare between the United States and the other NATO members. This disparity in long-range precision strike, stealth aircraft, and advanced command, control, communications, computers/intelligence, surveillance, reconnaissance (C4/ISR) systems was apparent to observers during Operation Allied Force, NATO's air campaign against the former Yugoslavia in 1999.[10] NATO's Defense Capabilities Initiative was intended to beef up Europe's military competencies in precision-strike, stealth, and battle space awareness and control during the next decade in order to close the technology gap.

NATO has been the most enduring, but by no means the only, US security alliance commitment since the end of World War II. But given the changing international landscape, permanent alliances may be the exception; the norm, ad hoc alliances and coalitions for a specific mission or purpose. During the 1991 Gulf War, for example, President George H.W. Bush was forced to improvise a "coalition of the willing" that cut across traditional Cold War alliances. President Clinton supported peace operations using US, NATO, and other forces in coalitions tailored for particular missions, even when NATO accepted formal responsibility for peacekeeping and peace enforcement. Such was the case with Operation Joint Endeavor in

Bosnia after 1995 and in Kosovo in 1999; in both cases a significant number of participants came from outside NATO, including Russia. Subsequently President George W. Bush used a coalition of the willing in Operation Iraqi Freedom to topple the regime of Saddam Hussein in 2003.

The US-European relationship may become strained as a result of increased integration within the EU, including the establishment of a common currency (the euro). The passage of NAFTA by Congress during the Clinton administration appeared to be one reaction to possible trade limitations on non-EU countries. In addition, there was some concern in the United States over what impact European integration would have on NATO membership and relationships. The US decision for war against Iraq in 2003 despite lack of UN Security Council or NATO support also alienated several long-standing US European allies, including France and Germany.

But other collective arrangements have strengthened the US-European relationship. The CSCE was formed in 1973 to provide a Europe-wide forum for considering human rights issues. It evolved into the OSCE and in the 1990s was Russia's preferred institutional locus for resolving European security issues. But the OSCE had only consultative machinery and lacked standing military assets of the kind that NATO could use to support peace enforcement and other activities. Several rounds of NATO enlargement pushed its membership to twenty-six countries by 2005. This demonstrated that NATO had become, despite Russia's wishes and some doubts among NATO traditionalists, the all-purpose security guarantor for post–Cold War Europe—and perhaps beyond. NATO's "out of the area" profile of activities was raised higher in the aftermath of US wars in Afghanistan and Iraq from 2001 to 2003. NATO assumed a major role in providing security for the fledgling Afghan regime of President Hamid Karzai and undertook a variety of support missions in postwar Iraq, including the training of 1,500 middle- and upper-level officers for the new Iraqi security forces.[11]

In the world order that evolved in the early 1990s, the Cold War alliance system unraveled and NATO underwent changes. A new system of alliances and relationships is emerging, with the United States and Russia, for example, establishing ties not contemplated several years earlier. Additionally, the US-China relationship is becoming increasingly important and is changing as China's economy approaches world-class standards and China's military power waxes in East Asia. Furthermore, regional groupings and regional alliances have emerged, often with little reference to the United States (e.g., the Association of Southeast Asian Nations). Economic associations and alliances have become increasingly important in light of global interdependence.

The Gulf War of 1991 demonstrated the effectiveness of temporary coalitions under the auspices of the United Nations in responding to overt aggression. This "coalitions of the willing" approach may be a model for future responses to international crises. And in such cases, it is likely that prevailing alignments will not deter the formation of temporary coalitions to achieve mutually acceptable objectives. The victorious Gulf War Coalition and other coalitions of the willing are dependent, however, on immediate circumstances, personal leadership, and influence among heads of state. It was doubtful that any US president other than George H.W. Bush could have put together the coalition that won the 1991 Gulf War; chances for a repeat in the twenty-first century are dim, as US experience against Iraq in 2003 and beyond has proved.

The September 11 attacks caused the George W. Bush administration to mobilize an unexpected coalition that included NATO, Russia, and China, with support from some Arab and Islamic states, against the Taliban of Afghanistan for sheltering and supporting the Osama bin Laden terrorist network. The level of international support for US policy in Afghanistan did not set a precedent for future conflicts, however. The US military operation to depose Saddam Hussein in 2003 was opposed by major NATO allies, by Russia, and by important US allies and friends in the Arab and Islamic worlds. Nevertheless the George W. Bush administration assembled its own minicoalition of the willing, including Britain as a major military contributor, for Operation Iraqi Freedom and its follow-on effort to pacify and rebuild Iraq.

Allies, Friends, and Temporary Alignments

National security interests demand that the United States do more than develop and maintain close relationships with its allied states that have committed through formal agreement to mutually acceptable goals. Several states, however, are reluctant to enter formal arrangements (such as treaties and executive agreements) with the United States; nevertheless, some short-term issues may require US involvement. Furthermore, circumstances may dictate indirect relationships to pursue independent but mutually supportive policies and strategies.

National interests can evolve and emerge in unanticipated ways—sometimes rising to crisis proportions. The lengthy and complicated treaty process may be inappropriate for timely and effective responses. Additionally, national security issues can arise when formal US arrangements with foreign states are not feasible, leaving informal arrangements as the only solution. Since the end of World War II the United States has signed many treaties, which require a two-thirds vote in the Senate for ratification. Treaties that involve long-range US commitments or other controversial matters are likely to provoke debate. Because there is no assurance that treaties will be ratified, presidents have turned to executive agreements, which allow them to commit the country to a course of action through formal agreement with foreign nations without Senate approval; this offers considerable flexibility.

In cases of controversy or failure, however, the president is vulnerable to criticism from the legislative branch and the body politic. In addition, many senators abhor the overuse of executive agreements, arguing that they violate the spirit of the Constitution and bypass elected representatives. Even though executive agreements give the president a degree of freedom, he will likely have to explain his actions to the public.

There are many examples of nontreaty agreements, including the 1991 Gulf War Coalition and our earlier support of anti-Vietnam forces in Cambodia, where the United States and China were pursuing similar policies. Likewise, US support of the mujahidin (Afghan resistance forces) in the 1980s during the Soviet invasion was consistent with the policies of China and Iran. The point is that national security policy can be pursued in many ways and, when necessary or expedient, through unexpected coalitions. And although Congress plays an important role, the moving force is the president, operating through the national security establishment.

Some states are not adversaries, although they certainly are not allies or even friendly, including states that promote or support fundamentalist Islamic movements and third world states that are neither democratic nor established totalitarian regimes as well as nationalist states that fear any alliance, especially with the West—a vestige of the colonial experience. It is in these relationships that unexpected alliances can evolve, causing concern and disagreement in US political circles. Similarly, indirect relationships with unfriendly states may require the president to explain the US role to the public. Such circumstances can create contradictory US national security policy and strategy.

For example, what was especially difficult for many Americans to understand during the 1980s was the US policy of supporting freedom fighters in Africa and Central America against established regimes, on the one hand, and the support of established regimes, as in El Salvador, against Marxist-Leninist revolutionaries, on the other hand. These complex relationships show that the United States was involved in treaty obligations and commitments through such structures as NATO while it also pursued national security interests through other relationships—friends, potential adversaries, and others. As for friendly Arab states, formal treaty arrangements might not be as feasible in light of Arab nationalism and the US-Israeli relationship. Nonetheless, an understanding was reached by the first President Bush in 1990 for positioning US forces in the Gulf and for overflying Arab airspace. His son, President George W. Bush, faced similar issues after September 11, 2001, in obtaining Saudi support for US military retaliation against transnational terrorists. Such friendly relationships can become well established and form an integral part of the US national security effort.

As for potential adversaries, the United States cannot simply adopt a military posture; it must establish formal relationships and use the range of diplomatic, political, economic, and psychological tools available to push for change in their posture and even their government, if necessary. Some regimes resist even the most persistent diplomatic overtures, especially if hard-pressed by revolution or civil war (the Taliban regime in Afghanistan in the late 1990s is a good example).

An important dimension of treaties, friends, and temporary alliances is that each imposes an obligation and commitment on each party, which constrains the ability to shift policies and strategies. Put simply, the more political actors that are involved, the more likely it is that the United States will have its options limited. Thus for any relationship established with foreign states in pursuit of US national security interests, the advantages must be weighed carefully against the need for flexibility and maintaining options.

These characteristics of national interests and policy goals illustrate that national security policy and strategy can appear contradictory and confusing. The general public, predisposed to straightforward distinctions between good and evil, can find national security policy to be incoherent, thereby generating domestic opposition, especially in Congress. This is a consequence of the disparate character of national interests and national security policy and the public's lack of understanding of these complex issues as well as an engrained partisanship among certain groups.

Finally, US commitments—whether they derive from formal or informal arrangements—must be honored by each succeeding president. Thus a new president takes office with the network of alliances and geostrategic commitments that are already in place. Usually, it is only through major changes in the security environment that such commitments are altered.

There is some general agreement among policymakers and scholars as to the more important dimensions of US national security policy in the future. The following might be considered the critical alliances and relationships for US national security interests:

- United States–Russia
- United States–Western Europe, which carries consequences for the United States–Russia relationship
- The United States–China–Japan triangle—considered important in shaping the nature of the security environment in the Pacific; US relationships on the Indian subcontinent with both India and Pakistan
- United States–India, a rising counterweight to China
- The Western Hemisphere, which cannot be taken for granted politically due to evolving US security relationships with Canada since

September 11 and with states in Latin America, including some new leftward-leaning governments in Bolivia and Venezuela
- United States–Middle East, evolving from the US-Israeli alliance and the Israeli-Palestinian peace process that accelerated during Bill Clinton's second term in office and again during George W. Bush's second term, with hiccups in between

These relationships are not listed in order of priority—indeed, the importance of each will vary over time. Balancing US efforts and dealing with each relationship, individually and collectively, make designing national security policy a complex and often frustrating task. Considerations range from trade to foreign policy to technology, yet each relationship will impact US national security. Third world areas, not listed above, are also important.

The end of the Cold War and the demise of the Soviet Union changed the character of the international system's relationships in complex patterns that have yet to fully reveal themselves. These include expanded NATO membership and reevaluation, Middle East peace initiatives, and the rush to armaments by several states, including probable nuclear proliferation in North Korea and Iran. North Korea's acknowledged status as a nuclear power has raised Asian uncertainties about future containment of nuclear weapons spread. In the aftermath of India's and Pakistan's nuclear testing and declared nuclear status in 1998, their relationships with one another, as well as with China, create a security arc of major importance to US policy and threaten regional security and stability. These developments, and others in Russia and Eastern Europe, raise questions about the utility and continued relevance of formal treaties and alliances entered into after World War II. Indeed, the very notion of friend, ally, and adversary has become muddled.

In sum, the new world order has created a strategic landscape that does not lend itself to Cold War–style alliances. In addition, there is a prevailing theme in US politics that resists alliances that enlarged the United States in uncertain political-military contingencies, such as Somalia in 1993, or involve a combat role. Alliances during the early twenty-first century may very well have an entirely new character: flexible in composition, adaptable to short-term missions, and reversible if conditions dictate.

Adversaries and Potential Adversaries

The United States at the turn of the twenty-first century was in the unusual position of having no official enemy or adversary state, or hostile coalition of states, against which to benchmark its security threat assessments. The singularity of its military power and economic potential also induced complacency on the topic of international security among members of Congress, the media, and the public at large. Relations with Russia, the core of former Soviet military power and influence, are now friendly or at least nonhostile. Threats to US security are now ad hoc, defying categorization except in broad terms: by type of action that might harm US interests (e.g., terrorism) instead of by potentially hostile countries and coalitions. Not even England during the nineteenth century, the period of Pax Britannica, presided over such a one-sided international system.

US military supremacy in information-based warfare, televised globally in Operation Desert Storm, guaranteed that few if any states would take on the United States and allied NATO forces on their own terms as Saddam Hussein did. But this is not a threat-free environment for US military planners. As Carl von Clausewitz taught, politics causes hostile intentions between states; military forces are merely the instruments that express that hostility. And the paradox of US power at this time is that it motivates envy and resentment on the part of dissatisfied state and nonstate actors. Security is highly context dependent. And part of that context is the uncertainty of future US relations with post–Cold War Russia.

The end of the Cold War and the dissolution of the Soviet Union do not diminish the significance of the relationship between the United States and Russia. To the contrary, Russia has become more important as a geostrategic centerpiece in US and allied efforts to stabilize East Central Europe and Central Eurasia. A nonhostile Russia also permits easier Western access to important natural resources and markets in the former Soviet Union; for example, US and other Western oil companies want to drill for oil in the Caspian Sea basin. Another factor is that a democratic and stable Russia is a more reliable security partner for the United States and NATO in controlling the nuclear arms race.

The world breathed a sigh of relief when the nuclear weapons temporarily dispersed among Belarus, Kazakhstan, and Ukraine by the demise of the Soviet Union were relocated under Russian control. After the election of Vladimir Putin to succeed Boris Yeltsin as president in 2001, the Russian Duma (parliament) ratified the Strategic Arms Reduction Talks (START) II agreement, reducing both sides' strategic nuclear forces to 3,000–3,500 warheads each. Although START II was never completed, many expected that the two states could proceed immediately toward a START III agreement, reducing their respective arsenals even more. In May 2002, US president George W. Bush and Russian president Vladimir Putin signed the Strategic Offensive Reductions Treaty (SORT), which required each party to reduce its operationally deployed nuclear warheads to between 1,700 and 2,200 by the end of the year 2012. Each state would set its own pace of reductions and was free to mix land-based, sea-based, and air-launched weapons as it saw fit.

The United States had an equal interest in the safety and security of Russia's nuclear weapons inventory and in the accurate accounting of Russia's fissile materials (enriched uranium and plutonium). The former Soviet system of accounting for warheads, and especially for fissile materials, left much to be desired. After the Soviet Union was dissolved in December 1991, US experts feared that former Soviet weapons or their constituent elements would trickle outside Russia's borders and into the hands of state and nonstate purchasers. These buyers of ill-gotten former Soviet nukes might include terrorists with agendas hostile to the United States or frustrated state actors with equally malign intentions. Therefore, through a variety of programs under the so-called Nunn-Lugar legislation passed by Congress during President Clinton's first term, the United States provided Russia with military aid and technical expertise to improve materials and weapons accountability, to increase the safe and secure transport and storage of fissile materials, and to retrain Russian nuclear scientists for work on environmental or other nondefense projects. The George W. Bush administration continued this program of Cooperative Threat Reduction (CTR) as a win-win for both sides but at a level of funding that many considered inadequate.

President Clinton in 1999 signed legislation that urged prompt US deployment of a nationwide ballistic missile defense (BMD) system. Clinton was less than enthusiastic about actually deploying missile defenses, but he was willing to let research and development proceed. President George W. Bush felt otherwise. Bush termed the antiballistic missile (ABM) Treaty a relic of the Cold War and declared his intent to begin deploying missile defenses in 2004. The Bush program initially deployed ground-based defenses in Alaska and California against light attacks or accidental launches. Meanwhile, the Pentagon's Missile Defense Agency pursued research and development on ground-based, airborne, and sea-based components of a more comprehensive system. US interest in theater missile defenses (TMD), against weapons of shorter range than intercontinental systems, also continued with refinements to the Patriot PAC-3 system.

Russia's military doctrine and national security concepts under the presidency of Vladimir Putin indicate that the United States looms large in Russia's security concerns. The United States is a security partner for Russia in the war on terror: Putin and Bush immediately found common ground on this issue, and Russia helped to clear the way for the operation of US military forces and intelligence-gathering in its historic sphere of influence in Central Asia. On the other hand, Russia's military establishment provides a threat assessment with a "retro" look. Important General Staff officers and Ministry of Defense (MOD) officials still regard the United States and NATO as Russia's notional, if not realistic, enemies for planning and force sizing.[12]

One reason for this backward-looking strategic perspective on the part of much of Russia's military is its diehard resistance to restructuring and reform. Despite Putin's popularity with the public and his centralization of power in the Kremlin compared to Yeltsin, Putin has been unable to prod the military into necessary major reforms.[13] In addition to its backward strategic outlook, the Russian military requires restructuring to create a true cadre of professional noncommissioned officers, to increase the percentages of contract soldiers compared to conscripts, and to reduce the frequency of crime and pathological behavior among soldiers—including alarming numbers of beatings, robberies, and murders.

Perhaps Russia's greatest failing in military reform has been its inability to adapt its forces to the requirements of irregular warfare on or near Russia's borders or within Russian Federation territory. Russia's military performance in Chechnya after 1999 was somewhat more impressive than its sorry showing in 1994–1996. But the second Chechen War, as well as the first, strained Russian military capabilities and finances.[14] More important for the morale of the Russian military was the determination shown by the Putin administration, in contrast to Yeltsin, to prevail at any cost against efforts to disconnect any part of the Russian Federation from Moscow's centralized political control. Putin also anticipated a lower profile of criticism from the Bush administration after September 11 on Russian policy in Chechnya.

Russia's rising oil and gas revenues in the new century have made available additional resources for all state purposes, including military modernization, training, and force restructuring. Russia needs to modernize its conventional and nuclear forces in order to replace obsolete equipment and to improve military command-and-control systems. In addition, Russia's concept of a military force based on massive numbers of conscripts and organized for a battle of attrition following the invasion of Russian state territory must be pushed into the dustbin of history. Europe is, for all intents and purposes, a war-free zone or security community.

Russia now faces threats from the East and South, the latter having the potential to exacerbate turbulence in Chechnya and elsewhere in the Caucasus or in former Soviet Central Asia. As well, Russia is now repositioning itself strategically and politically. Putin wants closer economic ties to the European Union and acceptance as a full-fledged member of the Group of Eight (G8), the elite market democracies. Russia also watches developments in Asia closely, including those involving China and India. In 2005, Russia and China conducted large joint military exercises that took place within a political backdrop of shared concern about US global military dominance. In addition, Russia wants to ensure that Central Asia remains mainly under its shadow as an extended security space and not a forward outpost for permanent US military ambitions. Russia's geopolitics are required to balance among regional actors of significant military power or potential (China, India); a Japanese economic powerhouse with growing military capability; an acknowledged new nuclear state (North Korea) whose example might be imitated by others in Asia, including South Korea and Japan; and the United States, with its strong commitments to the defense of allies in Asia (Japan, Taiwan, South Korea).

Others

Most of the states in the "other" category are non-European or fall outside the US-Western cultural system. The tendency to place all states outside Europe and North America into the third world prevails in much of the literature. The categorization is useful in broad terms but is of little use in close examination of US national security interests and in assessment of US policy. To place India, Chad, and Taiwan, for example, in the same third world category ignores the cultural, political, and economic differences, as well as geographic distinctions, among those three states. The same reasoning applies to many other developing and partly developed states in Africa, Asia, the Middle East, and Latin America.

China, with its vast human resources and geostrategic position in Asia, is in a special category. China's burgeoning economy and growing military power have raised US concerns that it could grow into a regional hegemon or even a peer competitor by the middle of the twenty-first century. Indeed, for many Western observers, little can be done in Asia and Southeast Asia without considering the role of China. China has an ambivalent relationship with the United States. On the plus side, both states benefit from trade and investment flows that assist in improving both economies. On the minus side, the two disagree over Taiwan, with the US insistence that Taiwan must not be forcibly annexed to the People's Republic of China (PRC). In addition, US military planners worry that a stronger China might engage in "access denial" of US power projection into the Pacific Rim.

US policy planners will have to deal with a twenty-first-century China that has escaped the confines of purely Maoist strategic military thinking built around people's war and national liberation.[15] China has modernized its armed forces and continues to improve its nuclear capabilities and ballistic missile forces. China's theater ballistic missiles could serve as deterrents to US conventional military deployments in the Pacific supported by the implicit threat of US nuclear arms (i.e., as antiaccess forces). The range of Chinese, Indian, and other Asian ballistic missiles and weapons of mass destruction (WMD) has the potential to redefine the entire concept of geostrategic space in Asia. Asian countries armed with WMD and medium- or long-range ballistic missiles might be transformed from "map takers" (states largely acted upon by others) to "map makers" (states that determine the geostrategic policy agenda in a region).[16]

Dealing with China requires nuanced diplomacy and sensitivity to Chinese culture. The impatience of Western negotiators with short-term objectives is often misplaced in China, whose diplomatic-strategic behavior befits the world's oldest civilization and focuses on long-term purposes. The Clinton administration made favorable US relations with China on trade and other issues a high priority, and to some extent it succeeded. But serious differences also surfaced, including China's resentment over the inadvertent US bombing of the Chinese embassy in Belgrade during NATO's air war against Serbia in 1999. Also, a scandal over alleged Chinese espionage against US nuclear weapons laboratories clouded US relations with Beijing during Clinton's second term. The uproar led to congressional Republican demands for investigation of alleged security lapses and resulted in some tweaking of Chinese diplomatic sensitivities. The US and Chinese governments also disagreed on other issues, including Chinese export of ballistic missile technology to rogue states with anti-US agendas and US claims of Chinese human rights abuses.

China, in turn, faced the problem of maintaining perestroika without glasnost: continuing to restructure and modernize its economy along capitalist, free-market lines without releasing the control over political life held by the Chinese Communist Party and central government. Capitalism without democracy might work in the short run, but the long-term incompatibility of free markets with totalitarian politics has been well documented by historians and political scientists. Freed of the myths that propped up Soviet power and fed up with the lack of consumer goods easily available to other Europeans, Russians and other nationalities revolted against the entire concept of the Soviet Union. The Chinese leadership wants to avoid Mikhail Gorbachev's fate at all costs, but it also wants to be a great power.

India is not a US adversary, but it will play a larger role in the next century in US security calculations. India is now an acknowledged nuclear power (it publicly tested a nuclear device in 1998, soon followed by Pakistan). India sees China and Pakistan as potential threats to its security, and nuclear weapons are now a part of their defense posture. Pakistan, in turn, sees India as the major military threat. China during the Cold War was mostly allied with Pakistan on security issues; the Soviet Union allied with India for the most part. Whether those patterns will persist in the twenty-first century is not clear, but China and Pakistan are assumed to have cooperated on the transfer of nuclear and missile technology to Iran and other states with potentially anti-US or anti-Western agendas. The US war on terror aligned the Pervez Musharraf government in Pakistan with the United States against Al-Qaida and other groups motivated by Islamic extremism.

The growing ballistic missile arsenals in the Middle East, South Asia, and North Asia, and the possibility of nuclear proliferation in those regions, change US geopolitical calculations. US regional conflict strategy is no longer as dependent on permanent forward basing, such as Subic Bay and Clark Air Force Base in the Philippines. Instead, it now assumes that rapid deployment of forces from the homeland or other bases such as Guam can meet a crisis, getting forces into the theater of operations in good time.

The potential spread of WMD and ballistic missiles in Asia, however, challenges the assumption of unopposed US power projection along the Pacific Rim or into the Middle East and Southwest Asia. If, for example, Saddam Hussein had been able to fire nuclear-capable ballistic missiles at Saudi Arabia in 1990, the massive US forces deployed in that country to expel Iraq from Kuwait would have been at risk.

The Middle East has its own set of political and geostrategic characteristics, many of which impact US national security interests. The US connection to Israel, combined with the US need to maintain reasonably friendly relationships with some Arab states, ensures that the Middle East is a fragile security area. Islamic links among the Arab states and sensitivity to non-Arab involvement in the Middle East give the area a degree of cultural homogeneity and offer a bastion against Israeli and Western power projections and influence. Included in the Middle East imbroglio are the Gulf and its oil reserves, the increasing political influence and military capability of Iran, and the prospect of further weapons proliferation (including possible Iranian nuclear weapons). The importance of this region to US national security has been well documented. The United States is a major actor in the area, whether it likes it or not.

The US military interventions in Afghanistan and in Iraq in 2003, and related US deployments in Central Asia, have redistributed power in the geopolitical "great game" that once was dominated by colonial European powers. Motivated by antiterrorism or desires for regime change in Iraq, the United States found itself depicted in much Arab and Islamic public discourse as an "imperial" or occupying power. The Bush administration had significant allied and international support in building a post-Taliban Afghanistan, including the willingness of NATO to undertake a major role in providing security.

But in Iraq after the fall of Saddam Hussein, the United States, Britain, and a coalition of smaller powers faced a protracted insurgency that had not been foreseen by Pentagon planners. Many critiques of US policy in Iraq pointed to devastating insufficiencies in plans and operations for postconflict reconstruction (PCR).[17] The situation was only redeemed by the high quality of US military performance in the field regardless of gaps in political and economic planning for the postwar period. US forces adapted to the demanding tasks of urban warfare or "close quarter battle," performed a wide variety of social and humanitarian tasks, rebuilt infrastructure, and tried to fight a counterinsurgency while distinguishing between genuine Iraqi nationalists and foreign terrorists sent into Iraq by Al-Qaida or other Islamic radicals for the purpose of destabilizing the state and destroying the new regime.

A key frustration to US policy in the Middle East remained the inability of Israelis and Palestinians to agree on a peace process leading to the creation of a democratically based Palestinian state coexisting with Israel. In the summer of 2000, President Clinton nearly brokered a peace agreement between Yasir Arafat's Palestinian Authority and the Israeli government to resolve the issues that divided the two sides. The status of Jerusalem was among the difficult questions that kept the negotiators short of fulfillment. Nevertheless, the intensive involvement of the United States created a favorable climate for peace. But the second Palestinian uprising—the intifada—began in September 2000 and was met by Israeli military escalation. The Ehud Barak government fell in 2001, replaced by the more hard-line administration of Prime Minister Ariel Sharon. The crisis came to a head in early 2001 as hundreds of casualties from Palestinian suicide bombs and Israeli military attacks were added to the decades-long death toll in troubled Palestine. The George W. Bush administration tried to restart the peace process but with mixed success. The Sharon government conceded Palestinian self-rule over Gaza in 2005 and promised to be more accommodating in negotiations on the final status of the West Bank. Health problems forced Sharon to withdraw from the political stage in 2006, however, and elections for the Palestinian legislature in January 2006 complicated the picture by returning a majority of candidates from Hamas, the Islamic social movement and terrorist organization.

The worst-ever terrorist attack on US soil, on September 11, 2001, added fuel to the combustible mixture of politics, religion, and nationalism that kept the Middle East and Southwest Asia in turmoil. Fighting this new, nonstate enemy without seeming to launch a holy war of Western Christendom against Islamic and Arab communities was the challenge facing President Bush and his successors. Military action in the war on terrorism, including special operations, airpower, carrier-based forces, and ground fighting, had to be contained within the larger policy framework of political de-escalation to avoid entrapping the United States in an open-ended series of unwinnable conflicts.

Conclusion

The United States is the world's only remaining superpower—a hyperpower of unprecedented military and economic strength. But not all situations are amenable to the use of US power, especially military power, whether in support of diplomacy or actual war. Military power is an effective persuader under certain, and very selective, conditions. These conditions can include the willingness of allies to help carry the burden. NATO has been among the most successful military alliances in modern history. The peaceful dissolution of the Soviet Union in 1991 opened the door for NATO to transform itself from a defense guarantor against Soviet attack into a promoter of a pan-European security community. Toward that end, NATO has worked with the EU to develop options for contingency operations that might not necessarily involve the United States or formally commit NATO forces. Nevertheless, in 1999 only NATO had the military capability and political clout to intervene in Kosovo to stop Serbian ethnic cleansing.

History shows that the decision to label other states as US allies, friends, enemies, or others is a matter of national interest, but it is also influenced by the cultural, social, and political characteristics of other regimes. Currently the United States has no official enemy comparable to the former Soviet Union. But the complexity of international politics in the twenty-first century argues against complacency. "Enemies" in the plural who are opposed to aspects of US policy will certainly appear, and some may be willing to risk everything—including annihilation—for their cause. The September 11 suicide hijackers are testimony to that.

But the United States can meet such challenges more effectively if it can call upon existing alliances such as NATO, or if it can assemble purpose-built coalitions, as during the Gulf War. Relations with allies can also lead to strain (e.g., over burden-sharing in peacekeeping and postconflict reconstruction in Iraq and Afghanistan). And the war against terrorism meant that new frameworks for cooperation had to be constructed. Nevertheless, the United States is apparently prepared to go forward by itself, if need be, to remove the tools of genocide from state and nonstate actors who may be willing to risk everything.

Notes

1. Susan L. Woodward, "Upside-Down Policy: The US Debate on the Use of Force and the Case of Bosnia," in H. W. Brands, ed., *The Use of Force After the Cold War* (College Station: Texas A&M University Press, 2000), pp. 111–136.

2. See Samuel P. Huntington, "The Clash of Civilizations?" *Foreign Affairs* 72, no. 3 (Summer 1993): 22–49.

3. The US role as sheriff of world order is explained in Colin S. Gray, *The Sheriff: America's Defense of the New World Order* (Lexington: University Press of Kentucky, 2004).

4. Stephen M. Walt, *Taming American Power: The Global Response to US Primacy* (New York: W. W. Norton, 2005), chap. 5.

5. Ibid., p. 222.

6. Ibid.

7. See, e.g., Daniel Burroughs, "Joining the Club: NATO Debates Terms for

Welcoming Former Foes," *Armed Forces Journal International* (December 1993): 25. See also John G. Roos, "Partnership for Peace: Cautious Movement Toward the 'Best Possible Future,'" *Armed Forces Journal International* (March 1994): 17–20.

8. Earl H. Fry, Stan A. Taylor, and Robert S. Wood, *America the Vincible: US Foreign Policy for the Twenty-First Century* (Englewood Cliffs, NJ: Prentice-Hall, 1994), p. 193.

9. Dr. Peter Schmidt, "ESDI: Separable but Not Separate?" *NATO Review* (Spring/Summer 2000): 12–15.

10. Dr. Elinor Sloan, "DCI: Responding to the US-Led Revolution in Military Affairs," *NATO Review* (Spring/Summer 2000): 4–7.

11. "NATO Trains Over 1,000 Iraqi Officers," *NATO Update*, January 18, 2006. Available at www.nato.int/docu/update/2006/01-january/e0118a.htm.

12. Stephen J. Blank, "Potemkin's Treadmill: Russian Military Modernization," in Ashley J. Tellis and Michael Wills, eds., *Strategic Asia 2005–06: Military Modernization in an Era of Uncertainty* (Washington, DC: National Bureau of Asian Research, 2005), pp. 175–205.

13. Pavel Baev, "The Trajectory of the Russian Military: Downsizing, Degeneration and Defeat," chap. 2 in Steven E. Miller and Dmitri V. Trenin, eds., *The Russian Military: Power and Policy* (Cambridge, MA: MIT Press, 2004), pp. 43–72.

14. For an expert assessment, see Pavel K. Baev, "Russia in the Caucasus: Sovereignty, Intervention, and Retreat," in Michael H. Crutcher, ed., *The Russian Armed Forces at the Dawn of the Millennium* (Carlisle Barracks, PA: Center for Strategic Leadership, US Army War College, December 2000), pp. 239–260.

15. Michael Pillsbury, "PLA Capabilities in the 21st Century: How Does China Assess Its Future Security Needs?" in Larry M. Wortzel, ed., *The Chinese Armed Forces in the 21st Century* (Carlisle Barracks, PA: Strategic Studies Institute, US Army War College, December 1999), pp. 89–158.

16. Paul Bracken, *Fire in the East: The Rise of Asian Military Power and the Second Nuclear Age* (New York: HarperCollins, 1999), passim.

17. See, for example, Thomas E. Ricks, *Fiasco: The American Military Adventure in Iraq* (New York: Penguin Press, 2006), and David C. Hendrickson and Robert W. Tucker, *Revisions in Need of Revising: What Went Wrong in the Iraq War* (Carlisle Barracks, PA: US Army War College, Strategic Studies Institute, December 2005).

PART 4

Conclusions

13

Long-Range Issues of National Security

THIS BOOK ANALYZES THE PROCESS OF MAKING US NATIONAL security policy. Without understanding the process of policymaking, the results would make little sense. Yet a complete picture must also take into account the substantive issues of national security over which policymakers struggle. Such issues matter, for the process is not simply an end in itself.

The six major categories of issues are national security as a concept, strategic cultures, geostrategy, homeland security, technology and economics, and the communications revolution. How such matters are viewed, interpreted, and implemented varies, but they need to be examined—not only to determine the proper course for US policy but also to assess their scope, importance, and difficulty within the national security system and policy process.

These six categories raise long-range issues not amenable to short-range perspectives and ad hoc responses. Each issue requires constant evaluation and analysis, followed by adjustments and refinements to national security policy and strategy. The interrelationships among the six categories compound the difficulty in designing policy, since a response to one category of issues will affect issues within other categories.

National Security as a Concept

Our concept of national security is broad, based on concepts and organizational structure characteristic of the post–Cold War and September 11 period. Recognizing the problems of defining and conceptualizing national security, we offered the following statement in Chapter 1: "*US national security is the ability of national institutions to prevent adversaries from using force to harm Americans or their national interests and the confi-*

dence of Americans in this capability." From this, the definition was expanded to include a variety of components, ranging from economics and humanitarian concerns to refugee assistance and institution-building. In fact, many of these components are not pure national security issues but fall more into foreign policy and finances.

Taking a page from Sun-tzu, if national security includes virtually everything, then it includes nothing. During the 1990s, the scope of national security became so broad after the Cold War that it risked a loss of meaning and conceptual coherence. In this context, the primary function of the Department of Defense and the military got lost in a muddled maze of fragmented policy, clouded strategy, and questionable, politically driven issues that in the long term may erode US capability. The George W. Bush administration also preferred an expansive definition of US national security as a concept and a robust definition of US security purposes. As a result the US military—especially the US Army—now faces an extremely difficult environment. The conceptual bases and meaning of US national security in the current environment are also complicated by modern understandings of warfare and its relationship to politics, society, and culture.[1]

We need to reexamine our definition with a view toward focusing the conceptual basis and clarifying the strategic purpose. It may be useful to revise the definition as follows: the use of military force to protect vital national interests based on core (first-order) priorities. In this respect, it is useful to revisit the Weinberger Doctrine (see Chapter 6), for it outlines important criteria for using the military and directly links those criteria to notions of national security and national interests.

An important part of the concept of national security is *strategic vision.* The link between national security and national security strategy is vision—seeing how one proceeds from one to the other. This has yet to be fully developed by the United States in the new security landscape. For example, in the 1990s the Department of Defense and the military services outlined broad aspects of future warfare and how the United States should prepare to deal with twenty-first-century security challenges. Unfortunately, these studies (primarily *Joint Vision 2010* and *Joint Vision 2020*) placed little emphasis on asymmetrical warfare, the kind practiced by terrorists on September 11. According to General Rupert Smith, who commanded the British Armored Division in the Gulf War of 1991, UN peace operations in Bosnia in 1995, and British forces in Northern Ireland from 1996 to 1998, among other key assignments, an altogether new concept of war is necessary for strategists and policymakers:

> It is now time to recognize that a paradigm shift in war has undoubtedly occurred: from armies with comparable forces doing battle on a field to strategic confrontation between a range of combatants, not all of which are

armies, and using different types of weapons, often improvised. The old paradigm was that of interstate industrial war. The new one is the paradigm of warfare amongst the people.[2]

General Smith's concept of "war amongst the people" goes beyond the ideas of military transformation, emphasizing technology, and asymmetrical warfare, which is somewhat trite because all warfare is asymmetrical in principle (each side seeks to win by doing the unexpected and unorthodox). "War amongst the people" emphasizes the difference between *deploying force* and *employing forces* to good effect. For example, over the past fifteen years or so, both the Western allies and Russia have deployed conventional military forces for battle in a number of military engagements, but those deployments have "spectacularly failed to achieve the results intended, namely a decisive military victory which would in turn deliver a solution to the original problem, which is usually political."[3] Some military historians would argue that this is not an entirely new discovery: conventional militaries have often bogged down or been defeated by unconventional or irregular warfare, from Napoleon's troubles in Spain to the US experience in Vietnam. Smith and others, such as military historian Martin van Creveld, suggest, however, that what has been thought of as regular or conventional war (fought between professional militaries under state control according to standardized tactics) may be the exception, not the rule, in future conflicts.[4]

In sum, there is a compelling need to rethink the concept of national security to ensure its relevancy in the post–Cold War period and to design a strategic vision and operating principles for the US military. At present, there is a serious gap between the political rhetoric of national security and the capability and effectiveness of the US government to respond to security challenges in the present century.

Strategic Cultures and Philosophical-Ideological Confrontations

During the Cold War it was often said that the real struggle—with a direct impact on US national security—was between the tenets of Western democracy and those of Marxism-Leninism as practiced in the Soviet Union and Eastern bloc. In the post–Cold War period, however, the tenets of democracy are confronting those of non-Western cultures such as Islam, Hinduism, Buddhism, and Confucianism. Religious fundamentalism, which can include anti-US virulence, is especially important in this context.

Philosophy establishes the moral tenets of a system. *Ideology* provides the political rationale and basis of legitimacy of that system. The struggles over these issues reach into virtually all parts of the world. The critical dimension is not so much the imposition of one culture over the other but whether the legitimacy and credibility of one type of political system prevail in the long run. This is not meant to imply that we are undergoing a war between civilizations, where one culture tries to overcome another. And this is not meant to imply that conflicts will necessarily have a military dimension. On the contrary, such struggles are primarily political-psychological. This is also not meant to argue that other states need to adopt one cultural system as their own. But there is an inherent and universal struggle between the open systems of the West and the closed systems of other cultures. As Samuel P. Huntington has written: "Western ideas of individualism, liberalism, constitutionalism, human rights, equality, liberty, the rule of law, democracy, free markets, the separation of Church and state, often have little resonance in Islamic, Confucian, Japanese, Hindu, Buddhist or Orthodox cultures."[5]

Philosophy and ideology have much to do with the degree of cultural affinity and commonality of purpose between the United States and a state. Obviously, US national security policy is best served by open political systems based on the Western Enlightenment-Renaissance heritage and democratic ideology. This is not to suggest, however, that commonality of purpose cannot be achieved with non-Western states such as India or those in the Middle East. If such states are striving for openness and a democratic ideology (not necessarily defined in Western terms), then it is important for US national security interests to develop friendly relationships with them.

The broader notion of strategic cultures can be better understood by reviewing Marxist-Leninist ideology and its attempt to establish a Communist cultural system. This background will help our understanding of what evolved from the Cold War and what remains in place in Russia, former Soviet republics, and elsewhere.

No single explanation does justice to the socio-ideological themes of Karl Marx and V. I. Lenin. The issue becomes even more difficult when the evolution of Marxist ideology is examined in the context of the Soviet state.[6] The Marxist-Leninist paradigm was based on several important concepts: the view that the party was the primary organ of power, the goal of establishing socialist systems throughout the world, and the notion that there was a basic contradiction between capitalism and Soviet communism that could lead only to the demise of the capitalist state. As Mikhail Gorbachev, the last Soviet head of state, revealed in his address in Moscow on November 2, 1987, marking the seventieth anniversary of the Bolshevik Revolution:

> The world communist movement grows and develops upon the soil of each
> of the countries concerned. . . . Born of the October Revolution, the move-

ment has turned into a school of internationalism and revolutionary brotherhood. And more—it has made internationalism an effective instrument furthering the interests of the working people and promoting the social progress of big and small nations.[7]

Gorbachev was a product of Soviet culture and the Marxist-Leninist legacy. This culture was nurtured over a period of seventy years and was rooted in central control and disciplined social behavior with control of the state by a small elite, perpetuating its own power and recruiting its own. The party remained the real power in a system in which the party established policy and supervised the instruments of the state in carrying out that policy.

There is a significant residue of Marxism-Leninism represented in the large number of Communist Party representatives in the Russian Duma today, in the resentment by many elderly and poor Russians at their decline in status since the Soviet Union disintegrated, and in the nostalgia held by some elites and others in Russia for the imperial trappings and international respect that were formerly accorded the Soviet Union. As an ideology capable of capturing the government and being reestablished as an official public doctrine or faith, however, Marxism-Leninism lacks some of the attributes that would be required for restoration. It cannot offer a blueprint for reforming the Russian economy or making it competitive in international trade and finance. To the contrary, Marxism-Leninism would be a retreat into history: in the actual (as opposed to the idealized) Soviet Union, a few party and government elites lived well while the masses lacked adequate consumer goods and any real political influence.

Other Ideologies and Philosophical Systems

The Chinese System

Variations on the Marxist-Leninist theme were the basis for the Chinese Communist system under Mao Zedong. With more than 1 billion Chinese on the mainland and a drive for modernity in the post-Mao period, the Chinese state has the potential to evolve into a superpower. Yet serious questions remain regarding the future of China. Chinese influence throughout Asia and Southeast Asia has increased since the Maoist era, especially in economics, and increasingly as a result of attempts to modernize the military system.[8] To be sure, the Confucian cultural system is part of China's overall development. Additionally, the Chinese mainland shares a long border with Russia, India, and states in Southeast Asia. Indeed, China is even contiguous to Afghanistan. Since the early 1980s, China has been involved in shooting confrontations with India, the Soviet Union, and the former North Vietnam.

Confucianism, a somewhat pragmatic approach to external relationships, combined with an underpinning of historical power considerations of the Middle Kingdom and mandate of heaven, establishes an amalgam of Chinese ideology and the substance of Chinese culture. Chinese culture dates back centuries before the time of Christ and remains deeply embedded in modern China, despite attacks by the ruling Chinese Communist Party. Yet it is clear that many changes are taking place that are transforming the country into an economic giant with a modern version of Chinese culture; such changes could also lead to civil strife or a balkanization of China, a modern version of the warlord system that predominated during the 1920s and 1930s.

The long history of Chinese influence throughout Asia and its potential as a hegemon in the twenty-first century make the People's Republic of China an important regional player, a pivot for US foreign policy in the region. The Clinton administration took advantage of China's economic modernization in the post-Mao era by aggressively promoting trade and cultural exchange with Beijing. China was also asked to play a part in supporting a US-led solution to the problem of containing North Korea's nuclear ambitions by giving Beijing's blessing to the so-called Framework Agreement of 1994. Later the George W. Bush administration would also enlist China's aid on this issue, after North Korea declared itself a nuclear power and the United States sought to reverse that status.

But the United States and China also tangled over nonproliferation issues in the 1990s. The United States sought to persuade Beijing not to provide nuclear know-how and missile technology to states of concern in Asia and the Middle East, especially Iran, Pakistan, and North Korea. Issues of proliferation reminded US officials that China's relationships with Russia, Japan, and the two Koreas were important variables affecting the US-China dialogue on arms control.

Although US pessimists argued in the 1990s that China sought superpower status, the Chinese political leadership expressed more moderate objectives. Much of China's economy remains underdeveloped by European, US, and Japanese standards. In addition, if China is to modernize its semimarketized economy in order to compete with the leading financial powers, the degree of authoritarian political control over investors and entrepreneurs will have to loosen. For example, China is imposing controls over Internet access and content for political purposes. And even though China's attempts to modernize its armed forces (driven by advances in computers, communications, and electronics) are bearing some fruit, its overall defense budget, large by international standards, pales in comparison to that of the United States.

The United States must pay special attention to China's relationships with Japan, Russia, and India. India officially joined the nuclear club in

1998, partly owing to a perceived threat from China (which is also a nuclear power). Russia, still powerful in North Asia, seeks rapprochement with Japan, including the settlement of territorial disputes outstanding from World War II. Japan is concerned with China's waxing military capability as well as any Chinese pretensions to superpower or hegemon status. China, of course, has its own grievances against Japan stemming from Japanese actions there before and during World War II. Additional Japan-Russia cooperation on security matters, leaving China on the outside looking in, is something that China will likely work to forestall. Russia under President Vladimir Putin has taken steps to improve dialogue on security issues with China. Both states suspect that US missile defenses will accelerate the nuclear arms race, and both Russia and China oppose a unipolar international order dominated by the United States.

The Middle East

The terrorist suicide attacks on the World Trade Center and Pentagon on September 11, 2001, stunned many US citizens and confounded many security experts. The sophisticated preparation required to carry out the attacks, combined with the high degree of fanaticism and self-sacrifice on the part of the perpetrators, offered a new variation on an old problem: terrorism and unconventional, or "asymmetrical," warfare. The terrorists cleverly exploited US vulnerabilities (e.g., US civil society and democratic openness) in the classical manner of Sun-tzu. Many people asked whether religious hatred motivated the terrorist attacks; the problem was not religion per se but rather politics with a religious undercurrent.

In the 1990s the Islamic and Arab worlds collided with globalization, or the internationalization of finance, information, and technology. Traditional geographic borders and regional and local cultures were penetrated by outside influences, with billions of investment dollars moving at the speed of light. Governments began to feel a loss of control over their own destiny and citizens. This vulnerability to the forces of globalization divided those who were prepared to benefit ideologically or financially and those who were not. The nonbeneficiaries often included traditional religious leaders.

Traditional elites and politicians now feel that their values are under siege, and many blame the United States and the West. Symbols of Westernization often go hand in hand with globalization—the Golden Arches, Mickey Mouse, and popular culture. For Muslims and Arabs with access to money and arms, their growing resentment expressed itself in revolts against secular regimes in their own states (e.g., Algeria and Egypt in the 1990s) and sometimes through their support of global terrorism (e.g., Osama bin Laden's Al-Qaida, responsible for the 2001 terrorist attacks).

In the immediate aftermath of September 11, some pundits foresaw a clash of civilizations between militant Islam and the West, between holy warriors and decadent capitalists. This pessimistic view mistakenly blames the entire Islamic culture for the actions of a few murderers using religion to justify terrorism. Islam, as in the case of Christianity, Judaism, Buddhism, and other belief systems, attracts followers with many different *political* agendas, and some of them use religious justifications for acts most would regard as sacrilegious. For example, many Christians today would acknowledge with embarrassment the atrocities of the Crusades from the eleventh through the fourteenth centuries as well as the Spanish Inquisition. None of the world's great belief systems, properly understood, justifies mass murder; but many have called forth religious rationales for imperialism, persecution, and terror. We should expect this pattern to continue.

To his credit, President George W. Bush spoke forcefully in September 2001 about US determination to bring the terrorists to justice while emphasizing US unwillingness to wage a war against Islamic and Arab communities. Bush emphasized US multiculturalism and inclusiveness and deplored the attacks by bigots against Arab and Islamic US citizens. In addition, Bush sought to develop a broad-based coalition for the US war against terrorism and states that support terrorism, including Arab and Islamic states. His success in lining up support from Saudi Arabia, Egypt, and other Islamic and Arab states was a message to US citizens as well as to potential enemies of the United States.

Yet early victories against the Taliban and Al-Qaida did not end challenges to US security, especially in the Middle East. The Palestinian intifada continued to reflect secular and religious hatreds, and US support for Israel remained a sore spot throughout the Muslim and Arab communities. Absent a miraculous breakthrough, the United States had to strike a careful balance between its security commitments to Israel and its desire for better relations with Arab and Islamic communities. The Arab and Islamic sentiment toward Israel is also clouded by Israel's reputation for military effectiveness, although Israel's inability to subdue Hezbollah in Lebanon in the war during the summer of 2006 caused this reputation to suffer. The United States has supplied aid and diplomatic support since the founding of the state.

Iraqi president Saddam Hussein and terrorist leader Osama bin Laden were the two leading examples of this continuing bitterness, but the fact is that the United States also supports conservative and moderate Islamic and Arab regimes. And despite some public chiding of Israeli military action by US officials in 2002, the "special" US-Israel relationship remained in place, a legacy of US domestic politics and the meaning of the Holocaust.

Other Systems

Other parts of the third world reflect combinations of socialism, democracy, communism, authoritarianism, military rule, and personalism, often influenced and shaped by Islam, Hinduism, Buddhism, Christianity, and animism. The point is that US and Western forms of democracy and open systems compete with a variety of other philosophical and ideological systems.

South America and Central America are important in terms of ideology and philosophical principles. The historical involvement of the United States in those areas has provided a notable element in the ideological and philosophical dimension of national security. To be sure, South America has a cultural dimension influenced by a colonial legacy from the Old World, including Britain, France, Spain, and Portugal—all states with a Christian heritage. This legacy reflects a range of political orientations, from monarchical to authoritarian to democratic. But many states in the region developed political cultures with distinct interpretations of Christianity and social structure, in which the concepts of openness and democracy take on a different connotation. There is a distinct Hispanic culture with roots in the Old World intermixed with indigenous cultures. Additionally, the increasing Hispanic population in the United States adds a cultural as well as emotional link to the Southern Hemisphere. The US census of 2000 revealed that the population of Hispanics grew by some 58 percent in the preceding decade.

Sub-Saharan Africa, although far from representing a coherent philosophical or ideological entity, presents a unique dimension nevertheless. Its colonial history and legacy of the slave trade have put sub-Saharan Africa in a special relationship with the United States. African Americans account for about 12 percent of the total US population. Many Americans of African ancestry feel a link with the continent of Africa, no matter how inchoate, which is reinforced by the history of slavery in the United States and the civil rights movement. Although in the short term there may not be a compelling national security issue in sub-Saharan Africa, in the long term this link is sure to be influential in shaping US national security interests. Although much political turbulence and regime change took place in sub-Saharan Africa in the 1990s, there were some developments favorable to the spread of open systems (e.g., in the government of South Africa). The breakup of failed states and the resulting chaos that may lead into local or regional wars are among the major challenges to US foreign policy in sub-Saharan Africa. For example, protracted civil wars partly motivated by ethno-religious strife in Congo and in Sudan pushed themselves onto the foreign policy agendas of the George W. Bush administration and the United Nations.

In summary, US security interests must deal with a variety of cultures and ideological and philosophical tenets that perceive the world in distinctly different terms. US values, norms, and political systems may be seen as a threat by some states, as imperialistic by others, and as interventionist by still others. Thus US security policy and strategy, although appearing reasonable, rational, and moral from the US perspective, are often seen as arrogant and immoral by others.

The design of US national security policy and strategy must therefore be based on intellectual and policy horizons that are not strictly bound by Western culture, ideologies, and philosophies. Thus, to design national security policy in the context of our homegrown democracy with the expectation that it will find favor elsewhere is naive and dangerous to US interests. The concept of democracy is shaped by the distinct experience and cultures of particular states. In dealing with the variety of cultures that exist in the world today, the United States must understand them and pursue US national security policy with prudence and patience. This does not require that the United States and Western cultures be compromised. But it does require an appreciation of the limits imposed by the external environment and a recognition that the pursuit of US national security policy takes time.

Geostrategy

Major powers usually place themselves at center stage in world politics. They see the world from their own physical location and with their own worldview. In the early twentieth century, this tendency became systematic, elevating geopolitics to a major dimension of the strategic maneuvering of major powers. Geopolitics stressed the importance of geography as a factor in determining the power of a state. In more current versions, geopolitics has spawned a geostrategic component, combining geography and strategy into a national security perspective.

The location of states, their natural resources, and their power relative to other states are critical elements of geostrategy.[9] For example, oil resources make many states in the Middle East extremely important to the national security of Western states dependent on foreign oil. Sitting astride important sea-lanes and trade routes (e.g., the Panama and Suez Canals, the Strait of Hormuz, the Caribbean passage) also enhances a state's geostrategic importance. The location and policy of a state with respect to major power strategies can also make it geostrategically important. Nicaragua, Cuba, and the eastern coast of Africa are but a few examples. Although minor states such as Nicaragua might not be geostrategically important in and of themselves, manipulation by other powers (i.e., as conduits for power projection and the pursuit of national security goals) carries national security implications for the United States.

Geostrategic components may well be the less difficult (but not necessarily the simplest) of any element of US national security policy and strategy, but they cannot be considered in isolation. Cultural issues influence geostrategic considerations and, in some instances, reinforce geostrategic importance. For example, the geostrategic importance of Israel is reinforced by the fact that it is a relatively open system whose values are generally compatible with those of the United States. In other instances, ideological and philosophical issues can be temporarily subordinated to geostrategic considerations, creating a condition in which the United States has few options other than to deal with a nondemocratic state. US support of the Pakistani government in 1987 and 1988 and again in 2001–2002 is a specific example.

In relating geostrategic elements to the specifics of national interests, the United States faces contradictory forces and contending ideologies. As a result, US policy and strategy can appear vacillating and unclear. Geostrategic considerations must be included in formulating policy and designing strategy, but they cannot simply be quick fixes and short-term responses. Rather, geostrategy must be included as part of a broader concept, one that provides a systematic application based upon a geostrategic vision. For example, the containment policy adopted by the Harry Truman administration just after World War II was rooted in geostrategic concepts that implied a principle of selection. The United States would not attempt to defend everything everywhere: primary security interests lay in preventing any single power, especially the Soviet Union, from imposing hegemony over Western Europe and Japan. When the idea of containment was extended (through the domino theory) to include every trouble spot under threat of Communist revolution, as in Vietnam, it became muddled, provided less compelling policy guidance, and got the United States into trouble.

The George W. Bush administration stirred considerable controversy at home and abroad as a result of its ambitious geostrategy in response to global terrorism and WMD threats. Bush declared the days were numbered for regimes making up the "Axis of Evil" (Iraq, Iran, and North Korea) and for other regimes that supported transnational terror or spread WMD to terrorists. Bush objectives included a realignment of Middle East politics and security through a transformed military landscape and a hoped for but as yet unrealized spread of democracy in its wake. The Middle East and Central Asia were no longer peripheral theaters of operations for US regional military commanders but central pivots for US policy and force operations planning.

As an integral part of national security policy and strategy, therefore, the United States must develop and articulate a broad geostrategic vision. This can be the guiding framework for those in the national security establishment to design strategy on a global scale. Equally important, we must evolve a sense of where the United States stands with respect to adversaries and potential adversaries, the international security environment, and its national security policy. It is in geostrategic terms that global vision, policy, and strategy are given specific meaning (i.e., commitment to a specific state or region in the context of US national security).

The Contemporary Period

The modern age of weapons technology appeared to reduce the relevance of geopolitical and geostrategic approaches to national security issues. Advanced aircraft, surface vessels, and submarines, combined with space technology and long-range, reconnaissance-strike systems, have tended to replace the views of Harold Mackinder ("heartland" and land power), Nicholas Spykman ("rimland" and sea power), Alfred Thayer Mahan (sea power and bases), and Giulio Douhet and the theorists (albeit to a lesser degree) with more advanced strategies of forward presence and crisis response as well as new concepts of land and sea warfare.[10] But the new approaches fail to grasp the fundamental global perspectives inherent in the earlier geopolitical-geostrategic views (although some elements have been borrowed and assimilated). New viewpoints focus more on war-fighting, operations other than war, and regional issues than on global visions of security relationships.

Critics of geopolitical models have long argued that geographical determinism is a dangerous concept because it assumes geography alone determines national power and policy. It is as great an error, according to critics, to translate geopolitical notions into geostrategic ones—that is, to make geopolitical factors into strategic ones by rationalizing their importance in national security. According to Henry Morgenthau, "geopolitics is a pseudo-science erecting the factor of geography into an absolute that is supposed to determine the power, and hence the fate, of nations."[11] Nonetheless, geostrategic theory has taken on prominence in the contemporary period primarily because of global industrialization and economic interdependence. Ironically, the demise of the superpower era created situations in which some states adopted policies precipitating less than major wars and engaging in unconventional conflicts to achieve political goals. All of these issues include geostrategic elements and clusters that have important consequences for US national security. Morgenthau countered, "There are areas that are crucial to the functioning of the world economy and our interests."[12] Put simply, this means that some geostrategic and power clusters are critical to US national security policy, but—like other factors—are not absolute.

A Global View: Competing Power Clusters

The global view of US national security, based on competing power clusters, recognizes that the world has moved away from the bipolarity of past decades. In addition, it acknowledges the emergence of a variety of states whose power and security postures preclude, or considerably reduce, the major powers' control and influence. With multiple centers forming power clusters, the focus of US policy and strategy, in geostrategic terms, should be to stabilize balances or create equilibrium among competing ideologies and systems in order to establish a basis for resolving conflicts through alliances. This approach assumes that conflict between major powers must be avoided, partly by recognizing legitimate interests, partly by removing conflicts from the battlefield, and finally by effectively resolving conflicts between competing power clusters. (This view incorporates elements of Spykman, Mackinder, and the balance-of-power theories.) For US national security, the global view of competing power clusters has some essential premises.

First, it does not reduce the US need to maintain a deterrent capability in its nuclear strategy or the US need to pursue arms reductions, arms control, and conflict limitation. But it does require a concentrated effort to develop realistic alliances and form mutually supporting power clusters within a modern vision of geopolitics and geostrategic perspectives. In such alliances, the United States does not always need to take a dominant role; indeed, a supportive role with very low visibility could often better serve US security interests.

Second, the overarching purpose is to create a directed balance of power against the most likely aggressor in the area. The Gulf War Coalition is an excellent case in point. But this directed balance should not be so rigid as to limit US flexibility in responding to unforeseen security challenges. Moreover, it cannot preclude the United States from developing political-psychological and economic support networks of mutual benefit among a variety of states, even those that are not democratic.

Third, an important part of US security policy and strategy is to ensure that centralized systems—totalitarian and authoritarian—and other groups with expansionist ideologies face a network of alliances shaped by geostrategic considerations. Alliances can serve as roadblocks as well as containment, deterrent, and defensive forces. These alliances, although primarily a security response to potential and real aggressive behavior and thus concentrating on security issues, also need to provide a framework for other policy issues. And finally, alliances can become part of an effective strategy only if states feel that entering such alliances will enhance their own national interests.

In summary, competing power clusters are an important characteristic of the world security setting. An effective response, including a security posture that can provide for sound policy initiatives, rests on the earlier global visions of Mackinder and Spykman, refined to accommodate characteristics of the contemporary period. These initiatives in turn are driven by the broader policy issues for a stable world order, peaceful conflict resolution, and democratic values. The global strategy evolving from the competing power-cluster view can serve as the context within which other support-ing strategies are designed and implemented.

The Limits of Geostrategy

Political, psychological, and economic considerations are beyond geostrate-gic influences. For example, the effectiveness of governments, ideologies, and nationalistic movements is not bound or necessarily influenced by geostrategic considerations. Islamic fundamentalism, for example, cannot be explained by geostrategic factors.

Furthermore, technological breakthroughs can reduce the impact of geostrategic factors. Technological advances have always had an impact on geostrategic perspectives; for example, airpower reduced the effectiveness of the physical containment based on land power inherent in the Mackinder thesis. Similarly, "system of systems" or information-driven military trans-formations, including enhanced long-range strike weapons, reconnaissance, and precision aiming, have reduced US requirements for massive numbers of troops with which to fight wars of attrition. In an important study of international relations, Quincy Wright examined political geography and concluded:

> It has been the hope of some geographers that because of the apparent per-manence of geographic conditions, geography might become the master science of international relations. This hope seems vain. Geography is pri-marily a descriptive discipline . . . [and] does not determine international relations. . . . The apparent permanence of geographical conditions is illu-sory. Civilized man uses his environment to serve ends which come from other sources. . . . Geography cannot develop concepts and conceptual sys-tems applicable beyond a limited time and area in which a given state of the arts, of population, and of society can be assumed.[13]

Geostrategy and National Security

A geostrategic vision is an important component in designing global strate-gy. The competing power-cluster approach to geostrategy, although shaped in somewhat new terms and requiring concentrated effort in developing alliances, is not so different from established US policy and strategy as to cause massive restructuring. It does, however, require some strategic rethinking. The approach does not demand the presence of US military forces in quantity to conduct effective military operations; rather it requires a specialization within alliances and various networks so that each state contributes its fair share (i.e., what it is good at and what it can afford). Conversely, the states within the alliance or network best equipped and positioned to implement a particular alliance strategy can be called upon to do so. Finally, Wright's criticism of political geography is equally appropriate for geostrategy. Geostrategic determinism distorts the importance of the dynamics of the security environment and ignores the changing nature of the physical environment. Furthermore, geostrategy cannot account for the nonphysical dimensions of security policy and strategy, such as national will, political resolve, and staying power, which in the long run are more important than geostrategic considerations. Yet geostrategic considerations have some influence on the posturing of forces and strategic alternatives and must be included as part of the security equation.

Homeland Security

September 11, 2001, changed the US national security agenda overnight. The terrorist attackers did not use weapons of mass destruction—nuclear, biological, or chemical weapons launched from offshore or released on US soil. That phase came later, in October, when either domestic or foreign terrorists mailed anthrax spores to various US government offices and prominent news media. The resulting publicity set off a national anthrax scare and numerous warnings from the US government that more attacks might be imminent. President George W. Bush established an Office of Homeland Security and, eventually, a cabinet-level Department of Homeland Security to coordinate domestic policy efforts against terrorism.

The phrase *weapons of mass destruction* conceals more than it reveals, however. Nuclear weapons remained the ultimate deterrent in the hands of five permanent members of the UN Security Council (the United States, Russia, China, Britain, and France). Other states aspired to acquire nuclear weapons as symbols of great power status: it is generally assumed that Israel has nuclear weapons, India and Pakistan went publicly nuclear in 1998, and North Korea declared its capability to produce and deploy bombs during the George W. Bush administration. The concomitant spread of nuclear weapons and long-range delivery systems (ballistic and cruise missiles and bombers) created the possibility of dangerous regional rivalries and attacks on the US homeland.

Biological and chemical weapons can also be used in long-range missile attacks. But chemical strikes would be destructive on a scale well below even small nuclear attacks. And the weaponization of biological pathogens for long-range missile attacks is a tricky business; atmospheric conditions and other uncertainties make the impacts very unpredictable. Nuclear weapons, in contrast, were road-tested in actual detonations and in simulations throughout the Cold War. Societies struck by even limited nuclear wars of the kind imagined by Cold War planners would be returned to prehistory.

The US national security and intelligence communities were unprepared for the October 2001 anthrax attacks, which used the US mail system and hit various US government and media offices. Some people suspected foreign terrorists, especially Al-Qaida. But US law enforcement did not rule out the possibility of domestic terrorists seeking to disguise their activities under the cloak of suspicion about foreign adversaries, and at least one US research scientist was investigated extensively for involvement with anthrax. Regardless of the identity of the perpetrators, the anthrax attacks led to demands for new powers of investigation for the Department of Justice against suspected terrorists, especially immigrants holding temporary visas that had expired.

By the end of October 2001, about 1,000 persons were being held in US detention facilities based on alleged ties to terrorist organizations, related charges, or immigration violations. Repeated warnings from Attorney General John Ashcroft and Homeland Security director Tom Ridge to the effect that more attacks at home or abroad could be expected raised public and media awareness of the lethal potential of biological weapons. Despite the media frenzy and public anxiety, military professionals cautioned that biological weapons were probably not as useful in combat operations as in creating mass fear among civilians. Even the world's largest militaries had little experience in testing biological warfare under realistic conditions. Biological warheads and chemical munitions on ballistic missiles might be used for strikes deep into an enemy's rear to disrupt command and control and logistics. Such attacks could force the defenders to don protective suits and shield equipment, thereby inhibiting personnel and vehicular movement, which might slow down forces at the front. Yet forward-deploying US forces might adopt several responses, not excluding their own use of WMD, against enemy forces. This was borne out by a report in early 2002 on the US nuclear posture review that stated that options for using nuclear weapons were expanding, not contracting.

Cruise missiles provide another weapon for attacking the US homeland and US forces with biological and chemical weapons. Cruise missiles are pilotless projectiles designed to exploit aerodynamic lift and precision guidance to attack surface targets on land or at sea. Widely available to some seventy countries by 2001, cruise missiles designed or modified for land attack can deliver biological and chemical munitions over distances up to about 1,800 miles (3,000 kilometers) against shore-based targets, including cities and military installations. Cruise missiles can be launched from land installations, from vessels at sea, and from aircraft. Cruise missiles can be guided during flight to attain precision targeting; they can also fly at high and low altitudes to confuse air defenses.[14] It would be easier for third world countries and terrorists to acquire, conceal, and modify cruise missiles, as opposed to ballistic missiles, for land attacks.

Strategic realism suggests that enemy states might be cautious about attacking the US homeland with long-range ballistic or cruise missiles and WMD. States have geographical locations and vulnerable populations that would surely be subjected to severe US retaliation. Saddam Hussein arguably did not employ chemical or biological weapons against US forces during Desert Storm because he feared possible US nuclear retaliation. Undisguised attacks on US soil that caused mass casualties would be suicide for heads of state and many of their citizens.

Terrorists are another matter, however. Terrorists have no permanent address and usually lack the assets, such as infrastructure, that can be threatened by retaliatory strikes. The best deterrent is preemptive—anticipating attacks and capturing or killing the planners and perpetrators. But preemption requires extensive human intelligence from inside the terrorist organization, something very difficult to acquire in a reliable and timely fashion. The effectiveness of deterrence through intelligence is still an open question, but if the absence of further attacks is the definition of success, then it has been successful, at least in the short term.

Terrorists' uses of WMD and other mass-casualty weapons (such as fuel-loaded airliners) are examples of asymmetrical warfare, something US adversaries may use more of in the future. US superiority in technology, conventional warfare, and military information systems such as C4/ISR would make it suicidal for state or nonstate actors to confront the US military one-on-one. Future US opponents will surely pursue the strategies established by Osama bin Laden and Al-Qaida. WMD in the hands of terrorists (even state actors) provide a potential force multiplier, an asymmetrical counterweight to US superiority. To defeat WMD and asymmetrical strategies, the United States must emphasize brains instead of brawn. Improved intelligence overall, better exploitation of human and technical sources, and intelligence support for theater commanders are necessary parts of any US response to asymmetrical threats.

WMD thus pose unique problems for US policymakers today. During the Cold War, nuclear weapons were symbols of great power status, the objects of envy by dissatisfied nonnuclear states. Today, nuclear weapons and other WMD are potential instruments of the weaker against the stronger. US and allied superiority in advanced technology conventional warfare will be tested by asymmetrical strategies that include the use of WMD as threats or actual methods of attack. The US homeland is no longer a sanctuary of safety, and homeland security is now a strategic mission of first importance. The use of WMD, including nuclear weapons, against US citizens en masse has become a frightening possibility.[15]

Technology and Economics

The US public has become accustomed to the daily conveniences of technology. Modern appliances; electronic gadgets at work, home, and school; and sophisticated medical treatments have become the rule rather than the exception. The enhanced quality of life has tended to personalize the impact of technology. As a result, the US public too often overlooks the impact of technology on the power of the state and its effect on the economy. In addition, many have little appreciation for the relationship between technological advances and the course of human history.

Technology reaches virtually all levels of society and the economy. Furthermore, technological developments tend to precipitate other technologies, creating a technological impetus that in turn can drive technology for technology's sake. Technology spawned the Industrial Revolution in the United States and Europe. Because industrial growth and technological change feed off one another, technology ultimately became part of the culture of industrial states. Indeed, competitiveness in the world economic system relies upon technology. In turn, technological capability depends upon a society that is postured to accept and demand technological change and growth. Similarly, this is dependent upon research and development within society and a commitment to scientific education. Put simply, continuing economic growth requires a society that is attuned to technology and can adapt to it while incorporating technology into the political-social culture of the system.

Two Dimensions of Technology

The two major national security dimensions of technology are *the power of a state* and *its military capability*. The initial period of the Industrial Revolution brought the rise of Great Britain as a world power and the era of Pax Britannica. Technological breakthroughs in steam power, metallurgy, and weapons development provided Great Britain a technological edge in developing its economy and military power, which led to the development of a superior navy and also protected British interests. Mechanization—the substitution of mechanical for human power—allowed the more efficient use of resources and nurtured the design of new industrial organizations to manage the production of goods. Improved means of communication brought societies closer together and allowed states to consolidate power and develop more effective control over the governing instruments.

The state possessing advanced technology could develop a dominant power position, allowing it to create conditions favorable to policy goals. Its quick reaction to events, its ability to gather information, its control over foreign policy, and its military were, to a large degree, dependent on technological developments in communications, transportation, economic capacity, and weapons development. The shift to mechanization, as well as efficient industrial organization, was the springboard to effectiveness in the international field.

The second national security dimension is military technology, which has shaped the conduct and characteristics of war. Thus the state possessing advanced military technology had a distinct advantage on the battlefield.

The invention of gunpowder and the refinement of rifling in guns changed battlefield tactics. The introduction of the Gatling gun, followed by the machine gun, had a dramatic impact on infantry tactics. More accurate and longer-range artillery engulfed civilians, threatening towns and cities well behind the defined battle area. The introduction of the battle tank in World War I opened the battlefield to further mechanization and tactics that stressed mobility and rapid movement. The rapid development of aircraft for military use changed the face of war. Similar advances in shipbuilding made naval warfare more destructive and far-reaching. These dramatic technological innovations of the nineteenth century and first part of the twentieth century have their contemporary counterparts: the nuclear era, the electronic revolution, and space-age capability have again altered the dynamics of the battlefield and pushed the qualitative as well as quantitative dimensions of war almost beyond comprehension. States possess a destructiveness well beyond anything envisioned in the past.

But technological advances do not guarantee a dominant power position. Historians are quick to point out that Great Britain lost its technological edge to Germany in the latter part of the nineteenth century, as German innovations in chemicals, electronics, and the steel industry gave rise to a powerful state. In the twentieth century the Industrial Revolution in the United States provided the economic base for it to develop into a superpower, militarily and economically. This technological advantage helped to vault the United States into the "postmodern" era of high technology in computers, electronics, and communications ahead of other powers.

This brings us to an important phenomenon of the technological dimension: the diffusion of technology from one state to other states. According to one authority, "the diffusion of military and economic technology from more advanced societies to less advanced societies is a key element in the international redistribution of power. Although technology is expensive and not easily created, once it is created it usually diffuses relatively easily."[16] Diffusion of technology allows new powers to emerge while reducing the power of existing technologically advanced states. It is clear that industrialization and a variety of "economic factors in particular have become an important source of national power and advantage." This in turn is contingent upon technology. But "in time . . . this technological advantage disappears."[17]

The diffusion of technology, with the resulting decline of one state and the rise of others, has led many to develop a sense of historical determinism about technology. Once a state reaches the limits of its expansion, then it begins a period of decline; "it has great difficulty in maintaining its position and arresting its eventual decline."[18] If one accepts this view, then retrenchment and consolidation follow, and an increasingly inward-looking culture evolves. Some point to US technological diffusion, a view reinforced by the limits of US power. If this is true, it follows that the United States must substantively change its national security posture, reducing its commitments and developing a better match between capabilities and national security policy.

Although technology is not the sole determinant of national power, there is no question that it is a very important one. It has a direct impact on industrial and postindustrial military capacity and has a pervasive effect on all aspects of life. The penetration of technological culture into society is a sure sign of its secular character. As one authority concluded, "taking mankind as a whole, there has been an irreversible movement of technological progress. Techniques once invented have seldom been wholly lost although they may have been lost in local areas."[19]

Technological Aspects

It is difficult to develop and maintain high technology without a strong economic base, although the ability of North Korea to develop nuclear weapons stands out as a dangerous exception. Furthermore, an industrialized or postindustrial society needs to develop and nurture a scientific commitment within its educational systems and research communities. With a broad-based scientific culture and an industrial base that can translate scientific advances into technological developments, society can improve quality of life.

Such advances are contingent upon a diverse and modern economy that is stimulated by consumer buying as well as continuous and growing investments in new plants and products. Government fiscal and monetary policies are important factors in shaping economic growth, as are market forces and international markets and trade. Thus a strong industrial economy, scientific culture, and technological advances are inextricable and essential in maintaining a state's ability to pursue national security goals.

In this environment technology benefits military development, which in turn benefits the economy. But these mutual benefits are dependent upon the nature of the political system and its ideological orientation. The link between the economy, technology, and military development can be considerably distorted by government action and ideological and cultural aspects of the system.

In the United States, a key indicator of technological effort is the resources committed to defense and military research and development. Since Vietnam, there has been much debate (and disagreement) over the proper balance between guns and butter. Critics contend that the defense budget and its emphasis on research and development have had a negative impact on the economy—that military expenditures tended to rob the civilian economy of financial resources and scientific talent. Defense research and development rose 64 percent during the 1981–1987 period; at the same time, "nondefense research and development fell 26 percent after inflation."[20] There are hidden benefits in defense spending on research and development, however. "Hundreds of US companies that engage in defense work in one form or another compete vigorously for contracts. . . . Firms will spend significant sums of their private research and development funds to prepare for making a bid on a defense contract."[21]

Some turn-of-the-century prophets forecast economic rather than military challenges as the Achilles' heel of the United States for the next century: "As the twentieth century draws to an end, the United States finds itself faced with few significant military threats. Instead, it is confronted with a global economic competition for which it is by no means as well or as uniquely qualified as competitors."[22]

This prediction was considerably wide of the mark. Economic and military challenges are not mutually exclusive. In fact, a state's rising economic power can lead to improvement in its military capabilities and, therefore, its aspirations on the global stage. The United States in the nineteenth and twentieth centuries and China in the twenty-first century offer examples of economic growth supporting increased military power and international ambition.

The issue is not simply military technology, but civilian technology from which the military can benefit. Thus technology, military developments, a strong military establishment, and the need for a strong economic base are sure to be persistent political issues within the US administration and political and military policymaking circles. To this date, there is little to suggest that anyone has designed a magic formula to balance these competing interests. There seems to be little question, however, that in the United States a strong industrial base, scientific culture, and technological commitment are essential in providing for an effective national security posture.

One fear is that technology, whether civilian or military, increasingly tends to drive itself: that is, a technological culture may develop to a point that technology will be seen as a good in its own right, with little reference to its impact on the quality of life, values, and morals of society. In its extreme form, the fear is that technology will advance without recourse to its social utility, and society will blindly adapt to it rather than technology's adapting to society. Biotechnology is a good example; some scientists claim that human cloning is inevitable and will someday become routine.

Several important issues emerge from these observations on technology. Technological developments are critical in nurturing economic progress, and military modernization and capability are contingent upon military technology. The links between technological progress in the economy and military modernity seem fairly obvious, as both factors are extremely important for US national security policy and capability. It is also clear that in an open system the strength of the economy is a basic priority in sustaining an effective national security posture. Another dimension is related to the economy as a whole. In the 1980s and the 1990s, there was serious concern about the increasing involvement of foreign firms in the US economy, even though most were from friendly countries. British, West German, French, and Japanese enterprises gained control over several US manufacturing firms—including defense-related industries—as well as supermarkets, banks, and other businesses. Large tracts of real estate in some major US cities—Washington, New York, Chicago, and Honolulu—were bought by foreign companies, and brokerage houses on Wall Street acquired several foreign partners. As a result of foreign economic penetration, some feared economic control by foreign companies as well as political control evolving from economic leverage. These fears raised more questions about allowing transfer of technology and access to defense products, even among friendly states. Some of these fears were confirmed during the 1991 Gulf War when it was revealed that the Patriot missile used in defending against Iraqi SCUD missile attacks had important internal guidance parts produced primarily by Japan.

Thus the fundamental problem facing the president and those in the US national security establishment is how to balance resources within the defense budget, ensure economic growth and technological advances on a broad scale, and minimize the unauthorized transfer of high-tech material and information to foreign states. At the same time, the US public must share certain technologies with allies to strengthen alliances and provide important national security benefits to the United States.

The problem is compounded by the fact that the president and members of his national security staff do not have the ability to direct or even shape all the instruments of national security; neither can they put policies into place without the cooperation of other political actors, especially Congress. Even when there is general agreement between the president and Congress about national security issues with respect to economics and technology, there is likely to be disagreement over military technology and the means to pursue national security goals—except in the most extreme cases when there is a direct threat to US national security interests. The controversy during the George W. Bush administration over letting a Dubai company manage a number of ports illustrated how economics, technology, and national security can intersect over a single controversy. Thus, except during crises, the US economy is driven by market forces that are outside the purview of government. The amorphous, free-market system—despite its efficiency—is not well suited to central direction and control.

Even in an economy as vast and diverse as that in the United States, government resources are not infinite. Therefore presidents, defense secretaries, and members of Congress must decide among competing needs for the military. The US defense budget must provide for *force structure, readi-*

ness and sustainability, modernization (investment for the next generation of weapons and infrastructure), and *connectivity* (linkages across the electronic spectrum and cyberspace that make joint operations involving more than one arm of service in a single military action or campaign possible). Important compromises must be negotiated among these various requirements and among the military arms of service (Army, Navy, Air Force, Marines). A trade-off of particular importance is that between readiness (how well we can fight now) and modernization (investment for tomorrow's wars). Finally, the various budget decisions relative to forces and missions are supposed to be made consistent with the president's overall national security strategy and defense policies.

Times of growth in US defense budgets can be as contentious politically as periods of decline. During the George W. Bush administration, US defense budgets were increased to support the war on terror and the wars in Afghanistan and Iraq. Defense Secretary Rumsfeld's vision of "transformation" anticipated a future in which "platform-centered" warfare (aircraft, ships, and tanks) would be supplanted by "network-centric" warfare based on information principles and technologies. This vision was highly controversial within the military services. In addition, as costs rose for the US postwar occupation of Iraq and counterinsurgent warfare, members of Congress began to question how long the United States would stay and to demand an explicit "exit strategy." Others argued that it would undermine US political resolve and demoralize the troops to leave Iraq precipitously. The war in Iraq also generated widely publicized criticism from soldiers in the field as to the adequacy of their equipment for combat and force protection, including complaints from soldiers about lack of suitable body armor and appropriate armor protection for Humvees.

During the Cold War a symbiotic relationship grew among the US military establishment, defense contractors, and members of Congress seeking defense spending in their districts. This triangle of influence will not disappear entirely, but it will be subjected to considerable turbulence as technology from the civilian sector begins to drive military innovation toward a revolution in military affairs. The computer, communications, and electronics revolutions were not driven by government laboratories but by entrepreneurial spirit and inventiveness in the private sector. The Internet and the globalization of information and finance now make it possible for medium and small powers to acquire advanced technology. A more diffuse international security power structure will almost certainly be one ramification of the information revolution. Hierarchies will be replaced by networks as the organizational frameworks of choice for much problem solving in military and government circles. Traditional approaches to intelligence collection and analysis, including military intelligence, based on compartmentation and specialization may not work well in this new era.[23]

The Communications Revolution

Given all the development surrounding the information superhighway, there is little question that the information age has arrived. A massive increase in news and entertainment sources is planned, much of it anchored in the hyperexpansion of available television channels. In addition, microchip and laser technology, computer advances, and satellite networks have made access to information and entertainment global in scope. In addition to the Internet, the ability of viewers to interact with television messages (interactive television) will offer a variety of options for making political, commercial, and buying decisions through the television set. Furthermore, numerous political, social, educational, and advocacy channels will be available to viewers. Add the ability of the print media as well as radio to extend their reach globally, and one can begin to appreciate the impact of the communications revolution.

The impact on national security will be no less dramatic. Continual monitoring of the conflict arena will provide commanders in the field with up-to-the-second and comprehensive visual scope of the battle arena. Penetration of the adversaries' military formations, political and social infrastructures, and target areas will be commonplace. Furthermore, access to the same information will be available to policymakers in Washington, global viewers, and the media. And in the case of terrorist attacks intended to cause mass casualties for the purpose of visible defiance and exposing US vulnerabilities, the media are the message. Vivid images of the destruction would be transmitted globally in an instant.

Moreover, the communications revolution will have a major impact on military command and control, and technology and communications will revolutionize weapons systems and the characteristics of conflicts—at least conventional conflicts. The electronic battlefield will be enhanced by sophisticated communications and standoff capabilities (e.g., an exchange of missiles using highly sophisticated targeting).[24] Military training and education will need to incorporate the lessons of the communications revolution into the battle arena. In summary, it is conceivable that conflicts can be more closely controlled from the safety of the operations room in Washington, with civilian leaders being able to see and talk directly to commanders on the battlefield down the chain of command.

One danger is that perceptions of war can take on the feel of a video game, depersonalizing it to the point that only those in harm's way will really understand the personal nature of ground combat. Those outside the immediate combat area could well make decisions that have little to do with realities on the ground.

In the broader sense, it will be difficult to maintain secrecy in the national security policy process. The media will be able to gain access to or penetrate virtually any communications network used in the policy process. At the same time, there will be almost simultaneous global access to events and decisions in the national security area. The entire national security policy process will be under tremendous pressure for immediate response and rapid implementation. In an age when video-driven national security and foreign policies are becoming almost commonplace (e.g., the emergence of Al-Jazeera as a message center for various groups in the Arab and Islamic communities, including Al-Qaida and other terrorists), the communications revolution carries serious implications for long-range national security planning as well as short-range policy and strategy. How all of this will affect the national security establishment in the next decade is not clear. Although policymakers are quick to blame the media for exciting the public with vivid images of atrocities, there is also a major impact of video on political leaders themselves. President George H.W. Bush's insistence on sending a US peace mission to Somalia in December 1992 was partly motivated (by his own admission) by news footage of starving Somalis.[25] Similarly, graphic media reports from Iraq have played a large role in altering US policies there.

Conclusion

War retains its fundamental nature throughout history: as the use or threat of organized violence to accomplish a political aim. But the character of war changes across centuries for many reasons.[26] Factors such as geography, economic power, and the political viability of state actors, as well as those states' own definitions of allies and enemies, must be taken into account by US defense and foreign policy planners and political leaders. Culture, which includes religious and regional factors, also influences whether states will be friendly or hostile toward the United States and its allies. For example, when the Soviet regime collapsed and nominally democratic Russia succeeded it, the political character of the regime changed, as did the political and social culture pertinent to Russian foreign policy. This change, in turn, had consequences for the United States and NATO.

The information and communications revolutions illustrate the potential of technology to create a new context for military strategy. Persons tutored on so-called second-wave industrial military logic now find their engrained habits stressed by "third-wave" or postindustrial technologies that leap across state borders at the speed of light. The new precision of the military art, made possible by the new technologies of smart warfare, has profound implications for the character and size of armies. Smart and highly specialized soldiers, fighting in smaller units and with a greater degree of self-control, will pose challenges to enemies as well as to their own superiors higher up the chain of command.[27] This change to smaller, smarter armed forces in turn creates organizational, sociological, and political issues within US and other armed forces. With fewer grunts and greater numbers of special operations volunteers, the US military may be better prepared for missions such as peace operations and low-intensity conflicts. Yet a smarter and more autonomous military can pose other problems in civil-military relations, including a possible incongruity with the values of the society.[28]

Notes

1. Sam C. Sarkesian and Robert E. Connor Jr., *The US Military Profession into the Twenty-First Century: War, Peace, and Politics* (London: Frank Cass, 1999), esp. pp. 67–69. See also the 2nd edition, 2006.

2. Rupert Smith, *The Utility of Force: The Art of War in the Modern World* (London: Penguin/Allen Lane, 2005), p. 3.

3. Ibid, p. 4.

4. Martin van Creveld, *The Transformation of War* (New York: The Free Press, 1991).

5. Samuel P. Huntington, "The Clash of Civilizations?" *Foreign Affairs* 72, no. 3 (Summer 1993): 40.

6. Dmitri Volkogonov, *Autopsy for an Empire: The Seven Leaders Who Built the Soviet Regime,* ed. and trans. Harold Shukman (New York: The Free Press, 1998).

7. Mikhail S. Gorbachev, "Document: The Revolution and Perestroika," *Foreign Affairs* 66, no. 2 (Winter 1987/1988): 425 (excerpts from his speech; English translation distributed by the Soviet press agency TASS).

8. See Susan M. Puska, ed., *People's Liberation Army After Next* (Carlisle Barracks, PA: Strategic Studies Institute, US Army War College, August 2000), for expert assessments of Chinese military modernization.

9. Colin S. Gray, *Modern Strategy* (Oxford, UK: Oxford University Press, 1999), pp. 165–166.

10. For a discussion of the various geopolitical theories, see Norman J. Padelford and George A. Lincoln, *The Dynamics of International Politics,* 2nd ed. (New York: Macmillan, 1967), pp. 106–112. See also Sir Harold J. Mackinder, *Democratic Ideals and Reality* (New York: Henry Holt, 1919), and Nicholas J. Spykman, *The Geography of Peace,* ed. Helen R. Nickel (New York: Archon Books, 1969).

11. Hans J. Morgenthau, *Politics Among Nations: The Struggle for Power and Peace,* 6th ed. rev. Kenneth W. Thompson (New York: Alfred A. Knopf, 1985), p. 634.

12. Ibid.

13. Quincy Wright, *The Study of International Relations* (New York: Appleton-Century-Crofts, 1955), p. 348.

14. For the potential of cruise missiles in WMD attacks, see Lt. Col. Rex R. Kiziah, USAF, *Assessment of the Emerging Biocruise Threat* (Maxwell Air Force Base, AL: USAF Counterproliferation Center, Counterproliferation Papers, Future Warfare Series, No. 6, August 2000).

15. Graham Allison, *Nuclear Terrorism: The Ultimate Preventable Catastrophe* (New York: Henry Holt/Times Books, 2004).

16. Robert Gilpin, *War and Change in World Politics* (Cambridge, MA: Cambridge University Press, 1983), p. 177. See also Paul Kennedy, *The Rise and Fall of the Great Powers: Economic Change and Military Conflict from 1500 to 2000* (New York: Random House, 1988).

17. Gilpin, *War and Change in World Politics,* p. 173.

18. Ibid., p. 185.

19. Wright, *The Study of International Relations,* p. 385.

20. William R. Neikirk, "Civilian Research Can't Break Pentagon's Grip," *Chicago Tribune,* December 30, 1987, pp. 1, 10. See also *Report of the Secretary of Defense Frank C. Carlucci to the Congress on the FY1988/FY1989 Biennial Budget and FY 1988–92 Defense Programs* (Washington, DC: US Government Printing Office, amended February 18, 1988), p. 297.

21. Neikirk, "Civilian Research," pp. 1, 10.

22. Leonard Sullivan Jr., "The Defense Budget in Transition," in Joseph Kruzel, ed., *American Defense Annual, 1993* (New York: Lexington Books, 1993), p. 51.

23. Bruce D. Berkowitz and Allan E. Goodman, *Best Truth: Intelligence in the Information Age* (New Haven: Yale University Press, 2000), esp. pp. 58–98.

24. Thomas A. Keaney and Eliot A. Cohen, *Revolution in Warfare? Air Power in the Persian Gulf* (Annapolis, MD: Naval Institute Press, 1995), pp. 188–226.

25. For perspective on this issue, see Christopher Jon Lamb, "The Impact of Information Age Technologies on Operations Other Than War," in Robert L. Pfaltzgraff and Richard H. Shultz Jr., eds., *War in the Information Age* (Washington, DC: Brassey's, 1997), pp. 247–278.

26. Colin S. Gray, *Another Bloody Century: Future Warfare* (London: Weidenfeld and Nicolson, 2005), pp. 29–37.

27. John Arquilla and David Ronfeldt, *Swarming and the Future of Conflict* (Santa Monica, CA: Rand, 2000).

28. Sarkesian and Connor, *The US Military Profession* (1999), esp. pp. 50–62. See also the 2nd edition, 2006.

14

National Security and Nuclear Weapons

SINCE 1945 THE AVAILABILITY OF NUCLEAR WEAPONS HAS BEEN a critical issue in US national security policy and strategy. For much of that time the primary concern was superpower relations. Later, the acquisition of nuclear weapons by other states complicated the balance of power between the United States and the Soviet Union. With the collapse of the Soviet empire, some accommodation has been made between the United States and Russia over the size of their nuclear arsenals. Nonetheless, the issue remains contentious.

- Assessment of the nuclear future is complicated by developments in the international landscape. This landscape is ill defined and is also characterized by access to nuclear technology and weapons by international terrorist groups and rogue states. And the dispute of India and Pakistan, both of which are nuclear powers, over Kashmir highlights problems that can evolve. Combined with US involvement in the war on terrorism in the aftermath of September 11, it is no wonder that nuclear weapons remain a critical issue. In this chapter we review the evolution of nuclear weapons as a critical component of US national security. To understand the current policy and strategy, we must study the evolution of nuclear weapons policies and strategies emerging from the US-Soviet rivalry to the current period.

During the Cold War the US homeland faced the possibility of nuclear attack, which never materialized. But on September 11, 2001, the US national security agenda changed overnight. A new context now exists for assessing threats to US national security posed by weapons of mass destruction, whether in the hands of terrorists or states. Nuclear weapons will receive specific attention here because nuclear danger remains the most geopolitically critical. This claim is supported by the decision of the George W. Bush administration to begin deploying US nationwide ballistic missile defenses (BMDs) in 2004 and to continue research and development on improved BMD technologies for possible future use. Are missile defenses the answer to Americans' prayers to be able to sleep more securely at night or a false security blanket? The complex relationships among US-Russian nuclear arms control, proliferation, missile defense, and homeland security provide a large challenge for US policy planners.

Nuclear Weapons Strategies

From 1945 to the end of the Cold War (1989–1991), theorists and military officers asked whether nuclear weapons had forever changed the relationship between war and politics.[1] This question remains relevant in the twenty-first century. Indeed, the issue of nuclear weapons and their proliferation remains a complex and uncertain dimension of US national security.

The end of the Cold War and the demise of the Soviet Union cast further doubt on the political utility of nuclear forces and, perhaps, the threat of nuclear force. Without a global opponent and favoring regionally oriented military strategies, US military planners are uncertain as to the relevance of nuclear weapons except as a last resort.

Nuclear weapons also appeared to reverse the traditional relationship between offensive and defensive military strategies. In traditional strategy, offensive attacks were thought to be riskier than defensive stands. But the speed and lethality of nuclear weapons made offensive technology, but not necessarily an offensive *strategy,* look more imposing. Nuclear weapons that survived a first strike could be used to retaliate, and unless the attacker could protect itself against retaliation, the difference between the attacker's and the defender's postwar worlds might be politically and militarily insignificant.

The paradoxical implications of nuclear weapons for military strategy and US national security led to Cold War advocacy of nuclear strategic policies that followed one of two paths: mutually assured destruction (MAD) or nuclear flexibility. Some US officials and military thinkers favored a strategy of assured retaliation as the necessary and sufficient deterrent against any Soviet provocation, including Soviet attacks on US allies with conventional weapons. Assured retaliation, or MAD, required that the United States be able to absorb a Soviet surprise first strike of any size and retaliate, destroying the Soviet Union as a viable society. Assured retaliation became official US declaratory policy under Secretary of Defense Robert S. McNamara in the Kennedy and Johnson administrations.

MAD had many critics in and out of government. Some thought MAD required too much of the US nuclear arsenal; others thought that MAD would not be enough to deter a Soviet attack under some circumstances. The view that MAD was an insufficient deterrent posture for US forces gained some ground during the Nixon, Ford, Carter, and Reagan administrations.

As for nuclear flexibility, under Richard Nixon and Gerald Ford, US nuclear weapons policy was revised to emphasize options short of all-out war between the superpowers. Under Jimmy Carter, Presidential Directive 59 expanded the previous guidance and called for the creation of nuclear retaliatory forces sufficiently flexible and durable to fight a protracted, or a limited, nuclear war, as might be directed by the US president in pressing circumstances. In addition, Carter policy called for the development of nuclear command-and-control systems that would permit the United States to fight an all-out nuclear war through various phases until victory was denied to the Soviet Union.

Critics of nuclear flexibility argued that its justifications were really disguised arguments for building up nuclear arsenals well beyond the requirements of deterrence. In addition, the Soviet Union showed little apparent interest in flexible nuclear response as a means of bargaining, especially in the case of strategic nuclear weapons exploded on Soviet territory. Nevertheless, a Soviet adversary determined to exploit any relative counterforce imbalance was frequently cited by policymakers as a necessary and sufficient case for counterforce and nuclear flexibility. Although Soviet military doctrine in its political-military aspects (grand strategy) remained essentially defensive and potentially open to the concept of limited war, other aspects of Soviet military doctrine offered little in the way of encouragement. The General Staff and Politburo showed little interest in the actual limitation of nuclear strikes once deterrence had failed.[2]

Nuclear Weapons as a Deterrent

The effectiveness of nuclear weapons as a deterrent was accepted as fact by most policymakers and analysts. But carrying out war plans if deterrence failed would have been left to organizations that operated with rigid, pre-planned, and detail-driven parameters, not subject to crisis control and wartime policymakers. Theorists and strategists conceived elegant ways to fight limited wars and to dominate the process of escalation, and Soviet–Warsaw Pact planners dreamed of blasting holes in NATO's forward defenses with tactical nuclear strikes during the initial phase of war. It was, for the most part, an effort to cover up mutual fears. The greatest fear was that there was no way to fight a nuclear war at an acceptable cost, making nuclear deterrence a potentially dangerous bluff.

Colin Gray was thus correct (up to a point) to insist that all nuclear deterrence strategies were tantamount to contingent nuclear war-fighting strategies.[3] Military chains of command were tasked to prepare plans for what to do if deterrence ever failed. As Cold War arsenals grew in size and complexity, some of these plans and the planning process itself took on lives of their own. The US Single Integrated Operational Plan (SIOP) for nuclear war was driven by calculations of "damage expectancy" against designated classes of targets, and damage expectancies had to be satisfied above and beyond other requirements of the war plan. US war plans were often characterized by a lack of clear policy guidance beyond vague statements to win or prevail, as if the definition were self-evident. Target planners at Strategic Air Command (now Strategic Command) in Omaha, Nebraska, were often forced to assign weapons to targets on the basis of hunches or rules of thumb. Few, if any, US presidents ever familiarized themselves with the details of nuclear war plans.[4]

The nuclear policy of the Nixon, Ford, and Carter years called for improved US counterforce capabilities: selective attacks on Soviet land-based missiles, missile submarines, and nuclear bombers as well as their supporting military command-and-control systems. None of the US nuclear policy guidance of the 1970s, however, offered any hope of protecting the US homeland in the event that deterrence failed. The Nixon administration, in signing the 1972 ABM Treaty, made US reliance on the threat of offensive retaliation for deterrence official. Defenses were marginalized by the ABM Treaty, which constrained the size of missile defenses as well as the kinds of defenses that could be built. Both constraints were intended to preclude any possibility that either side would later deploy an effective system for the defense of its national territory.

The Strategic Defense Initiative

In March 1983, President Ronald Reagan called for the US research-and-development community to transcend deterrence based on offensive retaliation. Reagan's proposed Strategic Defense Initiative (described pejoratively by many as "Star Wars") caught his own defense bureaucrats by surprise and alarmed Moscow.[5] The technology was not available during Reagan's terms in office, or even a decade later, to provide reliable protection against a large-scale missile attack against US territory. Continued deterrence through mutual vulnerability remained the only plausible option when the Cold War expired, and it remained so into the twenty-first century.

Several other strategic doctrines were considered by policymakers, experts, and critics: assured retaliation, escalation dominance, victory denial, defense dominance, and minimum deterrence.[6] In November 2001, a Texas meeting between Russian president Vladimir Putin and US president George W. Bush about nuclear weapons and the 1972 ABM Treaty changed the context for nuclear stability by opening the door to unprecedented offensive arms reductions. In December 2001, President Bush announced that the United States would no longer be bound by the 1972 ABM Treaty. The United States and Russia agreed in May 2002 to the Strategic Offensive Reductions Treaty, limiting each side to a maximum of 1,700–2,200 operationally deployed offensive nuclear weapons by December 2012. Russia's willingness to sign this agreement pointed to the post–September 11 rapprochement between Putin and Bush and to Russia's decision not to let missile defenses stand in the way of US-Russian cooperation on other issues. The United States began deploying defenses in 2004 in Alaska and California. US leaders emphasized that the current and foreseeable defenses were not aimed at Russia: instead, their purpose was to deflect accidental launches and to deter attacks from rogue states with small arsenals.

Nuclear Arms Control in the Cold War: From Confrontation to Stability

Following the October 1962 Cuban missile crisis, US and Soviet leaders perceived a mutual interest in strategic arms limitation, the avoidance of accidental and inadvertent nuclear war, and the prevention of the spread of nuclear weapons. This led to the Nuclear Test Ban Treaty of 1963 and the hot line, a direct communications link for emergency discussions between the US and Soviet heads of state. Discussions between Moscow and Washington about strategic arms limitation got under way during the latter years of the Johnson administration, continued under Nixon, and culminated in the Strategic Arms Limitation Talks Agreement of 1972 (SALT I). A year earlier, Washington and Moscow had concluded two agreements on the prevention of accidental and inadvertent war and the avoidance of unnecessary fears of surprise attack.[7]

The interim agreement on offensive arms limitation embodied in SALT I was superseded by SALT II, signed in 1979 and carried forward (although never formally ratified by the United States) until it was transformed into START during the Reagan administration. The ABM Treaty remained as the cornerstone of US-Soviet strategic arms limitation until the end of the Cold War. As amended by a 1974 protocol signed at Vladivostok, it limited both sides' national missile defense systems to one site of no more than 100 defensive interceptors. The United States chose to deploy its ABMs at Grand Forks, North Dakota; the Soviets, around Moscow. (The US system was closed down by Congress in the mid-1970s.)

The ABM Treaty became a powerful symbol of affinity for advocates of mutual deterrence based on offensive retaliation. When the Reagan administration proposed its Strategic Defense Initiative in 1983, opponents argued that it would overturn the ABM Treaty and reopen the race in offensive weapons being capped by the SALT/START process.

Even more entrenched than the ABM Treaty was the Nuclear Nonproliferation Treaty (NPT), ratified in 1970 and supported by both the

United States and the Soviet Union. The agreement was intended to prevent the spread of nuclear weapons and weapons-related technology. The NPT outlasted the Cold War and remains in force today, although under pressure from new and aspiring nuclear powers. The NPT was extended indefinitely in 1995 with near-unanimous approval, with the important exceptions of India, Pakistan, and Israel. All three of these states are now declared or opaque nuclear powers. The favorable climate established by the NPT extension carried forward into the 1996 multilateral agreement on a comprehensive test ban (CTB) on nuclear weapons testing, extending and deepening the impact of the original test-ban treaty and the subsequent treaties on threshold test bans and peaceful nuclear explosions.

After September 11, the United States was faced with the imminent possibility of terrorist attacks using nuclear or other weapons of mass destruction, including biological, chemical, and radiological weapons. Since terrorists are stateless and have no single "return address," deterrence by threat of retaliation is almost superfluous. Recognizing this, the George W. Bush administration redefined US national security policy and military strategy to emphasize the option of preemption against terrorists or rogue states planning attacks on the United States or its allies. This shift in policy and military strategy unsettled the administration's critics, who argued that a doctrine of preemption might "encourage other states to legitimize their own aggression under the guise of defensive measures."[8] Other skeptics feared that the Bush preemption doctrine was a disguised endorsement of preventive war. (Preemption is a decision to strike first against an opponent who is already planning or has set in motion a military strike. Preventive war is a decision for attack against another state whose intentions appear hostile and whose power represents a potential threat.)

Weapons Reduction

The nuclear arms control dialogue between East and West during the Cold War contributed to the reduction of political tensions in various ways. First, continuing arms control negotiations educated both sides during the Cold War about one another's strategic and defense cultures. Second, the strategic arms limitation agreements of the 1970s and 1980s (SALT/START) provided a framework that allowed both the Americans and the Soviets to avoid expensive deployments of systems that would have been militarily unnecessary and eventually obsolete in the face of improved technology. Third, cooperation between Washington and Moscow to limit the spread of nuclear weapons technology helped limit the number of nuclear aspirants during the Cold War and set a useful precedent for multilateral cooperation against proliferation afterward. US-Russia post–Cold War cooperation against the spread of nuclear weapons included the Cooperative Threat Reduction law, authorized by the US Congress in 1991 to encourage denuclearization and demilitarization within states of the former Soviet Union, especially the four successor states that inherited the Soviet nuclear arsenal (Russia, Belarus, Kazakhstan, and Ukraine).[9]

Efforts to limit the significance of nuclear weapons during the Cold War were complicated by the role of nuclear weapons in US and NATO strategy for the prevention of war in Europe and for the establishment of a credible defense plan if deterrence failed. Some US and European analysts and policymakers doubted that conventional deterrence was feasible; others feared that it might be. Those who doubted that conventional deterrence was feasible tended to see a viable Soviet threat of invasion, absent strong NATO military preparedness. Those who feared that conventional defense was feasible noted that a conventional war in Europe would involve very different sacrifices for Americans and Europeans. A conventional deterrent for NATO might not be as convincing as a conventional defense backed by nuclear deterrence.

NATO's willingness to settle for active-duty deployment in Western Europe of some thirty ground divisions was not forced by the economics of defense, as some politicians contended. NATO could have created conventional forces capable of credible deterrence against Soviet attack precisely because nuclear weapons made success problematic, to say the least. Nuclear weapons added a component of uncertainty and risk to Soviet calculations. Yet nuclear weapons were also a curse for NATO strategy. As the numbers of tactical nuclear weapons deployed with air and ground forces multiplied, the problem of NATO command and control, including obtaining political approval for first use, became more complicated. Whether NATO's inefficient policymaking process could ever have authorized nuclear release in time was widely debated. Regardless, the deployment of US nuclear weapons in Europe would link the defense of Europe and North America. In fact the United States, by spreading its nuclear deterrent outside of North America, risked an attack on the US homeland in order to defend Europe from a Soviet offensive.

US-Russian Nuclear Arms Control in a New Century

Neither Mikhail Gorbachev's political career nor the Soviet Union survived the end of the Cold War, but nuclear weapons did. The Russian Federation assumed responsibility for former Soviet nuclear weapons and for continuing the process of nuclear arms control with the United States in the START negotiations. US political relations with post-Soviet Russia were much improved. Under Nunn-Lugar and other projects, the United States provided funds to help Russia account for its fissile materials, transport and store its remaining nuclear weapons, dismantle obsolete or disarmed weapons and launchers, and employ displaced Russian nuclear scientists on other projects. In May 2002, as noted earlier, Bush and Putin signed the Moscow Treaty to reduce long-range nuclear weapons to a maximum of 2,200 deployed nuclear warheads for each state by the year 2012. This agreement, together with the creation of a new NATO-Russia Council for consultation on terrorism, nonproliferation, and other issues, signified for many the de facto end of the Cold War.

Russia prefers lower force ceilings under the Moscow Treaty than does the United States. Its economy will be hard-pressed to pay for the simultaneous modernization of its land-based, sea-based, and airborne launch platforms. Russia will probably be satisfied with a maximum nuclear deterrent force of 1,500 warheads on strategic launchers. Russia has various ways of mixing its forces at the 2,200- or 1,700-warhead level, as does the United States.[10] For the United States and Russia to reduce their arsenals of offensive weapons to Moscow Treaty levels by 2012, each will have to give up large numbers of operationally deployed weapons. The US and Russian nuclear arsenals as of 2004 are summarized in Table 14.1.

The Moscow Treaty imposes no limitations on the two sides' total holdings of nuclear weapons as distinct from those operationally deployed only. The treaty also has a post–Cold War cast in that it does not entail intrusive verification protocols or restrict either side's freedom to mix weapons and launcher types. Since the treaty dealt with offenses only, it leaves the door open to missile defenses for both sides. Russia indicated that it would modernize its offensive missile force to maintain essential parity with US forces. In addition, Putin also stated on several occasions that Russia would not permit any US defense system to nullify Russia's second-strike capability. According to Putin, future Russian strike forces would include types of weapons that could circumvent antimissile defenses.[11]

Such techniques might include maneuvering warheads or missiles that were capable of changing trajectories in flight. Russia might also consider its own defense system or cooperative security arrangements with the United States and NATO for the deployment of limited defenses on Russia's southern and eastern flanks.

Under the George W. Bush administration, the United States was thinking of missile defenses in the broader context of a reappraisal of the fundamentals of US national military strategy. According to national defense guidance and US nuclear policy statements, the former strategic nuclear "triad" of land-based, sea-based, and bomber-delivered weapons would be superseded in the new century by a "new triad" of (1) conventional and nuclear offensive strike weapons; (2) active and passive defenses; and (3) improved infrastructure, including command, control, and

Table 14.1 US and Russian Strategic Nuclear Forces, 2004

Type	Launchers	Warheads x Yield (in kilotons)	Total Warheads
		Russian Forces	
ICBMs[a]			
SS-18	120	10 x 550/750	1,200
SS-19	130	6 x 550/750	780
SS-24	15	10 x 550	150
SS-25	312	1 x 550	312
SS-27	36	1 x 550	36
Total	613		2,478
SLBMs[b]			
SS-N-18	96	3 x 200	288
SS-N-20	40	10 x 100	400
SS-N-23	96	4 x 100	384
Total	232		1,072
Bombers			
Tu-95 Bear H6	32	6 AS-15A ALCMs or bombs	192
Tu-95 Bear H16	32	16 AS-15A ALCMs or bombs	512
Tu-160 Blackjack	14	12 AS-15B ALCMs, AS-16 SRAMs, or bombs	168
Total	78		872
Total	923		4,442
		US Forces	
ICBMs			
Minuteman III/ Mark-12	150	1 x 170	150
Minuteman III/ Mark-12	50	3 x 170	150
Minuteman III/ Mark-12A	300	3 x 335	900
MX/Peacekeeper	29	10 x 300	290
Total	529		1,490
SLBMs			
Trident I C4	72	6 x 100	432
Trident II D5	288		
	Mk-4	8 x 100	1,920
	Mk-5	8 x 475	384
Total	360		2,736
Bombers[c]			
B-52H	56[d]	ALCM x 150	430
		ACM x 150	430

continues

Table 14.1 continued

Type	Launchers	Warheads x Yield (in kilotons)	Total Warheads
B-2	16	B61-7, B61-11, B-83-1 bombs	800
Total	72		1,660
Total	817		5,886

Source: National Resources Defense Council, *NRDC Nuclear Notebook,* Bulletin of the Atomic Scientists, May/June 2004, pp. 68–70. Available at http://www.thebulletin.org/issues/nukenotes/mj04nukenote.

Notes: a. ICBMs = intercontinental ballistic missiles.

b. SLBMs = submarine-launched ballistic missiles.

c. Bomber force loadings include a variety of weapons and mixes among air-launched cruise missiles (ALCMs), advanced cruise missiles (ACMs), and gravity bombs.

d. Bomber numbers include mission-assigned operational aircraft for nuclear or conventional missions, excluding those in training, testing, or backup.

communications, to support US military operations worldwide, including nuclear options.[12]

In addition, the Bush administration sought from Congress approval to develop specialized mininukes or micronukes with low yield for use against enemy fortified bunkers and caches of WMD.[13] Nuclear and conventional weapons, according to the Bush strategy, would function as more of a seamless web of options for deterrence or, if necessary, for military action.

The Bush policy shift reflected the reality of improved US conventional military forces compared to the Cold War and the information-driven character of modern weapons technology. It also responded to a new threat environment, one marked by asymmetrical threats involving weapons of mass destruction available to rogue states or terrorists. Missile defenses based on new principles, together with improved offensive and defensive forces, would provide the president with a range of options: preemption, deterrence, and defense and/or retaliation, if necessary. Bush critics argued that the new triad blurred the distinction between nuclear and conventional weapons to a dangerous degree, that it would encourage nuclear proliferation, and that the past performances of missile defense technology did not point to an optimistic future. In contrast, Department of Defense technology developers foresaw a mix of conventional and nuclear strike weapons that would make the United States less dependent on the nuclear option and more capable of posing credible threats supported by realistic options. For example, some experts recommended that the Secretary of Defense and the US Navy assign two missiles on each Trident ballistic missile submarine (SSBN) for delivering conventional payloads only and, perhaps, eliminate the nuclear role for Tomahawk cruise missiles and for forward-based, tactical, dual-capable aircraft.[14]

The purposes of a limited US National Missile Defense (NMD) system would be to deter and to defeat, if necessary, attacks on US territory by rogue states such as North Korea, to destroy any ballistic missiles accidentally launched at the US homeland, and to deter the use of such weapons by international terrorists and other nonstate actors. Testing of a ground-based midcourse defense (GMD) system using hit-to-kill, exoatmospheric nonnuclear interception—the most promising US technology—has produced inconsistent results, however. Although US NMD technology remained in its infancy, prominent Russian officials remained wary lest the United States create a first-strike capability against Russia's deterrent, backed by defenses good enough to absorb Russia's retaliatory strike. US nationwide and theater-range missile defense technologies in research and development under the Bush Pentagon include ground-based midcourse defenses, airborne optical lasers, and sea-based interceptors as well as advanced satellites and command-control-communications systems for launch detection, tracking, and battle management.[15]

The diminished quality of Russia's conventional military forces since the end of the Cold War pressured Moscow's military planners to increase their reliance on its remaining nuclear deterrent. Several versions of Russia's post-1991 military doctrine officially declared that Russia's nuclear forces might be used not only in response to a nuclear attack but also in a variety of other contingencies, including a conventional attack on Russian territory. In addition to an expanded NATO and a cash-starved Russian military, Russian nervousness about the instability of its borders gave nuclear weapons a higher priority among Russian military options. Although Russia reassured the United States and its NATO allies that every precaution had been taken against a failure of its nuclear command-and-control system, the United States offered its expertise to Russia in order to prevent computer failures and other disasters that might contribute to nuclear instability.

The Danger of Proliferation

The spread of nuclear weapons and other WMD in the twenty-first century poses new challenges for US and allied policymakers and their militaries. There is a justified concern on the part of the United States and other countries about the potential spread of ballistic missiles and other long-range delivery systems. The 1998 entries of India and Pakistan into the nuclear club showed that some states value nuclear weapons as symbols of power and status, contrary to the assumptions underlying the NPT (reaffirmed by signatories in 1995) and other arms control efforts. North Korea's decisions to depart the Nonproliferation Treaty, expel UN inspectors, and openly declare its nuclear status have added additional uncertainties to the mix.

Two schools of thought characterize the US approach to nuclear prolif-eration.[16] One school, continuous with the dominant tendency in Cold War thinking, holds that any spread of nuclear weapons is inherently bad. All states aspiring to obtain nuclear arsenals should be discouraged, and all states now possessing nuclear forces (with the exception of the five perma-nent members of the UN Security Council) should be urged to roll them back. The second school of thought sees the first approach as doomed to failure in the twenty-first century, regardless of its utility during the Cold War. This school favors selective US opposition to nuclear/WMD prolifera-tion, based on the willingness of the state to adhere to acceptable norms of international behavior.[17] Of course, the predominant norm is nonaggression. According to this approach, the United States and its allies would not neces-sarily attempt to dissuade or discourage nuclear proliferation in states satis-fied with the international status quo. Only those states determined to dis-rupt the geopolitical status quo, such as Iran, would be targeted for counterproliferation—active measures to prevent the state from obtaining nuclear weapons and to deny it the effective ability to use them once obtained (see Table 14.2, which summarizes nuclear weapons arsenals). Of course, a state's intention could change quickly, and a nuclear-capable "sta-tus quo" state could become a revolutionary "anti–status quo" state overnight.

Since the status quo works to the US advantage in the current and near-term international system, the selective approach to nonproliferation appears hypocritical to those on the receiving end. Why, for example, should India and (especially) Pakistan feel the sting of US disapproval

Table 14.2 World Nuclear Arsenals, 2005

Country	Suspected Strategic Nuclear Weapons	Suspected Nonstrategic Nuclear Weapons	Suspected Total Nuclear Weapons
China	280	120	~400
France	350	0	350
India	60	?	60+ (?)
Israel	100–200	?	200+ (?)
North Korea		8–11	8–11 (?)
Pakistan	24–48	?	24–48
Russia	~3,800	~3,400	~7,200
United Kingdom	180	5	185
United States	4,530	780	~5,300

Source: Center for Defense Information, May 2, 2005. Available at http.www.cdi.org/program/issue/document.cfm?Docum.

while Israel suffered nothing for its "bomb in the basement" nuclear status? In the case of US NATO allies such as Britain and France, it could be argued that the NATO defense pact gives US officials continuing contact with allied counterparts and might act, in some circumstances, as a restraint on an otherwise unilateral decision for nuclear use.

But Israel is part of no such alliance, and its nuclear decisions are accountable only to its own state interests. Israel, given its perceived defense predicament and small territorial size, makes a strong case for its own nuclear capacity: to deter any nuclear/WMD attack, to deny the possibility of another Holocaust, and to thwart adversaries who might engage in nuclear coercion.[18] Despite this logic, third world and other states aspiring to nuclear status cannot help but notice the selective application of US proliferation norms. This point, among others, has led some states to withhold their signatures from the Comprehensive Test Ban Treaty promoted by the Clinton administration and opened for signature in 1996.

Proponents of nuclear disarmament contend that selective nonproliferation shares the old fixation on partial instead of complete solutions to nuclear peril. The willingness to live with the existence of nuclear weapons, even in small quantities and in the hands of "reputable" states, runs the unacceptable risk of nuclear first use followed by a war of unprecedented destruction. Proponents of nuclear disarmament have a respectable intellectual and political tradition going back to the very beginning of the nuclear age.[19] But they are up against the practical objection that the level of international trust necessary for verified elimination of all nuclear forces does not yet exist. And even if states trusted one another to disarm completely, the knowledge of how to build nuclear weapons cannot be de-invented, and arsenals once destroyed can eventually be rebuilt. Thus some have proposed that states could disarm weapons already assembled and ready to fire, although arsenals could be reconstituted if necessary (so-called virtual nuclear arsenals).

Conclusion

Nuclear weapons, deterrence, and nonproliferation remain critical to US national security policy and strategy as well as to those of its allies and adversaries. At the same time, the availability of related technology—and perhaps actual weapons—to states or groups willing to use them has magnified the problems of deterrence and proliferation for the United States. And missiles, bombers, or other delivery systems for nuclear weapons can also be used for WMD such as chemical and biological munitions. The long reach of WMD in the hands of dissatisfied state or nonstate actors is another form of asymmetrical warfare or deterrence.

If new technology makes antinuclear defenses viable in the coming years, how will that change the relationship between deterrence and proliferation? This depends on how good the defense technology is and who owns it. Various technologies for airborne or ground-based interception of ballistic missiles seemed more promising at the end of the 1990s than they did a decade earlier. Technological innovation does not by itself, however, constitute a strategic breakthrough. Strategy involves a reactive opponent. Offensive countermeasures exist for many of the kinds of defenses that have been proposed. The era of offense-dominant nuclear strategy will probably continue unless space-based defenses operating at the speed of light can be deployed and protected. Until then, we are talking about a shift not from offense dominance to defense dominance, as President Ronald Reagan hoped for, but from offense dominance to offense-defense competitiveness.[20]

If antimissile defenses become cost-effective compared to ballistic missile offenses, then the effect will almost certainly be to dissuade interest in ballistic missile strikes, whether nuclear or not. There are other ways to deliver nuclear weapons, and one need not rely on missiles that lend themselves to interception and destruction. The terrorist attacks of September 11 were a reminder that mass destruction can be accomplished in the US homeland without missile attacks, nuclear weapons, or even regular armed forces. In addition, if antimissile defenses become good enough to make missile strikes obsolete, those defenses may also have ominous offensive (i.e., first-strike) capabilities against a variety of target sets and raise the problem of preemption to another technological level. Defenses that can intercept incoming ballistic missiles may also be able to destroy satellites, thereby disrupting communications and command and control and denying the enemy a clear picture of the battle space. Competent antimissile defenses or other space-based weapons may be the leading edge of an information warfare strategy for the twenty-first century.

Notes

1. On the development of nuclear strategy, see, e.g., Keith B. Payne, *Deterrence in the Second Nuclear Age* (Lexington: University Press of Kentucky, 1996); Colin S. Gray, *The Second Nuclear Age* (Boulder: Lynne Rienner Publishers, 1999); and Stephen J. Cimbala, *Nuclear Deterrence in the Twenty-First Century* (Westport, CT: Praeger, 2000). On the early years of US strategic theorizing, see Marc Trachtenberg, *History and Strategy* (Princeton, NJ: Princeton University Press, 1991), pp. 3–46. The logic of deterrence and deterrence rationality receives especially insightful treatment in Phil Williams, "Nuclear Deterrence," in John Baylis, Ken Booth, John Garnett, and Phil Williams, *Contemporary Strategy: I: Theories and Concepts* (New York: Holmes and Meier, 1987), pp. 113–139. The nuclear revolution is put into historical context in Bernard Brodie, *War and Politics* (New York:

Macmillan, 1973), pp. 375–496, and in Michael Mandelbaum, *The Nuclear Revolution: International Politics Before and After Hiroshima* (Cambridge: Cambridge University Press, 1981).

2. For evidence of Soviet views on controlling and possibly terminating a major war, see Raymond L. Garthoff, *Deterrence and the Revolution in Soviet Military Doctrine* (Washington, DC: Brookings Institution, 1991), chap. 5, and Garthoff, "New Soviet Thinking on Conflict Initiation, Control and Termination," in Stephen J. Cimbala and Sidney R. Waldman, eds., *Controlling and Ending Conflict* (Westport, CT: Greenwood, 1992), pp. 65–94.

3. Colin S. Gray, *Modern Strategy* (Oxford, UK: Oxford University Press, 1999), pp. 309–318.

4. Desmond Ball, "The Development of the SIOP, 1960–1983," in Desmond Ball and Jeffrey Richelson, eds., *Strategic Nuclear Targeting* (Ithaca: Cornell University Press, 1986), pp. 57–83. See also Richard Ned Lebow, *Nuclear Crisis Management: A Dangerous Illusion* (Ithaca: Cornell University Press, 1987), pp. 118–122.

5. Frances Fitzgerald, *Way Out There in the Blue: Reagan, Star Wars, and the End of the Cold War* (New York: Simon and Schuster, 2000), p. 198.

6. For an alternate perspective, see Charles Glaser, "Why Do Strategists Disagree About the Requirements of Strategic Nuclear Deterrence?" in Lynn Eden and Steven E. Miller, eds., *Nuclear Arguments: Understanding the Strategic Nuclear Arms and Arms Control Debates* (Ithaca: Cornell University Press, 1989), esp. pp. 113–117.

7. Nicolai N. Petro and Alvin Z. Rubinstein, *Russian Foreign Policy: From Empire to Nation-State* (New York: Addison-Wesley, 1997), pp. 135–136, 140–143.

8. Lawrence J. Korb, *A New National Security Strategy in an Age of Terrorists, Tyrants, and Weapons of Mass Destruction* (New York: Council on Foreign Relations, 2003), p. 7.

9. William J. Perry, Secretary of Defense, *Annual Report to the President and the Congress* (Washington, DC: US Government Printing Office, March 1996), pp. 63–70.

10. See Scott D. Sagan and Kenneth N. Waltz, eds., *The Spread of Nuclear Weapons: A Debate* (New York: W. W. Norton, 1995), for arguments and counterarguments with regard to nuclear proliferation.

11. "Putin Boasts of Russia's Missile Power," Associated Press, January 21, 2006. Available at CNN.com.

12. US Department of Defense, *Findings of the Nuclear Posture Review, Briefing* (Washington, DC: US Department of Defense, January 9, 2002). *See also DOD Briefing on the Nuclear Posture Review.* Available at http://www.globalsecurity.org/wmd/library/policy/dod/npr.htm (accessed April 22, 2005).

13. Robert W. Nelson, "Lowering the Threshold: Nuclear Bunker Busters and Mininukes," chap. 4 in Brian Alexander and Alistair Millar, eds., *Tactical Nuclear Weapons: Emergent Threats in an Evolving Security Environment* (Washington, DC: Brassey's, 2003), pp. 68–79.

14. Office of the Secretary of Defense, *Report of the Defense Science Board Task Force on Future Strategic Strike Forces* (Washington, DC: Office of the Under Secretary of Defense for Acquisition, Technology, and Logistics, February 2004), pp. 5–13.

15. On US missile defense technologies, see Department of Defense, Missile Defense Agency, *Fact Sheet*, available at www.mda.mil (regularly updated); Stephen A. Hildreth, Coordinator, Congressional Research Service, *Missile Defense: The Current Debate* (Washington, DC: Congressional Research Service, July 19, 2005);

and US Government Accountability Office, *Defense Acquisitions: Status of Ballistic Missile Defense Programs in 2004* (Washington, DC: GAO, March 2005).

16. Sagan and Waltz, *The Spread of Nuclear Weapons.*

17. See Stephen J. Cimbala, ed., *Deterrence and Proliferation in the Twenty-First Century* (Westport, CT: Praeger, 2001) for diverse perspectives on this topic by experts on arms control and military strategy. On the relationship between strategy and proliferation (or nonproliferation), see Gray, *The Second Nuclear Age,* pp. 47–78.

18. The case for an Israeli nuclear deterrent is summarized in Louis Rene Beres, *Security Threats and Effective Remedies: Israel's Strategic, Tactical, and Legal Options* (Shaarei Tikva, Israel: Ariel Center for Policy Research, April 2000), pp. 39–47.

19. Lawrence Freedman, "Eliminators, Marginalists, and the Politics of Disarmament," in John Baylis and Robert O'Neill, eds., *Alternative Nuclear Futures: The Role of Nuclear Weapons in the Post–Cold War World* (Oxford: Oxford University Press, 2000), pp. 56–69.

20. Stephen J. Cimbala, *Nuclear Weapons and Strategy: U.S. Nuclear Policy for the Twenty-First Century* (London: Routledge, 2005), chap. 2.

15

Making the System Work

GIVEN THE VARIETY OF AGENCIES AND INDIVIDUALS INVOLVED in US national security, it is no wonder that many consider it to be a confusing system with a muddled process. Designing coherent policy and strategy in such a system is like trying to complete a complex jigsaw puzzle: to be assembled correctly, it takes time, and sometimes the actors merely "muddle through." This is a disturbing overall view. To complicate matters, national security issues lead to serious disagreements within Congress, and the US public may be confused as to how the system actually works. Furthermore, bureaucratic turf battles and power struggles can lead to internecine warfare, causing serious problems in defining national interests and designing national security policy and strategy.

At first blush, September 11 promised to change all this, at least in the short term. The US "war on terror" was coupled with a policy of transformation in Middle Eastern politics, emphasizing the promotion of democracy in that troubled region. The Bush administration admitted that the struggle to defeat transnational terrorism and promote Middle Eastern democracy would be a protracted conflict for many years. Against this appearance of a singular focus in Bush policy and strategy, critics charged that the war against Iraq in 2003, and the insurgency in that country that roiled its postwar reconstruction, diverted US policy and strategy into wrong directions. The Bush administration felt that US efforts against global terrorism, and against state sponsors of terror or states that might give terrorists weapons of mass destruction (WMD), were all important pieces in solving the same puzzle. Regardless of how these arguments played out in US domestic politics, there was no question that a broad civil war in the Arab and Islamic worlds between traditionalists and modernizers would involve the United States, its allies, and its adversaries for years to come.

Despite outward appearances, US national security policymaking takes place within a well-established pattern and institutional system. The problem is that competing interests and divergent political perceptions and mind-sets often muddle the policy process. This was especially the case in the post–Cold War era and into the beginning of the twenty-first century. The passing of the Cold War swept away familiar frameworks of analysis and categories of thought about international politics. Scholars and policymakers alike have slipped their previous intellectual moorings, and certainties from the past have given way to ambiguities in the present.[1]

Coherence and effective functioning within the national security system are not self-executing—they require hard work. The sense of directed purpose and implementation is established only as a result of effective leadership putting the major pieces together. Without such leadership, the system becomes a series of political-bureaucratic fiefdoms, with each trying to dominate the others.

In these last two chapters, we examine the problems facing presidents in bringing together the agencies and individuals in the national security establishment in order to design coherent policy and strategy. Regardless of how well that is done, there are always disagreements and bureaucratic infighting. The key is to allow disparate points of view, to identify a variety of options, and to maintain a reasonably good working relationship with Congress while ensuring that the president's worldview and strategic perspective prevail.

It should be stressed that the national security establishment and those in the policy process cannot be viewed simply in theoretical terms, as intellectual curiosities. People are the foundation of the national security system, whether bureaucrats, staff members, political appointees, or members of Congress. They all come with imperfections, previous social and political relationships, divergent goals, ambitions, and human frailties. To speak of "the establishment" and "the process" in clinical terms, isolated from the real world and human dynamics, is to neglect the most important dimension of national security: the human factor. A realistic sense of the national security establishment and the effectiveness of the policy process must include how the human factor shapes and influences US national security. This dimension is too often neglected by those studying US national security.

We have examined the scope and complexity of national security, its institutional and political dimensions, and the variety of interests and forces involved in the policy process. That process has become even more complicated and broader in scope owing to the US determination to fight the war on terrorism. Thus there are many challenges to US security interests that defy simple solutions. Also, US national security policy has a great deal of continuity that reaches back more than five decades. Important elements shaping national security are part of the US political culture and are embedded in US history. What can be made of all of this? How can these be properly weighed and shaped to design the most effective US national security policy?

The search for answers can begin by applying what has been studied and analyzed in this book, recognizing that there are no perfect or immutable solutions to US national security. On the one hand, there are persistent US national interests; on the other, those interests must come to grips with a changing international security environment. *The key to success is the leadership exercised by the president and his ability to pull together all the pieces of the system.* The president must shape the boundaries, determine the directions, and establish the critical points to map out US national interests, priorities, policy, and strategy. If the president fails in this effort, national security will suffer accordingly.

The President and National Security: Retrospections

The scope of presidential power expanded over the course of the twentieth century, and the prerogatives of the presidency have been closely guarded by the executive, regardless of party affiliation and political orientation. Presidential power in national security, resting on such concepts as executive privilege and the interests of national security, was rarely challenged. In the period from the end of World War II until the Vietnam War, roles and responsibilities as commander in chief, chief executive, and head of state gave the president control over policy and intelligence-gathering instruments, and he was seen by most US citizens as the focal point for foreign and national security policies. But political and organizational developments during and after the US military intervention in Vietnam have sometimes constrained presidential initiative and prerogatives.

The International Arena in the Twenty-First Century

Compounding the problems of presidential leadership is the international security environment of the twenty-first century. It has become more difficult to define US national interests, national security policy, and strategy in the domestic and international arenas. After September 11, combating transnational terror networks such as Al-Qaida and their state sponsors became a consensus priority among US policymakers. But in the US system of government, the "how" is always controversial, even after broad agreement on the "what." Past controversies such as Vietnam and Watergate, as well as arguments over George W. Bush's domestic surveillance policies, have increased concerns about the extent of executive power. In the aftermath of Vietnam and Watergate, for example, Congress reasserted itself in foreign and national security affairs—the period of the "imperial Congress."

Although the White House regained some initiative during the Ronald Reagan presidency, the assertive role of Congress remains an important factor in limiting presidential power. George W. Bush's claims for broad presidential power were urged by Vice President Dick Cheney, who served as chief of staff for President Gerald Ford when presidential power suffered under the hammering of an aroused post-Vietnam and post-Watergate Congress.

The Vietnam legacy underpinned much of the congressional opposition and public resistance to extending US commitments beyond well-established treaty obligations. That legacy remains as an important conditioner of US attitudes, even though the victory in the 1991 Gulf War helped to erode the so-called Vietnam syndrome. But the failed US efforts in Somalia, with the humiliating deaths of US soldiers in Mogadishu, as well as US involvement in Bosnia and Kosovo, seemed to have rekindled the Vietnam syndrome, at least until September 11. Initially favorable military campaigns in Afghanistan and Iraq positioned the United States for a more influential profile in Middle Eastern politics, but they did not necessarily make the case for a fundamental change in US grand strategy. US grand strategy would have to reflect postconflict staying power and the willingness to follow success in battle with endurance in the murky political waters of the greater Middle East, from West Africa to Southeast Asia.

Many academic, policy community, and public attitudes also reflect a growing conviction that there are limits to US ability to influence events around the world. Indeed, some even argue for a revived isolationism. But the United States remains the lone superpower, with responsibilities that extend beyond the US homeland, and, arguably, the United States must assume the role of international "sheriff" for want of other candidates.[2] Nevertheless, the United States cannot succeed alone. The preceding point is underpinned by efforts to extend US values into other parts of the world and to establish democratic systems. Combined with lessened fears of major wars and the increasingly accepted idea that democracies do not fight one another, there is the notion that the United States should attempt to shape events around the world. But old demons have been replaced by new ones: "It was May 1989. . . . 'I'm running out of demons,' complained Army General Colin Powell. However, on 1 September 1993 when he unveiled DoD's Bottom-Up review, he amended his original statement: 'Fortunately, history and central casting have supplied me with new ones along the way.'"[3]

The new demons range from religious, ethnic, and nationalistic conflicts to international terrorism and drug cartels. Add to this the proliferation of nuclear weapons and increasing concerns about chemical and biological terrorism and information warfare, and the number of potential enemies is daunting. From the excessively well-structured (if dangerous) threat system of the Cold War, we have evolved into a less well-structured (if not chaotic) system of "distributed" threats. War can now take place in any of five dimensions: land, sea, air, space, and cyberspace.

The National Security System

Actors in the policy process have their own political constituencies and perspectives. They jealously guard their prerogatives, jockeying for power among themselves. The national security establishment, although directly under the control of the president, is still subject to congressional initiatives and oversight. Congressional initiatives, for example, have focused on intelligence activities and the defense budget process. Part of this effort reflects congressional reluctance to allow the establishment to operate outside congressional control. The legislation passed in 1996 requiring the secretary of defense to complete a Quadrennial Defense Review (QDR) every four years is but one example (see Chapter 6). Other examples include the post–September 11 reorganizations of US intelligence and national security to create a director of national intelligence (DNI) and a cabinet-level Department of Homeland Security. The US political system divides power and responsibility in ways that must impact on national security. Bureaucratic concerns about agency power and programs, interagency power struggles, budget constraints, congressional criticism, and domestic political considerations have solidified efforts to constrain the national security establishment. In the current period, presidential power in national security is being redefined by executive assertions, congressional initiatives, and court decisions, all happening simultaneously. Furthermore, various components of national security policy, such as budget considerations, weapons acquisitions, and strategy, are not solely determined by military and national security issues. The defense budget, for example, reflects a series of political compromises, many shaped by domestic policy issues rather than political-military policy and strategy. Nonetheless, the president has been given a broad mandate to fight terrorists, even preemptively.

The complexity and potential volatility of national security issues make the problem of presidential control and guidance even more difficult. The technical aspects of strategic weapons, information-age technology, the complexities of logistics, and the evolution of the electronic battlefield, for example, require that the president rely heavily on military and civilian experts for interpretations of weapons requirements, as well as advice on their strategic implications. One consequence is that there is a built-in propensity for struggle among agencies to gain access to the president and to convince him of the wisdom of their views. The internal struggles are compounded by gatekeepers who can be primarily concerned about preserving existing power structures. All of this makes the president vulnerable to agency biases, in some instances making him a captive of technicians, strategists, and midlevel bureaucrats. As Henry Kissinger once argued, "Because of our cult of specialization, sovereign departments negotiate national policy among themselves with no single authority, except an over-burdened President, able to take an over-all view or to apply decisions over a period of time."[4]

In summary, the power and posture of agencies within the national security establishment, the interplay of personalities within the executive, the power of Congress in the national security policy process, the tendency to politicize national security issues, and the demands of domestic politics and policy—all in a changing international security environment—have created a far more complicated situation compared to previous eras. The apparent simplicity of Cold War definitions of allies, enemies, and "others" has given way to a confused landscape of possibilities.

In the search for answers and a systematic approach to national security, we need to focus on two dimensions: the presidential power base and constituency, and the national security environment. Although fears have been raised about conflict on the Korean Peninsula and between India and Pakistan, conflicts such as the Gulf War of 1991 are not likely to characterize wars in the early twenty-first century.[5] The more likely scenarios are found in the NATO involvement in Bosnia (1995 and beyond) and later in Kosovo (1999 and beyond). The US interventions in Afghanistan in 2001 and in Iraq in 2003 are also characteristic of likely future conflicts. The past and ongoing conflicts over failed states in Africa reinforce this view. For example, Somalia in 2006 was besieged by Islamic militias struggling against warlords for control over major cities and ports, whereas the Somali "government" was more an expression of faith than an effective institution. Countering international terrorism with a global strategy adds a complex and challenging dimension to the conflict environment.

The Presidential Power Base and Constituency

The presidential power base is shaped by *four* elements: the legal and political dimensions of the presidency in national security, democratic ideology and open systems, domestic political actors and the domestic political environment, and presidential character and accountability (see Chapter 4).

First, since the end of World War II, presidents have generally assumed office with similar legal and political power to conduct national security policy—the War Powers Resolution notwithstanding. The president is the commander in chief, head of state, and chief executive. The legal and political powers derived from those roles have provided presidents the opportunity to engage in a range of initiatives in the conduct of national security. How such powers are used is a function of the president's personality and character, leadership style, and worldview. Thus each president places his own stamp on national security policy and the way that the national security establishment functions.

Second, the extent of presidential power in national security policy is limited and conditioned by the values and expectations of democratic ideology. The moral and ethical content of democracy and the public expectations that US international behavior should reflect values such as individual freedom, justice, and dignity limit the options in national security strategy, temper the means used, and establish an overarching presence in the way the president conducts national security policy. All this creates an inherent moral and ethical dichotomy between the ends-means relationships in US national security policy and strategy, that is, moral and ethical means to reach moral and ethical ends—a gap that presidents often find difficult to bridge. Furthermore, the president usually shares this commitment to democratic ideology and its moral and ethical imperatives, which shapes his mind-set and determines the boundaries within which he functions. In short, there are a self-imposed restraint and limitations on those reaching the Oval Office.

Third, there are several domestic political actors with power to affect national security policy, chief among them Congress. Vietnam, Watergate, Iran-contra, and Iraq, among other events, galvanized Congress to assert itself in the national security policy process. This was shown by criticism of the Clinton administration's efforts in Somalia, Haiti, Bosnia, and Kosovo, among others. Before and after September 11, the George W. Bush administration came in for its own criticism on several issues, including the perception that it tended to ignore international opinion and to avoid commitments on issues ranging from global warming to the control of antipersonnel mines. Congressional assertiveness is reinforced by the power of congressional incumbency—one that often goes beyond presidential terms in office.

In addition, the mass media have a significant influence in the policy process. Investigative reporting, brought to public notice in the Watergate affair, has become an institutionalized method of analyzing and reporting the news as well as for setting the agenda. Combined with the traditional adversarial relationship between the media and the national security establishment, this makes it difficult for the president to remain unchallenged in his policy pronouncements and in shaping that establishment. Equally important, representatives of the media have their own informal networks of information that penetrate the core of the national security establishment, making it difficult to develop policy out of public view when necessary.

Political predispositions of the media elite—whether perceived as left- or right-leaning—add to the problem, with certain national security policy and strategy issues presented in highly critical terms.[6] For example, some media critics suggested that reporters subdued their criticism of the Clinton administration because of Clinton's domestic social agenda, which conformed to the media's view.[7] On the other hand, the allegedly liberal bias of reporters and editors must be viewed within a broader context. Owners of flagship media tend to be wealthy entrepreneurs, not populists. In addition, the bias in news gathering and reporting is toward the negative and sensational, not against either political party. Presidents Bill Clinton and George W. Bush both felt the sting of negative reporting that arguably crossed the line between professional criticism and personal abuse. Indeed, outrageous and even irresponsible press behavior is a US tradition: it was even worse in the early years of mass-market newspapers whose rambunctious publisher William Randolph Hearst once boasted that he had started a war (the Spanish-American War)—an overstatement with a grain of truth.

Several groups and institutions in the public domain, including special interest groups and single-issue groups, seek to influence national security policy and strategy. Their involvement has increasingly politicized and publicized nuclear, environmental, and human rights issues, linking them to national security. This was the case even in the new war on terrorism. This creates a greater awareness about national security issues and defense policy, and the public becomes more sensitive to presidential postures on such issues. For example, both the Clinton and the George W. Bush administrations included persons who felt that acquired immunodeficiency syndrome (AIDS) was an important security as well as a health issue.

Furthermore, power clusters within the administration can also act as rallying points for advocating one or the other direction in national security policy and strategy, leading to struggles between the president's inner circle and the rest of the administration.

Fourth, even though the president has a freer hand in national security policy compared to some other issues, the nature of the office makes him accountable to the public. This is not limited to elections every four years but includes a variety of measures and instruments that counterbalance presidential actions and require explanation. There is a constant political and intellectual interplay that tests presidential accountability, including opinion polls, interest group activity, party cohesion, congressional-executive relationships, and the president's own staff and bureaucracy. The power clusters and the policy and strategic options they represent force the president to develop some degree of consensus and political coherence in policy and strategy, regardless of his leadership style and decisionmaking preferences.

Although several conclusions can be drawn from these observations, one stands out: the importance of presidential leadership. The president's leadership style and how he organizes and directs the national security establishment are primary determinants of the effectiveness of US national security policy and strategy. This shapes national will, political resolve, and staying power. The challenge of international terrorism will surely test the resolve of the US public and the president's leadership.

Presidential Leadership and the National Security Establishment

The boundaries within which the president must operate and the latitude of his legal and political power to deal with the national security system and environment are a consequence of his power base and constituency. The president's leadership, personality, and character are critical in determining his effectiveness. In this respect, *system* is defined to include the variety of political actors, the national security establishment, the policy process, and all of the informal procedures that are important parts of national security policymaking. The *environment* refers to the characteristics of the international security dimension of world politics, the capabilities and policies of external political actors, and the dynamics created by their interactions.

Although model-building and theoretical frameworks for analyzing the presidency are a useful and necessary undertaking, they have limits. Presidential performance is not bound by any single model; neither does the president necessarily engage in a conscious effort to adopt a particular model and shape his performance accordingly. Furthermore, the rigid application of models and theories can fail to account for a president's ability to change his approach and adopt ad hoc decisionmaking to resolve problems and challenges. Finally, choosing a single model as the sole basis for examining the presidency tends to favor a managerial perspective, highlighting the mechanics rather than the political and social components of presidential performance.

The psychopolitical-psychological approach is a useful vantage point from which to address the political, social, and humanistic components of presidential performance. Given the dominance of the political component in virtually all national security considerations, the psychopolitical-psychological framework can provide a useful and pointed focus on the president and his role in shaping the national security environment. This approach is based on the premise that presidential leadership—fashioned by the president's personality and character—and keen political instincts and intuitiveness are key elements in presidential performance. These qualities must flow from a mind-set that projects a national security posture that is coherent, purposeful, and in accord with the norms of democracy.

This is not to suggest that national security policy needs to be a noncontentious process. It does mean that a reasonably effective national security policy requires presidential leadership at major points in the national security establishment and in the policy process. Leadership, especially broad vision and goal setting, is more important than mastery of organizational procedures, managerial techniques, and knowledge of the details and technical aspects of national security issues.

Presidents who expect to be successful should begin with a deep understanding of the organizational dynamics within the national security establishment. This must go hand in hand with political acumen in dealing with

Congress and the public. Put simply, the president must be a creative political leader.

To ensure that the presidential presence permeates the national security establishment and that presidential views of national interests, policy, and strategy guide the system, the president must begin by placing his mark on three areas: the national security triad, the national security establishment, and the national security system. It must be remembered that none of this can be accomplished unless the president is first able to deal with his power base and constituency to create a domestic environment that is receptive and conducive to his leadership.

The president must appoint the triad—secretary of state, secretary of defense, and national security advisor—making sure that their worldviews are in general accord with his own. In the 2001 Bush administration, Secretary of State Colin Powell, Secretary of Defense Donald Rumsfeld, and National Security Advisor Condoleezza Rice fit the Bush worldview. This does not mean that members of the triad must be obsequious or without disagreement on some issues, for the entire system would suffer from lack of initiative and options. Each member of the triad must possess the personality, character, and leadership style that allow for effective engagement in the difficult process of designing national security policy and strategy. Each must be able to deal with the others in the triad in a firm but prudent way, with commitment to the most effective policy overriding any agency or department loyalty. Each member of the triad must combine political skills with national security expertise to ensure that the best posture will emerge as a result of the dynamics within the triad. Finally, members of the triad must not only be competent advisers to the president; they must be skilled managers and leaders to deal effectively with their own bureaucracies.

Although not part of the triad, the director of national intelligence (DNI) and the chairman of the Joint Chiefs of Staff (JCS) are key players in shaping the national security system. In each case, the president must appoint individuals whose philosophical range and worldviews are compatible with his own. As is the case with the triad, the DNI and the JCS chairman must be skilled advisers, politically wise, and capable of effective control and direction of their own structures. This also applies to the director of the Office of Homeland Security.

The personal strength and power of the members of the triad, the DNI, and the JCS chairman do not guarantee smooth dynamics or relationships within the national security establishment and system. But the strength of character, political acumen, and leadership skills of these individuals, combined with their commitment to the president and effective national security, are essential ingredients for coherent policy, realistic strategy, and effective implementation. This is true even if the public and the media see discord within the establishment, as was reported during the first term of George W. Bush, between the State Department under Colin Powell and the Defense Department under Donald Rumsfeld.

The president must also establish cooperative links with key members of the congressional establishment—members who have important roles in intelligence oversight, budget policies, and armed services matters. Cooperative links are established and reinforced by the president's sincere efforts to provide timely and relevant information on national security matters, articulate national interests and policy goals, and nurture and expand the president's power base and constituency support. The triad, DNI, and JCS chairman are important persons in these cooperative links; they are an extension of the president but are not presidential clones.

Finally, all of these matters must coalesce into workable ways to deal with the external security environment, in which sovereign states—many of which have differing ideologies and political systems contrary to US values and norms—look to their own self-interests. Their policies and conceptions of national security can contradict the goals of US security policy. The difficulties are magnified by the emergence of regional powers with their own policy agendas and relative immunity to pressure from external powers. With globalization complicating all of these developments, conflict in some form is inevitable. It remains to be seen how the threat of international terrorism will affect efforts to design an effective global security effort.

The complexities of the external security environment are compounded by the shifts in the locations of power (e.g., the power center emerging in Asia and the regional issues in relations among China, Japan, Russia, India, and other Asian powers). Europe has already established itself as a major power system, even though it faces bickering over the sovereignty of individual members within the framework of the European Union. Russia's effort to regain its position of power within the international community is another complicating matter in world politics. It is conceivable that new power relationships will emerge. These might include, for example, United States–Europe (including Russia); United States–Canada–Mexico; China-Japan; Russia and the states of Central Asia, the Caspian basin, and the Caucasus; and perhaps India and other Southeast Asian states. It is also conceivable that some Middle East states will form something more than the current oil cartel, focusing their attention even more on Israel. This may lead to Samuel Huntington's proposed "clash of civilizations."[8] Combined with existing competing power clusters, the security environment is undergoing major changes in the twenty-first century, requiring rethinking of the US security position and its global strategy. In this respect, international terrorist organizations add an especially challenging dimension.

The interplay of innumerable factors makes the national security arena difficult to understand and respond to. The US public tends to adopt simplistic perspectives and policy postures. This reflects frustration over the limited ability to achieve moralistic goals emerging from US ideology, a response to the complexity of such issues as nuclear strategy and weapons proliferation, and the complexities of information-age technology, as well as the public's lack of understanding and knowledge regarding the nature and character of modern warfare—especially unconventional conflicts and operations other than war.

To respond to the complex international security environment and its challenges, the United States must have an effective national security policymaking process. This requires a national security establishment staffed by skilled people who are properly organized and directed to respond and act effectively. But a perfectly skilled and bureaucratically efficient establishment and a Congress perfectly supportive of the president would be for naught if presidential leadership is found to be lacking. *Presidential leadership is the key to the effective functioning of the national security establishment.*

The Establishment and the Policy Process

Regardless of how well policy is articulated and world conditions are understood, the process by which policy is determined and strategies designed has an important impact on the end result. Furthermore, how well the national security establishment and the policymaking machinery function determines the relevance of policy and the effectiveness of strategy. If it is true that a flawed policy process is likely to lead to bad policy and strategy, how effective are the national security establishment and the policymaking process in coming to grips with the policy and strategic issues outlined here? How well can the establishment incorporate the necessary understanding and knowledge, balanced by keen intuitive insights, into the policymaking process? Is the current structure of the national security establishment relevant to the strategic landscape of the twenty-first century? These are the critical questions to which we now turn.

From the analyses of the national security policy process and the way the establishment functions, we offer three conclusions: (1) the national security process is cumbersome; (2) the diffusion of power makes it difficult to adopt innovative policies and strategies; and (3) the national security establishment as it existed in the Cold War is outmoded.

With respect to the way the US political system operates, Roger Hilsman concluded: "Reflecting on the complexity and difficulty of these problems and the untidy, frequently stalemated American political system, one wonders how the system can cope."9 He pointed out the fact that the policy process involves many power centers within the system. With respect to foreign and national security policy, "a long-run increase in the number of power centers, finally, seems inevitably to work to lessen the power of presidents in foreign affairs."[10] The same is true in national security policy. Hilsman went on to say, "So many centers of power make building a consensus for positive action a formidable task. . . . What is discouraging is how difficult it will be to get such a disparate myriad of power centers to agree on policies for meeting these complex problems."[11] This comment remains valid today. The exception is when there is a clear and serious threat to US national interests; this is reflected in national will, political resolve, and staying power.

Short of serious and recognized threats, some of the problem of myriad power centers stems from the emergence of Congress as a more powerful component in the national security policy process. This post-Watergate emergence has not necessarily concentrated more power in Congress as such, but has shifted power away from the executive and into the hands of bureaucratic gatekeepers, midlevel managers, and other decisionmakers. Gatekeepers filter information and policy recommendations and determine what can flow upward, usually for the purpose of protecting bureaucratic power bases, maintaining the status quo, and gaining more power. Furthermore, a coalition of a few members of Congress can frustrate the design of national security policy, because the policy process is extremely susceptible to a veto by small groups. Their power is strengthened by the inevitable iron triangle (key members of Congress, small sections of the bureaucracy, and special interest groups).

The irony, according to Hilsman, is that on the one hand there must be a certain concentration of power to come to grips with problems of policy; on the other hand, there must also be a balance of power to limit and restrain adventurous policy and strategy in foreign and national security affairs. The result is a virtual stalemate. "But power diffused can lead to evil as surely as power concentrated. Here is the irony."[12] In short, there are structural problems as well as political and intellectual ones not only in the national security establishment but also in the national security policy process.

Given the nature of the international security environment and the need to clarify national interests, policy choices, and strategic alternatives, what needs to be done to develop an effective structure for dealing with national security policy? The current establishment and policy process have evolved over five-plus decades, reflecting the lessons learned from the issues and crises during the Cold War and post–Cold War periods, the politics of congressional-executive struggles, and entrenched habits.

Periodically, there have been calls to change the national security establishment and the way that policy is formulated. Many such calls have been initiated by scholars, think tanks, and government sources. For example, during the Reagan presidency, recommendations came from the president's Special Review Board (the Tower Commission) in a 1987 report on the Iran-contra affair, and from the 1986 report by National Security Planning and Budgeting, "A Report to the President by the President's Blue Ribbon Commission on Defense Management" (the Packard Commission), whose suggestions focus on the national security establishment and its role in the national security policy process.[13] The Packard Commission recommended structural and procedural changes to the National Security Council, the secretary of defense, the JCS, Congress, and the defense budget process.[14] This was followed in 1988 by the Commission on Integrated Long-Term Strategy, which focused on national security strategy in the context of a changing international security environment.[15]

Although written years ago, these reports tried to create a starting point for shaping the national security establishment into a more efficient structure and for providing a more effective and expeditious national security policy process. Little was done to implement their recommendations.

Other studies called for structural and organizational changes in the national security establishment and the policy process.[16] For example, Carnes Lord suggested two changes: "the establishment of a separate staff component charged with planning, and the breakdown of compartmentalization throughout the staff."[17] Put simply, the establishment must be more streamlined and responsive to the initiatives of the executive as well as more adept at anticipating potential problems and creating innovative national security policy and strategy formulations. These include new procedures to develop a more integrated and long-range defense budget that is realistic as to resources, requirements, and capabilities. Congress must streamline the committee system and the budget process, and new structures should be developed to provide closer executive-legislative coordination and cooperation. Furthermore, these reports stated that national interests and national security objectives need to be spelled out more clearly and that a US strategy that can respond to conflicts across the spectrum on a long-term basis should be designed. These reports and studies are especially relevant in the new century. But there is little to indicate that these changes and procedures will be implemented.

More recent studies also emphasized transforming the national security system and national strategy. These include the 1997 report of the National Defense Panel, *Transforming Defense: National Security in the 21st Century*.[18] In 2000 and 2001, the United States Commission on National Security/21st Century created guidelines to restructure the national security establishment and national strategy (see Chapters 5 and 6).[19] For example, its report criticized the functioning of the National Security Council (NSC), saying that "in many ways the NSC staff has become more like a government agency than a Presidential staff."[20] Then it recommended the following:

> The National Security Council (NSC) should be responsible for advising the President and for coordinating the multiplicity of national security activities, broadly defined to include economic and domestic law enforcement activities as well as the traditional national security agenda. The NSC Advisor and staff should resist the temptation to assume a central policymaking and operational role.[21]

One of the more important periodic reports related to national security policy is the congressionally mandated Quadrennial Defense Review (QDR). The QDR is the Department of Defense's statement of its priorities in strategy and policy planning as well as the Department of Defense's assessment of how well it is doing to meet prior goals. In the QDR, changes in terminology can signal important shifts in political and military thinking by the top brass. For example, in the 2006 version of the QDR, the Department of Defense referred to the "long war" instead of the "war on terror" as a description of its major security challenge. The "long war" language suggests that the Department of Defense now acknowledges the need for a protracted conflict against terrorists and their state sponsors very much like the Cold War. Instead of a clear military solution, the "long war" of the twenty-first century may, like the Cold War, have to be endured for generations until it burns itself out. The United States could defeat or contain major transnational terrorists that pose direct threats to US or allied state territory. On the other hand, the likelihood of eliminating or controlling all terrorism and terrorist threats is small, even assuming a best case for US-allied cooperation. According to the QDR of 2006:

> Since 2001 the U.S. military has been continuously at war, but fighting a conflict that is markedly different from wars of the past. The enemies we face are not nation-states but rather dispersed non-state networks. In many cases, actions must occur on many continents in countries with which the United States is not at war. Unlike the image many have of war, this struggle cannot be won by military force alone, or even principally. And it is a struggle that may last for some years to come.[22]

What seems most instructive in all of these analyses and recommendations is that the role of the president is central to the policy process. He or she is charged with taking the initiative and developing the mechanisms to make the national security policy process work effectively. To be sure, Congress has a major role, but a body of 500-plus members cannot establish the necessary consensus and direction to lead the nation in national security policy. The fact remains that national security policymaking and execution rest primarily with the president.

And thus we come back to the issue raised by Hilsman—the irony of the diffusion of power and the concentration of power. Where is the balance between enough power for effective national security and not enough to override the will of the people?

For example, during the George W. Bush administration, critics charged that Congress after September 11 was too weak relative to a president armed with an ambitious agenda in national security policy. A Republican majority in Congress until 2007 guaranteed that Bush's national security strategy for the war on terror, including controversial detention and interrogation policies, as well as revised standards for domestic and international intelligence-gathering and covert action, would receive legislative approval. Democrats in Congress seemed in disarray during all of Bush's first term and well into his second, unable to offer coherent alternatives to the Bush national security policy and defense strategies. That situation changed with the Democratic takeover of Congress in 2007. On the other hand, if Democrats had controlled Congress during George W. Bush's first term, would the United States have been able to respond with such alacrity to wage war against the Taliban in Afghanistan and to reorganize the US government for warning and intelligence-gathering against future September 11–type attacks? Or would the policy have been imposed by having a Congress that seemed to check and balance the president's rationale for acting as a cheering section? Both the president and the Congress have been charged with being "too weak" or "too strong" from various perspectives and at various times, depending on the issues at hand and the biases of the observer.

Conclusion

Reform of structures and procedures is not enough for successful national security policy. Also required is a compelling political vision that provides coherent definitions of national interests, clarity of national security policy, and clear directions to the design of strategy. The president must provide this vision leading to clear policy and strategy. Equally important, there must be a new formulation and rethinking of the meaning of national interests and national security, including whether national security issues should include such items as the environment, refugee assistance, economics, and peacekeeping. In addition, the many power centers and forces involved in the political-psychological dimensions of national security make it difficult to give the necessary coherency to national security policy as it responds to the changing international security environment. But by exercising effective leadership and by providing a sense of purpose and vision in articulating national interests, the president can shape the boundaries, determine the directions, and establish the critical points to map out US national security policy and strategy.

Notes

1. Sean M. Lynn-Jones and Steven E. Miller, eds., *The Cold War and After: Prospects for Peace,* exp. ed. (Cambridge, MA: MIT Press, 1993), p. xxi.

2. Colin S. Gray, *The Sheriff: America's Defense of the New World Order* (Lexington: University Press of Kentucky, 2004).

3. David Silverberg, "Old Demons, New Demons," *Armed Forces Journal International* (November 1993): 14.

4. Henry A. Kissinger, *Nuclear Weapons and Foreign Policy,* abridged ed. (Garden City, NY: Doubleday Anchor Books, 1958), p. 198.

5. See, e.g., Donald Snow, *Distant Thunder: Third World Conflicts and the New International Order* (New York: St. Martin's, 1993).

6. S. Robert Lichter, Stanley Rothman, and Linda S. Lichter, *The Media Elite* (Bethesda, MD: Adler and Adler, 1986), pp. 20–21, 23, 294.

7. See ibid.

8. Samuel P. Huntington, "The Clash of Civilizations?" *Foreign Affairs* 72, no. 3 (Summer 1993): 22–49.

9. Roger Hilsman, *The Politics of Policymaking in Defense and Foreign Affairs: Conceptual Models and Bureaucratic Politics* (Englewood Cliffs, NJ: Prentice-Hall, 1987), p. 313.

10. Ibid., p. 316.

11. Ibid., p. 317.

12. Ibid., p. 318.

13. *Report of the President's Special Review Board* (Washington, DC: US Government Printing Office, February 26, 1987), and *National Security Planning and Budgeting: A Report to the President by the President's Blue Ribbon Commission on Defense Management* (Washington, DC: US Government Printing Office, June 1986).

14. *National Security Planning and Budgeting,* p. 1.

15. *Discriminate Deterrence: Report of the Commission on Integrated Long-Term Strategy* (Washington, DC: US Government Printing Office, January 1988).

16. See, e.g., James C. Gaston, ed., *Grand Strategy and the Decision-Making Process* (Washington, DC: National Defense University Press, 1992).

17. Carnes Lord, "Strategy and Organization at the National Level," in Gaston, *Grand Strategy,* p. 156.

18. Report of the National Defense Panel, *Transforming Defense: National Security in the 21st Century* (Arlington, VA: n.p., December 1997).

19. United States Commission on National Security/21st Century, *Seeking a National Strategy: A Concern for Preserving Security and Promoting Freedom,* phase 2 report (Washington, DC: US Department of Defense, April 15, 2000). Phase 1 of the commission's report was *New World Coming: American Security in the 21st Century* (Washington, DC: US Department of Defense, September 15, 1999). The final draft report of phase 3 was *Building for Peace* (Washington, DC: US Department of Defense, January 2001).

20. United States Commission on National Security/21st Century, *Road Map for National Security: Imperative for Change,* final draft report (Washington, DC: US Department of Defense, January 31, 2001), p. 50.

21. Ibid.

22. US Department of Defense, *Quadrennial Defense Review Report* (Washington, DC: Department of Defense, February 6, 2006), p. 9.

16

The Study of National Security: The Presidential Mandate

IN THIS FINAL CHAPTER WE REFOCUS OUR ATTENTION ON THE role of the president in national security. Notwithstanding the variety of perspectives and approaches, our framework, offered here, is based on the themes presented in this book.

Without some direction and coherency in research focus, one is likely to be overwhelmed by the vast amount of published literature on US national security. With this in mind, we offer a relatively simple study framework to help organize thinking on this complex topic. The cornerstones of this framework are shown in Figure 16.1. The major components are presidential character, personality, and leadership; the shape of the national security establishment; and the meaning of national interests and national security in the new era. How well the president deals with these major components has been the primary concern of this study.

Many components of the national security establishment are continuations from the Cold War era. Yet the meaning of national security, as well as its conceptual basis, has expanded to include nonmilitary factors such as the environment, refugee control, economics, domestic assistance, humanitarian and peacekeeping operations, immigration, and a role for the United Nations. September 11 reflected the primary role of the president in countering international terrorism and unifying the nation. This study considers national security in that context.

In the final analysis, the president is human; mistakes will be made, directions misinterpreted, and goals frustrated. The success of national security policy is, in no small way, a function of the president's ability to limit the damage of mistakes and bad judgments, reshape the directions of policy, and ensure proper functioning of the national security establishment while maintaining his presence and credibility throughout the establishment, with Congress, and with domestic and foreign constituencies.

Figure 16.1 Framework for the Study of National Security

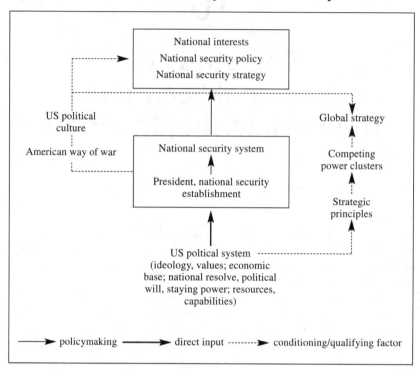

Although we cannot expect the president to be superhuman, we should expect a creative and competent political leader, one who can articulate national interests and shape policy to reflect them, and one who can project his presence to guide the national security establishment in carrying out effective strategies.

At the same time, the US public and the political actors involved in the national security policy process must be realistic about the presidency. There are limits to the office, even beyond those imposed by law. All things cannot be done all the time. This is especially true in the national security arena, where the United States must deal with sovereign states possessing ideologies and political systems that may not be compatible with ours. Moreover, the president can only rarely accomplish great things by himself; success generally begins with broad support from the public and a degree of consensus within the national security establishment. This brings us full circle: *Developing and maintaining broad support and consensus are primarily contingent upon the leadership style and ability of the president to set and maintain the tone and style of his administration, which after all reflects his own personality and character.* Whatever the president's leadership style, it is secondary to the impact of his personality and character and the scope and substance of his mind-set. In turn, what emerges in national security is the composite impact of these qualities on the agencies and policy instruments in the national security establishment, the other branches of government, political circles in Washington, the media, and the domestic and international political environments.[1]

Four conclusions are in order. First, presidential personality and character must be of a quality that promotes leadership in the broadest sense—the ability to lead in a manner consistent with democratic values and expectations so that a high degree of credibility is established within both domestic and foreign constituencies. Second, effective leadership depends on the president's ability to understand the capabilities of the national security establishment, its political tendencies, and its power; it depends as well on his political insights into the Washington political environment, congressional politics, the international arena, and the effective use of power to deal with that environment. Third, the president and the policy triad (secretary of state, secretary of defense, and national security advisor) must rethink US policy and strategy in light of the new international dynamics and changing strategic landscape. The twenty-first century requires a new strategic vision and organizational reshaping, particularly in terms of the "new war," countering international terrorism. Fourth, the president cannot succeed without skilled and committed leaders in the national security establishment. There must also be a high degree of trust and confidence between the president and the director of national intelligence and the chairman of the Joint Chiefs of Staff. In addition, there must be a special quality of trust and confidence among the president, the operational elements in the military, and the intelligence agencies.

But effectiveness and success in all of these areas will not necessarily lead to effective national security policy. Several important factors are beyond presidential power and control. Even the best intentions of personality and character give no assurance that the leadership style and exercise of presidential power will be effectively translated through the Oval Office to shape the national security establishment and the policy process accordingly.

Finally, national interests and policy coherence require a clear articulation of what the United States stands for and its role in the international arena. Furthermore, national will, political resolve, and staying power are needed to expend the resources effectively and use the instruments necessary to achieve national security goals. Given the nature of the international security environment and the imperatives of US national security policy, the president is placed in a position that requires a reconciliation of the ideals of democracy with the commitment necessary to further these goals—all in an environment that may have to resort to the military instrument and to the implementation of strategies that can stretch the notion of democracy.

As of this writing, President George Bush is still faced with many in the US public who disapprove of the US role in Iraq. In addition, the control of both houses of Congress by the Democratic Party makes it extremely difficult for President Bush to establish a unified national security strategy and policy for the continuing involvement in Iraq and in countering international terrorism.

Clinton Rossiter's study of the presidency assessed the power of the president in the following terms:

> Our pluralistic system of restraints is designed to keep him from going out of bounds, not to paralyze him in the field that has been reserved for his use. He will feel few checks upon his power if he uses that power as he should. This may well be the final definition of the strong and successful President: the one who knows just how far he can go in the direction he wants to go. If he cannot judge the limits of his power, he cannot call upon its strength. If he cannot sense the possible, he will exhaust himself attempting the impossible. The power of the Presidency moves as a mighty host only with the grain of liberty and morality.[2]

More than three decades ago, Erwin Hargrove and Roy Hoopes concluded as follows:

> The point to remember in assessing presidential power and the ability of a given president to wield it effectively—or perhaps even abuse it—is that the style and character of the president himself is every bit as important as the inherent power of the institution. And when we talk about the powers of the presidency, we must consider three factors: a president's sense of purpose; his political skills; and his character.[3]

None of this can be easily accomplished. Furthermore, the national security component of presidential responsibilities cannot easily be separated from all the other responsibilities of office. Regardless of the political actors involved in national security policy, the focal point is fixed on the presidency—the starting point for any analysis of US national security. It is the quality and capability of the president that determine the success and failure of US national security policy and strategy.

In the final analysis, the president is faced with the prospect of responding to an international strategic landscape that is characterized by a clash of civilizations, international terrorism, and a variety of challenges undercutting democracy and political freedom—threatening the very notion of US values and national interests. To respond effectively, it may be necessary for the president to be guided by an old Latin view, "Let him who desires peace, prepare for war."[4]

Notes

1. A number of books have been published on the presidential character and leadership. These include Erwin C. Hargrove and Roy Hoopes, *The Presidency: A Question of Power* (Boston: Little, Brown, 1975); James Q. Wilson, *American Government: Institutions and Policies*, 5th ed. (Lexington, MA: D. C. Heath, 1992); and Michael Nelson, "The Psychology Presidency," in Michael Nelson, ed., *The Presidency and the Political System* (Washington, DC: CQ Press, 1988).

2. Clinton Rossiter, *The American Presidency,* 2nd ed. (New York: Mentor Books, 1960), p. 69.

3. Hargrove and Hoopes, *The Presidency,* p. 47.

4. Norbert Gutelman, *Book of Latin Quotes* (New York: Doubleday, 1966), 3, prologue. Based on Flavius Vegetius Renatus, A.D. 379–A.D. 395.

Reading List

The following reading list is intended to complement the themes and focus of this book. It is not comprehensive; the inclusion or exclusion of any particular work is not an indication of its importance. For additional references, see the notes in each chapter.

Allison, Graham, and Philip Zelikow. *Essence of Decision: Explaining the Cuban Missile Crisis.* 2nd ed. New York: Longman, 1999.

Arquilla, John, and David Ronfeldt, eds. *In Athena's Camp: Preparing for Conflict in the Information Age.* Santa Monica, CA: RAND, 1997.

Bennett, Andrew, and George Shambaugh. *Taking Sides: Clashing Views on Controversial Issues in American Foreign Policy.* Dubuque, IA: McGraw-Hill/Dushkin, 2006.

Berkowitz, Bruce. *The New Face of War: How War Will Be Fought in the 21st Century.* New York: The Free Press, 2003.

Boot, Max. *The Savage Wars of Peace: Small Wars and the Rise of American Power.* New York: Basic Books, 2002.

Brzezinski, Zbigniew. *Second Chance: Three Presidents and the Crisis of American Superpower.* New York: Basic Books, 2007.

Carter, Ashton B., and William J. Perry. *Preventive Defense: A New Security Strategy for America.* Washington, DC: Brookings Institution, 1999.

Cimbala, Stephen J. *Nuclear Strategy in the Twenty-First Century.* New York: Praeger, 2000.

Clark, General Wesley K., USA (ret.). *Waging Modern War: Bosnia, Kosovo, and the Future of Combat.* New York: Public Affairs, 2001.

Combs, Cindy C. *Terrorism in the Twenty-First Century.* 3rd ed. New York: Prentice-Hall, 2003.

Crocker, Chester A., Fen Osler Hampson, and Pamela Aall, eds. *Turbulent Peace: The Challenge of Managing International Conflict.* Herndon, VA: United States Institute of Peace, 2001.

Dempsey, Gary T., with Roger W. Fontaine. *Fool's Errands: America's Recent Encounters with Nation Building.* Washington, DC: Cato Institute, 2001.

Evan, William M., ed. *War and Peace in an Age of Terrorism: A Reader.* Boston, MA: Pearson Education, 2006.

Feaver, Peter D., and Richard H. Kohn, eds. *Soldiers and Civilians: The Civil-Military Gap and American National Security.* Cambridge, MA: MIT Press, 2001.

Frum, David, and Richard Pearle. *An End to Evil: How to Win the War on Terror.* New York: Random House, 2003.

Graber, Doris A. *Media Power in Politics.* 5th ed. Washington, DC: Congressional Quarterly, 2006.

Gray, Colin S. *Modern Strategy.* Oxford, UK: Oxford University Press, 1999.

Huntington, Samuel P. *The Soldier and the State: The Theory and Practice of Civil-Military Relations.* New York: Vintage Books, 1957.

Janowitz, Morris. *The Professional Soldier: A Social and Political Portrait.* New York: The Free Press, 1971.

Joes, Anthony James. *America and Guerrilla Warfare.* Lexington: University Press of Kentucky, 2000.

Jordan, Amos A., William J. Taylor Jr., and Michael J. Mazarr. *American National Security.* 5th ed. Baltimore: Johns Hopkins University Press, 1999.

Kagan, Donald, and Frederick W. Kagan. *While America Sleeps: Self-Delusion, Military Weakness, and the Threat to Peace Today.* New York: St. Martin's, 2000.

Kegley, Charles W., Jr., and Gregory Raymond. *Exorcising the Ghost of Westphalia: Building World Order in the New Millennium.* Upper Saddle River, NJ: Prentice-Hall, 2002.

McCormick, James M. *American Foreign Policy and Process.* 3rd ed. Itasca, IL: F. E. Peacock, 1998.

Metz, Steven. *Armed Conflict in the 21st Century: The Information Revolution and Post-Modern Warfare.* Carlisle, PA: Strategic Studies Institute, US Army War College, April 2000.

Moskos, Charles C., John Allen Williams, and David R. Segal, eds. *The Postmodern Military: Armed Forces After the Cold War.* New York: Oxford University Press, 2000.

Nye, Joseph S., Jr. *Understanding International Conflicts: An Introduction to Theory and History.* 3rd ed. New York: Longman, 2000.

O'Hanlon, Michael. *Technological Change and the Future of Warfare.* Washington, DC: Brookings Institution, 2000.

Peters, Ralph. *Never Quit the Fight.* Mechanicsburg, PA: Stackpole Books, 2006.

Prados, John. *Keepers of the Keys: A History of the National Security Council from Truman to Bush.* New York: William Morrow, 1991.

Revel, Jean-François. *How Democracies Perish.* New York: Harper and Row, 1984.

Richelson, Jeffrey T. *The U.S. Intelligence Community.* 4th ed. Boulder: Westview, 1999.

Ricks, Thomas E. *Making the Corps.* New York: Touchstone, 1998.

Sagan, Scott D., and Kenneth N. Waltz. *The Spread of Nuclear Weapons: A Debate.* New York: W. W. Norton, 1995.

Sarkesian, Sam C., and Robert E. Connor Jr. *The U.S. Military Profession into the Twenty-First Century.* 2nd ed. London: Frank Cass, 2006.

Sarkesian, Sam C., and John Allen Williams, eds. *The US Army in a New Security Era.* Boulder: Lynne Rienner Publishers, 1990.

Sarkesian, Sam C., John Allen Williams, and Fred B. Bryant. *Soldiers, Society, and National Security.* Boulder: Lynne Rienner Publishers, 1995.

Snider, Don M., and Miranda A. Carlton-Carew. *U.S. Civil-Military Relations in Crisis or Transition?* Washington, DC: Center for Strategic and International Studies, 1995.

Snow, Donald M. *National Security for a New Era.* New York: St. Martin's, 2006.

Snow, Donald M., and Eugene Brown. *Puzzle Palace and Foggy Bottom: U.S. Foreign and Defense Policy-Making in the 1990s.* New York: St. Martin's, 1994.

Stoessinger, John G. *Why Nations Go to War.* 10th ed. Boston: Bedford/St. Martin's, 2007.

Van Creveld, Martin. *The Transformation of War.* New York: The Free Press, 1991.

Viotti, Paul R., and Mark V. Kauppi. *International Relations and World Politics: Security, Economy, Identity.* 2nd ed. Upper Saddle River, NJ: Prentice-Hall, 2001.

Weigley, Russell F. *The American Way of War: A History of United States Military Strategy and Policy.* Bloomington: Indiana University Press, 1973.

Zeigler, David W. *War, Peace, and International Politics.* 8th ed. New York: Longman, 2000.

Index

317

About the Book

COMPLETELY REVISED THROUGHOUT, THE FOURTH EDITION OF *US National Security* reflects the new strategic landscape as it has evolved in the aftermath of the September 11 terrorist attacks. The ongoing US military involvement in Afghanistan and Iraq, the focus on homeland security, the significant organizational changes in the intelligence bureaucracy, and the impact of the Bush Doctrine are among the current issues that inform the authors' clear presentation and appraisal of US security interests, politics, and processes.

Sam C. Sarkesian is professor emeritus of political science at Loyola University Chicago. He is the author of numerous books and articles on national security, unconventional conflicts, civil-military relations, and military professionalism. His publications include *The Military Profession into the Twenty-First Century* (with Robert Connor Jr.) and *Unconventional Conflicts in the New Security Era*. He has served as president and chair of the Inter-University Seminar on Armed Forces and Society and chair of the Academic Advisory Council of the National Strategy Forum. He served for twenty-three years in the active army with service in Germany, Korea, and Vietnam. Dr. Sarkesian is a retired lieutenant colonel of the US Army. **John Allen Williams** is professor of political science at Loyola University Chicago and chair and president of the Inter-University Seminar on Armed Forces and Society. A retired captain and strategic plans officer in the US Naval Reserve, he is chair of the Academic Advisory Council of the National Strategy Forum. He has published and lectured widely in the United States and abroad on national security, civil-military relations, and military professionalism issues. His publications include *The Postmodern Military: Armed Forces After the Cold War* (coedited with Charles C. Moskos and David R. Segal). **Stephen J. Cimbala** is Distinguished

Professor of Political Science at Pennsylvania State University–Delaware County Campus and is the author of numerous books and articles in international security studies, defense policy, nuclear weapons and arms control, intelligence, and other fields. He serves on the editorial boards of various professional journals, has consulted for a number of US government agencies and defense contractors, and is frequently quoted in the media on national security topics. Dr. Cimbala is a past recipient of Pennsylvania State University's Eisenhower Award for excellence in teaching.